OKLAHOMA PROJECT FOR DISCOURSE AND THEORY

Hollywood Fictions

The naive movie-hopeful who went to Hollywood expecting to find fame overnight was a familiar figure in art and literature by the early 1920s. *Hollywood Dreams* by Norman Rockwell, from *Ladies' Home Journal* (July 1930). Photo courtesy of The Norman Rockwell Museum at Stockbridge.

Hollywood Fictions

*The Dream Factory
in American Popular Literature*

John Parris Springer

UNIVERSITY OF OKLAHOMA PRESS : NORMAN

Library of Congress Cataloging-in-Publication Data

Springer, John Parris, 1955–
    Hollywood fictions : the dream factory in American popular literature /
John Parris Springer.
        p.   cm. — (Oklahoma project for discourse and theory ; v. 19)
    Includes bibliographical references and index.
    ISBN 0–8061–3203–5 (cloth : alk. paper)
    1. American fiction—20th century—History and criticism.   2. Motion
pictures in literature.   3. Popular literature—United States—History and
criticism.   4. Motion picture actors and actresses in literature.   5. Hollywood
(Los Angeles, Calif.)—In literature.   6. Motion picture industry in literature.
I. Title.   II. Series.
PS374.M55S67   2000
813'.509357—dc21   99–39591
                                                                                          CIP

Text design by Gail Carter.

Hollywood Fictions: The Dream Factory in American Popular Literature is Volume 19 of
the Oklahoma Project for Discourse and Theory.

1   2   3   4   5   6   7   8   9   10

A lot of silly things have been written about Hollywood. But nobody's ever written the real book yet.

STEVE FISHER
from his novel *I Wake Up Screaming* (1941)

I wish I could write the Hollywood novel that has never been written, but it takes a more photographic memory than I have. The whole scene is too complex and all of it would have to be in, or the thing would be just another distortion.

RAYMOND CHANDLER
in a letter to Edward Weeks, 27 February 1957

CONTENTS

SERIES EDITORS' FOREWORD

The Oklahoma Project for Discourse & Theory is a series of interdisciplinary texts whose purpose is to explore the cultural institutions that constitute the human sciences, to see them in relation to one another, and perhaps above all, to see them as products of particular discursive practices. To this end, we hope that the Oklahoma Project will promote dialogue within and across traditional disciplines—psychology, philology, linguistics, history, art history, aesthetics, logic, political economy, religion, philosophy, anthropology, communications, and the like—in texts that theoretically are located across disciplines. In recent years, in a host of new and traditional areas, there has been great interest in such discursive and theoretical frameworks. Yet we conceive of the Oklahoma Project as going beyond local inquiries, providing a larger forum for interdiscursive theoretical discussions and dialogue.

Our agenda in previous books and certainly in this one has been to present through the University of Oklahoma Press a series of critical volumes that set up a theoretical encounter among disciplines, an interchange not limited to literature but covering virtually the whole range of the human sciences. It is a critical series with an important reference in literary studies—thus mirroring the modern development of discourse theory—but including all approaches, other than quantitative studies, open to semiotic and post-semiotic analysis and to the wider concerns of cultural studies. Regardless of its particular domain, each book in the series will investigate characteristically post-Freudian, post-Saussurean, and post-

Marxist questions about culture and the discourses that constitute different cultural phenomena. The Oklahoma Project is a sustained dialogue intended to make a significant contribution to the contemporary understanding of the human sciences in the contexts of cultural theory and cultural studies.

The title of the series reflects, of course, its home base, the University of Oklahoma. But it also signals in a significant way the particularity of the *local* functions within historical and conceptual frameworks for understanding culture. *Oklahoma* is a haunting place-name in American culture. A Choctaw phrase meaning "red people," it goes back to the Treaty of Dancing Rabbit Creek in Mississippi in 1830. For Franz Kafka, it conjured up the idea of America itself, both the indigenous Indian peoples of North America and the vertiginous space of the vast plains. It is also the place-name, the "American" starting point, with which Wallace Stevens begins his *Collected Poems*. Historically, too, it is a place in which American territorial and political expansion was reenacted in a single day in a retracing called the Oklahoma land run. Geographically, it is the heartland of the continent.

As such—in the interdisciplinary Oklahoma Project for Discourse & Theory—we are hoping to describe, above all, multifaceted *interest* within and across various studies of discourse and culture. Such interests are akin to what Kierkegaard calls the "in-between" aspect of experience, the "inter esse," and, perhaps more pertinently, what Nietzsche describes as the always *political* functioning of concepts, art works, and language—the functioning of power as well as knowledge in discourse and theory. Such politics, occasioning dialogue and bringing together powerfully struggling and often unarticulated positions, disciplines, and assumptions, is always local, always particular. In some ways, such interests function in broad feminist critiques of language, theory, and culture as well as microphilosophical and microhistorical critiques of the definitions of truth and art existing within ideologies of "disinterested" meaning. They function in the interested examination of particular disciplines and general disciplinary histories. They function (to allude to two of our early titles) in the very interests of theory and the particularity of the postmodern age in which many of us find ourselves. In such interested particulars, we believe, the human sciences are articulated. We hope that the books of the Oklahoma Project will provide sites of such interest and that in them, individually and collectively, the monologues of traditional scholarly discourse will become heteroglosses, just as such place-names as *Oklahoma* and such commonplace words and concepts as *discourse* and *theory* can become sites for the dialogue and play of culture.

ROBERT CON DAVIS
RONALD SCHLEIFER

Norman, Oklahoma

ACKNOWLEDGMENTS

Movies and the mythology of Hollywood have long held me in their grasp, as they have many who grew up in the twentieth century. I daresay most of us have made that trip to Hollywood, where fame and success await our arrival—at least in our imaginations. Most of us eventually outgrow such ideas, our ambition cooled by reason or experience. But the loss of such dreams can be a bitter, disillusioning event both for an individual and for a society. On a historical scale, such events can produce whole communities of discourse and spawn new generic traditions in the wake of the social contradictions they set in motion.

Take the western, for example. Despite its roots in nineteenth-century dime novels and Wild West shows, the western is almost wholly a twentieth-century cultural form, the product of modern technologies such as motion pictures and television. As a genre, the western must be read as a twentieth-century response to the closing of the American frontier and to the loss of that expansive dream of limitless opportunity and personal freedom that the West promised. The genre of Hollywood fiction is based upon a similar sense of nostalgia and loss, tinged with sharp disappointment and anger— a pervasive feeling, at least among writers, that here some opportunity or potential has been lost or squandered, has gone astray, and that Hollywood represents something that is probably pervasive within American society and culture. In fact, Hollywood *is* American culture.

What became increasingly evident through my research was the degree to which popular myths of Hollywood have been shaped by a specific generic tradition—that of the Hollywood novel and the larger discursive context, which I refer to as *Hollywood fictions*. Such a realization makes one acutely aware of one's debt to that tradition, and of the extent to which one's thinking is dependent upon the visions and voices of others.

I would especially like to thank several people who read the manuscript at various stages and provided valuable advice and encouragement: Brooks Landon, Tom Lutz, John Raeburn, Barbara Welch-Breeder, and Carol de Saint Victor at the University of Iowa; Joanna Rapf at the University of Oklahoma; and James Welsh, the editor of *Literature/Film Quarterly*. David Cook and Anthony Slide provided generous support for the manuscript, and Janet Staiger made numerous helpful suggestions on chapter 4. I would like to thank Andrew Horton for his friendship and moral support during the final stages of the book's production. I would also like to thank my friends and colleagues Gary Don Rhodes, John Hoppe, Kerry Johnson, and Betty Robbins for their aid and advice along the way. My father, E. V. Springer, provided useful editorial suggestions at key moments in the project's history. And Dorothy Todd graciously provided her support throughout the project. Finally I am grateful to the directors of the Oklahoma Project for Discourse and Theory—Ronald Schleifer and Robert Con Davis—for their support over many years.

More personally, I would like to thank my mother and father—Marilyn Harris Springer and E. V. Springer—who, through the examples of their own artistic callings, instilled in me intellectual interests that have profoundly influenced my life and work. As a writer and an actor, respectively, both prepared me to write this book in more ways than I can ever acknowledge.

Finally I want to thank my wife, Laura, both for her invaluable help in preparing the manuscript and for always helping me to remember what is really most important.

John Parris Springer

Hollywood Fictions

HOLLYWOOD, HOLLYWOOD FICTION, AND AMERICAN MASS CULTURE

> Hollywood . . . is probably the most important and the most
> difficult subject for our time to deal with. Whether we like it or
> not it is in that great bargain sale of five and ten cent lusts and
> dreams that the new bottom level of our culture is being created.
>
> JOHN DOS PASSOS[1]

It is an obvious understatement to say that Hollywood has played an
important role in twentieth-century American culture. Hollywood itself, as
much as the films that it produced, has been a central component of our
national mythology, a complex, multivalent cultural symbol. Hollywood
has been a site, both real and symbolic, for the collision of contradictory
energies and agendas: commerce and art, work and leisure, success and
failure, sex and death. Hollywood has long possessed a Janus-faced identity
as both the "promised land" and the "wasteland," as an idyllic community
of luxurious homes, swimming pools, and verdant lawns yet also the
epicenter of cultural crisis and moral disintegration; as a town that kindles
dreams of opportunity, wealth, and fame yet most often produces disappointment, disillusionment, and despair.

This book represents an attempt to recover and explore Hollywood's
symbolic role in national life during the 1920s and 1930s—that is, to trace
the various ways in which Hollywood was constructed and understood,
examine conflicting ideas concerning its identity and significance, and

3

position these competing views within the social and cultural arguments that surrounded the film capital in that period. As such, this work discusses *Hollywood fictions* in two senses: first, as a set of popular literary texts that took Hollywood and the film industry as their principal subject, and second, as a larger discourse about movies and mass culture that informed popular attitudes toward Hollywood and shaped its literary representation. Much of the contemporary writing about Hollywood in the twenties and thirties was devoted quite openly to the fabrication of fictions, offering in hyperbolic terms both positive and negative assessments of the film capital and the motion pictures produced there. Hollywood, both as an idea and as an actual social space, could be best understood through a series of narratives, stories that often articulated larger ideological and cultural concerns. Thus, Hollywood fiction should be read within the context of more general attitudes and arguments about American mass culture and society.

It was, of course, the classical Hollywood cinema[2]—a body of films and a style of film making that has dominated motion-picture production throughout the world for some seventy years[3]—that constituted Hollywood's most direct contribution to American culture. However, the influence of Hollywood goes beyond that of the movies produced there, and has permeated American social and cultural life to an extent that is seldom acknowledged. "It is quite possible," Anita Loos wrote, "that we would have vastly different ideas about many things—physical beauty, glamour, clothing, decor, hobbies, ethics, manners, and mannerisms—without Hollywood."[4] As Loos's comments suggests, it is not merely on the level of style that Hollywood's influence can be discerned; it has been a potent shaper of ideas and behavior, articulating fundamental social and ideological myths, giving form to powerful collective aspirations and anxieties, and thus helping to mold American culture in profound ways. Hollywood was (and still is) a source of values and beliefs, a focus for mass desires and expectations, the center of a complex cultural pedagogy that has left few aspects of the American scene untouched. The conflicting images and ideas about Hollywood that circulated during its so-called golden age in the twenties and thirties reveal the complexity of its identity and, at the same time, reflect the conditions and contradictions of American social and cultural life at large during those years. As the novelist John Dos Passos observed, "whether we like it or not," Hollywood is one of those places where "our culture is being created," and it is difficult to overstate its impact on American society. Speculating on its centrality in American life, Loos concluded, "If there was no Hollywood, no doubt we'd have to invent it, a place to project our fantasies and reflect our dreams, no matter how outlandish" (161).

Hollywood in the twenties and thirties was arguably the most important cultural institution in American life. As the production center for the largest entertainment industry ever created, Hollywood enjoyed a unique capacity to shape the dreams and desires of its mass audience. The studio system, which was at the height of its power in this period, was producing an average of 385 motion pictures a year,[5] delivering them to the public with all the publicity and ballyhoo expected from a business that had built itself on spectacle and showmanship. At the same time a colorful array of fan magazines and trade papers fed the public's appetite for behind-the-scenes information about the film industry and the glamorous lives of those who worked in it. In 1928 an estimated 20,500 movie theaters were showing Hollywood films in towns and cities across the country.[6] James R. Quirk, the voluble editor of *Photoplay*, noted, "The eyes of the world are actually centered on Hollywood every day when millions of people crowd into theaters all over the world."[7] By the late thirties the Hollywood press corps had become the third largest in the country (trailing only those in New York and Washington), with a contingent of nearly four hundred newspapermen, columnists, and feature writers covering the Hollywood beat for the press and major magazines worldwide.[8] In the words of Perley Poore Sheehan, one of its most enthusiastic boosters, Hollywood was a "world center,"[9] the focal point of an unprecedented curiosity and interest, by turns both envied and reviled.

Hollywood in these decades was a highly charged symbolic site in the American landscape, not merely stimulating but embodying a complex, contradictory set of cultural arguments and social values that would transform it into a symbolic microcosm of the best and worst in American life. As Hortense Powdermaker observed, Hollywood is "a part of that modern cultural continent we all inhabit, a place where in exaggerated form we can see our own communities."[10]

Hollywood frequently evoked the sense of a culmination, an ending: not just the terminal point in this historical process of western expansion but the conclusion of a journey toward national identity, either the fulfillment or the betrayal of the American dream. For some, Hollywood seemed a distillation, the purest embodiment of our national character, exuding a facile confidence and superficial optimism; to others it was the locus of cultural forces that appeared fundamentally "foreign," a potentially dangerous influence necessitating censorship and regulation. Above all Hollywood has been America's "dream factory," both the center and the source of national fantasies and myths, and consequently its image was often tied to the success or failure, to the richness or the sterility, of the dreams it offered audiences.

Thus, during the period of its greatest influence and prestige in national life, Hollywood's image was controversial and unstable, and it was most often a site of cultural argument, a locus of conflict and struggle where various social and cultural issues were articulated and rehearsed for the country at large. In his sociological portrait of Hollywood in the thirties, Leo Rosten observed that "the aberrations of our culture are simply more vivid, more conspicuous, and more dramatic in Hollywood than in New Bedford or Palo Alto. Our values are extended to the strident and the unmistakable in Hollywood's way of life. It is for this reason that a study of Hollywood can cast the profile of American society into sharper relief."[11] To revise the normative social theory that underlies Rosten's comment, I would suggest that it is the *contradictions* of our culture that are "more vivid, more conspicuous, and more dramatic in Hollywood" than anywhere else, and for that reason any attempt to understand twentieth-century American culture must take Hollywood, and all of its different meanings, into account.

"HOLLYWOOD"

The word "Hollywood" can refer to either the American film industry or its product, the movies. In its most generic sense the term refers to the West Coast film studios and the creative and technical personnel involved in film production there. Until 1903, when it became an incorporated city of the sixth class, Hollywood was merely a sparsely populated real-estate subdivision at the base of the Santa Monica foothills. In 1910 it was annexed by the City of Los Angeles,[12] yet it always maintained a distinct identity within the larger urban environment. By the twenties Hollywood was being referred to as a "state of mind," the phrase "going Hollywood" had entered the popular argot, and the "film capital," as it was widely known, had begun to take on the significance of a full-blown national symbol. While Hollywood has long been the subject of both nostalgic and scholarly attention, compelling analyses of its symbolic role in American thought and culture have been rare.[13] In much of the writing about Hollywood, the word is used as a synonym for the movie business, a synecdoche for American film in general. Certainly it was the presence of movie making, with all of its attendant illusions and excesses, that contributed the most to Hollywood's cultural identity.

However, the system of narrative and aesthetic devices that constitutes the classical Hollywood cinema and the commercial and production practices that define Hollywood film making as an industry are quite different from Hollywood considered as a town, a life-style, or a cultural trope. I would suggest that to understand Hollywood's influence on American culture it is necessary to examine these more elusive aspects of its identity and history. Certainly neoformalist criticism has taught us much about the narrative language of Hollywood films, and the work of economic and industry historians has led to significant advancements and revisions in our knowledge of American film history. Yet, along with gaining some understanding of film history, we must also examine a series of representations of Hollywood and a history of arguments about it. And while it is necessary to distinguish between Hollywood as an idea and Hollywood as a sociogeographical space, texts and places are equally social products, thoroughly embedded in processes of representation and narrative.

As a cultural signifier, "Hollywood" has always borne an excessive semantic weight. Powdermaker observed:

> It means many things to many people. For the majority it is the home of favored, godlike creatures. For others, it is a "den of iniquity"—or it may be considered a hotbed of communism or the seat of conservative reaction; a center for creative genius, or a place where mediocrity flourishes and able men sell their creative souls for gold; an important industry with worldwide significance or an environment of trivialities

7

characterized by aimlessness; a mecca where everyone is happy, or a place where cynical disillusionment prevails.[14]

What makes Hollywood such a potentially valuable interpretive metaphor for the study of twentieth-century American culture is precisely this complex freight of meanings that it supports, its luxuriantly overdetermined cultural legacy. The problem confronting the cultural historian who would investigate and analyze that legacy is one of scope. Writings about Hollywood have been extensive but often ephemeral, produced by journalists, gossip columnists, studio publicists, and movie critics and scattered throughout newspapers, popular magazines, fan publications, and industry trade journals.

One of the most important discursive sites in which ideas about Hollywood have been presented and argued is popular fiction—novels and short stories. Indeed, for many American writers as for the public at large, Hollywood has generated an intense fascination, which has remained undiminished despite changes that have attenuated its economic power and challenged its cultural authority. The extent to which literary representations—particularly that category of popular fiction known as the Hollywood novel—have shaped and defined Hollywood's image suggests its importance as a subject of discussion in American culture. These texts permit a unique analysis of Hollywood as a cultural construct, an organizing myth of twentieth-century American social and cultural life. Katharine Fullerton Gerould, one of the most astute commentators on Hollywood, observed in 1923, "Hollywood, California, you may say, is most often a text,"[15] and it is this textual construction of Hollywood within works of popular fiction that is the central subject of this study.

HOLLYWOOD FICTION

Fiction about movie making first appeared in the early teens as juvenile literature. Appearing under the publishing-house pseudonyms of Victor Appleton and Laura Lee Hope were several series of books designed to appeal to young people and based upon the technological novelty of moving pictures. The first "movie" novel was Appleton's *Tom Swift and His*

Wizard Camera; Or Thrilling Adventures While Taking Moving Pictures, published in 1912. This was followed by two Victor Appleton series, *The Motion Picture Chums* (seven titles published between 1913 and 1916) and *The Moving Picture Boys* (eight titles published between 1913 and 1918), and one Laura Lee Hope series, *The Moving Picture Girls* (six titles published between 1914 and 1915).[16] All of these works emphasized the scientific and technological aspects of film making in narratives marked by exotic adventure and romance. Drawing on such diverse fictional sources as the proto-science fictions of Jules Verne, the rags-to-riches narratives of Horatio Alger, and the melodramatic plots of American dime novels, these works evinced an interest in and an optimism about technological progress and entrepreneurial initiative that were wholly nineteenth-century in spirit.

Nancy Brooker-Bowers in her annotated bibliography, *The Hollywood Novel and Other Novels About Film, 1912–1982,* cites the 1916 adventure-romance *The Phantom Herd* by B. M. Bower as "the first true Hollywood novel."[17] In it, an ambitious young director of western pictures grows impatient with the formulaic stories he is given to direct and goes into independent production, taking an inexperienced crew of cowboys on location to New Mexico, where he can get the authentic settings that will give his picture a greater aura of "realism." After hardships and setbacks, the film is completed and premieres at the Texas Cattlemen's convention, where it is a success. The cattlemen's endorsement of "The Phantom Herd" as "the first really authentic Western drama ever produced" (317) ensures the film's commercial success and produces the requisite happy ending for the novel.

The search for origins is a project fraught with peril and uncertainty for the historian, if only because new research continually threatens current findings. In the case of fiction about Hollywood, efforts to secure a single origin are particularly reductive if they fail to take into account the relationship between literary works and the larger cultural discourse that surrounded the film capital and motion pictures in general. Moreover, Brooker-Bowers's research was limited to a single literary form—the novel—and excluded other Hollywood fictions that appeared in short stories and magazine serials. In fact, the forms of cultural response to Hollywood have defied the conventional categories of literary study, making the search for a single origin in the novel even more problematic.

9

Rather than being the "first true Hollywood novel" (a claim advanced by Brooker-Bowers because about a third of the book is set in the Los Angeles studio of the "Acme Film Company"), I would argue that *The Phantom Herd* has more in common with the works of Appleton and Hope. True, complaints in the book concerning the essential phoniness of the "moving-picture West," about "chasing outlaws all over a ten-acre lot . . . and driving out into Griffith Park" to find locations (41–42), show how early fictions that dealt with movie making could produce questions about the authenticity and value of film as an artistic and cultural form—questions that would be central to subsequent Hollywood fictions. More important, however, is the fact that, like the Appleton and Hope series, Bower's novel is grounded in an ideology of entrepreneurial optimism that finds inherent in the new medium, as both a technology and a commercial enterprise, a sense of adventure and romance.

Despite their attention to the apparatus of the motion-picture camera and the contingencies of early film making and exhibition, the early novels by Appleton, Hope, and Bower should be viewed as distinct from the twentieth-century tradition of Hollywood fiction. The latter has demonstrated little interest in film as a technology and little faith in the movie business as a beneficial social enterprise. Rather, twentieth-century fiction about Hollywood has most often served as a vehicle for cultural complaint, particularly in regard to the influence of Hollywood and the mass culture of the movies on American life and values.

Hollywood fictions first appeared in movie fan magazines, as a supplement to their standard offering of film plots and star profiles. Then came the works of a number of American writers who visited California in the twenties and experienced the heady atmosphere of the film capital firsthand. For many of them, the "Hollywood novel" became an almost obligatory gesture of either devotion to or disdain for the film industry. Fictional accounts of Hollywood and the film industry, often from the jaundiced viewpoint of an outsider or industry critic, became standard fare in the many magazines that published fiction in the 1920s. As a popular literary genre (if we can define "popular" as corresponding to the interests of readers of national periodicals such as *Collier's*, *Cosmopolitan*, *Red Book*, and the *Saturday Evening Post*, where many of these works originally appeared), Hollywood fiction on the whole was uniquely critical of its subject and obsessive in its attention to the negative effects of Hollywood's values on both the individual and society as a whole. As Tom Dardis has observed, "popular fiction has done much to convince its readers that Hollywood is a truly monstrous place."[18] Even in its most pedestrian examples, Hollywood fiction draws upon a modern literary tradition built upon a sense of disillusionment with contemporary life and an alienation from its social and cultural forms.

Authors of Hollywood fictions in the twenties and thirties were generally interested in film and film making only as examples of Hollywood's eccentricity and excess; stories were opportunities to expose the superficiality and artifice within the film industry and attack the vapidity of film as popular entertainment. These works can be seen as a series of efforts to explore Hollywood's significance within the larger framework of American life and values. Characteristic of them is the tendency to transform the film capital from a neutral backdrop for the narrative into a hyperbolic cultural symbol in which, for good or bad, Hollywood functions as an organizing metaphor for certain aspects of American social and cultural life. Its thematic significance goes beyond that typically assigned to *setting* in fiction; in fact, Hollywood frequently becomes a central character, loaded with metaphorical weight. What unifies the texts that take up the subject of Hollywood is a sense of its importance as a reference point for certain social and cultural issues—the implicit conviction that in some sense Hollywood provides a key to an understanding of the American scene and the values and experiences that shape it.

This excessive ideological and thematic significance has, of course, worked to the detriment of the critical reputation of Hollywood fiction. In many Hollywood novels, the overdevelopment of Hollywood as metaphor proceeds at the expense of narrative and characterization, and the preoccupation with Hollywood's significance produces the tendency toward didacticism and polemic that characterizes many of these works. Yet it is precisely as statements, as occasions for self-conscious cultural complaint, that Hollywood fiction can contribute to an analysis of Hollywood and of American life.

Given the critical, condemnatory emphasis in Hollywood fiction, I would propose that a more viable contender than Bower's book for the earliest Hollywood novel is Francis William Sullivan's *The Glory Road,* which was serialized in *Photoplay* magazine starting in July of 1916—the same year *The Phantom Herd* was published.[19] In Sullivan's book, an explicit concern with Hollywood's moral values scarcely conceals a conservative reaction to modern socioeconomic changes involving women and work. *The Glory Road* was announced in *Photoplay* as "the first great novel written around the motion picture capital of the World—Los Angeles. Its chapters exude the living atmosphere of the studios, reflect their romantic glamour— and reveal at times the brassiness of the glitter."[20]

This attention to the romance and glamour of movie making in combination with the promise to reveal "the brassiness of the glitter" constitutes the earliest formulation of what would become the standard appeal of Hollywood fiction—the merging, in a neat narrative package, of a fascination with Hollywood as a way of life with suspicion toward its moral and social influence.

The Glory Road presents the experiences of June Magregor, a beautiful and inexperienced young woman whom the "Graphic Film Company" brings to Hollywood to test her potential for screen stardom. What June finds there is a community of relaxed social mores and carefree pleasures facilitated by the affluence and informality of the fledgling film industry. Yet Sullivan's description of that environment is dominated by what was to become the central theme in Hollywood fiction: the deceptiveness of appearances in a milieu that blurs the distinction between illusion and reality. For June, such blurring leads to moral ambiguity and sexual danger. In chapter 14, Hollywood is described as a fantastic domain cut off from ordinary social life.

> Los Angeles in three years has become the Carnival City of the World. . . . But though Los Angeles is the Carnival City, within her lies another and truer land of Masque where the pageant people live their two-dimension lives.
>
> Its buildings are of canvas and plaster and wood, roofless and without backs. Its rooms want ceilings, and the rented furniture has a strange, unhomelike look. Its citizens rarely go to bed, and then only that they may awaken at once and emote. . . .
>
> The streets of this metropolis are trod by the peoples of all history, yet all speak with one tongue. Its flag is a dollar sign rampant on a

field *d'or*, and its government is autocratic. The ruler has the title of Director, and his reign must be prosperous or he is overthrown.

Dynasties change often and without appeal. Publicity is the Order of Merit in this land, and the honor is bestowed by a functionary called the Press Agent. Altogether it is a happy land, and when for any cause its motley life spills from its flimsy walls into the great and solid and real city, it enlivens the soberer streets with a fantastic touch that is always welcome.[21]

Despite the many attractive features of life in Hollywood, June rapidly discovers that "beneath the colorful, gay surface . . . there were dark and hidden things" (9:107), and she is gradually drawn into a position fraught with moral and physical peril. This is, in part, because of "the character of the work" (13:114), which unavoidably places her in situations where conventional moral limits are tested. Although she is engaged to the handsome Graphic star Paul Temple, June agrees to put off their marriage until she either succeeds or fails as a motion-picture actress, an arrangement that places her career goals above the more traditional roles of wife and mother. When the company sends Paul to the East Coast, June increasingly finds herself prey to the interests of the powerful studio boss Stephen Holt, whose growing sexual demands place her in the middle of a dangerous romantic triangle. Complicating her dilemma is her devotion to the brilliant director Tom Briscoe, who sees their new film as an important breakthrough in screen art.

It is characteristic of Hollywood fiction to intertwine questions of art and morality in this way; as Tom and June complete production on the film that will prove to all the critics and doubters that "the pictures are an art" (12:108), Holt threatens to destroy the film before it is released if June does not surrender to his demands. In this way June's romantic crisis becomes implicated in the larger issue of the cultural fate of motion pictures as an art form. In the end Paul Temple returns to Hollywood and reclaims June's affections. Tom's film is finally released to critical and commercial acclaim; yet June's experiences in the fallen moral world of Hollywood lead her to renounce her imminent stardom and devote herself to a quiet domestic life as Paul's wife. She declares, "I'd sooner be a nobody with you than be alone and have my name a household word" (18:108). *The Glory Road* was paradigmatic for many of the Hollywood fictions that followed it in presenting the threat of sexual danger in Hollywood as a consequence of new opportunities for employment and success offered to women by the motion-picture industry.

Throughout the 1920s Hollywood fiction was, predictably, preoccupied with the debate over the moral influence of movies and the ethics of the film industry. Writers often used Hollywood to examine issues raised by the "new morality" in post-World War I American society.[22] For many writers in this period, Hollywood represented a modern alternative to outdated Victorian mores, promising a new and romantic realm of personal freedom and opportunity. In the 1920s, in the wake of scandals that for a time seemed to threaten the future of Hollywood as a center of motion-picture production, the Hollywood romance emerged as a type of Hollywood fiction specifically dedicated to defending, even glorifying, Hollywood. However, the counterimage of Hollywood as a scene of decadence and dissipation caused other writers (and perhaps most Americans) to see the film capital as representing a climate of debauchery and moral corruption that promised only social disorder and cultural decline.

Hollywood was, as well, an apt site for an examination of the emerging ethos of leisure and consumption in American society. The great propaganda machines of the studio publicity departments and the fan magazines presented glamorous, compelling portraits of an ideal way of life based on affluence and consumption. In this way the life-styles of the Hollywood elite were often used as dramatic examples of the transformative virtues of modern economic and social values. Through the figure of the star in Hollywood fiction, the new consumerist values were both celebrated and held up for interrogation and critique.

Concomitant with the tendency to magnify and elaborate Hollywood's metaphorical significance in fiction about the film capital was the tendency to outline a moral or aesthetic position in regard to Hollywood. As *The Glory Road* demonstrates, questions of moral and aesthetic value were often implicitly intertwined in Hollywood fiction. Particularly in the 1930s, while the rest of the country staggered under the effects of the Depression, Hollywood commonly figured as an emblem of cultural decline, a milieu in which greed and appetite—crass material values—dominated, bullying into submission whatever true artistic ideals struggled for expression in the movies. Hence, Hollywood came to represent a mode of cultural production predicated on artifice and illusion, a threat to artistic integrity and accomplishment, and the perceived shallowness of its aesthetic—its failure as art—often found a parallel in the moral emptiness and social breakdown with which so many Hollywood writers were preoccupied. In much of the fiction of this period, then, Hollywood became an organizing metaphor for the collapse of traditional moral values and artistic standards, an emblem of widespread cultural crisis.

In contrast with the positive, often enthusiastic appraisal of the movies and film industry offered by the romances of the 1920s, the Hollywood fictions of the 1930s were generally more pessimistic in their attention to the corrupting influence of the film industry; they expressed a widening sense of disillusionment with the fantasy and official optimism that characterized American mass culture in the 1930s. Indeed, the canon of Hollywood fiction has been a discursive site for the most widespread and sustained critiques of mass culture, which was the product of new technologies of communication and visual representation that had emerged in the late nineteenth century.

HOLLYWOOD AND MASS CULTURE

Representations of Hollywood in fiction have generally functioned, with varying degrees of purpose and insight, as commentaries on American mass culture, and the tenor of this commentary has been largely (although not exclusively) critical. While much postmodern cultural theory sets out to reclaim the products of mass culture through deconstructive or resistant readings aimed at uncovering contradictory or oppositional elements at work there, the tradition of Hollywood fiction has most often embraced an analysis of mass culture that finds in it a mechanism of control and deception. Hollywood fictions often reveal what Warren Susman termed "the great fear" running through much of the writing of the twenties and thirties: a pervasive cultural anxiety over "whether any great industrial and democratic mass society can maintain a significant level of civilization, and whether mass education and mass communication will allow any civilization to survive.[23] For most writers who approached the subject, "Hollywood" was synonymous with vulgarity, sham, and deception, and it was a convenient symbol for what they perceived as a morally and aesthetically vapid ersatz American culture. Whether or not they shared this harsh judgment, writers interested in exploring the American scene could never ignore Hollywood. In fact, Hollywood fiction has often provided writers with a forum in which to negotiate and explore their relationship to mass culture and the "entertainment" provided by the movies.

The notion of "mass culture" (as opposed to "popular culture," which implies a more direct relationship to the lives of ordinary people) first appeared in the work of scholars associated with the Frankfurt School of Social Research in Germany during the 1930s, such as the critical social theorists Max Horkheimer and Theodor Adorno. They advanced a view of mass culture as an instrument of coercion and control, a system of "mass deception" imposed from above that offered its audiences little more than "entertainment and distraction" from "an unbearable reality."[24] Their arguments, which constituted a Marxist critique of cultural production under capitalism, derived a sense of urgency from the tangible dangers posed by the cultural policies of the German state under Nazism. Underlying their sometimes compelling analyses, however, was an unacknowledged cultural elitism that imprisoned popular culture in a sterile dichotomy with high "Art," dismissing the styles and values of mass entertainment as less authentic than traditional artistic forms and therefore as essentially alienating.

Subsequent cultural theorists have rightly challenged this unidirectional, monolithic conception of mass culture (and its reception). Indeed, the phrase "mass culture" has become increasingly problematic because of its evocation of a sociologically flat and theoretically reductive notion of an undifferentiated and homogeneous "mass society." "There are in fact no masses," Raymond Williams cogently argued; "there are only ways of seeing people as masses."[25] Despite the limitations of the Frankfurt Schools' analysis of mass culture, the phrase retains validity if one understands the word "mass" not as referring to an assumed audience, but rather as describing the mode of cultural production under a particular arrangement of industrial and economic interests. Mass culture, so conceived, means *mass-produced culture*—a shift in emphasis that avoids the pejorative connotations usually attached to it within contemporary cultural studies.[26] In this sense, Hollywood can be seen as the locus of mass culture par excellence. Hollywood from the late twenties on was a model of industrial rationalization—a vertically integrated factory system that coordinated production, distribution, and exhibition through powerful corporate empires, which attempted to produce commodities that would appeal to the broadest possible market.

Setting aside, for the moment, this conception of mass culture as mass-produced culture, it is perhaps more important to note that many of the literary works that attacked Hollywood in the twenties and thirties seem to have had in mind something similar to Adorno's notion of a "cultural industry," on the basis of their depictions of the Hollywood film industry as ruthlessly imposing its skewed vision of the world upon an audience made passive and impressionable by the movies' relentless domination of their cultural and psychic lives.

A cultural history of Hollywood fiction should begin by recognizing that fiction about Hollywood represents the sustained efforts of those within one area of cultural production (popular fiction and the New York publishing business) to describe and evaluate a rival area of cultural production (motion pictures and the Hollywood film industry). The relationship between literature and film has, of course, been dynamic and complex, characterized as much by mutual influence and dependence upon each other's narrative forms and devices as by competition and an insistence on their fundamental differences as modes of narrative discourse.[27] Moreover, as the two most prevalent forms of narrative art in the twentieth century, popular fiction and the movies have often reiterated and supported each other at the level of the commodity: popular novels and short stories have served as a staple source for motion-picture scenarios, and novelizations of popular films have become a key marketing strategy for capitalizing on box-office success.[28] As one would expect from a literature preoccupied with movies and their influence, Hollywood fictions often display the formal traces of a film aesthetic in their approach to narrative structure and characterization. The marked influence of scenario writing on Hollywood fiction is not surprising, considering the number of Hollywood writers who also wrote for the movies. Hollywood fictions often evoke cinematic effects and principles of construction, and display a heightened awareness of the codes and conventions of Hollywood film making.

Hollywood fictions constitute a set of prose narratives written in a variety of literary styles (comic, tragic, realist, romantic, satiric) and displaying a wide range of aesthetic purposes and effects. Given this heterogeneity, it is fair to ask whether Hollywood fiction can be viewed as a distinct literary genre or if, rather, it has been merely a lucrative marketing category for a publishing industry eager to profit on the public's fascination with Hollywood and the lives of those who work there. Certainly there are no specific literary elements that would provide an internal, formal unity for Hollywood fiction per se. On the other hand, there is a significant thematic consensus among Hollywood fictions, and in many of them an almost stylized approach to character and setting in which stereotypical Hollywood characters (the avaricious producer, the libidinal starlet, the ambitious director, the disillusioned writer, the down-and-out extra) are walked through almost ritual set pieces and situations (the Hollywood party, the story conference or production meeting, the studio back lot, the Hollywood premiere). This recurrent iconography of character and setting does provide Hollywood fiction with a set of stable (perhaps clichéd) generic reference points so that, like all genre-driven forms of narrative, Hollywood fiction offers its readers the pleasures of familiarity and repetition. The force of its cultural arguments stems from the accumulation and arrangement of familiar motifs and thematic conflicts.

The central cultural paradox disclosed by Hollywood fiction is the fundamental ambivalence of Americans toward their own "popular" culture: their simultaneous delight in and suspicion of the formulas of mass entertainment and their attraction to, yet distance from, the organizing ideologies and styles of mass culture. Hollywood fictions articulate the social and sexual fantasies emanating from the film capital as well as deep-seated anxieties and concerns about the influence of Hollywood and the movies on traditional social and cultural values. However, the attacks on mass culture found in Hollywood fictions have often been trivialized and dismissed, precisely because they arise from a popular literature whose own cultural value has often been questioned and discounted.

Granted, much Hollywood fiction is writing of the most ephemeral and aesthetically vapid sort, and critics of these works have often questioned their artistic worth. Today it is less difficult to justify the study of popular literature.[29] Questions of aesthetic value aside, however, any discussion of

Hollywood fiction needs to recognize its perennial appeal for readers, for—like the "western" or the "hard-boiled detective" story—Hollywood fiction is a uniquely American literary genre that has become a publishing staple, revealing an ongoing and deep-seated fascination with Hollywood and its influence upon American culture.

THE POLITICS OF POPULAR CULTURE

American popular culture has always been a terrain of controversy and debate drawn along lines of class, ethnicity, age, and gender. The essential features of this debate have generally been disguised by a rhetoric of "taste" and artistic "value" that originates as much in the class structure of late-nineteenth-century American society as in a particular philosophical or aesthetic tradition.[30] During the late nineteenth century, America underwent a period of intense social and economic upheaval, a central feature of which was the emergence of mass-produced forms of culture made possible by scientific discoveries and improvements in industrial manufacturing. Advances in printing technology placed newspapers, periodicals, and books in the hands of millions of Americans, creating a rapidly expanding mass market for fiction, the chief commodity forms of which were popular novels and magazines. The phonograph and, by the 1920s, commercial radio helped to popularize new styles of American music and dance forms. New modes of visual representation appeared as well, as photography and motion pictures contributed to an ongoing perceptual revolution in which a logic of the visible was elaborated and codified. Color chromos, stereopticons, photographic portraits, postcards, comic strips, and movies all exemplify the commodification and marketing of visual images in this period. With the adaptation of narrative protocols based on popular nineteenth-century literary and dramatic forms and their increasing acceptance by middle-class audiences, by the 1920s motion pictures emerged as one of the most important and profitable elements within a thoroughly commercialized mass culture.[31]

With the ascendancy of mass cultural forms in the twentieth century, an apparently homogenizing system of cultural production emerged that appeared to level and more effectively efface the social, sexual, and racial dynamics that energized popular culture. The enigma of mass culture, and the dilemma for those who would study it, is that it seems to come at once from everywhere and nowhere, its sources obscured by the technologies of mass production and the anonymity of corporate management, its ideologies concealed by the putative goals of entertainment and reportage. Ubiquitous, transient, and transparent, mass culture has dominated the cultural landscape of twentieth-century American life. And, ironically, traditional cultural elites and radical social critics have at times found themselves in uneasy agreement in their condemnation of mass culture,[32] characterizing the new media and their cultural forms with a rhetoric of crisis and upheaval charged with an implicit moral or political imperative.[33]

Of course, mass culture has had its celebrants as well. It is possible to see in its broad appeal the realization of a Whitmanesque call for a truly democratic art, the achievement of a common cultural vocabulary through which diverse social groups and cultural traditions could begin to discover shared experiences and values and produce that most cherished of American social and political ideals—consensus. The fact that mass culture has never exactly worked in that way, that it has, in fact, always privileged the values and cultural forms of particular social groups, has not diminished the optimism of those who see in it a force for the democratization of American culture.[34]

Mass culture, it must be acknowledged, played an important role as an agent of modernization in American life. The movies, jazz, and popular fiction all helped to loosen the hold of a rigidly hierarchical and decorous nineteenth-century Victorianism on American thought and manners. Upsetting received aesthetic categories, challenging traditional cultural forms, and revolutionizing social values and behavioral codes, mass culture was a vital element among the historical forces that shaped twentieth-century experience. Most important, it articulated and disseminated an emerging ethos of leisure and consumption in American society—a cultural mission that gave it both an ideological purpose and an economic structure, as the commodity form of cultural production. As Richard Ohmann has argued, from its inception mass culture "was a discourse inseparable from the circulation of commodities." Whether it is sold (like books or movie tickets) or is used to sell (like radio and television), mass culture is structurally tied to the economic ideologies and relations of production under capitalist systems of exchange.[35]

When one examines the canon of Hollywood fiction, it becomes evident that within it Hollywood functioned as a totalized and demonic figure for mass culture—the hyperbolic symbol of an increasingly powerful culture industry that was seen as both a source of collective fantasy and an apparatus of mass deception. Like mass culture generally, Hollywood was associated with the loosening of traditional moral codes and the breakdown of established cultural forms and values. It was, as well, linked to an ideology of success that was based on a myth of opportunity and individual initiative endemic to American democratic and economic experience. In terms reminiscent of Horatio Alger, anyone—through either luck or talent—could be "discovered" in Hollywood and realize the American dream of wealth and fame. However, when the dream proved elusive, as it so often does in Hollywood fiction, the whole ideological apparatus of American values and beliefs could be called into question. When Hollywood fictions began to question the efficacy of consumption as a path to personal happiness or professional achievement, one of the central ideological messages of mass culture came under interrogation and critique. Increasingly, the myths of Hollywood came to be treated as coequal to the myths of American culture at large, transforming this seemingly minor popular literary genre into one of the most consistently polemical bodies of fiction in American literature.

Most studies of Hollywood fiction, in their emphasis on a single literary form (the novel), have not considered other literary representations of Hollywood. Hollywood short stories, for example, which appeared by the hundreds in popular magazines of the twenties and thirties, have never received the attention they deserve. The same is true for the rich corpus of essays, editorials, and occasional pieces that Hollywood inspired in those decades. Fan magazines and autobiographies are an equally fascinating source of information and opinion about Hollywood and its place in American life. In short, students of the Hollywood novel have not always acknowledged that it is part of a larger literary and cultural discourse about the film capital and the mass culture of the movies. To understand Hollywood's role in American culture, it is necessary to consider this larger discursive context, as daunting as that might seem in light of the sheer quantity of material involved. Thus, while I have been guided by the handful of scholars who have preceded me into this vast, little-explored area of American literary and cultural history,[36] I have nonetheless found it necessary to extend my research in new directions. Prior studies of Hollywood fiction have been, for the most part, rather specifically literary in their approach to the subject. In contrast, I have attempted to view the texts as a series of cultural statements, rejoinders in the social arguments that raged around the film capital in this period.

In writing about a body of texts that are largely forgotten or unknown, and in attempting to recover the cultural arguments and debates to which they were responses or contributions, I have focused my attention on the *content* of these works—the plots and characters—to a greater extent than would be necessary if they were more familiar. Naturally, I have not avoided considerations of form and language when they were relevant to my argument, but in general I have found it necessary to make at least brief summaries of these works in order to elaborate and support my views. Much critical and theoretical work needs to be done before we can claim to understand the narrative invention and linguistic resources of popular writing. In what follows, I am primarily concerned with showing how the elevation in Hollywood fiction of such themes as sin and romance, success and failure, betrayal and loss, art and commerce, and illusion and reality to the level of cultural argument has served to interrogate and undermine fundamental American ideological assumptions and values. Only an analysis that recognizes the complex social and cultural dialogue that has surrounded Hollywood can begin to account for its place and significance in American life.

CHAPTER ONE

SUNSHINE AND SHADOW

The Paradox of Hollywood in the 1920s

Hollywood, you see, is not simply a suburb of Los Angeles; it is
a suburb of every town in the country.

KATHARINE FULLERTON GEROULD[1]

In 1886 Horace and Daeida Wilcox purchased 160 acres of fig and apricot
orchards in the Cahuenga Valley at the base of the Santa Monica foothills
north of Los Angeles and subdivided the property for residential development, bestowing upon it the name "Hollywood." Horace, a successful
businessman from Topeka, Kansas, had brought his second wife, Daeida, to
Los Angeles because of its year-round good weather and its burgeoning
opportunities for real-estate speculation.[2] It was Daeida who suggested the
name "Hollywood," and to justify the appellation for such a dry, rugged
environment as the Cahuenga Valley, she planted a pair of English holly
trees. The trees died, but the Wilcoxes' real-estate investments slowly
prospered.[3] By 1900 Hollywood was a sleepy arcadian village of some
five hundred inhabitants, many of them retired businessmen and shopkeepers from the Midwest whose chief interests were religion and
horticulture. Two-story white frame houses like those found in Iowa or
Kansas nestled among the orange groves, along broad dirt roads lined with
pepper and eucalyptus trees. By 1920 Hollywood was a booming city of
36,000, and only nine years later its population would reach 157,000.[4] Yet

its phenomenal growth during these years only hints at its growing symbolic importance within American culture.

Hollywood was always more than just a place where movies were made. Indeed, there have been many "Hollywoods." In the 1920s, just as it was emerging into the full glare of public attention, Hollywood could evoke a whole series of conflicting images and ideas. While to critics it was "a sink of iniquity, a modern Sodom," for movie fans it was the glamorous and romantic abode of the stars, "the dreamer's dream come true," or simply "a decent law-abiding community of good, fine home folk."[5] As a cultural signifier, Hollywood has always been defined by contradiction, a semantic field of conflicting ideas and perceptions, and yet its influence has been felt across an array of cultural discourses and social practices in American life. Katharine Fullerton Gerould, a novelist and professor of English at Bryn Mawr College, argued as early as 1923 that, because of its larger symbolic significance, Hollywood should be considered not a "geographical entity" but rather "a state of mind." "Hollywood is more than itself," she proclaimed; "Hollywood is one of the national points of view . . . an instance, a manifestation of something ubiquitously present in America, not an isolated phenomenon."[6] Gerould's estimation of Hollywood was later echoed by film director John Ford when he joked, "Hollywood is a place you can't geographically define. We don't really know where it is."[7] The difficulty of precisely locating Hollywood's influence and importance in American culture stems from the complex, often contradictory role it has played in our national life. Still, much of Hollywood's significance derives from the allure of its locale, and it is therefore necessary to begin a discussion of Hollywood's role in American culture by considering the reasons why the American film industry chose to locate its production center in this southern California community.

WHY HOLLYWOOD?

From its beginnings in the 1890s, the film industry had been located primarily on the East Coast, in New York and New Jersey, with Philadelphia and Chicago as important secondary sites for production and distribution. This placed the emerging industry in proximity to the manufacturers of cameras and projecting equipment and to the vaudeville stages and theater circuits that provided exhibition spaces and a talent pool for film work. However, starting around 1907, film makers and production companies began to converge on southern California and the quiet Los Angeles suburb of Hollywood. First to arrive, attracted by the Los Angeles Chamber of Commerce's claim of 350 days of sunshine a year, was a production unit from Chicago's Selig Company.[8] Initially movie work in California was seasonal, the camera crews and players migrating west only during the winter, when weather made filming in New York or Chicago difficult. In 1911 David Horsley and Al Christie of the Centaur Film Company (which released films under the Nestor banner) established the first permanent studio in Hollywood at the corner of Sunset Boulevard and Gower Street, using the old Blondeau Tavern for a front office and constructing a crude stage in the back for film production.[9] Gradually more and more companies established production facilities, and movie making established itself as a West Coast occupation. Even so, the industry's migration to California was never complete. The financial end of the business remained in New York, an arrangement with important consequences for Hollywood's conception of itself. The dichotomy between art and commerce was seen, in part, as a result of the bicoastal structure of the film industry, which imposed a sharp division between production (West Coast) and financing and distribution (East Coast).[10]

An obvious explanation for the selection of Hollywood was the consistently favorable weather conditions in southern California in an era before freeways and smog. At a time when, for technological and economic reasons, most film making took place outdoors, the sunny California climate allowed movie makers virtual year-round production. Another obvious attraction was the diverse topography of the region. For location work, film makers had at their disposal oceans and mountains, forests and deserts, all within a day's drive from downtown Los Angeles. In an article appearing in the February 1916 issue of *Photoplay*, Jesse L. Lasky outlined the advantages of West Coast production: "(1) There is the clear atmosphere . . . (2) The Climate . . . (3) . . . the abundance and variety of natural scenery."[11] To these geographical and climatological advantages he added two sociological factors. First, after an initial shortage of trained actors and actresses in Los Angeles, Lasky reported that "today every train brings in new arrivals to be added to the great colony of legitimate players who have adopted motion pictures as a permanent means of earning their livelihood and continuing their art" (99). While actors with a stage background were not as important to film production as Lasky's statement suggests, his reference to "legitimate players" must be understood within the context of the film industry's struggle for cultural respectability in the first decades of the century. The second sociological factor was "the difference in the manner of living as compared to the East." In striking contrast with what would soon become Hollywood's image of sin and decadence, Lasky depicted the West Coast production center as a haven from urban vice and dissipation.

> In Hollywood and vicinity, which is the real motion picture center of California, the majority of artists and directors live in their own bungalows. They are not subjected to the distractions and dissipations of a large city. The absence of a Broadway and the gayeties of the Rialto means that they retire earlier, live healthier, cleaner lives and are generally more physically fit for their duties than they would be were they pursuing the same calling in the East. (162)

A more dramatic explanation for the concentration of motion-picture production in Los Angeles was that it provided to independent producers, who were engaged in a bitter legal battle with Edison's Motion Picture Patents Company (MPPC), a base of operations with quick access to an international border in case MPPC lawyers or their hired thugs showed up to interfere with production.[12] One problem with this account is that two of the first companies to move to California were in fact prominent members of MPPC: Selig in 1907 and Biograph in 1909.[13] Moreover, the Mexican border is almost two hundred miles from Los Angeles—hardly a convenient getaway.

Film historian Robert Sklar offers a more persuasive argument: that Los Angeles became the centers for film production for basic economic reasons. In the early decades of this century, land was plentiful and inexpensive around Los Angeles, and East Coast companies, looking to expand and improve their production facilities, found that locating in southern California made good business sense. In addition, Los Angeles was well known to be an open-shop, nonunion city, and the steady stream of people migrating from all over the United States into southern California guaranteed a ready supply of cheap labor. For these reasons, Sklar maintains, "lower costs became an increasingly important factor in locating production in Los Angeles."[14] A decisive moment in this process was the winter of 1918, when an East Coast fuel shortage led several of the major manufacturers to permanently relocate their production operations in southern California.[15]

Perhaps the most compelling arguments, however, stem from a recognition of the symbolic importance of California in American life. California had long been conceived of as a land of opportunity, and Horace Greeley's famous editorial advice to "Go West, Young Man!" set the imprimatur of official wisdom on what was already the historical fact of western movement in the late nineteenth century. The West was seen as a place where past identities could be left behind in pursuit of new prospects and a better way of life. Hollywood eventually came to be conceived of in similar terms, as a place of easy opportunity and sudden wealth where people could reinvent themselves in the glamorous terms of movie life. The historian Kevin Starr has argued that by linking its identity to that of southern California, the film industry was associating itself with a part of the country that had already been a land of dreams and aspirations for over half a century.[16]

Hollywood, "as a town, an industry, a state of mind, a self-actualizing myth" (334), quickly became an intensely symbolic American place. The images of Los Angeles disseminated by Hollywood films—"a city where everyone seemed to live in a bungalow on a broad avenue lined with palm, pepper or eucalyptus trees, where there was never any snow on the ground or other evidence of bad weather" (294)—offered a remarkably appealing "visual signature" to the rest of the country. From its beginning, Hollywood represented an acute version of the American dream. It is not surprising that America's *dream factories* found that a home there was particularly suited to their role in national life.[17]

"WHAT'S WRONG WITH THE MOVIES?"

The cultural arguments that surrounded Hollywood in the 1920s were the culmination of a larger debate over motion pictures, which had begun almost as soon as they were established as a form of popular entertainment. Indeed, the history of American film in this period is fundamentally a history of the social, economic, and cultural processes whereby an emerging technology of mass communication is defined and becomes integrated into national life. The fact that in the case of motion pictures this period was marked by controversy and struggle points to the tremendous impact the new medium had on American society and to its power as a cultural form. At stake in the debates were not just the reputations of Hollywood and the American film industry but the fate of a new and increasingly powerful form of mass culture.

A widespread belief in the ability of motion pictures to influence social behavior and shape moral values eventually drew into conflict those who saw movies as a threat to traditional moral precepts or standards of taste and those who believed in the commercial and artistic potentials of the new medium. Progressive reformers, religious enthusiasts, and highbrow critics of motion pictures squared off against movie fans and supporters of the film industry in a debate that had broad social and cultural consequences. So heated were the arguments and so high were the stakes that by the early twenties, as a writer for *Time* magazine observed, the debate over the question "What's wrong with the movies?" had begun to take on the proportions of a "national pastime."[18]

Initial complaints focused upon the content of motion pictures, and arguments were made on both moral and aesthetic grounds. In an era of postwar uncertainty and disillusionment in which traditional moral values were in flux, and before the film industry was forced to abide by strict production codes, many critics felt that movies too often dealt with shocking and offensive subject matter. Opponents of motion pictures insisted that melodramatic and violent plots encouraged crime and glamourized vice, and that frank depictions of sexual situations and emotional problems flouted established moral precepts and standards of decency. Senator Henry Lee Myers of Montana, for example, railed against the moral effects of motion pictures from the floor of the Senate.

> I believe that a great deal of the extravagance of the day, a great deal of the disposition to live beyond one's means, yea, a great deal of the crime of the day, comes from moving pictures. Through them young

people gain ideas of fast life, shady ways, laxity of living, loose morals. Crime is freely depicted in alluring colors. Lax morals are held up lightly before them. The sensual is strongly appealed to. Many of the pictures are certainly not elevating; some at least, are not fit to be seen.[19]

Indeed, even brief scenes of smoking, drinking, and gambling could arouse the wrath of local and state censor boards who were concerned about the power of motion pictures to influence social behavior.[20] This view of the movies is succinctly expressed in a passage from Rupert Hughes's Hollywood novel *Souls for Sale*, in which the Reverend Doctor Steddon, archcritic of Hollywood and the movies, stares in horror at the facade of a local movie theater.

> He had gazed aghast at the appalling posters with their revolting blazon of the new word "Sex"; their insolent questions about "Your Wife," "Your Husband"; their frenzied scenes of embraces, wrestling matches, conventionalized rape, defiances, innumerable revolvers, daggers, train wrecks, automobile accidents, slaughters, plunging horses, Bacchic revels, bathing suits, gambling and drinking and smoking scenes—everything and everybody desperately wicked or desperately good.[21]

The real danger of all this perceived immorality was that it was being disseminated by a new medium of popular entertainment with an unparalleled capacity to reach and influence a mass audience. One critic observed, "Through reaching millions on millions of impressionable minds daily, in thousands of big and little movie theaters throughout the country, the movies are to-day influencing your children and mine, your neighbors and mine, your employees and mine, your future and mine."[22] The content of motion pictures as well as their appeal to an increasingly large and undifferentiated audience of moviegoers led critics of the new medium to conclude that films were seriously undermining traditional moral and social codes. Katharine Fullerton Gerould, writing about the problems of movie censorship for the *Saturday Evening Post*, attributed the controversy over the morality of the motion pictures entirely to their success as a *mass* medium. "Neither the spoken drama nor literature reaches the millions that are reached by any successful film. Therefore the film is everybody's business.

It penetrates the whole fabric of American life. As its sponsors have always wished it to do."[23]

It was because motion pictures were recognized as an increasingly powerful form of mass culture that a different set of critics, more concerned with the movies' artistic shortcomings than with their moral ones, complained about their deleterious effects on the public. These critics attacked the movies for their "cheap sentimentalism" and "shoddy melodrama," for their lack of realism and the "distorted views of life and character" they offered, and found them to be a serious menace to the standards of taste and artistic sensibility of their audiences. It was with no apparent sense of exaggeration that the anonymous author of a series of bitterly critical exposés of motion pictures and the film industry that appeared in *Collier's* in 1922 wrote that "on account of their stupidity the movies today are one of the greatest dangers threatening our entire social fabric."[24] George Jean Nathan complained in *The Smart Set:* "More than any other force, more than any other ten forces all compact, have the moving pictures in the last dozen years succeeded brilliantly in reducing further the taste, the sense and the general culture of the American nation."[25] Maurice Maeterlinck in his article "The Spiritual Future of America and the Movies," written for *Photoplay* in 1921, complained that out of some one hundred films he had seen on a recent trip to California, "there were only four or five truly good ones, based on a big idea or an original thought, following a logical, human and interesting plot—in short well built, with exposition, complication, climax and denouement."[26]

Apologists for the movies routinely accounted for their lack of artistic finish by pointing out their youth in comparison with other art forms, or blamed their low artistic achievement on the climate of commercialism within American society.[27] But these excuses did little to defuse the complaints of highbrow critics, whose real target, more often than not, was the mass audience, "that uncritical crowd—just 'kick' hungry—seeking surcease from its boredom."[28] Here the critics of motion pictures often revealed the class and gender biases that underlay their aesthetic assumptions. George Humphrey, a professor of psychology at Wesleyan University, offered this analysis: "The stories which unfold themselves on the screen are really a picture of the inside of the mind of the lazy woman, the overworked clerk, the tired shopgirl. Working out in the darkness, one may see the un-intelligent, animal wishes of the people in the chairs."[29]

Humphrey was one of many critics who believed that the problem with the movies lay largely with the people who consumed them. "We shall never get away from a mass of cheap and melodramatic films," complained another writer, "for there will always be a large class that demands such pictures"; and the solution to this problem was to place more of the control of the industry into the hands of the "intelligent minority of artistically sensitive and intellectually superior industry critics.[30] In a similarly elitist vein, Maeterlinck's suggestion was that an "aristocracy of millionaires" be given the authority to "intervene from above" by taking control of the business and establishing a "model studio" that would set the standards for artistic achievement and good taste.[31] The promotion of elite control over popular amusements which these critics advanced paralleled the battles that surrounded other sites of popular diversion, such as the amusement park and the urban dance hall.[32] In such arguments the focus of criticism was shifting from the content of motion pictures to the composition and structure of the film industry itself.

By 1921 criticisms of the film industry, often originating within its ranks, dominated the cultural debate over motion pictures. This was due largely to the fact that the industry was experiencing a severe economic slump, during which many theaters closed and the studios suffered a huge drop in revenues.[33] The criticisms were often directed at industry leaders, fueled by a barely concealed envy for the newly prosperous and now culturally powerful Jewish moguls who ran the major studios—"little fellows, boosted by circumstances into jobs that are too big for them."[34] Their critics often relied on racial stereotypes and anti-Semitism in condemning them for their "shortsighted commercialism" and "greed." New York's Canon William Sheafe Chase, one of the national leaders of the movement for movie censorship and a bitter enemy of the film industry, argued that "the real trouble is that the business is in the hands of a few men—producers who have a strangle grip on the art, the morality and the freedom of individuals connected to the industry. These men think they can make money by giving pictures which are below the morality of the general public."[35]

Others, however, made more impartial and legitimate assessments of the film industry's shortcomings. Homer Croy, in his article "The Gold Cure," attacked the excesses of movie-industry spending that so often substituted for the "art and intelligence" needed to produce good pictures.

And he cited no less of an industry insider than Jesse Lasky to support his views.

> The day for a complete "showdown" has come. Abnormal and exorbitant salaries, needless and wasteful extravagance, so-called "bankers' hours," and all the various illogical and un-businesslike methods that have obtained to a greater or lesser degree in the motion-picture business, and for which it has been more or less justly criticized from time to time, must come to an abrupt end.[36]

W. W. Hodkinson, a leading film distributor, explained in an article entitled "Why You Don't Get Better Films" that the industry's emphasis on quantity rather than quality had led to motion pictures' being treated, to their detriment, like a "factory-made product."[37] The novelist George Randolph Chester complained in a piece entitled "Too Many Cooks Spoil the Pictures" about the difficulty of making good films through a production process that was necessarily collaborative and collective and was determined, in the final analysis, by what the audience would pay to see.[38]

Chester was a prolific writer of Hollywood fiction in the twenties; his works were uniquely concerned with the administrative and economic problems of running a studio and producing films that are both popular and artistically successful. In collaboration with his wife, Lillian, he wrote the novel *On the Lot and Off* (1924) and a series of short stories that was published in the *Saturday Evening Post*.[39] All chronicle the experiences of an ambitious "boy wonder" movie executive named Izzy Iskovitch (a comic forerunner of Budd Schulberg's Sammy Glick). In intricately plotted narratives characterized by clever twists and sudden reversals of fortune that betray a wry, gently satirical view of Hollywood, the stories follow Izzy as he fights industry waste and inefficiency while dodging temperamental stars, extravagant directors, and rival studios to become the number-one producer in Hollywood. As a studio executive and businessman, Izzy is a somewhat anomalous character in Hollywood fiction. Not until the appearance of Monroe Stahr in F. Scott Fitzgerald's *The Last Tycoon* would a studio executive receive a similarly favorable treatment.

In 1922 arguments over the efficiency and organization of the film industry were upstaged by three important events: the murder trial of Roscoe "Fatty"

Arbuckle, the mysterious murder of director William Desmond Taylor, and the drug addiction and death of popular screen star and "all-American boy" Wallace Reid.[40] These "star scandals" galvanized the American public and precipitated a fire storm of controversy, extending anxiety over the moral influence of motion pictures to the "debauchery behind the screen," as well.[41] Suddenly Hollywood, including the life-styles and values of those who worked there, was a focus of national scrutiny and outrage. Critics described Hollywood as "the graveyard of virtue,"[42] a place where "debauchery, drunkenness, ribaldry, dissipation and free love seem to be conspicuous."[43] It was asserted—with little supporting evidence besides the notoriety of the scandals—that "[Hollywood's] daily life is a devil's playground, its inhabitants morally bankrupt, and its amusements of a character to invite condemnation."[44] Even so ardent a supporter of the film industry as James R. Quirk, the editor of the popular fan magazine *Photoplay*, called for a "Moral House-Cleaning in Hollywood."[45] Hollywood itself had swiftly become an emblem of all the things the critics said were wrong with the movies. The immorality, the lack of artistic value, the excesses and ineffi-ciencies of the film industry—all of these could be localized and to some extent contained by linking them to Hollywood. There were even those within the movie business who were quick to seize upon Hollywood as a convenient scapegoat for the industry's woes. The director Herbert Brenon, for one, argued that "Hollywood as a moving picture colony must go."

> The trouble is that out in Hollywood the motion picture people are thrown upon themselves for recreation. They live, think and talk pictures all the time. They do not lead the normal lives with outside diversion which we in the East do. The minority, who have made money quickly, persons with little character and less morals, have had their head turned and have cast aside all restraint.[46]

Spurred by women's clubs, church leaders, and reform organizations, indignation against Hollywood grew; the film capital found itself at the center of a national moral hysteria. Industry leaders became increasingly uneasy about the effects of the controversy, fearing that it might even lead to the end of the film business. "If this keeps up there won't be any motion picture industry," Louis B. Mayer is reported to have said after the Taylor murder.[47] The industry responded by appointing former Postmaster General and Republican Party leader Will H. Hays as president of the newly formed Motion Picture Producers and Distributors Association and immediately dispatching him to Hollywood, where he promised to turn the film capital into a "model industrial community."[48] There was even some discussion about the feasibility of moving motion-picture production back to the East Coast, although the moral benefits to be gained by such a relocation seemed dubious.[49]

At the same time, there were many who stepped forward to defend Hollywood.[50] In Los Angeles, following Fatty Arbuckle's arrest, community and religious leaders released a statement insisting that the movie colony was made up of "clean and upright citizens. Taken as a whole, the people in the Hollywood film world are upright, law-abiding residents. They own mile after mile of the best homes. They have bank accounts. They have A-1 credit. Hollywood is a section of well-conducted house-holds, well patronized churches and model schools."[51] John Emerson—actor, director, screenwriter, and husband of Anita Loos—likewise defended Hollywood in the *New York Times,* just days after the Taylor murder, as "a perfectly normal, upstanding and self-respecting community, . . . no better and no worse, in proportion to its size, than any other American city."[52] By Emerson's account, Hollywood's idyllic climate and natural beauty encouraged "a healthy, normal out-of-door mode of living," supported by the comforts of beautiful homes and a gracious social life. When screen stars Norma and Constance Talmadge arrived in New York from the West Coast a week later, they gave a similarly positive account of Hollywood as a place of innocent amusements and healthful athleticism. "The midnight parties and the wild life there is greatly exaggerated. Since there are no theaters, few restaurants and other indoor diversions, we find our recreation out of doors. We give tennis parties, golf parties and spend hours swimming. Such a life is sure to make one healthy and clean-minded."[53]

Defenders of Hollywood were quick to blame its notoriety on the "dishonest, scavenger press,"[54] which in an era of tabloid journalism was eager to exploit any sensational story that might boost circulation. In the ensuing years, however, articles debunking the myth of "flaming Hollywood" became standard journalistic fare in the national magazines.[55] When asked about the wild night life of the town, H. L. Mencken responded that

"Hollywood seemed to me to be one of the most respectable towns in America. Even Baltimore can't beat it."[56]

Yet there was a symbolic dimension to the criticism of Hollywood that did not escape some observers. Canon Chase found that "the looseness characteristic of the moving-picture industry is not very far different from that into which the American people as a whole have fallen since the war,"[57] linking Hollywood to the larger moral and social changes the country was undergoing. Distinct from the quiet residential neighborhoods, drugstores, cafeterias, real-estate offices, and movie studios that composed the actual community, Hollywood had become a cultural myth, a symbolic site of tremendous importance in the social landscape of the twenties. An editorial in the *New York Times* expressed the situation this way: "The stories of 'orgies' have been greatly exaggerated, as some readers have all along suspected. But we fear that this testimony won't do Hollywood much good. The great American people loves its myths and legends. It has become convinced that Hollywood is a scene of iniquity, and it will remain in that conviction."[58]

Of course, there were more perceptive cultural analyses of Hollywood at the time, many of them appearing in works of fiction. One of the most cogent assessments of Hollywood's role in national life came from Katharine Fullerton Gerould, who was the first critic to recognize Hollywood's larger cultural significance. In an article published in 1923, entitled "Hollywood: An American State of Mind," Gerould suggested that Hollywood be understood "as a mental condition, an attitude of some millions of souls."[59] For her, Hollywood was symptomatic of a false optimism and a tendency toward self-deception in American culture that was fed by a climate of commercialism and speculation; in other words, it was an embodiment of a desperate need to believe in the possibilities of success, happiness, and the ability to recreate oneself in more flattering or prosperous terms. Gerould saw Hollywood fostering a rhetoric of hyperbole and sensationalism, as reflected in the ballyhoo and boosterism of the 1920s.

> Hollywood, you see, even better than the women's magazines, illustrates our general lack of the sense of proportion, our tendency to distort values. And Hollywood is wherever the young and ignorant expect to get the triumph without the toil, the reputation without the virtues, the fame without the achievement, the reward without the

sacrifice, the knowledge without the study. . . . It is not Hollywood, California, that we need to be worried about: it is the Hollywood in the heart of us all. The little high-school girl from mid-Dakota who goes to the Coast in the hope that after a few years she may return twinkling with jewels to give her obscure fellow citizens the "once-over," is sister to the woman who believes that if she can find the right complexion clay she will be an American Venus, to the man who believes that if he will take a correspondence course, he will be truly educated, to all the people who believe that if they buy a book, they will develop "personality—charm—power." (694)

A professed admirer of the movies, Gerould felt that they nonetheless represented a kind of "canned culture," which contributed to "this mental laziness which we have allowed to invade the national soul." She complained about their "vulgarity," by which she meant not their sexual content but the sentimentalism and sensationalism that so often characterized movie narratives.[60] Still she could confess, "I myself have found more beauty, in the last half dozen years, in motion pictures than in any other art form except the great field of English prose."[61] Although critical of the cult of celebrity that surrounded motion-picture stars, she admitted being a fan of the actor Rudolph Valentino. "Hollywood," in her use, became an organizing metaphor for American social and cultural life—figuratively, "a suburb of every town in the country."[62] In her remarks about motion pictures and the film industry Gerould revealed her insight and her ambivalence, displaying both a keen appreciation and a sense of unease about the movies as a new and powerful form of mass culture. "Our greatest danger," she wrote, "lies in believing our own fairy tales." The paradox of Hollywood for Gerould, as for American culture in general, was precisely this ambivalence, the alternating currents of attraction and scorn, fascination and outrage that Hollywood evoked.

THE PARADOX OF HOLLYWOOD

In a short story published in 1924, entitled "Fancy Turns," Samuel Merwin explored some of the contradictions that clung to Hollywood's cultural identity in the early twenties.[63] In the story, a young artist travels to Hollywood from New York in order to search for a beautiful young woman whom he has seen in the western film "Hickory Heart." He comes fully expecting to find the "flaming Hollywood" of all-night parties and drunken orgies, and is surprised to find instead "a Spanish-tinged Iowa with palms."

> Hollywood! A flat valley under abrupt hanging hills. A long and wide avenue. Buildings only two and three stories high. Trolley-cars. Crowds of automobiles. A camera-man on the curb grinding out a scene for a comedy, while a fat director in puttees shouted through a megaphone and a few idle boys looked on. Real estate offices. Drug stores. Men's furnishings. Drygoods. Automobile showrooms. Photographers. Shining banks, all glass and mahogany. Great quiet studio inclosures on side-streets with scaffolding and tawdry painted scenery rising above tight fences. Long studio buildings with glass roofs on steel frames. Everywhere glaring sunshine, but a chill in the shaded places. Everywhere quiet and order. Surprising! (120)

So completely does Hollywood fail to live up to the young man's expectations that he at last concludes that "the wicked Hollywood was a paradox"; the Hollywood of his imagination and the real Hollywood are two different things. He eventually finds his ideal woman at a respectable Thursday-night dance at the Hollywood Hotel, where she is chaperoned by her mother. After an abbreviated courtship, they are married and return to New York, where he discovers that his new bride never appeared in the western "Hickory Heart." He has married the wrong girl but, in proper Hollywood style, has found true love. On one level, this story is an example of the linking of Hollywood to the promise of romance that was a common theme in the Hollywood fiction of the twenties. On another level, the story engages in a more serious cultural argument over the moral character of Hollywood and the film industry, at a time when they were under serious public attack.

By the 1920s Hollywood had become fixed in the popular imagination as an almost mythical domain of romance, glamour, and luxury, a landscape dominated by palatial homes and populated by beautiful, elegantly dressed people who drove the most expensive automobiles and enjoyed a gay life of wild parties and astonishing affluence. As we have seen, for some this image of Hollywood was a potent symbol of the American dream fulfilled, while for others it was an emblem of crumbling moral and social values. Actually, in many respects Hollywood retained a small-town ambience and character throughout much of the decade, and comments about its sleepy provincialism were legion. Many complained, but others enjoyed the peace and quiet it offered. As one observer noted, "It is a positive fact that the thing which stands out more than any other single feature of Hollywood is the quietness of the place. Comes ten o'clock P.M. and the streets are deserted."[64] Some of the most acerbic comments concerning Hollywood as a small town came from Karl K. Kitchen, a reporter for the *New York World* who made several trips to Hollywood to investigate its wild life and was always thoroughly disappointed that he could not find it. Kitchen described Hollywood as a "dreary, desolate suburb of Los Angeles," in which he could find "no evidences of any life—wicked or of the night variety—anywhere within its precincts." He went on: "If in the daytime more than two people walk abreast on Hollywood or Sunset Boulevards—broad avenues that lead nowhere—the inhabitants mistake them for a parade."[65] And no less a spokesperson than actress and studio executive Mary Pickford felt compelled to write in defense of Hollywood.

> The usual complaint of the visitor from the East or Middle West is that Hollywood is dull and lacks the life and gayety to which he is accustomed. He discovers, to his amazement, that it is far from being a community of outlaws and adventurers, that most motion-picture people lead rather humdrum lives, go to bed early, and contrive to amuse themselves without the aid of alcohol, drugs, or wild parties, and that young girls may actually engage in the industry without losing their decency and self-respect.[66]

However mundane the real Hollywood might have been in this period, it was the tensions between the contradictory perceptions of the film capital that organized the cultural and social arguments surrounding it. Hollywood in the twenties was at once a symbol of the most extravagant Jazz Age fantasies and an embodiment of Middle America's self-image, a modern Babylon and an equally mythologized Main Street rolled into one. And the fundamental social fact behind this paradoxical cultural identity was the presence of the film industry.

By 1920, forty million Americans were attending motion pictures every week, and most of the films they saw were made in Hollywood by some twenty different movie studios.[67] Hollywood had become the universally acknowledged "film capital of the world," home to the largest mass entertainment industry ever created. In 1921 it was estimated that in the United States alone ten million people a day sat in darkened movie theaters watching films produced in Hollywood,[68] the mass-market narratives of a new industrial art form. As one of the era's leading purveyors of mass culture, Hollywood held powerful fascination for both its critics and its admirers, and became a site of controversy and struggle over the social and cultural changes that made the twenties a decade of transition and turbulence in America.

Hollywood fiction often addressed these larger issues and concerns. For some writers, Hollywood represented a healthy, modern alternative to outdated social strictures and suggested a utopic realm of personal freedom and opportunity. For others, Hollywood represented a condition of moral and artistic debasement, a palpable threat to the social and cultural health of the country. In particular, Hollywood challenged prevailing social and sexual codes and reflected changing perceptions of work and gender. At the same time, Hollywood was linked to the emerging ethos of leisure and consumption in American society, and Hollywood fiction often examined the relationship of the new social and economic values to various conceptions of the "American dream." In the fiction of the twenties Hollywood was treated as a place where the changes that were sweeping American society as a whole could be forecast and observed in monumental proportions. As Lionel Barrymore wryly observed in an article for the *Ladies' Home Journal*, "Hollywood is a mirror that reflects the habits and virtues and vices of the world at large—neatly censored."[69]

By 1922, both the critics and the admirers of motion pictures had found in Hollywood a symbolic center for their arguments, malleable to their various purposes and agendas. As we have seen, Hollywood could be conceived of on several levels of generalization: as synonymous with the movies themselves and embodying a mode of representation founded upon (or lacking) specific artistic and narrative features; as the American film industry, understood as a model of cultural production based upon specific industrial and commercial practices; and as a community in which to live and work that embodied a particular set of social values and life-style choices, ranging from fashions in clothing and residential architecture to behavioral patterns and social codes. For its critics, Hollywood was an organizing metaphor for their perception of the moral and aesthetic emptiness of ersatz American culture. Admirers found in Hollywood a model of the American dream of success and self-fulfillment, an exhilarating example of a modern mode of life linked to new opportunities, pleasures, and freedoms. Carey McWilliams, perhaps the most astute historian of southern California, observed about Los Angeles: "Not a neutral land, it has long aroused emotional reactions ranging from intense admiration to profound disgust."[70] Hollywood's divided identity—either a sunny paradise suffused with an ambience of success, luxury and glamour, or the dark epicenter of cultural crisis and moral disintegration—made it an obvious point of convergence for the arguments surrounding mass culture. For, like Hollywood, mass culture produced responses that ranged from extreme admiration to utter disdain.[71]

After 1922, fiction about Hollywood became a publishing staple, appearing in novels, short stories, and serial fictions in popular magazines. The rise of Hollywood fiction in this period can be directly linked to the controversies surrounding the film capital and the explosion of public interest in Hollywood and the lives of those who worked there. Notwithstanding the diversity of literary styles, aesthetic purposes, and thematic concerns represented by this body of work, all the texts of the period use the figure of Hollywood to address central cultural issues. Hollywood fictions fed an insatiable public curiosity about the movie business and life in the film capital. Not uncommonly, these works catered to one of the two extreme reactions we have already identified—either prurient interest or moral indignation—in their representations of the film industry and the exotic social milieu it had spawned. But, along with the appeals to salacity and righteousness, Hollywood fiction managed to raise fundamental questions about American life and the tremendous changes it was undergoing in the 1920s.

CHAPTER TWO

"The Eden of the Movies"

The Redemptive Myth of the Hollywood Romance

You reflect on what Hollywood has given you—the physical well-being, the tranquility of soul, the resurrection of hopes and visions, of faith, of charity—and you love this beautiful bestower of gifts with a love that is akin to a flaming sacred passion.

PERLEY POORE SHEEHAN[1]

Two opposing versions of the Hollywood myth shaped the cultural debate that surrounded the film capital in the 1920s. For many, Hollywood was a symbol of crumbling moral values and cultural decline, the center of a presumably corrupt entertainment industry that proffered a form of mass amusement based on distortion and deception. Such negative assessments of Hollywood were often linked to complaints about mass culture, for which the film capital came to serve as a convenient emblem. In criticisms of Hollywood, objections to its moral influence and to its artistic value were often intertwined, and the conflation of these categories of complaint generally served the interests of those who saw the film capital as a powerful agent of mass culture. This was particularly true in Hollywood fiction, where the notion of Hollywood as a moral wasteland marked by greed, lust, and ambition was often linked to a notion of the Hollywood cinema as an art form predicated on artifice and illusion.

From the early twenties, Hollywood signified the breakdown of traditional moral rules and restraints. Writers frequently conveyed this aspect of its cultural identity through images of sexual danger. This was because Hollywood was widely perceived as a place where modern sexual and social roles were being defined and disseminated—not just in movies but in fan magazines and studio publicity that emphasized the glamorous and romantic lives of the stars. At a time when thousands of young people were being drawn by "the lure of easy life and big money in the Hollywood picture game," many saw Hollywood as a direct path to moral and physical ruin. Cautionary tracts such as Marilynn Conners's *What Chance Have I in Hollywood?*[2] warned of the fate awaiting movie-struck young girls in the film capital—starvation, drug addiction, prostitution, and white slavery. One commentator observed: "To far away people who know little about the place except 'scare lines' which they see in newspapers, 'Hollywood' and another shorter word beginning with H are practically twins."[3]

The star scandals that rocked the film industry in 1921 and 1922 enlarged Hollywood's reputation as a "hotbed of sin, lust, and depravity." Those events linked Hollywood irremediably to an image of sexual license and personal excess that has remained the most potent element of the film capital's cultural identity. This dark image of "Hollywood the Destroyer"[4]—seductive, illusory, and dangerous—has dominated literary representations of the film capital.

THE GIRL FROM HOLLYWOOD

The myth of "Hollywood the Destroyer" found its most hyperbolic expression in Edgar Rice Burroughs's novel *The Girl from Hollywood*, which was subtitled *A Modern Drama of City and Country Life in Southern California*. First published as a serial in *Munsey's Magazine* in June 1922, at the height of the furor over the Hollywood scandals, the novel was a rare attempt by Burroughs to write about ordinary people in a contemporary American setting.[5] (It was published between two of his more typical works: *The Chessmen of Mars* and *Tarzan and the Golden Lion*.) Burroughs had moved to Los Angeles with his family in 1918. After observing the Hollywood scene for three years from the comfortable distance of his 540-acre estate in the San Fernando Valley, he produced *The Girl from Hollywood*, in which he aired his conservative moral and social views with the film capital used as a backdrop. The critics slammed *The Girl from Hollywood* as they did most of his works, describing it as "so much sensational hash" with "neither moral nor artistic value."[6] Yet Burroughs's daughter Joan recalled later that he had done "considerable research" on the novel, and that "he believed very much in this story and always felt that it was killed quickly by certain Hollywood elements" (although how the book was "killed" is not clear, for it went through four printings between 1923 and 1925 and was also published in England).[7] In this novel, Hollywood is a highly overdrawn symbol of urban corruption and vice, for which the illusions of movie making provide an attractive but dangerously deceptive facade. As a city of actors and movie studios, where nothing is exactly what it appears, Hollywood's capacity for deception is represented as holding very real moral and physical dangers.

In contrast with the criminality of the film capital, Burroughs depicts the bucolic innocence of Rancho del Ganado. He modeled this rural retreat after his own estate, Mil Flores, which he had purchased from General Harrison Gray Otis (publisher of the *Los Angeles Times*) and subsequently renamed Tarzana. The book is both structurally and thematically organized by this rigid country-city division of experience—Burroughs's morally dichotomized social landscape.

From the idyllic haven of Rancho del Ganado, beautiful Grace Evans is drawn to Hollywood by her (as Burroughs would have it understood) misguided sense of career and the desire to "live a little" (15). Forsaking her engagement to Custer Pennington, the handsome scion of the rancho, Grace flouts the conventions of rural life and seeks independence and opportunity as an actress in Hollywood. Burroughs first illustrates the difficulties and dangers entailed by such ambitions through the experiences of Shannon Burke ("the girl from Hollywood").

> Two years ago she came to Hollywood from a little town in the Middle West. . . . She was fired by high purpose then. Her child's heart, burning with lofty ambition, had set its desire upon a noble goal. The broken bodies of a thousand other children dotted the road to the same goal, but she did not see them, or seeing, did not understand. (43)

Upon her arrival in Hollywood, Shannon adopts the exotic name "Gaza de Lure" and begins making the rounds at the studios. Despite her natural talent, she has trouble finding work because she rebuffs the frequent sexual advances made by directors interested in furthering her career at the expense of her virtue. The latter practice was commonly alleged by critics of the film industry. Canon William Sheafe Chase, for example, claimed to possess sworn testimony from "young women artists who have been compelled to perform immoral acts in order to retain their business positions."[8] Karl Kitchen, however, after his investigation of "the gay life in the studios," refuted such reports, calling them "the pitiful excuses of the unsuccessful."[9] Whatever the actual conditions were, for most Americans the image of Hollywood as a place of sexual danger for young women was sufficiently confirmed by the star scandals, and for Burroughs it was the essential feature of Hollywood life.

The novel's archvillain is the actor and director Wilson Crumb, who wins Shannon's trust with a studio contract before hooking her on cocaine and forcing her into cohabitation. Crumb is the quintessential Hollywood villain; his superficial courtesy and refined manners conceal a shocking criminality and a fatal ability to manipulate and control. He represents the difficulty of distinguishing the real from the unreal, the moral from the immoral, within the purview of the Hollywood ethos. Because of her drug addiction and moral fall, Shannon is forced to give up her movie career, becoming a virtual prisoner in Crumb's Hollywood bungalow.

Crumb's bungalow—the book's central symbol of Hollywood corruption—is a florid example of the city's "new school of Hollywood architecture, which appears to be a hysterical effort to combine Queen Anne, Italian, Swiss chalet, Moorish, Mission, and Martian" (40). In a work as severely nativist as Burroughs's novel, this eclectic combination of "foreign" styles is a particularly apt site for crime. The interior of the bungalow is reminiscent of an opium den, rich with "Chinese rugs, dark hangings, and ponderous, overstuffed furniture" (41), and here Crumb surrounds himself with an assortment of ethnic criminal cohorts, from Japanese houseboys to Mexican "greasers." In the book's dichotomized moral vision of country and city life, the exoticism of Hollywood's architectural styles signifies its moral ambiguity and corruption.

Crumb's criminal schemes include blackmail, drug trafficking, and bootlegging, presented within a melodramatic plot of mistaken identities, hidden motives, and sudden revelations of character. But the novel's deepest fears concerning Hollywood immorality are played out on the level of sexual threat—first against Shannon, whose escape from Hollywood to Rancho del Ganado signals the beginning of her moral and physical rehabilitation, and finally against Grace, whose fate becomes a cautionary tale of Hollywood failure. Indeed, Grace gradually becomes an exemplary figure for Burroughs's cultural arguments, a vehicle for the novel's shrill moral warnings.

After Grace arrives in Hollywood, Crumb persuades her to do a nude screen test, a humiliating experience that "outraged every instinct of decency and refinement in her, just as it has outraged the same characteristics in countless other girls" (82). By proposing that Grace's experiences are typical (shared by "countless other girls"), Burroughs makes a sweeping indictment of the film industry, positioning his text within the larger debate over the morality of the movies and the ethics and motives of those who produce them. Once started on the road to moral ruin, Grace falls quickly into Crumb's power, driven by "the fear that the girl holds of offending a potent ally, and the hope of propitiating a power in which lies the potentiality of success upon the screen" (239).

This desire for "success upon the screen"—certainly one of the most widespread and appealing social fantasies of the period—reflects Grace's fatal moral flaw, a willingness to compromise virtue in pursuit of career and success. And the fact that these are her only alternatives (she must choose either virtue *or* success) reveals the patriarchal and conservative moral logic that organizes Burroughs's narrative. At last, her beauty faded, pregnant and rejected by Crumb, Grace dies as a direct result of his abuse, a fate loaded with significance for the thousands of young people who flooded into Hollywood in the 1920s. In *The Girl from Hollywood*, the film capital is presented as an environment rife with temptation and peril for the innocent, and the themes of sexual danger and betrayal that it announced have remained central within the canon of Hollywood fiction. In this work Burroughs took a clear position in the cultural battle that was engulfing Hollywood in the early 1920s. A reviewer for the *New York Times* wryly observed about *The Girl from Hollywood:* "We are so genuinely sorry to learn all these terrible things about Hollywood. It makes us tremble for the future of the motion picture industry. If the directors and stars spend all their time sinning, who is going to make the pictures that have become almost a necessity in our drab and dreary lives?"[10]

THE HOLLYWOOD ROMANCE

In response to widespread condemnation of the film industry such as Burroughs expressed in his novel, there emerged a countermyth of Hollywood as an embodiment of romantic dreams and utopian possibilities. The Hollywood romance promised to redeem Hollywood's moral and artistic reputation through a celebration of modern social and sexual roles and a validation of the movies as a "universal" art. In this positive and optimistic assessment, Hollywood became a paradigm for the American dream of success and personal happiness. In particular, Hollywood was linked to an ethos of leisure and consumption, and was depicted as a society of unique opportunity and privilege for women, In the Hollywood romance, the tendencies toward make-believe and illusion that characterized life in the film capital were seen as therapeutic inducements to fantasy and wish fulfillment, and Hollywood became a physical embodiment of widespread social and sexual desires. This version of the Hollywood myth evoked powerful longings for personal and romantic fulfillment while sharply rebutting the criticisms of Hollywood's morality.

In Samuel Merwin's story "Theme with Variations," the two contrasting versions of the Hollywood myth are set side by side for comparison before a romantic solution to the Hollywood paradox is offered.[11] The story follows Adrian Yule, a writer embittered by a recent divorce, who decides to rebuild his life in California. On the long train journey to Los Angeles, he overhears different versions of what Hollywood is like. From a "professional reformer" and a group of middle-aged club women he hears of the need for "a thorough moral survey of Hollywood," and although it sounds to him like "moral snobbery," he is finally persuaded that "they had a case, these worthy folk."

Next he encounters a group of men employed in motion pictures who gossip and joke amongst themselves, lasciviously comparing the women on the train and making vulgar insinuations about a beautiful young star, Marjorie Drew, who is traveling for the first time without the protection of her mother. Yule is offended by their ribaldry and arrogance, and he begins to seriously ponder the dangerous moral influence of the film industry.

> The success of it had swept on so far beyond all human experience. Certainly no poet or playwright or painter or singer or actor had ever so widely touched the world. . . . This immense new force would be at the moment, in their hands, curiously molding the taste of a new age: queer scheming little fur-men and rag-men and button-men from Lemberg and Kishinev and Ekaterinoslav, salesgirls that happily photographed well, electricians with an inventive gift, ambitious office-boys and dubious beauties from the cities, and proudly resisting actors from New York and Paris and London, and financial adventurers and experimental playwrights and men from the newspapers, and (again) swarming little girls without breeding or morals— men from nowhere who gathered swift easy millions because they were fat or thin or wall-eyed. Tribute from every continent and every remote island pouring in; a thousand a week to an old actor whose face wrinkled amusingly, five thousand a week to a child of six, ten thousand a week to a girl because she looked like Mary Pickford! Money. . . . (39)

Alarmed by the conversation of the movie men, Yule retreats to the observation car, where he is joined by a distinguished-looking gentleman who, he is surprised to discover, is the renowned motion-picture director David Dean. Together they commiserate over the problems of the film industry, in a discussion similar to the "What's wrong with the movies?" articles that were filling the national magazines in 1923, the year this story appeared in *Red Book Magazine*. At the end of their talk, Dean offers Yule the following conclusion.

> The fact is . . . Hollywood is variously described as a state of nerves, passion's playground, all that sort of drivel. But a thoughtful man comes in time to see that it is really a frontier. Not so different from the California of 'forty-nine! Everybody comes, the wrong people and all.

It is rough and difficult for a good many individuals. Any number of ignorant little devils with too much easy money. And it goes through phases so rapidly that no mind can quite keep up with it. But the germs of beautiful things are there. Yes, it is a frontier—the frontier of a new art. (40)

Thus, Hollywood's reputation is redeemed under the auspice of art.

Steadied by this assessment of the film capital, Yule goes on to meet and quickly fall in love with the young film star Marjorie Drew. By the end of the story he had decided to go into pictures as a partner with Drew and Dean. The Hollywood "frontier" holds out to him the promises of both emotional and economic success. Despite its melodramatic plot and romantic denouement, "Theme with Variations" exemplifies the level of cultural argument in Hollywood fiction. At issue in this story is the rehabilitation of Hollywood's reputation as well as that of the film industry and its movies. The key to this rehabilitation is a linking of Hollywood to the promises of healthy romance, brisk economic opportunity, and artistic achievement.

The ideology of romance and opportunity is most succinctly articulated in a short story by Arthur Somers Roche, "Alms of Love," in which Hollywood is shown to be a place of singular opportunity and freedom for women.[12] In the story, the beautiful Kitty Wheeler reluctantly divorces her philandering husband and moves to California to start life over with her two children. While in her garden one day, she is observed by a film director, Macready, who is struck by her beauty and persuades her to come to the studio for a test. Launched upon her career as a screen actress, Kitty works hard and, under Macready's guidance, achieves stardom. Predictably, Macready falls in love with Kitty; when she explains that she cannot return his feelings, he shakes off his disappointment and insists that they continue as good friends and colleagues. In contrast with the cautionary stories about sexual harassment of young women in the film industry, Macready's behavior toward Kitty is above reproach, and he becomes her protector in matters both professional and personal.

At this point Kitty's ex-husband arrives in Hollywood and attempts to reclaim her affections. Having seen her in a picture in New York, he suddenly finds her fascinating again and wishes to resume their marriage. Initially Kitty resists, but she is finally persuaded to remarry. Macready serves as the best man at their wedding and graciously releases her from her contract. Kitty's renewed marital bliss is short-lived, however; it ends when she observes her husband whispering into the ear of a pretty blonde at a Hollywood party Macready has thrown for her on the eve of the couple's return to New York. On the way to the train station the next morning, Kitty decides that she will have better luck holding her husband's interest if she remains in Hollywood and pursues her career. "If she went with him, he would forget her existence. He had come back to her because she was no longer Kitty Wheeler the wife, but Kitty Wheeler the great success in the world of films, the woman admired by millions. He would always come back to her if she were the famous actress" (130).

This story is representative of a great many Hollywood fictions of the 1920s in which the film capital is used as a setting for the romantic adventures of a heroine who comes to Hollywood to assert her independence or to build a new life away from a troubled or misunderstood past. Kitty discovers that the emotional and sexual power that attends screen success is a potent inducer of male devotion and love, and Hollywood becomes the guarantor of marital harmony. Because in the film industry good looks and the ability to "act natural" were primary prerequisites of success, Hollywood often appeared to be a place of unique opportunity for young women, even if the odds of success on the screen were remote for most aspirants. For the lucky ones who did succeed, the fan magazines and studio publicists never lost an opportunity to show that the rewards of stardom were affluence, glamour, and romance, often with the most admired male stars in Hollywood. It was an intoxicating blend of social, economic, and sexual appeals, and Hollywood fictions played a major role in concocting these fantasies for their readers.

Along with the allures of romance, wealth, and fame, Hollywood in the 1920s offered a material environment redolent of fantasy and enchantment, and this became an important element in the myth of the Hollywood romance, as Hollywood was gradually transformed into "America's real live Fairyland,—the dreamer's dream come true."[13] In this version of the Hollywood myth—which was most aggressively espoused in romantic fictions and travel guides—Hollywood was a place of breathtaking physical beauty and civic charms, a secular paradise of elegant homes, handsome shops, and lush gardens. Much of its beauty was recognized as essentially false: "The reason for the beautiful verdure may be laid at the door of artificiality. All is planted, seldom is any growth natural."[14] Nonetheless, admirers of Hollywood continually rhapsodized its natural beauty: "Hollywood is eternally green. Winter is unknown. A thousand varieties of flowers, shrubs, vines and trees make a riot of color on plain and hill, and their perfume is forever wafted on the gentle zephyrs from the sea."[15]

By all accounts, Hollywood in the 1920s presented an unusually exotic and fanciful material environment, which easily lent itself to an ambience of romance and dreams. For British visitor Alice Williamson, who wrote enthusiastically of her trip in 1927, Hollywood was "the new Wonderland"—a comparison that emphasized both its beauty and its strangeness. In her book *Alice in Movieland* (which is equal parts travel diary and fan-magazine gush), Williamson displays a constant infatuation with the dreamlike qualities of Hollywood's fantastic architectural landscape that is quite different from Burroughs's moral alarms.

> Dare you believe in the solidity of these adorable houses and bungalows, built behind lawns along straight, endless boulevards, or vanishing into a blue horizon at the end of fairylike, tree-shaded streets?—houses large and small, houses of every architecture: Tudor, Spanish, Mexican, Italian, Georgian, Pullman? . . . It is too amusing to walk from street to street, and see a Marie Antoinette pavilion next door to an Egyptian temple or a Chinese pagoda (really it's a house!) or a simple Colonial dwelling, a miniature copy of Mount Vernon, elbowing a tiny Escorial, or a pocket edition of a Florentine palace. . . . You hardly know which you would choose if you could.[16]

Of course, the architectural fantasies that lined Hollywood's streets were fabrications like the sets within the strange and magical worlds of the studios, the real centers of Hollywood illusion. In the romantic version of the Hollywood myth, the film studios are stripped of the industrial trappings that identify them as places of often dreary and uninspiring labor, and they become playgrounds in which fantasy worlds are created, imbued with an aura of exoticism, glamour, and romance. As Marilynn Conners observed:

> [Hollywood] is romantic. But it is even more a "make-believe land of romance." The reason is that so many cities, towns, locations, atmospheres of the south, north, east and west are reproduced by artistic camouflage in the studios themselves. These 'atmospheres' seen on silver screens carry the beholder in a theater anywhere in the world off his feet, he is taken out of himself, launched in a different environment, and variety is the spice of life. For that hour in another land, he works days, weeks, months and years in some seemingly unromantic locality, in his office or in the home, very familiar to him, over paths and through streets of his home town that he has walked 365 days in the year.[17]

Whether it took place in the movies, at the studios, or on the streets of the film capital, this invitation to dream one's self out of the everyday routines of a mundane life characterized the idealized and romantic images of Hollywood in the 1920s.

Linked to this utopic image was its seeming opposite, the image of an average American town—a place, as Charles Donald Fox put it in *Mirrors of Hollywood* (his account of Hollywood life in the twenties), "where everybody lives just like everybody else lives, everywhere."[18]

> Framed against the backdrop of Hollywood's hills, the whole city—all the palm-lined streets, with their impossibly picturesque and gayly colored bungalows ... looks more like one of the huge movie sets that have brought it fame, than it does like the peaceful city of normal community activities and interests, of children, of mothers and fathers, of sisters and brothers, which this magic city of the West really is. (3)

In fact, this conception of Hollywood as a typical American community, "not much different from the average small town" (4), relies upon the same impulse toward fantasy and make-believe that supports its image as an exotic wonderland. In this case Hollywood represents a beautified and idealized notion of American life in which the signs of its "normality"— invariably familial and domestic—suggest a social environment free of both moral ambiguity and economic contradiction. "What other place has no slums? In what other place is almost everyone young and practically everyone rich?"[19]

One "other place" was the commercial advertising of the period, which constructed a similar version of American life. Hollywood and the commercial advertising of the 1920s shared a common visual rhetoric and cultural purpose. Like motion pictures, advertising was a powerful and influential form of mass culture that offered consumers attractive, idealized images of American life.[20] Hollywood movies and advertisements had many similar cultural tasks as agents of a modern commercial culture committed to both promoting and exploiting the emerging appetite for leisure and consumption in American society; each contributed to and helped to define the proclivity for fantasy and simulation within American culture. Whether conceived of as an idyllic small town or as a romantic fantasy land, Hollywood was at the center of a system of ideas and images—a visual rhetoric and an iconography derived from advertising—that served to validate the values of consumption and leisure through a fetishized depiction of the Hollywood good life.

One of the best fictional explorations of the cultural appeal of the Hollywood good life is Frank Condon's comic tale of the temptations of the film capital, "Hollywood," which was published by *Photoplay* in 1923.[21] In it Condon chronicles the experiences of Joel Whitaker, a respectable middle-aged widower living with his pretty daughter Angela and two spinster sisters in the morally upright community of Auburndale, Ohio. Over the breakfast table one morning, Joel and his sisters are shocked by Angela's announcement that she is leaving for Hollywood. "I want to be somebody and do something. I'm fairly good-looking and I certainly have ambition." Her aunts strenuously oppose the plan on the grounds that "Hollywood, as everyone knows, is a morass of iniquity," and Joel initially concurs.

> "Motion picture people are loose in their habits. Their conduct is, as we have seen in the paper, a national disgrace. I read about one party where the guests went in bathing at midnight and drank champagne from silk slippers. Another thing—they never go to church. They stay out all night, carousing. They get divorced and remarried so fast that nobody knows where he lives. . . . I warn you. The motion picture is a fiery dragon sinking its ruthless claws into the innocent young womanhood of America." (40)

When Angela refuses to be swayed by these arguments, Joel is compelled to go along and guard her from the perils of life in the film capital. Father and daughter arrive in Hollywood "expectant, but disappointed over the scarcity of visible debauchery" (41), and after a week they determine that the stories of Hollywood's wild life are greatly exaggerated. Eventually Joel strikes up an acquaintance with a character actor, and they become good friends. Joel is introduced to others in the movie colony and begins to join them for games of tennis and golf and for luncheons at their club. Through his new friends he is introduced to a Hollywood life of leisure and recreation. His initiation is completed when he is asked to play a small part in a movie and begins a career as an extra and bit player.

Now father and daughter decide to rent a bungalow ("in tan stucco, with a Spanish wall"), and Joel updates his wardrobe with the latest Hollywood fashions: "baggy knickerbockers, and British golf hose with bright green tassels." Hollywood has transformed him from a "stubby little gentleman in a frock coat" to a stylish and leisured denizen of the studios, and his transformation is complete when he places a down payment on a "chummy roadster," light blue with red wheels. The narrative displays a systematic interest in the acquisition of consumer goods, which serve to usher Joel into a modern world of leisurely pleasures.

Angela, on the other hand, becomes increasingly distraught over her father's success and her own failure to break into the movies. She decides to summon her aunts to Hollywood in order to curtail her father's new way of life. When the aunts arrive, one of them chaperones Angela to a studio and is promptly offered work as an extra, while Angela is turned away because, she is told, "Hollywood just now is filled up with young girls" (109). The aunt, after some reflection, decides to accept the job in order to buy herself some new clothes. Eventually both aunts secure jobs in the studios and convert to the Hollywood good life, bobbing their hair and enjoying the luxury of a Japanese cook. Angela, on the other hand, decides she is not cut out for the movies and returns to Auburndale.

This comic reversal comments upon the unpredictability of success in the movies and suggests the broad appeal of Hollywood's good life to middle Americans. What Joel and his sisters discover and embrace in Hollywood is nothing less than a modern way of life based upon the values of leisure and consumption, and Hollywood serves to both sanction and exemplify the transformative virtues of these new social values. In Condon's short story, Hollywood is used to illustrate the new patterns of social and economic life that were everywhere transforming American life. Its message of middle-age success and personal fulfillment is a celebration of the new social and economic order.

The *reductio ad absurdum* of Condon's version of the Hollywood myth is Perley Poore Sheehan's *Hollywood as a World Center*, published in 1924—a visionary treatise on the spiritual meaning of Hollywood, based on Sheehan's own millenarian and racial views. Sheehan, a journalist and an author of fantasy and romance fiction, had been a foreign correspondent for the *New York Times* and editor of the Paris edition of the *New York Herald* before settling in Hollywood in 1922.[22] There he supervised the filming of his book *If You Believe It, It's So* and produced screen adaptations of other works, most notably Universal Studio's 1923 version of *The Hunchback of Notre Dame*, which starred Lon Chaney. He was a founding member of the Hollywood Writer's Club and for the next twenty years, until his death in 1943, was a part of the Los Angeles literary community.

In *Hollywood as a World Center*, Sheehan portrays Hollywood, through a bizarre combination of boosterism and mysticism, as the spiritual and cultural center of a new civilization brought about by the "last great migration of the Aryan race."[23] Among the orange groves and pepper trees of the Hollywood hills, Sheehan argues, Aryans have built a "distinctive civilization" of worldwide significance. "Just as Alexandria, Athens, Venice, expressed the soul of empires now gone, were the fountain-heads and syntheses of characteristic civilizations covering wide sections of the world, so with Hollywood today" (24). Sheehan's Hollywood is, of course, a place of singular natural beauty: "To think of Hollywood is to think of the warm sands and blue capes of her shoreline, the mountains and valleys that surround her, the mystical deserts, the endless boulevards that spin away through enchanted landscapes . . ." (24). This paradise is also an enclave of Aryan racial purity:[24] "They are pleasant folk, these neighbors of yours in Hollywood. They speak English" (37). In terse aphorisms Sheehan chants the virtues of the Hollywood good life, its unequaled capacities for prosperity and personal fulfillment.

Success is happiness. Happiness is success. . . . Success is a thing of the spirit. . . . It is this elation of spirit that is one of Hollywood's most outstanding characteristics. . . . It might well be written that Holly-wood is also a state of mind—the center of a regional psychology wherein have been declared nul and fraudulent the claims of those hoary ghosts of Poverty, Sickness, and Old Age. (38–39).

Sheehan observes that the ultimate significance of Hollywood conceived of as a redemptive utopia is "not narrowly industrial and aesthetic but grandly spiritual" (61), and the vehicle of this spiritual mission is the motion picture understood as a universal language. This was a central aesthetic assumption of those who made silent films,[25] and significantly, it was under this banner of universal art that the mass culture of the movies first began to acquire a degree of cultural cachet.

Perhaps the most important cultural task for Hollywood's romantic myth was this validation of mass culture in the sacral terms of a universal aesthetic. For Sheehan, motion pictures were instruments of a "universal religion" (95) that heralded the "Golden Age"; for Charles Donald Fox they represented the realization of a democratic and international mass culture whose "appeal is to everyone from the worldly-wise of the great cities to the simple folk of the smallest hamlets" (75). Laurance Hill offered the following summation in his pro-Hollywood tract *Can Anything Good Come Out of Hollywood?* "The pictures that move have brought the ends of the earth together and made them shake hands, so that the great human family is for the first time really getting acquainted with itself. Could there be a more tremendous force for world peace?" (52). In the "new Jerusalem" of Hollywood, the poets and prophets of this new secular religion of the movies lived their high-minded and blissful lives, surrounded by superfluities of wealth and beauty.

SOULS FOR SALE

The social and cultural messages of the Hollywood romance were put on vivid display in Rupert Hughes's novel *Souls for Sale*—subtitled in *Red Book Magazine*, where it was originally serialized, *The Story of a Girl's Redemption Through the Motion Pictures.*[26] As an author and editor, Hughes was one of the most popular and prolific of American writers in the first half of the twentieth century, contributing short stories, articles, verse, and criticism to numerous periodicals for over forty years. In addition, he was a moderately successful playwright, historian, musicologist, and biographer, his three-volume biography of George Washington being his most enduring work. Early in his career Hughes found a receptive audience for his fiction among motion-picture producers, who purchased the rights to many of his stories for film adaptation. In 1919 producer Samuel Goldwyn established a new division of his company called Eminent Authors Pictures, which was intended to capitalize on the talents of some of America's foremost novelists. Along with such well-known writers as Gertrude Atherton and Mary Roberts Rinehart, Hughes joined the Goldwyn outfit in Hollywood. In 1921 one of its most successful pictures was made from his novel *The Old Nest*. In 1922, the same year *Souls for Sale* was published as a novel, Hughes wrote and directed a film version of it for Goldwyn. Increasingly Hughes found himself in demand as both a scenario writer and a director. After several long visits, he finally moved permanently to Hollywood in 1923 and built a lavish mansion inspired by illustrations in *The Arabian Nights*.[27] Through his affiliation with the film industry, Hughes became one of its most outspoken and influential supporters.

Despite its title, *Souls for Sale* is perhaps the most vehement and sustained defense of Hollywood to be found in the canon of Hollywood fiction. Hughes organized its arguments by reversing the moral dichotomies that so often govern Hollywood's cultural identity. In this work it is the small town of Calverly, not Hollywood, that holds real moral and spiritual danger for Mem Steddon, the daughter of the Reverend Doctor Steddon, a twentieth-century puritan who preaches against Hollywood's sin and immorality. Pregnant and unmarried at the beginning of the novel, Mem travels west, fleeing her father's judgment and the community's moral censure. During her employment as a domestic in Palm Springs, she accidentally falls and miscarries. But it is her good fortune to end up in Hollywood, where she is quickly befriended, finds work in the studios, and begins her ascent to stardom.

Mem enters the film capital with some trepidation, still under the sway of her father's preaching. For Doctor Steddon, Hollywood is "the new Babylon," "the central factory of Satan and his minions, the enemy of our homes, the corrupter of our young men and women—the school of crime" (1). But at every stage of her movie career Mem discovers the opposite: the people are kind and considerate, the work is often difficult but always above reproach, and the moral climate, if somewhat less formal than that in Calverly, is decent enough and poses no serious physical or spiritual threat. In Hollywood she flourishes and is happy as never before, in an atmosphere of freedom and relaxed enjoyment of life that would have been unimaginable in her home town.

Mem steadily moves up the ranks in the studio until she achieves the pinnacle of Hollywood success—stardom. In this respect she exemplifies the new opportunities for career and success offered to women in the early film industry. In a business where natural good looks and a spontaneous charm were the primary requirements for success, Mem finds herself possessed of a valuable commodity "for which the grateful public would pay with gratitude and fame and much money" (185).

The myth of the Hollywood romance is typically constructed around both a narrative of individual success and a narrative of romantic fulfillment linked to the promise of heterosexual love. Mem is an interesting exception. In the course of the novel she is courted by three eligible Hollywood bachelors. Handsome leading man and movie star Tom Holby proposes marriage to her, but Mem cannot tolerate having to share him with his millions of female admirers: "Mem turned green at the thought of a husband whose real lips she must share with actresses on the scene and whose pictured lips would be kissed good night all around the world" (331). Thus, Holby's romantic advances fail because of his celebrity—a condition that in Mem's eyes dooms him to the role of "a universal husband, a syndicated consort." She is also courted by Claymore, the powerful director who gives her a first break at the studio and schools her in the techniques of screen acting. But for Mem, their relationship is a "spiritual union" dedicated to "the art of the motion picture," and her feelings for him are shattered after an incident in which his cowardice is revealed. Finally there is the brilliant comedian Ned Ling, whose genius and professionalism inspire Mem to push her talents to the limit but who proves to be infantile and demanding off the screen. Mem refuses to fall in love with any of them.

Like the dalliances of Anita Loos's quintessential twenties femme fatale, Lorelei Lee (who also begins her career as a movie star in Hollywood),[28] Mem's relationships with her would-be suitors represent a sexual politics in which women dominate men through their beauty, their talent, and their sexual appeal. In the novels of Hollywood stardom this version of the woman as sexually dominant led to the figure of the "Blonde Goddess,"[29] an image of female sexual aggression and power that often becomes a symbol for the corruption and moral ambiguity produced by the confusion of social and sexual roles in Hollywood. In Hughes's novel, however, Mem's refusal to marry represents something more positive and progressive: a rejection of the traditional limitations placed upon women in a patriarchal society and a refusal to sacrifice her career for the conventional roles of wife and mother. In the course of the narrative Mem becomes emblematic of the "New Woman" in American society, "an allegory of all recent womanhood" (195), in her pursuit of independence and self-actualization. In Hollywood she discovers a modern set of social values and moral standards that offers an alternative to the oppressive puritanism of her father and an opportunity to "climb as high" as she can in the world.

> Well, she was fulfilling the newly discovered destiny of her sex. . . . To-day all the American women were voters; millions of them were independent money makers. And this seemed right to Mem, though preachers had shrieked that it meant the end of all morality. . . . The obscene old ideal, that reproduction was the prime obligation of womanhood, revolted Mem. . . . Marriage had never been the whole duty of man, and Mem was sure that never again would it be the whole duty of woman. . . . Terrible euphemisms for slavishness, miscalled meekness, submissiveness, modesty, piety, propriety had been held as lashes over women for ages. Now whipping was out of style. A girl could go where she pleased and go alone. She could take care of herself better than men had ever taken care of her. (378–79)

The central importance of Hollywood in defining these modern sexual values cannot be overstated. In *Souls for Sale* Hollywood is an embodiment of the new social and sexual freedoms that were sweeping American life in the 1920s, a remarkably appealing example of the personal and public benefits of the "new morality" and a clear alternative to Victorian values and rules of decorum. Hollywood represents for Mem a "new world" of physical beauty and graceful living based upon an ethos of self-fulfillment and pleasure, and it provides her with a powerfully attractive model of a new way of life. "Mem's greatest shock was the abrupt arrival in a world where the enjoyment of life was made its chief business. She had been brought up to believe in duty first—in self-denial, abstention, modesty, demurity, simplicity, meekness, prayer, remorse. Here people worshipped the sun, flowers, dancing, speed, hilarity, laughter, and love" (168).

Although Mem is at first shocked by Hollywood's "contempt for conventions," she soon learns that "many of those who loved to break the rules of outward propriety were solid as white marble in their standards" (168). At every turn she receives new confirmations of Hollywood's essential goodness. She is surprised to discover that Hollywood, "the city which her father had damned with such wholesale horror, was nine-tenths composed of mid-Westerners like himself, people who had brought their churches and churchliness with them" (169). Increasingly Hollywood comes to signify a regime of official optimism and health, a "leisure utopia"[30] in which the pursuit of pleasure finds social sanction through a culture based on athleticism and heterosocial amusements. Hollywood becomes for Mem a paradise of exhilarating new freedoms and exciting social possibilities, and she soon finds herself swept up in its diversions: "It became a commonplace for Mem to jig about in young men's arms. She learned to dance. She learned to play a little golf, a little tennis" (182).

> In swimming, dancing, mountain climbing, horse-back riding, motoring, singing, laughing, days and nights reeled by. . . . She looked back on her earlier existence at home as a slothful indolence at best, a waste of gifts, a burying of genius. . . . To be busy, to achieve, to build her soul and sell it—that was her new passion. She gave up all thought of going home to Calverly. She would never be content with village life again. (186)

Clearly, in her conversion to the Hollywood good life, Mem traces a social path that was followed by many in the twenties who turned their backs on restrictive social conventions and moral precepts to embrace the pleasures of a modern commercial culture based on the dual promises of leisure and consumption. In *Souls for Sale*, these modern cultural values are given flattering expression. In Hughes's Hollywood, there is no dark side to this world of enjoyment and sensual pleasure, no price to pay for constant ease and happiness.

Souls for Sale served as an explicit and outspoken defense of the film industry in the face of the star scandals and the widespread complaints about motion pictures. Responding to the "lynching mood" of the country toward Hollywood and its films, the novel devotes pages to impassioned arguments in defense of the movies and of Hollywood's morals.

> I tell you the average morality is just as high in Hollywood or Culver City as anywhere else in the world. . . . The moving picture did more to keep girls and boys off the streets than all the prayer meetings ever held. They drove the saloon out of business more than any other power. The screen is the biggest educational and moral force ever discovered and it hasn't got a fault that is all its own. (250)

Hughes singles out the Arbuckle scandal, in particular, as an example of unjustified and intolerant moral hysteria directed at the movie colony. Movie censors come in for some of the most fierce deriding in the book. The novel attacks these "busy agents of vicarious virtue" (91) for their narrow-minded and misplaced notions of good and evil. Significantly, their chief offense is obstructing the growth of motion pictures as a serious art form.

> Just as hard times are coming on [for the film industry], the censors rise up like a sandstorm and blow from all directions. You can hardly find a story that can stand their sand blast. They eat away the plot till it falls with a crash. . . . Hideous, isn't it, that grown people in a grown-up country called the land of the free and the home of the brave should be bullied and handcuffed till we can't even tell a story? We can't play Shakespeare, of course, or the Bible stories, or any of the big literary works anymore. And they do it all in the name of protecting morals!—as if girls and boys never went wrong until the movies came along; as if you could stop human beings from being human by closing up the theaters and telling lies to the children. (148)

It was in defending the mass culture of the movies as a universal and democratic form of art that the myth of Hollywood romance accomplished its most important cultural task, and *Souls for Sale* is exemplary in this regard. For Mem, Hollywood stardom means more than just wealth and fame; it signifies the discovery and nurturing of an artistic vocation: "She was living the artist's life, goaded to expression, rejoicing in utterance and afterwards anguished with regrets that she had not phrased herself in a little differently" (335). Claymore, Holby, and Ling all represent, in different ways, the seriousness of Hollywood moviemakers and their dedication to their emerging art. However, the most extravagant claims for film art are made by the author "Mr. Hobbes"—an obvious spokesman for Hughes— who praises the movies as "the greatest art that ever was, the all-in-all art" (368). It is through the movies' presumed capacity to function as a "universal language," the "long-sought Esperanto" (377) (that myth of the silent film as an international medium of universal expression), that they secure their aesthetic credentials and cultural authority. In this way *Souls for Sale* celebrates and upholds the mass culture of Hollywood as a cultural and aesthetic phenomenon of unmistakable importance.

The myth of the Hollywood romance required this belief in the cultural and aesthetic value of motion pictures—this notion of the movies as secular religion—to justify the obvious benefits and gratifications of life in the film capital. In Hollywood, those who dedicated themselves to the uplift and entertainment of the mass audience, who gave shape and meaning to the mass dreams of our collective cultural life, were rewarded for their efforts by an offscreen life of unique pleasures and privileges. Hollywood—"the Eden of the movies" (65), as it is constructed in *Souls for Sale*—functions as a powerfully appealing and persuasive cultural pedagogy. There the ideologies of a rapidly consolidating commercial culture found their most perfect representation in a glamorous life-style based upon the modern transformative virtues of leisure and consumption.

This is a version of the Hollywood myth that, while it can be said to pander to obvious social and sexual fantasies, organizes and articulates powerful utopian ideas through which Hollywood is linked to the promises of opportunity, happiness, and freedom. Yet it existed alongside other definitions of Hollywood's cultural significance. The idea of Hollywood as a sociocultural environment predicated on artifice and illusion produced a perspective through which the values of the consumer society, as well as the instruments of mass culture that support them, could be interrogated and critiqued. As the remainder of this book will show, most Hollywood fictions went to extreme lengths to expose the illusory and deceptive promises of the Hollywood romance.

CHAPTER THREE

ILLUSION AND REALITY

Hollywood and the Peril of Disillusionment

Hollywood is an Aladdin's dream. Penniless youth rubs a lamp
and becomes rich and famous over night, only to discover that
it's all a dream—the gold of no value and the fame a monster,
treacherous and enslaving.

HERBERT HOWE[1]

Probably the defining theme in fiction about the film capital is the confusion
of illusion and reality. David Fine observed that "this collapse of the
boundary between reality and illusion, fact and fantasy, has been the central
theme of novels about Los Angeles and Hollywood from the 1930s to the
present."[2] In fact, this has been the dominant theme of Hollywood fiction
since its beginnings in Sullivan's *The Glory Road* (1916). As the symbolic
center of movie make-believe and mass fantasies, Hollywood has always
evoked for observers what Edmund Wilson called "the strange spell of
unreality."[3] Writing about this facet of Hollywood in 1929, P. G. Wodehouse
commented:

> The whole atmosphere there is one of insidious deceit and subterfuge.
> In Hollywood nothing is what it affects to be. What looks like a tree
> is really a slab of wood backed with barrels. What appears on the
> screen as the towering palace of Haroun-al-Rashid is actually a card-
> board model occupying four feet by three of space. The languorous

lagoon is a smelly tank with a stage hand named Ed wading about in it in a bathing suit.[4]

Isolated, in many respects, from the "real world" by the business of movie making and the affluence and celebrity that attended the film industry, Hollywood in the 1920s and 1930s became the national locus for an epistemology of fantasy and dreams. One observer noted, "there is too much of dreams about—the town is saturated with their vanity. The result is that Hollywood is a world by itself—a world out of known dimensions."[5] Like some great national amusement park,[6] Hollywood represented a zone of unreality—a place where anything was possible, where appearances were deceiving and the facts of American life could be (temporarily) suspended. This atmosphere of rampant illusion and make-believe was most apparent in Hollywood's films,[7] but it was reproduced in other areas of cultural practice as well—such as the city's material landscape, which was dominated by architectural whimsy and a penchant for eclecticism and the exotic.[8]

Raised to the level of cultural argument by Hollywood fiction, this theme had both positive and negative variants. For the Hollywood romance, the blurring of fact and fantasy functioned as a benign invitation to dream, to set aside dull cares and concerns by entering a world graced by beauty and the utopic promises of self-fulfillment and happiness. More directly, the Hollywood romance was a response to the criticisms of Hollywood and the film industry in the early 1920s, and as such it was linked to the larger debate over mass culture and the role motion pictures were to play in American life.

On the other hand, for many writers drawn to the subject, the blurring of fact and fantasy in Hollywood created a social and cultural milieu of pervasive artificiality and inauthenticity. This assessment was frequently related to the question of Hollywood's morality: the difficulty of discerning the real from the unreal parallels the problem of separating the moral from the immoral in a social environment governed by ambition and desire. In most Hollywood fictions, the confusion of reality and illusion was an idea filled with anxiety that could grow into nightmarish uncertainty and fears of hallucinatory proportions. One consequence of this was that the stable subject of realist fiction, already being undermined within literary modernism, became increasingly problematic in a literature obsessed by the disjuncture between appearance and reality. The collapse of the presumably stable and discrete categories of fact and fantasy in Hollywood fiction produced a crisis of identity, pressing the characters into a heightened and disturbed subjectivity. Moreover, the realization of a discrepancy between screen fantasy and real life inevitably produced a profound sense of disappointment in and disillusionment with the sustaining dreams of the movies, resulting in a very personal sense of betrayal and loss. In the fictions that treated this theme, Hollywood often became an organizing metaphor for widespread social and cultural crisis, linked to the private disillusionment and failure of a central character.

Two novels from the early 1920s, Harry Leon Wilson's *Merton of the Movies* and Stephen Vincent Benét's *The Beginning of Wisdom*, examined the dangers and deceptions implicit in Hollywood's confusion of reality and illusion and explored the consequences of that confusion for Hollywood and American culture.

MERTON OF THE MOVIES

Harry Leon Wilson's comic novel *Merton of the Movies* is one of those exceptional works that serve to consolidate a literary tradition by defining its essential features. Though not the first Hollywood novel, it was certainly the most influential, and it articulated what would become the key themes of Hollywood fiction in the 1920s. *Merton of the Movies* first appeared as a serial in the *Saturday Evening Post* from February to April of 1922, at the height of the national debate over Hollywood and the movies.[9] That same year it was published as a novel, and George S. Kaufman and Marc Connelly adapted it for the stage.[10] It was subsequently filmed no less than three times—in 1924 and 1932 by Paramount and in 1947 by Metro-Goldwyn-Mayer (MGM).[11]

Merton of the Movies offers both positive and negative views of Hollywood illusion, revealing Wilson's fundamental ambivalence toward motion pictures and the film industry.[12] A comic version of the "revolt from the village" theme in American literature, exemplified by authors such as Sherwood Anderson and Sinclair Lewis, *Merton of the Movies* chronicles the adventures of Merton Gill, a movie-struck sales clerk who abandons his job in Simsbury, Illinois, to pursue Hollywood stardom. In light of the book's popularity, it is worth noting that *Merton of the Movies* was hailed by no less an apostle of literary modernism than Gertrude Stein as "the best book about twentieth-century American youth that has yet been done," and when Stein visited California in 1935 she asked to be introduced to only one celebrity: Harry Leon Wilson.[13]

The novel opens with a device that is frequently used in Hollywood fiction to confound the reader's sense of a stable fictional world: the juxtaposition of different levels of narrative reality. Like Nathanael West's *The Day of the Locust* (in which a Napoleonic army on the march described in convincing detail, is gradually revealed to be a procession of dress extras moving across the back lot on their way to a sound stage), *Merton of the Movies* begins with a remarkable moment of narrative uncertainty and disorientation, almost modernist in its shaking of the book's realist premise.

> At the very beginning of the tale there comes a moment of puzzled hesitation. One way of approach is set beside another for choice, and a third contrived for better choice. Still the puzzle persists, all because the one precisely right way might seem—shall we say intense, high keyed, clamorous? Yet if one way is the only right way, why pause? Courage! Slightly dazed, though certain, let us be on, into the shrill thick of it. So then——[14]

This moment of authorial indecision leads directly into an episode set in the "great open spaces" of the American West, involving the abduction of the beautiful Estelle St. Clair by Snake le Vasquez and her rescue by Buck Benson, the "strong, silent man of the open." Resembling a western dime novel in style and subject matter, the narrative proceeds for five pages.

At the moment in which Buck is about to vanquish Snake le Vasquez, "a new voice from the doorway" stops him: "Merton Gill, what in the sacred name of time are you meaning to do with that Dummy? For the good land's sake! Have you gone plumb crazy, or what? Put that thing down!"(5). A third level of fictional reality is thus introduced with the stern voice of Amos Gashwiler, Merton's employer and owner of the Gashwiler Emporium. Here we first glimpse Merton, bravely holding over his head a costumer's dress mannequin, "Snake le Vasquez." By drawing the reader into Merton's fantasy and making it appear to be the primary world of the fiction until it is ruptured by Gashwiler's entrance, Wilson adumbrates one of the book's central concerns—the confusion of illusion and reality and the inevitable moment of disappointment to which this confusion leads.

The opening pages of the novel brilliantly illustrate what George Kummer has cited as a basic principle of Wilson's comic art: "the ability to see a person or a situation from two points of view simultaneously."[15] Indeed, much of the book's humor arises from the reader's double perception of Merton, based on the discrepancies between his imaginary fantasy life and his actual situation and abilities. Yet this view of Merton also exemplifies one of mass culture's most important characteristics: its ability to interrupt direct experience and interpose its own mediated and inauthentic versions of self and world. The mass media, and movies in particular, provide potent, value-laden vicarious experiences for their audiences— experiences whose forms and messages function by organizing the audience's understanding and perception of the world. Mass culture often proffers substitutes for or simulations of "reality" that seem more aesthetically, ethically, and emotionally satisfying than the mundane and imperfect life in which we generally find ourselves. And our experience of mass culture and the internalization of its values are heightened in the movies.

Isolated from the sights and sounds of the outside world and evoking the visionary quality of dreams in the darkness of the theater, the experience of seeing a motion picture is often capable of initiating and energizing the psychological responses of identification and projection in its audience, becoming a vehicle for mass fantasy and escape. A contemporary article in *Collier's* offered an analysis of the psychological effects of motion pictures that paralleled Wilson's portrait of Merton.

> But what happens when a person spends all his spare time at the pictures? One-fifth of the population of the United States is said to go every day. It would be a great mistake to underrate the power of this seduction. Especially for the young and immature, who have not enough fact and experience of the world to counteract such mental lotus eating, every thinking man must recognize a great danger. There seems little doubt that in the course of time the boy or girl movie fan gets out of the habit of thinking with facts, and into the habit of

thinking pleasantly. Thus develops a type of person who is necessarily out of touch with his surroundings, essentially unhappy, for whom the world must be out of joint because it cannot be made over to his impossible wishes.[16]

In this respect, Hollywood takes on an added level of meaning as the *dream factory*—the source of collective fantasies that can seem more "real" than the actuality from which they are meant to divert us. Merton's misapprehension of himself and others, brought on by his identification with movie plots and characters, is a central comedic device in the novel; indeed, his whole perception of reality is shown to be filtered through the distorting lens of movie westerns and screen romances, the simplistic yet often profoundly appealing narrative formulas of mass culture.

Gashwiler's interruption of Merton's western fantasy triggers not a return to the "real" world of his work but the deployment of a second layer of pleasing illusion: Merton's alter ego, "Clifford Armytage"—movie star. The idiom of the dime novel that was parodied in the Buck Benson episode gives way to the idiom of movie marketing and promotion before finally being driven back to the more mundane idiom of commercial advertising, which signals a return to the everyday reality of Gashwiler's Emporium.

> And now, gone the vivid tale of the great out-of-doors, the wide plains of the West, the clash of primitive-hearted men for a good woman's love. Gone, perhaps, the greatest heart picture of a generation, the picture at which you laugh with a lump in your throat and smile with a tear in your eye, the story of plausible punches, a big, vital theme masterfully handled—thrills, action, beauty, excitement—carried to a sensational finish by the genius of that sterling star of the shadowed world, Clifford Armytage—once known as Merton Gill in the little hamlet of Simsbury, Illinois, where, for a time, ere yet he was called to screen triumphs, he served as a humble clerk in the so-called emporium of Amos G. Gashwiler—Everything For The Home. Our Prices Always Right. (6)

This radically multivoiced passage, with its imbrication of several languages of movie ballyhoo, fan magazine interviews, and commercial advertising, is a complex parody of the cultural discourses it so carefully evokes: the dime-novel narrative of the western romance is interrupted by the "local color" vernacular of Amos Gashwiler, which in turn is superseded by the fan-magazine rhetoric of Hollywood stardom, which at last gives way to the discourse of retail advertising.

Characteristically for much Hollywood fiction (and anticipating the disappearance of the stable subject in contemporary critical theory), Merton Gill—the ostensibly "real" person at the center of these events—is barely visible behind the masks of his personae, an absent cause discernible only in the traces of his projected dream life. Buck Benson, "the strong, silent, two-gun man of the open spaces," and Clifford Armytage, "the sterling star of the shadowed world," are equally the products of mass culture, a culture that Wilson parodies and critiques by casting it in the most hackneyed of popular forms.

Merton's comic appeal in the novel stems from his too-fervent devotion to the "fine and beautiful art of the motion pictures" (20), and the importance he attaches to the movies becomes a recurring sign of his naïveté. While his solemn dedication to motion-picture "art" makes him seem odd and out of place in Simsbury, in Hollywood his passionate convictions seem ridiculous to those inside the film industry. He is enthralled by the most formulaic of movie narratives, the serials and westerns, in which he discovers the models of heroic and self-sacrificing masculine behavior upon which he later bases his own screen career. And he is an ardent admirer of the serial star Beulah Baxter, "the slim little girl with a wistful smile" (32) who, week after week in her roles, defeats a seemingly endless procession of villains and saves herself from a series of increasingly horrific and improbable dangers. Wilson's depiction of Merton's vicarious identification with the characters and plots of the most obvious and contrived movie narratives ridicules the movie fan's obsessions and demonstrates how the mass fantasies emanating from Hollywood could become a substitute for reality.

Merton prepares himself for his chosen profession by reading movie and fan magazines and by taking a correspondence course on movie acting. The fan magazines and self-improvement courses Merton consumes are products of a commercial culture that, like the movies themselves, are purveyors of mass dreams and desires.[17] Throughout the novel, Merton's rural innocence serves as a comic counterpoint for his artistic pretensions and his pathetic susceptibility to cinematic illusions. Repeatedly we are shown that his capacity for self-deception is surpassed only by his willingness to be deceived by the instruments of mass culture—movie magazines and motion pictures. However, the book explores not just the comic but also the tragic potential of these deceptions. Beneath the narrative's optimistic and sentimental surface runs a current of alarm and skepticism. At the moment when Merton prays, "Oh God, make me a good movie actor! Make me one of the best! For Jesus' sake, amen!" (29), the unlikeliness of his success in Hollywood overwhelms the force of his revealed ambition.

Merton's penchant for role playing and posturing is displayed early in the novel, when he tries on mail-order costumes, poses for "art studies" shot by a local photographer, and conducts imaginary interviews with himself as "Clifford Armytage." These passages, like the Buck Benson episode, reveal Wilson's genius for vernacular and his mastery of the dialect of the fan magazine. Picturing himself enthroned in the luxury of his "palatial bungalow in distant Hollywood" (17), Merton/Clifford muses on the Hollywood good life in terms of "expensive cigars in elaborate humidors and costly gold-tipped cigarettes in silver things on low tables," the pleasures of tobacco smoking being severely curtailed in the Gashwiler home, where he lives. Hollywood is linked to the promises of leisure, consumption, and personal freedom, if only in the diminished forms Merton can imagine.

Not surprisingly, his Hollywood dream is a romantic one, in which the sexually innocent Merton has found the love of a woman who (he tells the imaginary interviewer) "is more than a wife—she is my best pal and, I may add, she is also my severest critic." Echoing the movie magazines, this image of matrimonial harmony and domestic bliss does more than parody the rhetoric so often employed to conceal the troubled emotional and sexual lives of the stars. It is also consistent with the comedic structure of the novel, which ends with Merton's marriage to the actress and stunt woman Sarah Montague ("the Montague girl") and a repetition of these same lines to a (this time) real interviewer visiting him at his "luxurious Hollywood Bungalow" (330). While *Merton of the Movies* exposes much that is inauthentic and deceptive about Hollywood, ultimately its good life is shown to be realizable—even for one as obviously unequal to it as Merton—and therefore worthy of emulation and pursuit.

Unlike many Hollywood novels that ritualize the cross-country trip to California, transforming it into a liminal passage in which the past is abandoned and a new identity is fashioned (often accompanied by a screen name), in *Merton of the Movies* Merton's trip is elided. The suddenness of his appearance in California underscores the fact that the distance between Simsbury and Hollywood is more than just geographical. Merton has traversed a social and cultural distance for which he is not entirely prepared.

The novel's initial view of Hollywood announces a fundamental trope of Hollywood fiction, made possible by its paradoxical cultural identity: the fantastic contained by the ordinary. "The street leading to the Holden motion picture studio, considered by itself, lacks beauty" (56). Surrounded by vacant lots and the occasional modest bungalow, the studio is enclosed by a tall and unassuming fence—the boundary between a depressingly prosaic real world and a domain of exoticism and mystery, the juncture of illusion and reality. "Back of this fence is secreted a microcosmos, a world in little, where one may encounter strange races of people in their native dress and behold, by walking a block, cities actually apart by league upon league of the earth's surface and separated by centuries of time" (56).

On his first visit to the studio Merton is forcefully turned away by the studio guard, who bars the gate to all but the "inner elect." Thus Merton encounters a social fact often explored in Hollywood fiction: like American society at large, for which it often serves as a demonic double, Hollywood is ruled by rigid structures of inclusion and exclusion. It is a society of "insiders" and "outsiders," often cruel in its elitism and indifference. So Merton becomes a "watcher at the gate," reinforcing his role as a passive consumer of Hollywood dreams. More important, his predicament is reproduced in the subject position that the narrative constructs for the reader—who, like Merton, must await an opportunity to penetrate the mysterious world of the studio.

What makes Merton Gill such a rich character is the way in which he activates for the reader a conflicting sense of both identification and disdain. Merton comes to represent the reader's own curiosity about the workings of a Hollywood studio, and at the same time he is a comic object of ridicule for the reader, who presumably knows that one cannot find success in

Hollywood by haunting the studio gate. Hollywood fiction frequently evokes this interplay of mixed narrative responses: on the one hand, attraction and identification; on the other, skepticism and doubt. And, despite the fact that he is often the butt of the joke, Merton is a literary version of a very real (and ongoing) social phenomenon in Hollywood—the flood of thousands of young men and women into Los Angeles in the 1920s, drawn by the glittering promises of Hollywood fame and success. In 1923, according to one estimate, ten thousand people a month invaded Hollywood to find work in the movie business.[18] Merton is a representative figure for this army of movie hopefuls sustained primarily by ambition and dreams.

In Hollywood Merton discovers that "never had he achieved so much downright actuality" (58). Now in the physical presence of the film studios and the movie stars whom he has worshipped in distant Simsbury, Merton experiences a heightened sense of what, to him, are the most meaningful and significant aspects of his existence—the romance and adventure of the movies. His sense of closeness to the screen world, of really being "where the pictures are made" (63), is a reward that far outweighs the postponements and discomforts he endured to get there. Wilson's obvious irony is that Merton discovers this heightened sense of "actuality" *in Hollywood*, with its illusions and artificiality, where the tricks and deceptions of movie making permeate both the material and social environments. In fact, this suggests the extent to which Hollywood illusion has become Merton's primary reality, as he basks in the imaginary plenitude of his most cherished dreams and desires. Merton's sense of "actuality" is an ironic reminder that mass culture undermines the real, making its own mass-market fantasies and the epiphenomenon of celebrity more "real" for Merton than the drab routines of life in Simsbury.[19]

After weeks of feverish anticipation, Merton is admitted to the Holden studio as a visitor. At last he can mingle with the actors and wander agog through the stages and standing sets of a frontier town, a row of New York brownstones, and a Baghdad street. At once a process of disillusionment begins, as he is shocked to learn about the stage effects and cinematic fakery that he had accepted as real on the screen. The sets are "pretentiously false," "fragile contrivances of button-lath and thin plaster" (74), and instantly their allure as emblems of romance and adventure begins to evaporate for him, their "real falseness" (77) all too apparent. His interest is renewed somewhat by the action on the sets, as he studies the actors, directors, and technicians engaged in the intricacies of film production. But he is soon disappointed with the tedium and inefficiency of film work, as actors loll in boredom while waiting for a prop or a camera setup, and directors huddle endlessly with carpenters and dressmakers. Echoing the complaints about film-industry excesses that were appearing in national magazines at this time, Wilson's novel exposes and ridicules Hollywood as a mode of production, finding it to be a system of massive inefficiencies and delays. While the book is circumstantial in regard to the routines and difficulties of film work in the silent era, the accumulated weight of these details only hastens Merton's disillusionment with the "art" of the motion picture.

Eventually Merton is employed as an extra in a potboiler, "The Blight of Broadway," where he is paired with the Montague girl for some close-ups. But, when his money runs out and he can no longer pay his rent, he hides out on the studio lot, sleeping in empty sets by night and aimlessly wandering the stages by day, his already overactive imagination now accelerated by lack of food and fear of discovery. At last Merton has a chance to live in a world of movie illusion, only to discover that it is a rather harsh and unhealthful place to be.

The comic tone of the novel is significantly undermined at this point by Merton's dilemmas. Slowly starving, living on moldy prop food and sleeping in abandoned sets, unwashed and unshaven, he is a figure of increasing pathos and despair. As he teeters on the edge of physical collapse and mental breakdown, his dreams of Hollywood fame and romance are clearly shown to be chimerical, and for the first time in the novel he is confronted with the prospect of failure and a retreat to Simsbury.

In this section Wilson presents a portrait of a mind at odds with its own illusions, engaged in a battle that seems all but lost when, a short time later, Merton is described as mere "clay to the moulding of the subconscious" (158), a creature now driven by the most basic needs for food and shelter. This portrait of a wraithlike figure haunting the back lot, lost and alone in his Hollywood dreams, is Wilson's most significant achievement in the novel, a disturbing portrayal of the empty promises of Hollywood's mass fantasies.

As Merton slips deeper into self-doubt and starvation, he is only beginning the process of disillusionment that the novel chronicles. While observing a film crew, he is shocked to discover that the dramatic rearing of a horse, which had so often thrilled him in the Buck Benson westerns, is produced by a nearby shotgun blast in response to a signal from the director. "So that was it. The panic of the old horse had been but a simple reaction to a couple of charges of—perhaps rocksalt. Merton Gill hoped it had been nothing sterner. For the first time in his screen career he became cynical about his art. A thing of shame, of machinery, of subterfuge. Nothing would be real, perhaps not even the art" (166). This revelation of movie trickery begins to erode Merton's belief in film art, and the phoniness and cheap illusions practiced on the lot begin to overwhelm him.

His doubts are suppressed when he is dazzled by a glimpse of his screen idol Beulah Baxter, and he comforts himself with the assurance that "she, at least, was real." In fact, this assurance is short-lived: Merton discovers that his "wonder woman" is doubled in her stunt work by the Montague girl, the "slangy chit" whose humor and irreverence on the lot have shocked him since he arrived in Hollywood. He is further dismayed to discover that Beulah Baxter is happily married (for the third time) to her director, Sig Rosenblatt. This, "the swift and utter destruction of his loftiest ideal" (175), leaves Merton dazed. It also signals the real beginning of his Hollywood career.

Hollywood fiction has always been preoccupied with success and failure, and it has thereby helped to shape the narrative formulas through which our culture thinks about these basic social and economic experiences. Hollywood has been conceived of as a place of both sudden and unexpected success (often undeserved) and equally sudden and disastrous failure. As a founding text in the canon of Hollywood fiction, *Merton of the Movies* presents definitive accounts of both possibilities through Merton's grim "outlaw" days on the Holden lot and his eventual success and enjoyment of the Hollywood good life, following his discovery by Sarah Montague.

Sarah, the "Montague girl," embodies all the experience and cynical wisdom about the movies that Merton so clearly lacks, and throughout the novel she is a narrative foil for his seriousness and pretension. At the same time she is a vehicle for the book's sentimentalism, as her affection for Merton slowly evolves into a motherly but nonetheless romantic attachment to him. A seasoned veteran of the circus and stage, she knows every trick in the movie game, and her experience with stunt work makes her a valuable and popular person on the lot. In contrast with the ethereal and vapid screen beauties whom Merton admires, the "Montague girl" is an unusually capable and high-spirited young woman who, to Merton's dismay, takes mischievous delight in puncturing the pompous absurdities and artistic pretensions of the movies. She is, in fact, a Hollywood version of the "New Woman," exemplifying the opportunities for achievement that were available to women in the pioneer film industry. She is the equal of any man on the lot and possesses a genuine strength and confidence that make her the most attractive character in the novel. Her middle name—Nevada—is an intentional reference to the freedoms of the American West. It is Sarah who rescues Merton from starvation and discovers in his zeal for the art of the motion picture his potential for stardom.

Merton of the Movies is on one level a catalogue of hackneyed movie plots and situations, and only someone as attuned to the formulas and devices of popular culture as Wilson could perform the parodic subversion of its narrative forms with such precision. Interpolated throughout the novel are fragments of movie plots that, while serving to underscore the sensational and formulaic qualities of Hollywood narratives, are credible as films of the period. Their banality and repetition, however, make it clear that Wilson is condemning Hollywood for making the same films over and over again. His judgment was echoed by the critics of motion pictures at the time, who complained that producers and directors looked for ideas in the movies that had been successful, and scenarios were tailored to fit the already-established persona of the screen star.

In this respect, *Merton of the Movies* is an attack upon the "art" of the motion picture and the melodramatic narrative formulas that dominated early movie making. Within the canon of Hollywood fiction, Wilson's novel displays a special interest in characterizing and criticizing the kinds of movies Hollywood offered its mass audiences.[20] A central device of this critique is Merton's own taste in films. His aesthetic standards are based on a valorization of the most melodramatic and sentimental narrative formulas, which produce for him "something better and finer" than the "coarse pantomime and heavy horseplay" (87) associated with another school of film making—the slapstick comedy. Indeed, the novel's central cultural argument hinges on the disjuncture between these two forms of popular art and the differences in their structures of appeal: on the one hand, a romantic identification with the heroes and situations of a ritualized and sentimental melodrama, and on the other hand, the ironic distancing provoked by an aesthetically anarchic, morally ambiguous, and socially disruptive slapstick comedy. Wilson seems to suggest that if the mass culture of the movies has any redeeming feature, it is to be found in the gleeful chaos and irreverence of movie comedy.

For Merton, screen comedy is a vulgar cultural "other" that debases the "fine and beautiful art" of the motion pictures. In evoking the "genteel tradition" of aesthetic judgment (which, ironically, would be horrified by the melodramatic movie plots he admires), Merton clings to an elitist notion of screen art for which the novel has little sympathy. The chief objects of his scorn are the Buckeye Comedies produced on the Holden lot by Jeff Baird, a Mack Sennett-like character. In Baird's stock company is a "cross-eyed man" whose antics, Merton notes with characteristic disdain, invariably appeal to "the coarser element among screen patrons" (90). Merton's comic fate is to become the unwitting partner of the cross-eyed man and to achieve stardom in precisely the kind of movies he most despises.

Because of Merton's resemblance to matinee idol Harold Parmalee, Baird casts him in a "five reeler" that parodies the melodramas Merton admires. Merton unwittingly enhances the satire through an absurdly overblown imitation of the mannerisms and gestures of his matinee idols. Merton believes that he is at last doing something "serious" and "important," while in fact Baird is constructing "mere comedy" by juxtaposing Merton's humorously earnest efforts at screen art with the antics of the Buckeye cast. Incredibly, Merton remains impervious to the massive joke being played upon him until the film's premiere, where the sudden revelation sends him into a tizzy of indignation.

Yet even at this, his ultimate moment of disillusionment, Merton discovers a way to preserve his illusions. Throughout the novel, Wilson uses conversations between the director Henshaw and a high-ranking studio executive called "the Governor" as a running commentary on the commercialism and superficiality of Hollywood and the film industry. Eavesdropping on their table in the studio cafeteria the day after the preview, Merton discovers that they have mistaken his bad dramatic acting for a brilliant comedic performance. Henshaw complains, "But see what he does: he takes the good old reliable, sure-fire stuff and makes fun of it. I admit it's funny to start with, but what'll happen to us if the picture public ever finds that out? What'll we do then for drama—after they've learned to laugh at the old stuff?" (317). The Governor, however—with the cynical wisdom of the experienced Hollywood showman—counters that, despite the effectiveness of Merton's lampoon, the tired formulas of movie drama will always have an audience. "Now take your picture public. Twenty million people every day; not the same ones every day, but with the same average cranial index, which is low for all but about seven out of every hundred. That's natural because there aren't twenty million people in the world with real taste or intelligence—probably not five million. . . . Don't worry; that reliable field marshal, old General Hokum, leads an unbeatable army" (317).

The critique of motion pictures that the book elaborates becomes, at last, a critique of the mass audience: "To make money we must sell to the mob. And the mob reaches full mental bloom at the age of fifteen" (320). The book's final rebuttal of Merton's idealistic belief in the "fine and beautiful art" of the motion picture is the Governor's description of film as "the Peter Pan of the arts," unable to grow up and marked by, as Ariel Dorfman has characterized it, "a tendency to infantilize . . . to diminish the most complex dilemmas to simplified and simpleminded formulas."[21]

Of course, the critique of Hollywood in *Merton of the Movies* is profoundly ambivalent precisely because it hangs on the complicated figure of Merton, who represents both the (mass) audience of readers and its parodic double, the "mob" led by "General Hokum." The significance of Merton as a character is that he embodies the projected desires of the audience (represented by his success in Hollywood) and at the same time is a comic emblem of the absurdity and emptiness of those desires. Merton acts out pervasive social fantasies associated with Hollywood as a cultural myth and at the same time allows us to laugh at them.

So completely does Merton become a figure for the desires of his audience that Robert Littell, when he reviewed the book in 1922, worried that "there are millions who might read this story and see nothing in it to laugh at all."[22] Significantly, Merton arrives at the end of the book with his illusions intact; rather than becoming disillusioned with motion pictures he simply reinvents himself as a "tragic comedian" and finds contentment in screen success, confirming what he has always known and what the readers of Wilson's popular and ultimately sentimental fiction want to believe—Hollywood dreams can come true.

For this reason *Merton of the Movies* is of central importance within the canon of Hollywood fiction. It illustrates the way in which fictions about Hollywood appeal to some of our deepest and most widely held desires (for success, fame, wealth—ideas crucially linked to Hollywood as a cultural myth) and at the same time critique the social values and the agencies of mass culture that produce and reproduce those desires for a mass audience. In other words, *Merton of the Movies* articulates our fundamental ambivalence toward Hollywood.

THE BEGINNING OF WISDOM

Writing to his wife from California in 1929, Stephen Vincent Benét offered a trenchant description of Hollywood, a place that he often referred to in his letters as "a madhouse."

> In the first place Hollywood—Los Angeles, Glendale, Pasadena etc etc—is one loud, struggling Main Street, low-roofed, mainly unsky-scrapered town that straggles along for twenty-five miles or so, full of stop & go lights, automobiles, palm-trees, Spanishy—& God knows what all houses—orange-drink stands with real orange juice—studios—movie theaters—everything but bookstores. . . . There are some swell hotels—up in the hills or between L.A. & Hollywood—and a few night-clubs. But in general, everything is dead, deserted at 11:30 P.M.[23]

Benét had come to Hollywood to write a scenario on the life of Abraham Lincoln for D. W. Griffith. After two months' work at a salary of $1,000 per week, he fled back to New York, eager to escape the velvet trap of life in Hollywood.[24] Benét was lonely and uncomfortable in California, and in his correspondence he often launched into visceral attacks on Hollywood and the film industry:

> Of all the Christbitten places and business[es] on the two hemispheres this one is the last curly kink on the pig's tail. . . . I don't know which

makes me vomit worst—the horned toads from the cloak and suit trade, the shanty Irish, or the gentlemen who talk of Screen Art . . . nowhere have I seen such shining waste, stupidity and conceit as in the business and managing end of this industry. Whoopee! . . . If I don't get out of here soon I am going crazy. Perhaps I am crazy now. I wouldn't be surprised.[25]

Benét's response to Hollywood typifies the frustration and sense of alienation experienced by many of the artists, writers, and intellectuals who sojourned there. But his attitudes also resemble those of the protagonist of his first novel, Philip Sellaby, an ironic and embittered young poet who finds himself in Hollywood in 1917 and gets swept up in a whirlwind of make-believe and fame.

Begun when Benét was a senior at Yale, *The Beginning of Wisdom* is a semiautobiographical novel that traces Philip's growth and education, from his birth in 1892 through his youthful experiences in a military academy and on to college at Yale, where he develops his poetic sensibilities.[26] He forms fast friendships, goes to movies and dance halls, struggles with academic work and school traditions, and falls in love with a local girl, whom he secretly marries. Her sudden death from pneumonia shatters Philip's happiness and precipitates a period of restless soul-searching, as he struggles to understand the meaning of his life.

In its portrait of innocence and experience framed by the vicissitudes of college life, the novel seems clearly influenced by F. Scott Fitzgerald's *This Side of Paradise*, which was published in 1920, the year before Benét's work. Yet the narrative quickly pulls Philip from the college scene in order to explore other aspects of American life. Diagnosed with tuberculosis and unable to enlist in the army with his college friends in 1916, he instead goes to Arizona to work for a mining company. There he befriends members of the Industrial Workers of the World (I.W.W.) who are engaged in a labor struggle against the company, with the result that he is railroaded out of town for supporting their cause. Returning to his family home in California, he breaks with his father over his involvement in the strike and his inability to join the army. Now destitute, cut off from family and friends, disillusioned with his country but frustrated by his inability to serve it, Philip drifts south to Los Angeles, where he suddenly finds himself in a world of bizarre unreality, the "Movie Paradise" of Hollywood (226).

Experimental in form and content, the novel intersperses fragments of poetry, journal entries, philosophical and aesthetic musings, impressionistic descriptions, and allegorical dream scenes with realistic sections that propel the narrative and present a broad portrait of American life in the first decades of the twentieth century. Unlike the sentimental realism of Wilson's *Merton of the Movies*, Benéts American *bildungsroman* is, in many respects, an artifact of high culture, acutely self-conscious in its literary ambitions and artistic gambits. Yet, like Wilson's more popular work, Benét's novel displays an interest in the forms of contemporary popular culture, particularly the movies, and expresses a similar ambivalence about mass culture, reveling in its democratic jocularity and its irreverence toward tradition yet suspicious of its shallow optimism and aesthetic vapidity. As in *Merton of the Movies*, the focus of these arguments is Hollywood. Yet the confusion of reality and illusion that Philip experiences in *The Beginning of Wisdom* suggests a moral ambiguity and personal confusion much darker than that in Wilson's novel. For Philip, "the whole movie-world was . . . a phantasm of unreality . . ." (235), and he is both fascinated and repelled by its glittering lies. The differences in the representations of Hollywood in these two texts are best exemplified by the attitudes of their central characters: for Merton, Hollywood is a projection of his ideal self—romantic, artistic, adventurous; for Philip, Hollywood comes to represent a serious crisis of identity, a haunting symbol of inauthenticity and self-deception.

Significantly, Philip's Hollywood experiences occur during a period of self-doubt, when he is particularly susceptible to the city's temptations. Unlike Merton, he drifts casually into movie work, where he is quickly singled out by the director because of his clean-cut, collegiate good looks. After making a couple of pictures, Philip slides easily into "the conventions of stardom," acquiring "a valet, a suite at the Grantmore and a red Stutz" (240) and taking the movie name "Peter Sands." In Hollywood fiction, as in the star-making machinery of studio publicity, the adoption of a screen name is an often obligatory rite of passage, a symbolic break with the past and with family and community ties. For Merton this was an exhilarating moment of freedom and of transformation into an ideal version of himself as "Clifford Armytage." For Philip, however, "Peter Sands" is a sign of both cynical capitulation to Hollywood convention and his determination not to lose sight of his past: "Peter" is the name of a college friend now fighting in Europe, and "Sands" is a reference to his recent experiences with the I.W.W. in the Arizona desert. Anxious about the meaning of his past and uncertain about his future, Philip finds Hollywood a particularly congenial and fascinating spot to reinvent himself. Initially he throws himself energetically into "the whole arabesque and painted world into which he had stumbled."

> The clue to it all was artificiality and easy money from studios that were steel and stucco copies of Renaissance chateaus to febrile, sex-precocious little girls, who drew salaries in the thousands and lived in the conjugal intimacy of a bedroom-farce when they should have been getting ready to put their hair up and bid hidden, weeping farewells to their favorite dolls. It was a world that revolved like the spinning wheel of stiff horses in a merry-go-round to a syncopation of all the jazziest musical comedy tunes. It was a world in which temperament abounded like an overdose of paprika on fish—a world where every one seemed to revel in pink-and-purple striped limousines, cellars full of expensive cordials and permanent cases of actor's head. Not that its inhabitants did not work and work hard—when they worked it was with the hypnotic energy of slaves on a sinking galley, when they played it was with the spectacular abandon of hasheesh eaters. (238)

The falsities and deceptions of Hollywood life shock Philip again and again, and increasingly it is his own self-contradictions that bear the weight of his disdain. "Philip recognized himself on the screen, but that was all; when he looked in the mirror the contrast was too pitiful for words" (234). On the set he observes the faces of extras, "ghastly with screaming paints that would make beautifully natural complexions on the deceptive screen" (229). It is the discrepancy between screen illusion and real life that most disturbs him. "There were vampires on the screen with good-natured husbands and bobbing little girls in private—there were *ingenues* with the open faces of pansies and a vocabulary in which a Parisian Apache would have felt at home" (239). The distance between the screen person—a creature of equal parts fantasy and formula—and the actual person behind the celluloid mask represents for Philip the gaps and inconsistencies between his own fragile and uncertain sense of self and his "new incarnation" (234) as movie star Peter Sands.

Philip achieves stardom in roles as the average American doughboy, "the hero just a fraction better than normal" (236), in films produced to capitalize on the public's interest in the war. Initially he conceals his discomfort in these roles beneath an attitude of grim irony and, on the surface, an open enjoyment of success, with "the money that flowed in so effortlessly, and all the other monogrammed silk-underwear appurtenances of a star" (245). However, as Los Angeles begins to fill with uniformed soldiers, real-life "normal heroes," Philip becomes increasingly impatient and angry with "the play-acting, false-fronted cosmos into which he had slipped" (241). His stardom becomes a constant and painful reminder of his exemption from military service and of the sacrifices being made at the front by his college friends. Costumed in a soldier's uniform, Philip feels like a "buffoon," "a soiled masquerader in stolen clothes" (246–47). News of his best friend's death in combat finally plunges him into a crisis of self-worth and personal integrity.

Benét staged Philip's crisis of self-doubt in two of the most powerfully symbolic Hollywood settings: a raucous studio party and the luxurious boudoir of a beautiful movie star. Since the Fatty Arbuckle scandal of 1921, in which the popular screen comedian had been accused of making a fatal sexual assault on a starlet during a drunken bash at the St. Francis Hotel in San Francisco, the wild Hollywood party had been the chief exemplum of filmdom's decadence and debauchery.[27] For Prohibition America, the Hollywood party was a source of fascination and horror, a scene of extravagant consumption, strenuous indulgence, and sexual excess—in short, a social stage in which new moral and behavioral codes could be acted out. In Hollywood fiction the party is an almost ritual set piece, an obligatory symbol of the social and cultural dangers implicit in the Hollywood good life and an emblem of the moral depravity of mass culture. For Philip in his morass of guilt and confusion, the gay studio party is "like an aimless walk through a second-rate part of hell" (251).

He leaves the party for a sexual liaison with the screen vamp Pancha Verschoyle, who has pursued him since his arrival in Hollywood. Pancha represents a familiar type in Hollywood fiction: the amoral, ambitious, and sexually aggressive female star—a blonde sex goddess, predatory and merciless in her conquest of men. She embodies both male sexual fear and sexual desire in her bold pursuit of pleasure, free from the entanglements and responsibilities of love and marriage. Yet for Philip, Pancha's erotic power turns out to be just another example of Hollywood illusion; in reality the exotic screen siren is Hilda Swenson, ex-burlesque dancer, whose temper and lack of talent are only partially concealed by her publicity and her screen performances. Stumbling in the darkness of her boudoir amid overstuffed, violet-scented furnishings, Philip suddenly remembers his dead wife. Struck by guilt, he flees Pancha's Hollywood bungalow, severely spraining his ankle in the process. A doctor who examines him the following day tells him of an operation that will cure his respiratory condition and render him eligible for military service. Philip immediately agrees to the surgery. After recovering, he enlists in the army and happily leaves Hollywood for good.

Philip's almost instant Hollywood stardom in the novel is only slightly less improbable than his sudden abandonment of that stardom to join the army. But, in a work as centrally concerned with the symbolic dimensions of American life as *The Beginning of Wisdom,* this can hardly be a serious complaint, for in this novel Hollywood—understood both as a way of life and as a mode of cultural production—clearly functions as an emblem of larger concerns. It symbolizes a mass culture that offers its vast audiences only mediated and inauthentic versions of self and world, and thus also symbolizes that culture's failure as "art." "The films," Philip concludes, "bore in general the same ingenuous and illegitimate relation to the arts that advertising copy did to literature" (309). Constructed upon a system of false values and an aesthetics of illusion, Hollywood in Benét's work functions as an agent of cultural corruption and decline. Eight years after the publication of *The Beginning of Wisdom,* Benét wrote to his wife from Hollywood complaining, "It is still unreal, unreal, unreal."[28] However, for fiction about the film capital, as for American culture at large, unreality could be both a source of horror and a compellingly attractive feature of life in the "movie paradise." Ambivalence continued to dominate both depictions of Hollywood.

As both *Merton of the Movies* and *The Beginning of Wisdom* show, the confusion of illusion and reality thematized by Hollywood fiction often worked to foreground the contradictions of mass culture, pointing to the incongruities between Hollywood's screen fantasies and actual life. However, the real danger of Hollywood's confusion of illusion and reality lay in the peril of disillusionment, the loss of faith and hope in oneself and in the sustaining dreams of our culture. This was an end of innocence for which Hollywood became emblematic, and whose most tragic representative figure was the star.

CHAPTER FOUR

FALLING STARS

Hollywood Fiction and the Lessons of Stardom

Where are the stars of yesterday? The famous people who lived in Hollywood mansions, rode in shining, big limousines, and whose faces flashed across the screens of the world? They received the adulation of the public, they trod the paths of glory, and then disappeared. New faces. New times. . . . Hollywood doesn't like to talk of its failures. Success is all that really matters in Hollywood.

MARQUIS BUSBY[1]

Hollywood invented the phenomenon of modern celebrity and, in so doing, created a cultural figure of enduring fascination and ambivalence—the movie star.[2] Like Hollywood itself, stardom was often at the center of conflicting ideas and contested values. In the 1920s and 1930s, stardom exemplified the American dream of success, and the life-styles of film celebrities helped to define an emerging ethos of leisure and consumption in American society. Yet stardom was also marked by scandal and personal tragedy, and the lives of film stars often revealed the hidden perils of success. As agents of social modernity, film stars embodied conflicting ideological imperatives concerning issues of work and leisure, sexual and social behavior, gender and career, private life and public image. While stars, studios, and fan magazines energetically strove to manage and shape these competing messages to suit their own interests, the social and cultural dynamics of movie stardom often eluded their control, producing a focal point for audience interest that could upstage the movies themselves.

Film stars were more than just actors and actresses who made motion pictures; they were exemplary figures, objects of mass adoration and emulation, centers of collective aspiration and desire. Often they were symbolic figures—embodiments of national character, emblematic social types, or idealized models of masculine and feminine behavior. In light of their symbolic roles, both on screen and off, it can well be asserted, as Raymond Durgnat has done, that "the social history of a nation can be written in terms of its film stars."[3] Movie stars embodied the prevailing canons of taste and style. They illuminated the dominant values of society, sometimes through their apparent opposition to them; yet their lives often revealed the contradictions and inconsistencies that underlay those values. As social and cultural creations, Hollywood stars were, as Alexander Walker has noted, "the direct or indirect reflection of the needs, drives and dreams of American society,"[4] yet they reflected those dreams obliquely, as in a fun-house mirror that exaggerates and distorts.

It is this notion of Hollywood stardom, as a social phenomenon loaded with unresolved cultural and ideological tensions, that I want to examine through the Hollywood fictions of the 1920s that focused upon movie stars.[5] However, to understand the presentations of film stars in Hollywood fictions, we must begin by considering the broader social, cultural, and institutional frameworks for stardom that informed their construction. In fact, we must begin by recognizing that the movie-star persona was itself always a type of cultural fiction, articulated across a range of media texts and answering the real or manufactured needs of the audience for a certain kind of hero.

At the same time, however, movie stars were often problematic heroes. The glamorous facade of their highly publicized personal lives could crumble into scandal and notoriety, much to the public's shock and delight. A star's popularity with movie audiences was always alloyed with a degree of suspicion and resentment, arising as much from their privileged way of life as from their occasional sexual or social misconduct, and revealing an emotional substratum of hostility beneath the fan's obsessive interest. Clark Gable remarked on the relationship between the film star and his audience.

We all have a contract with the public—in us they see themselves or what they would like to be. On the screen and in our private lives, we are the standards by which they measure their own ideas of everything—sex, guts, humor, stupidity, cowardice, crumminess—you name it. They love to put us on a pedestal and worship us and form fan clubs and write thousands of letters telling us how great we are. But *they've* read the small print, and most of us haven't—they expect us to pay the price for it all. . . . We have to get it in the end.[6]

Admired, envied, and despised by their public, the great movie stars of the 1920s and 1930s were the most visible cultural icons of their day, and the narrative of stardom that they enacted served as a paradigm for success in American life. Yet it was a narrative also haunted by a sense of anxiety and guilt and by the nagging fear that movie stars "have to get it in the end." Thus, the lives of stars often disclosed in exaggerated dimensions the fundamental desires and fears of American life.

The phenomenon of film stardom was first analyzed in fan magazines and in Hollywood novels and short stories, which shared both a fascination with and an ambivalence toward the figure of the star. An examination of these parallel fictions about movie stars reveals the conflicting images of Hollywood fame that they offered—in particular, the ambivalent images of women as film stars.

SUCCESS, CONSUMPTION

Most generally, Hollywood stars represented the American myth of success, serving as living examples of the possibility of a Horatio Alger-like rise to wealth and fame. The twentieth-century phenomenon of film stardom helped to keep alive nineteenth-century notions of individual initiative, opportunity, and success, which were tied to a democratic myth of American life that was increasingly being undermined by modern social and economic conditions. The historian Daniel Boorstin commented upon the potency of this social myth: "The film-star legend of the accidentally discovered soda-fountain girl who was quickly elevated to stardom soon took its place alongside the log-cabin-to-White-House legend as a leitmotif of American democratic folklore."[7] In theory, anyone could become a star; indeed, the lure of stardom—and of Hollywood itself—resided in the unpredictability of "discovery" and the suddenness of screen success. In practice, however, the equation for Hollywood stardom was variable and uncertain, and while a career in pictures seemed to be open to people of all economic classes and backgrounds, the possibility of success was certainly not based on either equal opportunity or the possession of talent.[8]

The lives of film stars were inevitably defined by the amounts of time and money they could devote to the pursuit of leisure and consumption. These modern social and economic values had transformed American life by the 1920s, giving rise to a pervasive "culture of consumption"[9] and replacing the traditional Protestant work ethic, which had been based on self-denial and thrift. The life-styles of Hollywood movie stars contributed to this shift by defining a set of social and economic values based on the promise of leisure spending, recreation, and pursuit of pleasure.[10] Out in Hollywood, the stars had their lavish homes, wardrobes, and automobiles as well as busy social lives, filled with parties and premieres yet also permitting time for artistic and recreational pursuits. The stars' lives provided attractive models of consumer life for society at large. Film stars became "national models as leisure experts"[11] and living examples of the transformative virtues of consumption. Hollywood celebrities taught the lesson that, through stardom, one could achieve in real life what previously had only been dreamed about—a life of affluence, romance, and glamour—and the key was consumption on a grand scale. Hollywood soon emerged as a symbolic center for consumerist versions of American life, and the film star became one of the chief representatives of these modern social and economic values.

In many respects the Hollywood stars of the twenties and thirties were an apt example of what Thorstein Veblen had termed the "leisure class." In *The Theory of the Leisure Class,* published in 1899, Veblen analyzed the extravagances of the wealthy in turn-of-the-century American society.[12] He defined the leisure class as a privileged social group exempt from the economic imperative to work and devoted to a life of ceremonial and largely symbolic consumption. Veblen's famous phrase "conspicuous consumption" referred to the way in which the purchase of goods and services could function as a means of displaying one's wealth and social standing within a "regime of status" founded on pecuniary values. The ultimate guarantor

of social worth within the leisure class was the nonutilitarian, nonpro-
ductive nature of one's activities—evidence of freedom from the need to
labor. Athletic or artistic achievements, for example, were worthwhile only
insofar as they served to demonstrate one's wealth and free time. In this
sense "sport" and "culture" were the perquisites of the upper class. Veblen
analyzed at length the symbolic role of social and cultural phenomena such
as fashion, athleticism, and the arts, and it was precisely these interests that
were taken up by the movie fan magazines in their treatments of film
celebrities, whose clothes, sporting lives, and artistic hobbies became the
formulaic elements of the star's identity.

Certainly movie stars engaged in a dramatic display of conspicuous
consumption. Yet there is an important difference between Veblen's notion
of a leisure class and Hollywood movie stars. Veblen argued that consumption was a mark of class distinction and social difference that underscored
the remoteness of the leisure class from all other social groups. Film stars,
on the other hand, became objects of emulation and identification for their
mass audience when they achieved success, thereby representing at once
the privileged life-style of the leisure class and the democratic possibility
of its attainment by the average person.

In his study Veblen was in fact describing patterns of economic and
social behavior that were emerging in American society as a whole, where
leisure and consumption were increasingly the prerogatives of the vast
middle class, as well. Throughout the late nineteenth and early twentieth
centuries, the rule of conspicuous consumption was gradually being
imitated throughout society, as the consumption of mass-produced goods
played an increasingly important social and economic role at all levels of
American life.[13] In opposition to Veblen's class-bound and rigidly hierarchical notion of a leisure class, film stars were available for the emulation
and identification of their mass audience.

A satisfactory sociological explanation of the role of film stars in
American culture should account for how they were able to signify both a
similarity to and a difference from the general conditions of social life. In
other words, how was it that film stars could lead lives so clearly different
from everyone else's and yet be seen, at least in the sphere of private life, as
"just like you and me"? Leo Lowenthal's essay "The Triumph of the Mass
Idols"[14] offers an analysis of this paradoxical social role. In this seminal

study Lowenthal examined biographical articles that appeared in two popular magazines, *Saturday Evening Post* and *Collier's*, from 1901 to 1941. He found that, until about 1922 (a date that corresponds with the emergence of Hollywood as a topic of cultural debate), biographies in popular magazines focused primarily on individuals from political, business, and professional life. Lowenthal referred to these individuals as the "idols of production," and he contended that the purpose of presenting their lives was to educate the public about the important political, economic, and scientific figures of the day. Moreover, their lives were frequently offered as models of accomplishment that could inspire the average reader— "examples of success which can be imitated." In this way popular biographies served both educational and ideological purposes, reconciling the ordinary person's "interest in the important trends of history and in the personal lives of others" (113). This was the "great man" view of history in the service of an ideology of individualism and personal initiative.

After 1922, however, Lowenthal observed a marked decrease in the number of biographies devoted to individuals from "the serious and important professions and a corresponding increase of entertainers" (111). "The idols of production" were increasingly pushed off the pages of popular magazines by what he termed the "idols of consumption"—those who were "directly or indirectly related to the sphere of leisure time" (115), among whom film stars played a disproportionately large and important role. With a dismay characteristic of his Frankfurt School origins, Lowenthal noted that "the idols of the masses are not, as they were in the past, the leading names in the battle of production, but the headliners of the movies, the ball parks, and the night clubs. . . . They seem to lead to *a dream world of the masses* [my emphasis] who no longer are capable or willing to conceive of biographies primarily as a means of orientation and education" (116).

A significant consequence of this shift was an obsessive interest in the most trivial details of the stars' private lives, such as food preferences and hobbies. The attention to "personal habits, from smoking to poker playing, from stamp collecting to cocktail parties" (121), revealed the extent to which consumption had replaced production as the focus of reader interest. Indeed, celebrity entertainers were often enthusiastic advocates of consumption for society at large. Film stars, in particular, were frequent endorsers of commercial products in the pages of popular magazines.[15]

I would suggest that Lowenthal's arguments provide a framework within which we can begin to understand how movie stars, the "mass idols" of our culture, could lead lives that seemed both remote and familiar to their fans. On the one hand, they lived in what was surely a "dream world of the masses," a realm of fantasy and wish fulfillment, luxury and wealth, at which the average person could only stare in wonder and envy. On the other hand, the emphasis on consumption in their lives made them seem familiar and invited imitation and vicarious identification. More important, in their apparent similarity to the average moviegoer, movie stars provided an ideological escape hatch from the diminished expectations and the haunting specter of failure in a competitive, capitalist society. Lowenthal observed:

> It is some comfort for the little man [sic] who has been expelled from the Horatio Alger dream, who despairs of penetrating the thicket of grand strategy in politics and business, to see his heroes as a lot of guys who like or dislike highballs, cigarettes, tomato juice, golf, and social gatherings—just like himself. He knows how to converse in the sphere of consumption and here he can make no mistakes. By narrowing his focus of attention, he can experience the gratification of being confirmed in his own pleasures and discomforts by participating in the pleasures and discomforts of the great. (135)

Consumption became the common language of film stars and their audiences, providing a symbolic link between the fabulous life-styles of those who made movies and the more mundane existence of those who watched them.

WORK, INDIVIDUALISM

Pursuing the pleasures that a $10,000-per-week salary could provide was often seen as the primary occupation of a movie star, and the distinction between work and play in the film celebrity's life was often tenuously drawn at best. The idea persisted that what movie stars did was not really work at all. This gave rise to the belief that the compensations and perquisites of stardom were entirely out of proportion with the real importance of the job and the competency it required. Resentment against film stars for their fabulous salaries dovetailed neatly with complaints about their immorality, as a 1922 editorial in the *New York Times* shows.

> Hollywood's residents are certainly no worse than would be any similar number of attractive, uneducated young people who had suddenly come into great wealth and a peculiarly heady sort of fame. Most of us, in their situation, would do as they do; since we are not in their situation, but one far less prosperous, we make the best of our comparative moral grandeur. Because the temptations of wealth and luxury have never assailed us we fall on those who have succumbed. . . . So what we take out on Hollywood is our resentment, not at its wickedness, but at its wealth.[16]

Fans displayed ambivalent attitudes toward film stars. On the one hand, they enjoyed reading about the stars' glamorous and affluent lives, as even the most cursory glance at the fan magazines of the period demonstrates. On the other hand, there were frequent complaints in the same magazines that movie stars "do not earn the high salaries they receive, and for which the public must pay."[17] Articles in fan magazines sometimes emphasized the amount of work required of film stars by the studios and their directors, but more often such articles contributed to the belief that stars led pampered lives of wealth and ease.[18] While the work of movie stars was commonly seen as play, in truth their offscreen leisure activities were often merely extensions of their work, "dressed up" as play for the studio publicity department and the fan magazines. Thus the movie star was positioned in a cultural double bind, in a job where traditional social and economic ideologies jostled with modern redefinitions of work and leisure. Consequently, the life of a star was often a site of turmoil and confusion, within which one had to negotiate the shifting imperatives of a culture whose social and economic values were in transition.

Linked to this ambivalent notion of what it meant to work and be successful in Hollywood was an idea that perhaps was the dominant myth of movie stardom: that film stars in pursuit of the American dream inevitably found only unhappiness. No doubt this was a reassuring thought to those excluded from the charmed circles of wealth and glamour in the film capital. And it was an idea to which Hollywood fictions eagerly contributed. The Hollywood novels that dealt primarily with the lives of movie stars often portrayed them as flawed and lonely individuals, and cast their stories in the form of a rise and fall, offering the definitive modern version of an ancient narrative formula. The cultural critic Camille Paglia recently put it thus:

> The glamorous, tawdry lives of Hollywood stars are the hero sagas of modern life. Born in obscurity, driven by a dream, the great stars fight their way to fame and win their dates with destiny. But fortune's wheel is ever turning: a combination of hostile external forces and swirling internal pressures transforms triumph and adulation into disaster and despair.[19]

It was this paradigm of success and failure, "half Greek tragedy and half soap opera," that made the movie star such a potent figure in American culture, helping to both ratify and undermine a faith in economic opportunity and social mobility.

At the same time, stardom was also about "the promotion of the individual,"[20] and the cultural issues that stardom raised were generally framed by a problematic of the self and an ideology of individualism. Richard Dyer has argued that film stars served as models of social behavior, representing "typical ways of behaving, feeling and thinking in contemporary society"[21] and negotiating the complex demands of work and play, public and private life, for a mass audience hungry to learn how to be modern individuals.[22] In this cultural work stars articulated the prevalent "ideas of personhood, in large measure shoring up the notion of the individual but also at times registering the doubts and anxieties attendant upon it" (10). Certainly for the studios the social role of the movie star was to be a model of the well-integrated, successful individual—an ideal to which fans could aspire. Generally the fan magazines advertised and celebrated this ideal enthusiastically. But stardom, as the fan magazines were also eager to show, came only at a physical, emotional, and psychological cost. The life of a movie star seldom seemed to produce real contentment.

In many ways the star system itself constituted an assault upon individual autonomy and the notion of a stable identity. Personalities and names became commodities—manufactured wholesale by publicity departments and owned by studios—to which performers could find themselves chained throughout their careers and beyond. The actress Myrna Loy was quoted as cautioning movie aspirants to that effect in a fan-magazine article entitled "So You'd Like to Be a Star?"

> I'm not my own man, girls. I daren't take chances with Myrna Loy, for she isn't my property. . . . The studio has spent millions of dollars on the personality known as Myrna Loy. And I can't let the studio down by slipping off my expensive mask of glamor. I've got to be, on all public occasions, the personality they sell at the box office.[23]

In her memoir of life as a Hollywood star, the actress Louise Brooks put the case more bluntly: "There was no other occupation in the world that so closely resembled enslavement as the career of a film star."[24]

THE STAR SYSTEM AND THE ORIGIN OF HOLLYWOOD FICTION

Although entertainment celebrities first appeared live on theater stages and in concert halls, stardom required the twentieth-century technologies of mass communication in order to circulate performers' images and identities on the scale that could produce the "larger-than-life" characteristics of stars. The star, Christine Gledhill has observed, is "a product of mass culture," yet in obvious ways stars perpetuate "theatrical concerns with acting, performance and art."[25] Richard deCordova's *Picture Personalities: The Emergence of the Star System in America* provides the most detailed analysis to date of the emergence of film stardom from the theatrical models that preceded it.[26] Although the rise of the star system in American cinema is not my primary interest here, deCordova's study deserves close examination because it links the origin of Hollywood fiction to the appearance of the motion-picture star.

For deCordova, the emergence of the star system in American film is a history of the expanding intertextual field in which the identity of the motion-picture performer could be constructed. Any attempt to understand the phenomenon of stardom must begin by recognizing that the identity of the film star is constructed from a variety of texts, most notably their films but also movie posters and promotional materials, feature articles and interviews in fan magazines, newspaper stories, publicity photos, and studio press releases. As Richard Dyer has noted, "star images are always extensive, multimedia, intertextual, and it is in this complex intertextual network that the fiction of the star's identity is elaborated and defined. In this regard Hollywood fictions have played a crucial role in articulating the dominant myths and antimyths of movie stardom. DeCordova examines the appearance and development of this discursive field through a variety of industry practices that sought to construct and regulate the identity of the motion-picture performer.

Naturally enough, the social identity of the film actor was initially closely linked to the conventions of theatrical life; the most famous early film actors were "legitimate" stage actors who occasionally ventured into film production. However, deCordova argues that by 1910 the "discourse on acting" began to give way to a different set of audience concerns, and the film actor was superseded by the "picture personality" (50). The need to satisfy the ever-growing demands of exhibitors for new films and the shift to narrative films by production companies led to a reliance on formulaic plots in which actors often found themselves typecast, playing a similar character from one film to the next. Out of this continuity of character type emerged the picture personality, a motion-picture performer whose identity was established and maintained by playing similar roles from film to film. Hence, whereas the identity of the film actor was based on his or her existence outside the narrative of the film and within the traditions of the stage, the intertextual field that supported the picture personality was produced and maintained largely by the cinema. This was accomplished through the stability of a screen persona that was established across a number of performances and sustained by the publicity surrounding the films—a situation that made actors particularly vulnerable to the control of the producers.

The earliest picture personalities were often anonymous, known only as "the Biograph girl" or "Little Mary" to their fans,[27] and for some time the producing companies resisted the pressures from the public and exhibitors to publicize their names.[28] By 1911 screen credits for motion-picture actors had become common practice. Still, the kinds of information that constructed the identities of picture personalities were severely limited by studio publicity departments, and a logic of concealment and disclosure surrounded their emergence. In effect, the images projected by picture personalities were almost wholly a product of their screen roles, and they were represented as being the same off screen as they were on.

As the film industry expanded, moving from the East Coast to Hollywood, and as the conventions of film narrative became more sophisticated, the picture personality, like the film actor, was eventually supplanted by the "star." DeCordova argues that the emergence of the star represented a marked expansion of the kinds of information that were seen to constitute the intertextual field in which the film performer was located. He notes that, "with the emergence of the star, the question of the player's existence outside his or her work in film became the primary focus of discourse" (98); increasingly the motion-picture performer's private life became the center of attention and interest. This interest was reflected in the growing attention that fan magazines devoted to the personal lives and experiences of people working in motion pictures. Initially these stories appeared as nonfictional confessions or biographies, often authored anonymously or under pseudonyms. DeCordova cites as the earliest example of this kind of writing the serial *My Experiences as a Film Favorite*, which first appeared in the November 1913 issue of *Photoplay*.

Another early example, one not mentioned by deCordova, is *My Strange Life: The Intimate Life Story of a Moving Picture Actress*, which was published anonymously in 1915.[29] This book follows the pattern of early journalistic writing on stars by tracing the career of a young woman from her early experiences on the stage, through insignificant roles as a studio "super" (supernumerary, or extra), to her eventual stardom as "the most popular moving picture actress in America" (261), focusing on the ups and downs of her private and emotional life in the movie business. In its attention to the "intimate life" of the movie star, *My Strange Life* articulated some questions to which the nascent star system was giving rise. "What conception can you have of what it means to work in the movies? Of what goes on behind the beautiful, romantic screens in the theaters, of what goes into the making of a picture, of what goes into the making of a moving-picture star?" (5).

Significantly, *My Strange Life* is ambiguous regarding its fictional status. No author's name appears on the title page of the work, suggesting the fan-magazine convention of concealing or disguising the film star's identity. To confuse matters further, the text is interspersed with photographs of leading motion-picture actresses, inviting the reader to speculate on which of them (if any) is the actual subject of the book. At the same time, the stock characters and conventionally sentimental narrative of *My Strange Life* make it seem like a work of fiction cast in the form of an epistolary novel. The ambiguous literary status of this text illustrates the way in which ostensibly factual accounts of movie stars' private lives could serve as models for a new type of fictional narrative concerned with the experiences of people working in motion pictures. DeCordova argues, in fact, that the genre of Hollywood fiction "actually began with these stories"[30] in the expanded intertextual field in which the movie star's identity was being created—the performer's private life as represented by fan magazines.

Of course, this movement from factual account to fictional narrative is not new in literary history; indeed, it has been argued that the origins of the modern novel are to be found in precisely such permutations of journalistic sources.[31] But deCordova's account of the origin of Hollywood fiction treats it as a consequence of the relatively local needs of film studios and fan magazines to produce an expanded intertextual identity for the film star—a purpose that tends to produce a single kind of star narrative, characteristically sentimental or romantic, and that reflects the industry's desire to control and shape the star's persona. Indeed, the first fictional treatment of the film star, Robert Kerr's 1914 *Photoplay* serial entitled "Loree Starr—Photoplay Idol,"[32] is a dubious prototype for the Hollywood novel. To begin with, it is set entirely within the milieu of the New York theater scene, a very different social and cultural environment from that which informs Hollywood fiction. Moreover, it pays little attention to the movie business and lacks the critical, self-reflective interest in the medium of motion pictures that I have argued is a defining element of Hollywood fiction (even of works that have an essentially romantic and optimistic view of the film industry), focusing instead on the emotional entanglements of the protagonist. *Loree Starr* relies more on the stock elements in cultural representations of stage life than on the conventions of the Hollywood novel. By subsuming the origins of Hollywood fiction within the discursive practices of the emerging star system, deCordova minimizes its cultural significance and actually succeeds in explaining its appearance in one only area of cultural discourse, the fan magazine, which was devoted to publicizing and promoting star images anyway.

More than just the demands of the star system, it was the *cultural debate over Hollywood* that expanded the readership for Hollywood fictions beyond that of the fan magazines and made the genre more than just an adjunct of studio publicity. This debate arose in part from the notoriety of the star scandals in the early 1920s and from the controversy they engendered; deCordova rightly argues in his concluding chapter that the star scandals were a defining moment in the intertextual construction of stardom, locating the final truth about the star's identity in sexual experience. It was during this period that fictions about Hollywood and about the lives of those who worked there (not always necessarily stars) began to proliferate in novels as well as in short stories and serials in national magazines. The appearance of Hollywood fictions in periodicals such as *Collier's, Cosmopolitan, Red Book,* and the *Saturday Evening Post* has less to do with the discursive demands of the star system than with the national debate over motion pictures and the values of mass culture. Nonetheless, it is fair to say that initially the fan magazines provided a fertile seedbed for the emerging genre of Hollywood fiction.

THE STUDIO SYSTEM AND
THE FAN MAGAZINES

The star system was created and operated within a particular framework of institutions, specifically the film studios and the fan magazines. By definition, stars were performers working under long-term contracts with film studios that took charge of virtually every aspect of their lives. Movie stars usually signed five-year contracts, at the end of which the studios maintained the "option" to either renew or cancel their contracts, which meant that many stars lived under the threat of job loss and the humiliating prospect of being dumped by the studio. They could also be lent to a rival studio, a common form of punishment for actors who were less than compliant with studio demands.

As employees, stars were subject to almost complete control by their employers: their physical appearances were meticulously designed and groomed by studio personnel; their images were discreetly protected and placed on continual display by studio publicists; their careers were advanced through roles carefully selected for them by the studio to represent a particular type of screen persona; when in production, they could be expected to work for seventeen or eighteen hours a day; off screen their personal lives were regulated by "morality clauses," a standard feature of studio contracts. The vast resources of the studio's star-making machinery were formidable, and there can be little doubt that its purpose was to transform human beings into commodities that could be marketed and sold. "You know, because of the studios, we were like pieces of merchandise— soap or jello," Claudette Colbert once remarked.[33]

The process through which stars were created by studios was of tremendous interest to fans, who often saw the endless round of makeup and wardrobe tests, photo sessions, and publicity events as examples of Hollywood glamour.[34] But the "studio treatment" had a more pragmatic goal, as David Niven observed in his Hollywood memoir, *Bring On the Empty Horses*.

> The policy of the studios was to sell their pictures on the names of their stars; they had a vested interest in their performers, and it was to their advantage to build them up. If they did so successfully, their investment was returned with interest, but the contracts of the actors were long, and the work of the publicity departments was painstaking; it was a case of piling up grains of publicity sand until they became mountains, and at the end of it the public might say, "Joe Doakes beats his wife," or "he drinks his bath water," but it did not ask, "*Who* is Joe Doakes?"[35]

In other words, the "mountains" of publicity produced by the studio could not fail to make the performer well known to the public. And Niven's comment suggests another reading: *Who is* the person buried beneath this mountain of publicity? What happens to the individuals at the receiving end of this attention, manipulation, and control? At what cost have they purchased—or has the studio imposed upon them—this fame and public attention? Katherine Albert, one of the leading fan-magazine writers of the 1920s and 1930s, offered one answer in a 1929 *Photoplay* article, "Don't Envy the Stars," in which she observed that Hollywood's celebrity performers were, "for the most part, miserable and discontented."[36] For performers caught in the grip of studio control, being a star could be a suffocating experience, a fact to which many Hollywood memoirs attest.[37] As Pola Negri eloquently observed:

> The Hollywood I knew [in the 1920s] was the Hollywood of dreams. . . . But even then there was, beneath the illusions, the harsh reality of a desperate place. The surface was so glitteringly beautiful; the underside, an amalgam of fear and personal tragedy. Gorgeous smiles enchanted the entire world but often hid insecurities that drove these chosen few to the excesses of depravity. Would an option be picked up? Would a star made overnight dim swiftly in the morning? Would the next picture make money? Would that barometer of box office, which measures all emotional and economic storms, suddenly drop? The prizes to be won were very nearly beyond belief. But the stakes necessary to play were equally steep, though of a different currency.[38]

The myth of Hollywood stardom was always haunted by an equally powerful antimyth. While film studios struggled to maintain an uncomplicated image of stardom as something to be admired and sought after, the fan magazines articulated a more complex attitude, one that shared with the fans an ambivalence toward the larger-than-life image of the movie star.

By and large, the fan magazines were eager collaborators with the studios in presenting a positive public image of Hollywood and its stars as well as in promoting motion pictures, both as entertainment and as a serious art form. Exemplary in this regard was *Photoplay*. Founded in 1911, the magazine struggled at first to distinguish itself from its chief competitor, *Motion Picture Story* (also founded in 1911). Both periodicals began by publishing plot synopses of current films, along with rotogravured portraits of film stars and feature articles that catered to readers' interest in the new medium. In 1914 *Photoplay* moved from Chicago to New York and was taken under the editorial control of publisher James R. Quirk, whose policies guided the publication until his death in 1932.[39]

Under Quirk's management, *Photoplay* became the most popular and influential fan magazine in the country, its format and style clearly setting the standard for the entire fan-magazine industry during the 1920s and 1930s. In 1920 Quirk initiated the annual *Photoplay* Gold Medal Awards, which were the most prestigious markers of accomplishment in the film industry until the founding of the Academy of Motion Picture Arts and Sciences and its establishment of its own award for achievement in 1928. Quirk's *Photoplay* was one of the earliest magazines to offer its readers serious film criticism, and it made an important contribution to film history by presenting a series of articles outlining the historical development of American film, written by Terry Ramsaye. The series was subsequently published as *A Million and One Nights* in 1926. The pages of *Photoplay* featured articles and fiction by many of the foremost writers of the period, including Sherwood Anderson, Theodore Dreiser, F. Scott Fitzgerald, Rupert Hughes, Anita Loos, H. L. Mencken, George Jean Nathan, Channing Pollock, and Donald Ogden Stewart.

Throughout his tenure with the magazine, Quirk was an ardent defender of the film industry and of motion pictures as a serious art form, as evidenced by a 1918 editorial in which he sermonized to industry leaders: "Will you think of your art as a business or your business as an art? Will you say, 'Make this picture because it will sell'? or 'Make this picture because it deserves to sell'?"[40] Quirk's influence could cut both ways, however, as remarks made by Will Hays in a 1949 interview reveal.

> He [Quirk] tried to protect Hollywood and raise its sights, not exploit the weaknesses of its personalities as did other journalists. He did not batten off Hollywood's troubles for mercenary gain at the newsstands, as did some of his colleagues. Along with me, he could be firm in dealing with the recalcitrant elements in Hollywood, and the power of his typewriter was greatly feared, for he could be coldly chastising when chastisement was needed, but to the public he tried to present a fair, balanced—and basically compassionate—picture of Hollywood's problems during its growing pains in the 1920s.[41]

The portrait of Quirk that emerges from Hays's description is that of a person with considerable influence in both the film industry and the larger

Hollywood community. What Hays's comments do not touch on, however, is the influence exerted by *Photoplay* and other fan magazines on their readers. Did Quirk's editorial opinions concerning film as art or Hollywood morality lead public opinion or follow it? While we can only speculate, one thing is certain: fan magazines were inordinately solicitous of their readers' views, as indicated by their frequent letter-writing contests and opinion polls, which ranged from "What the Motion Pictures Mean to Me" (*Photoplay*, March 1920) to popularity polls on the readers' favorite stars.[42] Whether it was a matter of editorial policy or simply a fortunate confluence of interests, fan magazines articulated the currents of fascination, envy, and contempt that surrounded Hollywood and those who lived and worked there.

The fan magazines actively contributed to the positive myth of stardom and Hollywood life with stories that emphasized the glamour and fun of being a film star. Articles such as "How Stars Spend Their Fortunes," from *Screen Book*, or "How Constance [Bennett] Really Spends Her Money," from *Modern Screen*, celebrated the wealth of movie celebrities with a litany of star salaries, expensive homes, and extravagant purchases. Articles like *Photoplay*'s "Hollywood at Play" chronicled the leisure time and romantic offscreen lives of the stars.[43] While profiles of male stars in the fan magazines generally focused on their offscreen hobbies or recreational pursuits, female stars or their agents often cultivated a domestic image that seemed at odds with the popular conceptions of Hollywood life. For example, in the *Screen Book* article "Motherhood . . . What It Means to Helen Twelvetrees," the actress lamented the self-absorption of movie stars and contrasted their careers with the more fulfilling duties of a "quiet domestic life"; and in a piece in *Modern Screen* entitled "My Husband Is My Best Friend," Irene Dunne explained to readers how she "deftly handles her life so that a brilliant career and a happy marriage dovetail despite enforced separations during work."[44] Pieces such as these idealized the lives of movie stars and presented them as models of social and personal behavior, spurring the reader's emulation and kindling the hope of a similarly fulfilling life.

While the effect of articles such as these was to evoke both a sense of difference and a sense of familiarity in readers, making stars objects of admiration and identification (as Lowenthal's analysis of the "mass idols" of American culture suggests), they were counterbalanced in the fan magazines with another type of article that articulated the antimyth of

Hollywood stardom, exploring what Richard Griffith has aptly termed "the pathology of stardom."[45] Many of these pieces fastened on the love lives of the stars (i.e., on their sexual histories) in order to demonstrate their unhappiness and to allude, subtly, to their immorality. Articles such as Katherine Albert's "What's Wrong with Hollywood Love?," published in *Modern Screen*, and *Photoplay*'s controversial piece "Hollywood's Unmarried Husbands and Wives" focused on the inability of film stars to find meaningful or socially acceptable romantic-sexual relationships.[46] A 1930 *Photoplay* article by Louis E. Bisch, entitled "Why Hollywood Scandal Fascinates Us," offered four reasons for the public's interest in these kinds of stories: (1) curiosity ("the Peeping Tom tendency"), (2) jealousy ("few men and scarcely any women exist who would not like to be stars in the movie heavens"), (3) sadism ("it pleases me every time I hear one of those movie stars getting it in the neck"), and (4) guilt ("it is a well-known fact that, if you find somebody else as bad as you are, you feel gratified. And if you find him even worse than you are, your gratification may amount to jubilation").[47] Bisch's article represents a kind of contemporary pop psychology of fan interest in film stars' unhappiness. Here, at least, was one area of experience where readers could feel a degree of superiority over, even pity for, those who led such otherwise enviable lives.

A number of articles focused on the phenomenon of stardom itself as the source of film celebrities' unhappiness—separate from the divorces and scandals that were the fan magazines' usual bill of fare. In 1915 *Photoplay* featured a piece entitled "Confessions of a Star," which concerned the discontentments of a famous screen actress who—in accordance with what was then conventional practice—remained unnamed in the article. In it she complained about the limitations imposed upon her in the film industry because of her beauty, and her inability to do serious acting on the screen as a result of the studio's typecasting her in ingenue parts.

> I'm a star, it's true, but only a movie star—a movie heroine. You might think that I would have just as good opportunity to act—but I haven't. . . . The only reason why I've got the job I now hold is because I'm good-looking on the screen,—because I have film personality. . . . The reason I'm discontented, in spite of my big salary, in spite of the fact that I have a world-wide reputation, in spite of the fact that

I get nearly a hundred love letters a day, is that I'm not allowed to
act. . . . Then, too, there is the annoyance of having to play the same
role in every picture in which I appear.[48]

In prototypical manner this article shows how arguments about film stardom
often hinged on arguments about film—as an art form or as a mass medium.
Moreover, it reveals how arguments about stardom often confronted fundamental ideological assumptions about the nature and value of success: the
importance of a "big salary" and a "world-wide reputation" are here discounted because they entail a loss of self and a compromise of artistic
integrity. In a 1926 *Photoplay* article entitled "The Price They Paid for
Stardom," one fan-magazine writer questioned whether, "after all, it is wise
and right to buy fame and money at the price of contentment; if in the
struggle for success, it is good to kill all those emotions and feelings that
make life worth living"[49]—sentiments that would not be out of place in the
fiction of Dreiser, Fitzgerald, and Lewis, all of whom explored the cost of
success in 1920s America.

Success in Hollywood was always marked in the fan magazines with a
kind of fatalistic doom: "How long will it last?" "Can it coincide with real
happiness?" Hollywood was, as *Photoplay* correspondent Herbert Howe
grimly observed, "the land where dreams come true—and turn out to be
nightmares." In his article, appropriately entitled "See Hollywood and
Die," Howe sketched a portrait of film stardom as an inevitable and tragic
loss of self.

The man in pictures not only sees himself constantly but hears, day in
and day out, a discussion of himself. Everyone talks to him about him.
His own image is constantly before him. As his popularity grows the
vicious circle tightens; if he makes an attempt to escape he is quickly
driven back into himself; eventually the will to escape is destroyed
and he is held fast, hopelessly and forever his own prisoner. . . . He
who enters Hollywood leaves self—the real self—behind. It is the
land of Let's Pretend, and the hardest acting is done off screen.[50]

Hollywood stars were often portrayed as victims of their own "excessive,
overpowering, devastating ambition," trapped in an environment where,

as veteran fan-magazine correspondent Ruth Waterbury remarked, "there is only self, self, self, and the glorification of self."[51] At the same time the stars were subject to frequent and massive assaults upon their privacy and personal security, as Katherine Albert observed in "Don't Envy the Stars."

> A star is on the public's payroll. It is his duty to be a good fellow at whatever cost. And the cost is tremendous! . . . Immediately that a star reaches the pinnacle, he is a lofty target for vituperatives from the public, from the press, and from his fellow-stars. Small wonder that the picture folk have a haunted look in their eyes. There is no happiness for them.[52]

All of the images and ideas concerning Hollywood stardom that were circulated by movie fan magazines offered readers, who were excluded from this world of privilege and fame, a sense of moral superiority that allowed them to negotiate their own ambivalence—that is, their simultaneous desire for and distance from the mass idols of American culture. Fan magazines refined the essential myths and antimyths of stardom not only through celebrity profiles, interviews, and feature articles but in fictional short stories and serials that took up and developed the same ideas, offering narrative elaborations on the idea of the pathology of stardom. In fact, it was the construction of stardom in the nominally journalistic forum of the fan magazines that provided the discursive context for subsequent literary representations of film stars.

STAR FICTION IN *PHOTOPLAY*

One of James Quirk's first editorial changes after taking control of *Photoplay* was to begin a gradual elimination of the "short stories" adapted from the plots of motion pictures that were currently in release (which were detailed synopses, illustrated with production stills and serving to promote the cast and the producing company) and their replacement with stories and serial fictions that dealt with the experiences of those who lived and worked in the Hollywood studios. It was in these latter works, in which movie stars were generally the central characters, that the contradictory representations of stardom described earlier first appeared. In short stories such as Adela Rogers St. Johns's "The Last Straw" (*Photoplay*, May 1922), film stars were depicted as vain, arrogant, self-absorbed individuals whose selfishness often threatened their own happiness and the happiness of those around them.

In "The Last Straw," the long-suffering wife of a domineering male star threatens to end their marriage after he informs her that he plans to have an affair with his leading lady, reminding her that "this is Hollywood in the twentieth century."[53] While reinforcing Hollywood's reputation for loosened sexual and marital mores, the story neatly reinscribes traditional values by staging a last-minute reconciliation between husband and wife, sealed with the purchase of a new car and the hiring of a maid—rituals of consumption that seem to have been intended to demonstrate the now-renewed blessings of domestic life. Although the star is humbled and ultimately redeemed by his separation from his wife, St. Johns's story derives most of its humor from exposing the excesses of his temperament and egotism, a theme that is echoed in many *Photoplay* stories.[54] "The Last Straw" effectively satirizes the self-importance of film stars and suggests that they can be humbled through the routines of domestic life, an idea that no doubt was appealing to the story's readers.

Another common theme in *Photoplay*'s fictions was the idea that stars existed behind a false mask, a persona derived from their screen roles that was often very different from who they actually were.[55] This idea received a comic treatment in Faith Service's "False Faces" (*Photoplay*, May 1926). In it we are introduced to Lilith Flame, "ultra" screen vamp and quintessential movie star, around whom the studio publicity department has created an aura of sensuality and exoticism. In actuality, she is "Mildred P. Means from East Machias, Ohio," daughter of a traveling salesman and of a mother who raised eleven children of whom she was "the unwanted sixth."[56] Realizing that "as Mildred P. Means she hadn't a chance, not a chance in the world" (96), she dyes her hair bronze and reinvents herself as Lilith Flame, then presents herself at the "X-Ellent Studios," where she swiftly becomes a star. However, after four years of "efflorescent glory," she suddenly finds herself in love with her leading man, the aristocratic Gaillard De Koven. He is the son of a wealthy family that has fallen on hard times, causing him to seek his fortune in motion pictures. When Gaillard asks Lilith to marry him, she is plunged into a crisis of identity, wanting to reveal her real self but afraid that her working-class background will dampen his interest. Determined to be honest with him, Lilith confesses, and—though shaken—Gaillard finally accepts her for who she is. The moment of comic denouement occurs when the maid interrupts them and, seeing Gaillard for the first time, recognizes him as "old Pete Hodgkin's boy, Pete Junior" (110). Gaillard too, it seems, has fashioned a new identity for himself. When, as film stars, the two discover the truth about each other's backgrounds, they tacitly agree to protect their screen images, "carefully and tenderly" readjusting each other's movie-star masks.

Service's comic story operates on several levels of cultural argument. On the one hand, it underwrites the democratic myth of stardom as a vehicle of social mobility and success, as it shows lower-class characters raising their social standing—and their income—by recreating themselves within the make-believe world of the studios. There it doesn't matter which side of the tracks you're from; all that counts is the power of the image that the publicity department and your own ingenuity can create. At the same time, the story suggests that that image can become a kind of trap, sealing you off from the past and confining you to a life of dissemblance that has ethical and emotional consequences.

The tragic dimension of those consequences is explored in Dana Gatlin's story "It's Different in Life" (*Photoplay*, December 1928). In this story, Hollywood stars Zenia Mott and Paul Marvin find themselves on the verge of an offscreen affair after having made several successful movies as romantic costars. Desperately in love, Paul begs Zenia to divorce her husband, Gus Boldt, the artistic producer who has supervised their last three pictures. The two stars find themselves living the great romantic drama they have enacted upon the screen. However, Zenia, out of loyalty and genuine affection for Gus (who, after all, discovered her and made her a star), sacrifices their happiness by refusing Paul's proposal. Although in their movies loves wins out and always produces a happy ending, the two stars discover that "it's different in life." Off screen there will be no happy ending, and their love is doomed to remain unrequited. In Gatlin's story the star's screen image becomes an emotional prison, confining Paul and Zenia to roles they can only act out in movies never truly live. The ironic message of the story is that the often-envied romantic life of film stars is predicated upon an illusion that is wholly inadequate to meet their genuine emotional needs as human beings—an idea that confirms the reader's sense of emotional superiority over the flawed lives of Hollywood stars.

While "The Last Straw," "False Faces," and "It's Different in Life" explored the negative aspects of Hollywood fame, many of *Photoplay*'s other stories offered a positive view of stardom, especially for characters who achieved success only after setbacks and failure. In these stories stardom was explicitly linked to an idea of Hollywood as a place of sudden opportunity. Jean Dupont's "Life for a Night" (*Photoplay*, March 1927) is one of the best examples of this conflation of Hollywood, stardom, and success. It opens with what is certainly one of its most memorable expositions.

> "Manana" land! That's Hollywood. . . . In the Cinema City, "tomorrow" is the day of hope, a glorious day. It may bring you a square meal or a Rolls-Royce. Today you may be dodging your landlady. Tomorrow you may be flirting with the newest real estate subdivision. Boston may dwell in the past, New York clutch madly at the present, but Hollywood lives for tomorrow.[57]

"Life for a Night" concerns a typical Hollywood hopeful, the beautiful Amber Evans, who for two years has vainly pursued "vivid dreams of the joy that stardom would bring her." Finding her good looks to be no advantage in Hollywood and failing to rise above the rank of extra in the occasional film work she has done, Amber finally decides to accept a proposal of marriage and a one-way ticket home from her high-school sweetheart who has built up a successful hardware business in her absence. For Amber it is either "Hollywood or hardware," and her decision to leave the film capital signals the end of her dreams and a retreat to "safety, security, and a stuccoed bungalow"—in other words, a life of mundane domesticity in a small town. However, on the night before she is to leave, Amber finds a ticket to a Hollywood premiere. Encouraged by her friends to have one last fling, Amber borrows a dress and attends the glittering opening at the Egyptian Theater, a scene in which Dupont expertly captures the social interplay of celebrity spectacle and mass audience.

> This was premiere night in Hollywood. The uninvited curious came thronging to watch the pageantry, to gaze upon those who had been

blessed beyond belief with beauty and fame and wealth all at once. The huge theater was a focal point of light. Kleigs and sun-arcs had been mounted for the occasion. They beat a shaft of light straight down the great out-door court which was the lobby. A dazzling promenade to glorify the smart men and women already descending from their cars. Expensive cars worthy of a show by themselves. A sun-art, swinging back and forth, picked up here and there patches of upturned faces, draining the color from them, little green-white patches which were curious eyes and open mouths. Persons of no importance gathered to watch the personages promenade, peacock-wise, down the path of light. (132)

When the announcer introduces her as "Miss Amber Evans—Hollywood's Golden Girl," the crowd stares at her, uncertain of who she is. Dazed by the attention, Amber enters the theater, relishing the feeling of importance and thinking, "It would be like this if I were a star. Like this all the time." As she approaches her empty seat, Amber discovers that her companion for the evening is to be "America's great lover." "He was Romance, he was Conquering Love, incarnate. He was Julio Conrad!" (133). Amber has the opportunity to experience, "for a night," a potent social fantasy, one meant to activate the reader's own vicarious pleasure: for the rest of the evening she becomes the beautiful and admired companion of a handsome Hollywood star. After the premiere Julio invites her to a cafe for a late supper, drawing her further into a world of wish fulfillment that is shared by the reader. "Women had fainted and been trampled on in an effort to shake his hand. Who was Amber to turn down a date with him?" (134). When they arrive in the "super-gorgeous chariot" of his car, she is again the object of attention. "They didn't know who she was, but Julio made her a personage. . . . Women subjected her to penetrating inspection, men speculated, trying to remember whether she was somebody they should have known" (134). Suddenly Amber finds herself the center of interest. Influential directors and producers, some of whom she has been trying to see for months, invite her to drop by the office and discuss a contract. Amber's unexpected and brief experience of stardom finally leads, in Cinderella fashion, to the promise of success and future happiness, and she tears up her one-way ticket back to the hardware store.

In "Life for a Night," Hollywood is presented as a place of hope and unexpected opportunity, where the dreams of stardom can come true—maybe for a night, maybe for a lifetime. Yet even in the euphoria of Dupont's star fantasy a dark note is sounded in the final conversation between Julio and Amber, which resonates with irony and unspoken doom.

> "Sorry you stayed?" . . .
> "No, oh, No. I'll never forget it, never." He could never dream what it meant to her.
> "Neither will I," replied Julio agreeably, his eyes over Amber's head turned upon Sonya, newest importation from Poland.
> "It's been almost like being a star myself," Amber said.
> "How long have you been here?" Julio recalled himself politely.
> "Two years—"
> "And you still want to go on with it? Hit the top and glitter around for a while?" He assumed high contempt for the luster which he spent his every waking hour to preserve.
> "I want to be a star," Amber said.
> "You poor kid." He looked at her directly after that . . . and then they started home. (134)

In the play of Julio's gaze beyond Amber and toward Hollywood's newest discovery, Dupont has inscribed the restlessness and insecurity of stardom even as Amber experiences it for the first time, and Julio's final comment hints at the unhappiness that awaits her in Hollywood.

HATTIE OF HOLLYWOOD

From July to December of 1922, *Photoplay* presented its readers with Samuel Merwin's novel *Hattie of Hollywood,* the first serial to be carried by the magazine since Sullivan's *The Glory Road* five years earlier. Like Hughes's *Souls for Sale* and Wilson's *Merton of the Movies*—also published in 1922—Merwin's *Hattie* was in large measure a response to the controversy surrounding Hollywood at that time and exploited the public's interest in the behind-the-scenes details of motion-picture life in order to comment upon film as a mass medium and as a form of popular art. Yet, more directly than Hughes's and Wilson's novels, Merwin's *Hattie* focuses upon the dangers and liabilities of stardom, establishing the rather dark tone that would be echoed in many of the star fictions to follow.

Hattie of Hollywood adhered to what had become, even as early as 1922, the basic narrative pattern of Hollywood fiction. Hattie Johnson, a young working woman of modest social background, is persuaded by a friend to make a screen test for an East Coast studio, Earthwide Films. She is tested by the brilliant director Armand de Brissac, and her work is so promising that she is offered a studio contract and sent to Hollywood, where, after overcoming career setbacks and scandal, she finally achieves stardom. Yet Merwin's tale is hardly a simple success story; essentially it is the story of Hattie's growing disillusionment with a career for which she feels no enthusiasm or interest.

Initially Hattie must overcome the conflicting objections of her family— a grasping sister and brother-in-law who seek to benefit from her growing income and a puritanical grandmother whose moral outrage at the idea of Hattie's career in motion pictures is slowly dissolved in the sunny prospects of a life filled with luxury and ease. Throughout the novel the relatives are presented as parasites, "family hangers-on, that cluster inevitably about the successful stars, particularly the inexperienced girl stars, and live off them."[58] One of the most disillusioning facts about Hollywood stardom for Hattie is this dependence of her family, who are eager to enjoy the benefits of her success at the expense of her happiness. But this is simply the first in a series of realizations that mark Hattie's shifting conceptions of Hollywood and what it means to be a success there, as she moves from naive excitement to fear and finally resignation. Her first ideas about Hollywood are derived from the gossip of her friends and the stories she has read in the "picture magazines":

> "Hollywood"—a queerly make-believe far-off place, out of which whispery stories drifted like smoke. The girls in the store talked pruriently of it. And what unhappy influences mightn't a lot of happy-go-lucky picture people have on a colorless little girl like Hattie? Not that they need be worse than other people. They couldn't be worse than New Yorkers. . . . [Yet] about Hollywood hovered a

glamour. It was even possible that the money might come too easily. Money did change people; lots of it, pouring in all at once. And in the pictures everyone seemed to deal in tens and hundreds of thousands. Even in millions. Millions! . . . (First installment, 86)

Hattie's earliest impressions revolve around two sets of concerns: morality and money. That dichotomy asserts itself as a powerful subtext in Merwin's (and others') Hollywood fictions—stardom as prostitution. Predicated on the display of the body and the mobilization of the erotic potential of the screen image, and balanced precariously between conflicting notions of work and play, the life of the movie star always existed within the shadow of this sexual subtext, the image of whore or gigolo, which was supported by tales of casting-couch seductions and sexual favors exchanged for preferential treatment by producers and directors.[59]

Hattie's anxieties about the sexual role she is to play as a film actress are immediately brought into focus by the presence of her Svengali-like director, the brilliant and libertine de Brissac, who accompanies her to Hollywood. On the train de Brissac outlines his plan to make her a star, which includes his personal supervision of her emotional and sexual growth. He provides her with books to read (Flaubert's *Sentimental Education* and Havelock Ellis), changes her name to the more distinguished "Harriet John," and describes in no uncertain terms his desire for complete control over her life. "'Now, my dear,' he said, taking her hand and playing with her soft little fingers as he spoke, 'you and I had better understand each other right at the start. If you'll do exactly as I say—place yourself unquestioningly in my hands—I will make you. If you won't, I can't help you'" (first installment, 88).

The director plots not a seduction of Hattie but her transformation into a great screen star, a process that he believes must include a widening of her emotional and sexual experience. And, although he does fall in love with her and uses his power to place her in morally compromising situations (such as a scandalous triangle with a former lover), de Brissac's attentions stem mainly from his dedication to film work and his "unconventional" artistic methods. While throughout the novel Hattie struggles to understand her own feelings as well as de Brissac's motives, the reader is permitted to see that his goal is not mere sexual conquest but artistic achievement. In this respect de Brissac is like Hollywood itself, as Merwin would have us understand it: outwardly he displays the signs of sexual notoriety through a flamboyant bohemianism, yet behind the scandalous surface of appearances lies the struggle for artistic expression and cultural recognition that characterized Hollywood in the early twenties.

Upon Hattie's arrival in Los Angeles, her view of Hollywood suffers a series of disillusioning revisions. Expecting "the Hollywood of mystery, of whispered romance and scandal, of (recent) murders and underworld conspiracies . . ." (second installment, 27), she is surprised to find instead "an uninspiring bit of everyday" (28). The studio is "a vastly more respectable place" than she had imagined, and she makes the "odd discovery" that "Hollywood exhibited to the outer eye no night life whatsoever. It was as quiet as a country village" (97). Merwin's commentary on Hollywood here, as in his short stories "Fancy Turns" and "Theme with Variations" (discussed in chapters 2 and 3), seems to be a clear attempt to challenge its image as "a modern Sodom" by emphasizing its small-town character, dismissing it as a "somewhat ragged little city, this overgrown village sprawling over a desert plain at the feet of pretentious little mountains." Within this mundane environment Hattie suffers a growing disappointment, a process that is complete after she becomes inured to the routines of studio life. In fact, Merwin offers a portrait of the film studio as Fordist nightmare that has few equals in Hollywood fiction.

> Disillusionment was now complete. Even at the studio; particularly there. For the studio proved to be a great factory, in which de Brissac and his assistants fought against time and against a terrific overhead charge for the use of space and light and material and the time of the mechanical staff; in which swarms of preoccupied men and women went to work, at nine in the morning and kept at it, at times, until far into the night; in which all of life was routinized and systematized until it seemed hardly worth going on with. (97)

Increasingly, Hattie feels trapped by studio life, tied to a three-year contract yet uncertain of her talent and wary of the easy familiarities that exist among film people. Above all, she longs for a simple domestic life. But when de Brissac's film is released, the bewildered Hattie becomes a star overnight; suddenly she is the idol of millions and one of the brightest names on the lot. Although success eases the financial burden of supporting her family, Hattie finds the attention of fans and studio executives overwhelming, and as she slaves over a pile of fan letters one night she muses that "probably this was success, all those letters that had to be somehow laboriously answered, all the cheap prints of still pictures that would have to be sent. She didn't feel successful, she felt hunted" (fourth installment, 46). So great is her unhappiness that for a moment she considers suicide, but finally her family persuades her to accept a new contract (for $1,000 a week) with de Brissac, who has left the studio and gone into independent production—a career move fraught with sexual peril for Hattie. Her future as a famous Hollywood star looms before her, yet she is "a frightened little person" (fifth installment, 40) who has begun to wonder whether "fame might prove a substitute for happiness" (41).

Now enjoying considerable affluence, which has given her a respite from the avarice of her family, Hattie continues to submit to the routines of film work and the advances of de Brissac, often comforting herself with the advice offered by a jaded fellow movie actress: "Morals don't matter, mistakes do" (fourth installment, 45). Still she clings to the "appearance of respectability" (fifth installment, 42) and does her best to keep de Brissac's attentions centered on the new film they are working on. In *Hattie* one of the chief dangers of Hollywood stardom for young women is its unrelenting assault upon their moral values and standards of behavior.

As the narrative, through its inexorable melodramatic logic, moves Hattie closer to moral calamity, she is introduced to an East Coast writer, Julian Dempster—a well-known "highbrow" critic of motion pictures who has come to Hollywood to research a magazine article he is writing. Although critical of most films, Dempster finds Hattie/Harriet's work curiously unaffected and real, "simple and sweet . . . like a fragrant little wild rose here in this big hothouse called Hollywood" (103), and they quickly fall into a relationship of growing tenderness and mutual respect that saves Hattie from the imminent danger she faces with de Brissac.

Through the character of Dempster, Merwin articulates his own views on the status of movies as art.

> "It's hardly more of an art than the packing business of Armour and Swift. Hollywood is a group of big factories. Quantity production, all

the drive and efficiency of a first class automobile plant. Factory men running it and hiring showmen to give it flavor. The most ingenious devices for finding out what the public wants and then giving it to them. And that public is being ground out of the public school hoppers by the million—without culture, without tradition—and swarming in by shiploads from the backwaters of Europe. It's just what you said, Harriet—a machine, a big machine." (Sixth installment, 42)

This image of the "machine" of mass culture, crushing revered artistic and cultural traditions beneath the weight of vulgarity and homogeneity, is grounded in the xenophobic and class-bound politics of Progressivism, for which Merwin had been a spokesman throughout his literary career. But beneath his only slightly veiled cultural politics lies the perhaps deeper resentment of the print-genre worker confronting a cultural form that relegates the writer to a subordinate position within the creative process.

"Don't you see, Harriet, where the writing man gets off in all this? He's simply smothered to death. . . . —whatever place there is for the creative sort of person, the artist, goes to the director. The writer has to work under him, try to please him. . . . They have to be showmen, these directors, and they're all busy exploiting themselves—that and fighting overhead and working out mechanical and technical problems and driving the job along. I haven't met three of them who are really interested in interpreting an author's quality. They're too busy interpreting themselves." (42)

For his tirades against the film industry Dempster finds a sympathetic audience in Hattie, who has had her own experiences with directorial temperament.

Predictably, Hattie and Julian fall in live and elope to New York, where they plan to marry after the premiere of the new film she has completed with de Brissac. But upon their arrival, the two are overwhelmed by the signs of Hattie's fame: crowds of reporters and fans gather wherever she goes, and at every corner huge twenty-four-sheet posters bear her image. Faced with the embarrassment of his own modest income and the inescapable presence of Hattie's fame, Dempster breaks their engagement, admitting that she now "belonged to the public, to her own amazing success" (102). When he sees her for the last time, amid the thunderous acclaim of premiere night, she has become for him, once again, "a remote celebrity" (105). Hattie, now engaged to de Brissac (through an arrangement engineered by her brother-in-law) and hopelessly entangled in the net of publicity surrounding the announcement of their marriage and the success of their last film, is last shown to the reader wearing the "sweetly pretty mask of recent habit," a prisoner of success, hopelessly isolated within her stardom.

WOMEN AND STARDOM

As *Hattie of Hollywood* illustrates, stardom represented a particular danger to women.[60] In the popular novels of Hollywood life written in the 1920s and 1930s, the perils of stardom fell heavily upon the shoulders of women, and the narrative trajectory of their lives—the rise toward success as a film star followed by the inevitable fall into unhappiness and loss—became a familiar cautionary tale of patriarchal culture, revealing the hidden dangers of success, ambition, and career. In fact, the Hollywood star emerged in the twenties as a cultural emblem of the new opportunities available to women—an embodiment of the social promise as well as sexual threat posed by the New Woman in American society.

Hollywood in this period was a symbolic stage for the social and sexual freedoms that transformed American life in the first half of the twentieth century. New economic circumstances and changing standards of social conduct, together with women's demand for the vote, challenged traditional notions of women's work, widening their roles in social and economic life.[61] The film industry was one place where the opportunities for work and economic independence that had opened up for women were dramatically displayed to the rest of the country. Here, as Merwin observed in *Hattie of Hollywood*, "a little cash girl out of a store may wander in by chance and arrive in a day,"[62] enjoying a level of success undreamt of by most Americans. Notwithstanding its reputation for the sexual exploitation of young women, Hollywood also represented a profession that seemed specifically suited to the "feminine" traits of aestheticized fantasy and make-believe, and therefore seemed especially open to career opportunities for women. The novelist Joseph Hergesheimer, writing about Hollywood in a series of articles for the *Saturday Evening Post* entitled "Shapes in Light," articulated precisely this idea of the film capital, as a realm of feminine freedom and opportunity.

> Suddenly I realized that we were part of an amazing and unprecedented scene, the extraordinary existence brought about by moving pictures. Neither the stage nor any other art had created such a life for itself, at once exotic and free and impersonal; I mean in essence:
>
> I was living in a community of specialized and lovely women where there were no social obligations outside a strict relationship to their work; the tyrannical institution of family, tiresome relationships with censorious and superficial worldly connections, stupid and rigid conventions, had no existence here. This, as I have intimated, was a world of bright creatures with charming houses, elaborate motor cars, hung like a rainbow over the cameras of their profession.[63]

Images of Hollywood and women's role in it like the one sketched by Hergesheimer were echoed and elaborated on in the fan magazines. Such images provide the necessary cultural context for understanding the literary construction of the film star as a figure doomed by her success. On the one hand, the myth of stardom gave shape to powerful utopian aspirations and desires, and stars could be said to engage in an ongoing social pedagogy: their enactment of a life-style based on ritual displays of affluence and leisure eroticized Veblen's notion of conspicuous consumption by casting it within the logic of display typical of consumer culture. However, the image of the star was haunted by unresolved social and cultural tensions that surrounded the issues of gender and career at a time when these were undergoing shifts of seismic proportions.

In Hollywood fiction of the 1920s and 1930s, women as film stars became signs of an "excessive" desire, and their success was invariably depicted as being founded upon their abandonment of more traditional roles as wives and mothers—Hergesheimer's "tyrannical institution of family." Thus, Hollywood fictions that showed stars being punished for what they had achieved satisfied readers who felt threatened by the advances women were making in society generally. It is certainly fair to say that the depictions of women-as-stars in the Hollywood fictions of the 1920s and 1930s were thoroughly grounded in a sense of envy and hostility as well as in a suspicion toward modernity and mass culture.

More generally, the life of the movie star often served as an acute example of the problem of success in American life—the difficulty of negotiating the complex moral, emotional, and social obligations produced by sudden wealth and power. This was a dilemma that was compounded for film stars by their ostensible dedication to aesthetic principles—their commitment to their "art." In Hollywood fiction, the film star's embrace of a life based on leisure and consumption usually signaled a fatal loss of integrity, a selling out of talent, often paralleled by a literal or figurative prostitution. Caught in a cultural double bind where traditional social and economic ideologies jostled modern redefinitions of work and leisure, and working in a profession that was emblematic of the shifts and uncertainties in sexual and social behavior in American society, the fictional film star often appeared trapped within an irresistible cultural and narrative logic that led inevitably to unhappiness, disillusionment, and destruction.

THE SKYROCKET

Perhaps the most prolific author of Hollywood fiction in the 1920s was Adela Rogers St. Johns. The daughter of famed defense lawyer Earl Rogers, St. Johns grew up in Los Angeles, where, as a cub reported for the Hearst-owned *Los Angeles Herald,* she observed the growth of the film industry. St. Johns's Hollywood fictions always evinced a remarkable familiarity and insight into the social mores, emotional lives, and psychological tensions of those who lived and worked in Hollywood—a community that, as recorded in her autobiography *The Honeycomb,* she had seen develop from "a fragrant, idyllic peaceful country village in the midst of orange groves" to an American cultural symbol, "the trade name for the Art and Industry of the Motion Picture."[64] As a newspaperwoman and the first West Coast correspondent for Quirk's *Photoplay,* St. Johns knew virtually everybody who was anybody in the Hollywood of the 1920s, many of them as good friends and confidants—an enviable position for a fan-magazine writer and one that led Quirk to dub her the "Mother Confessor of Hollywood." As a Hollywood journalist and an author of Hollywood fiction, St. Johns contributed significantly to the literary and cultural image of the film capital in this period, and her work exemplifies the interconnections between fan-magazine writing and Hollywood fiction.

St. Johns appears to have been a woman of startling contradictions. She first gained national attention when, at the age of eighteen, she publicly debated the formidable Alice Ames Winters, president of the General Federation of Women's Clubs, on the question "Is modern woman a failure?" St. Johns took the conservative position that "the women of today are miserable in their new so-called freedom. They know it's built on selfishness and indulgence." She went on to argue that in pursuit of career and economic independence the modern woman was "sacrificing the tremendous privilege of home, social and religious culture and the education of her children to run after false gods."[65] On the other hand, St. Johns was active in the women's suffrage movement and was herself a lifelong career woman as a correspondent for the Hearst newspaper chain and an author of magazine fiction and feature stories. She was even sued (unsuccessfully) by her second husband for custody of their children because he claimed that her coverage of the Lindbergh kidnapping trial had led her to neglect her family.

In 1922, through Quirk and through her association with Hearst newspapers, St. Johns was introduced to Ray Long, editor of the Hearst-owned *Cosmopolitan* magazine. As recounted in her autobiography, they first met at the Hearst "ranch" (soon to be known as San Simeon), where Long urged St. Johns to supplement her reportorial work for *Photoplay* by submitting stories to *Cosmopolitan*, a monthly periodical with a voracious appetite for new fiction. Long's interest was in a particular kind of fiction—an interest symptomatic of the attention Hollywood was getting, which would lead directly to the development of Hollywood fiction as a category of American writing. Rarely does literary history provide us with such moments as St. Johns describes, in which the author's background and experience, the economic needs of the publishing industry, and the interests of the reading public coincide so fortuitously to produce a new kind of literary subject.

As Ray Long and I sat smoking leisurely under the oleanders on that morning of glory, he kept urging me to spend more time on fiction. Especially, he said, Hollywood fiction. These tales were new and Hollywood was an entirely fresh setting and the public was growing more and more curious and interested. I began thinking. . . . They seemed to me awful, those stories. False and phony and fake—yet they weren't, most of them were built on fact and often became fiction only to avoid libel laws. . . . Fiction, as I discovered then and later, had that one distinct advantage. In some instances it was the only way in which you could print the truth.[66]

Actually, in many cases St. Johns's Hollywood fictions do ring "false and phony," particularly in their conclusions, where she seems too eager to resolve conflicts and provide a happy ending—one that typically restores women to their post as domestic helpmates of men (as we have seen in her short story "The Last Straw"). In this regard it must be remembered that, through both personal conviction and editorial policy, St. Johns was an ardent defender of the film industry. This kind of ending served the interests of an embattled industry struggling to defend its reputation and insure box-office returns within a climate of moral outrage, which had been precipitated by the "star scandals" of the early twenties. Still, St. Johns realized that the public's interest in Hollywood mingled adoration and contempt, and in the stream of Hollywood short stories and serials she produced for popular magazines such as *Collier's, Cosmopolitan, Good House-keeping,* and *Photoplay* through the 1920s and 1930s, she attempted to provide a portrait of Hollywood life that balanced its vices and virtues. Writing primarily for women's magazines, St. Johns set herself the task of evoking for readers the aura of transgression that surrounded Hollywood stardom while at the same time assuring them that the film industry posed no essential threat to the dominant social and sexual ideologies.

A striking example of her work is the Hollywood novel *The Skyrocket,* which was serialized in *Cosmopolitan* from January to April of 1925.[67] *The Skyrocket* follows the basic formula of romance novels about Hollywood life by recuperating the woman-as-star through a restoration of domestic values. At the same time, the book is a stinging attack on the institution of Hollywood celebrity and the values that underlay stardom as a life-style, setting out to expose, as did the fan magazines, the pathology of stardom. The novel follows the career of an ambitious young woman, Sharon Kimm, from her start as a bathing beauty and out-of-work extra to the height of Hollywood fame and back, through an ignominious fall into financial ruin. While the novel offers a vivid portrait of Hollywood life in the 1920s, its realistic surface is periodically ruptured by the heavy-handed symbolism of Sharon as a character, which St. Johns effectively summed up in her introduction to the first installment of the serial in *Cosmopolitan.*

> All Hollywood knows them—the true stories of those meteoric rises and headlong falls that have startled and horrified the world are whispered along the boulevard. . . . They are like skyrockets. Gathered from everywhere and nowhere—planted in the quicksands of most amazing temptations—fed by flattery and adulation—fired by too sudden wealth and all too sudden fame—they flame in swift and spangled glory across the sky. . . . only to crash back to the earth from which they came, charred and broken. . . . Hollywood skyrockets—poor little shooting stars—children of glory and romance and—disaster.[68]

Clearly, Sharon Kimm is an allegorical figure for Hollywood. St. Johns expressed this directly in the novel: "Sharon belonged to Hollywood. She had given herself to Hollywood . . . and in return Hollywood was to give her many things, not all of them good. But the two of them were bound together so close that the history of Sharon Kimm is almost the heart-history of Hollywood."[69] Like all characters who bear the burden of allegory, Sharon is at times a rather flat, one-dimensional creation, a quality exacerbated by a mechanical naturalism in the novel through which her actions are linked to childhood deprivation and the tragic influence of her mother. Using flashbacks, St. Johns reveals the brutal poverty of Sharon's childhood as the only daughter of a woman trapped in a loveless marriage with an older man who could not support his family. Despondent over the family's privation and desperate to preserve her own vanishing youth and beauty, Sharon's mother spent hard-earned Christmas money on a new dress for herself, then, in a fit of remorse, committed suicide. Throughout the rest of the novel, Sharon is haunted by the memory of her mother's unhappy marriage and desire for beautiful things that she could never afford. It is this background of impoverishment and familial tragedy that impels Sharon to eschew love and marriage and pursue a career as a movie star, where she can indulge her desire for the expensive clothes and luxurious life that were denied her mother.

In the course of the novel, Sharon encounters the career setbacks and near scandals that are the conventional elements of the star narrative, in the process becoming emotionally involved with two men who come to represent the moral poles of life in Hollywood. The first is the handsome actor Mickey Reid, who, though only moderately successful in films, is able to help Sharon get a foothold in the business. Mickey falls in love with Sharon and asks her to marry him, but she is selfishly devoted to her career. "I wouldn't marry anybody. Marriage is the bunk. . . . I'm not going to tie myself down to some man and have kids and all that. I want to be a star and have money and beautiful things and diamonds and dresses and be some-body" (82). It becomes clear that by renouncing Mickey as she becomes more successful, Sharon has given up her one chance for real happiness. In St. Johns's treatment, Sharon's demands for sexual and economic independence align her with the social agenda of the New Woman in American life and ensure her eventual fall.

Sharon's second emotional entanglement is with the director William Dvorak, a star maker and power broker in the Hollywood studios who appears to be emotionally unstable and sexually dysfunctional. To Sharon he offers the enticing possibility of achieving the highest level of Hollywood stardom through his patronage. Dvorak, like Merwin's de Brissac in *Hattie of Hollywood*, is a familiar figure in Hollywood fiction: a powerful and charismatic character who embodies the brilliant creative genius as well as the libertine moral values of the artist; an individual who sees himself as outside society's strictures in his devotion to his own iconoclastic artistic vision. Gradually Dvorak insinuates himself into Sharon's personal life, remaining physically aloof despite his growing sexual obsession with her. At one point he hires a handsome male star to make love to her as his proxy, but his jealousy causes him to abandon the plan. He finally settles for being Sharon's guide and tutor as he leads her into a life of "material pleasures and desires" that "debauches her soul and her mind" (180).

The real interest in *The Skyrocket* lies in its description of Sharon's growing affluence, accompanied by the increasingly hollow rituals of a life based on conspicuous consumption. And it is on this level that the novel operates as a critique of Hollywood stardom and of the ethos of leisure and consumption that it represents. St. Johns tells us that Sharon's "arrival" as a film star ignites "a raging fire of desire, a small blaze that was to be fed continually with the tinsel of Hollywood success" (100). This desire grows within her until it becomes a destructive passion. "Desire. Reckless, enormous, red-hot desire for things, for possessions, for ornaments with which to deck this beauty of hers. Desire for a throne from which she might scorn lesser mortals" (152). It is a sickness that infects the entire Hollywood community, for which Sharon is a symbol.

> [Hollywood] is like some fantastic fair, where dicing on one side of the midway provides unexpected wealth, and irresistible opportunities for squandering amid the baubles of the gaudy booths on the other side tempt it back again.
>
> There is no place in the world where it is so easy to learn to spend money—where the spending of money is so necessary to keep up the show, and where spending money is one of the few pastimes for a hard working people. New York, Long Island itself, can display no more lavish scale of living than Hollywood, and because Hollywood is so small, the contrast and comparison of one's possessions with another's is inevitable.
>
> Splurge. Front. Show. They are monstrous. (170)

It is not the implied sexual threat posed by Dvorak that endangers Sharon's well-being but "self-indulgence, and flattery, and luxury, and popularity, and the lying tongues of sychophants, and the honeyed words of parasites" (172), the symptoms of "that dread Hollywood plague—egomania" (169). Her salary jumps from $75 a week to $125, $350, $500, $750, and finally reaches $3,000 a week, a level of wealth Sharon can scarcely conceive of. Guided by the shallow "friends" who now crowd in on her, she engages in a reckless spending spree, masterfully chronicled by St. Johns, that culminates in her acquisition of a palatial Beverly Hills estate, ironically named "Paradise," where she begins a round of extravagant parties and entertainments. St. Johns revels in the ironies of "Paradise," the ultimate symbol of Sharon's profligacy, as she notes, "There never seemed to be any happiness in Paradise. Certainly never any peace. . . . It was, in its magnificent way, something of a madhouse" (218). Ultimately Sharon's unchecked "desire for things" (224) leads her into bankruptcy and scandal. The ability to buy things provides her not a royal road to happiness, as she thought it would, but rather a spiraling fall into isolation and self-destruction.

Echoing the fan magazines' ambivalent portrayal of Hollywood stardom, St. Johns's novel invites the reader to consider "whether those among the great stars who were happy were not so in spite of their success with its burdens and temptations rather than because of it" (259). In *The Skyrocket*, the narrative of stardom becomes a cautionary tale of consumer culture, which, by pushing the "desire for things" to its logical conclusion through the vast pecuniary resources of the film star, exposes the emptiness and alienation at the heart of consumerist versions of American life.

In the final pages of the novel, St. Johns introduces the familiar subtext of stardom as prostitution. Faced with financial ruin, Sharon is forced to consider submitting to the sexual demands of Dvorak as a way of avoiding financial scandal, and she finally decides to yield to his ambiguous demands in exchange for his help. But, while shooting location scenes in downtown Los Angeles, Sharon sees a prostitute on the street. Struck by the parallel in their situations, she resolves to renounce the "false gods, false standards" of Hollywood stardom (316), in terms that echo St. Johns's own denunciation of "modern women."

Sharon Kimm's eleventh-hour salvation from Hollywood is sealed by her decision to abandon her career and marry Mickey Reid, embracing the humble domestic role of wife and homemaker. With Mickey's help, she shoulders the massive debts that her excessive life as a Hollywood star created and at last finds happiness. Although the ending strains the narrative's credibility and undercuts the elements of the story that readers would be likely to find the most interesting—namely, those contained in St. Johns's lively account of Hollywood life—it is an ending that satisfies a conservative impulse to punish women for their career ambitions.

St. Johns's artificial happy ending established a precedent for the romantic star fictions that followed it. Anne Gardner's *Reputation* (1929), Jack Preston's *Screen Star* (1932), and Maysie Greig's *Romance for Sale* (1934) were all works in which, after adversity, setbacks, and scandal, the film star was shown to finally achieve the goal of happiness—defined by a successful romantic relationship that, according to fan-magazine formula, balanced the demands of career with a richly rewarding domestic life. Yet, even in these romance novels, the hidden dangers of success were often more vividly presented than the soft-focus happy ending, which typically resolved three hundred pages of torment and struggle in an unconvincing final chapter.

Ultimately, the narrative of stardom offered a cultural vehicle both for the representation of "feminine" desire and for its containment by the familiar ideologies of patriarchal culture (marriage, family, and repro-duction). The narrative pattern of the film star's rise and fall represents an implicitly misogynistic view aimed at forestalling and limiting the advances made by women in society. Many star fictions thus functioned as explicit warnings to women against pursuing an ideal image of themselves, an image that was being shaped by fan magazines and movies and by the demands of consumer culture. Yet this ideal image was also about women taking control of their lives by choosing career over marriage and achieving success. In this respect, the narrative of stardom was based on a logic of transgression that, even as it attempted to shore up crumbling patriarchal values, articulated the utopian promise of autonomy and independence for women. Still, the pathology of stardom, as it was defined by the fan magazines and in popular fiction, served a fundamentally conservative cultural politics in reaction against the modern sexual and social changes represented by the movie star in American life.

More generally, the film star became a figure that condensed a deep-seated ambivalence concerning the nature of success, thereby calling into question fundamental social and ideological values. The narrative trajectory of the film star's rise and fall raised profound doubts about the value of success in American life, and this ambivalence was all too obvious in works that eschewed the romantic mythology of the fan magazines for a perhaps equally mythologized view of film stars as captives of their privileged lives. In novels such as Frances Marion's *Minnie Flynn* (1925), Keane McGrath's *Hollywood Siren* (1932), Vicki Baum's *Falling Star* (1934), and Katharine Albert's *Remember Valerie March* (1939), film stars are tragic figures, often victims of their own emotional instabilities or sexual appetites, their lives controlled by the studios and their happiness constantly endangered by conflicting social, economic, and artistic demands: sacrificial lambs, finally, for the mass audience whose own excessive desires produced around film stars a culture of admiration, envy, and scorn. In the last analysis, the lessons of stardom in Hollywood fiction were expressions of a nagging skepticism concerning the nature and value of success, a suspicion of mass culture and a concern for its effects on both the individual (the star) and society (the fans), and a critical judgment against the ethos of leisure and consumption at the precise historical moment when it was establishing its dominance in American social and economic life.

CHAPTER FIVE

"THE MOST TERRIFYING TOWN IN THE WORLD"

Hollywood Fiction of the 1930s

The lure of the screen brings thousands of girls and boys to Hollywood from every part of the world. They come in a constant stream from cities and villages and countryside of America and Europe, come with dreams of fortune and fame, wholly ignorant of what awaits them and destined to disillusionment if not to utter failure and shame.

REV. EDWIN P. RYLAND[1]

Hollywood's mythic identity has always had a greater influence over popular perceptions of the film capital than have the generally mundane, if at times somewhat sordid, facts of life there. In the 1932 essay "Hollywood: The Blessed and the Cursed," playwright Robert E. Sherwood observed that, as a place, Hollywood was "effectually obscured by the penumbra of fable" that surrounded it,[2] the realities of living and working there being less tangible somehow than the city's aura of glamour and romance. And even when Hollywood's myths became tales of disillusionment and loss, they continued to contribute to a fascination with the city and with an industry where the rewards of success as well as the risks of failure were so great. Everything that was believed about Hollywood, whether good or bad, fact or fantasy, fueled a popular interest in the place. Sherwood went on to say,

It is not as a town, a paltry dot on the map of California, that [Hollywood] exists in the imagination of mankind; it is an idea— glamorous, insane, alluring or wildly ridiculous, but always tremendously important and fantastically unreal.

You may regard Hollywood as the blessed realm of dreams come true, or as civilization's worst nightmare; but you can hardly afford to ignore it or the inestimable influence that it has exerted. (67)

This contradictory image of Hollywood as "the blessed and the cursed" effectively defined the range of cultural responses to the film capital throughout the 1920s—from breathless enthusiasm to righteous indignation. But by the 1930s the moral dichotomies of the past decade seemed out of date in an America sunk in the misery of the Depression. Although the movie capital may still have been perceived by many as a sexual playground for the film community, the fan magazines had so successfully institutionalized the idea of Hollywood scandal that whatever notoriety was generated by the seemingly endless succession of divorces and extramarital affairs was unlikely to give rise to much shock or outrage. The anomaly of a bohemian "film colony" springing up in the largely rural suburbs of Los Angeles like some exotic flowering shrub seemed a distant memory to those accustomed to the hectic routines of what had become a factory town in full swing.

The extravagances and excesses of Hollywood in the 1920s gave way to a sense of uncertainty and restraint before the new technological and economic conditions brought about by the introduction of sound and the dominance of Wall Street investment capital in the film industry.[3] *Photoplay* correspondent Herbert Howe, who observed the changing circumstances of life in "filmland," reported, "Today Hollywood is as unhappy as Tahiti. The missionaries have come, Will Hays and the efficiency experts. The happy children of the jungle have been made to take life seriously."[4]

GOING HOLLYWOOD

What made Hollywood unique as a cultural idea (here Sherwood was wrong, I believe) was that you could actually go there. The fact that it was a place, "a paltry dot on the map," is tremendously important to an understanding of its cultural significance in this period. A person could follow the map and arrive at the dream, or so it was hoped. Certainly such a journey was attempted during the 1920s and 1930s by those who poured into southern California in great waves. This westward migration, which had started slowly at the end of the nineteenth century, played a key role in shaping the social and cultural landscape of Los Angeles.

Mike Davis has pointed out that Los Angeles "was first and above all the creature of real-estate capitalism."[5] The postwar prosperity of the late teens made possible a population movement from the agricultural Midwest into southern California, setting off a real-estate boom that would shape the identity and scale of the city. The staid farmers and retired grocers from Iowa and Indiana who moved to Los Angeles brought with them a middle-class conservatism and religiosity that gradually came to dominate the city's social and cultural life. By 1930 the pronounced midwestern character of the city led the "local-color" author Hamlin Garland to remark that "Los Angeles is the largest town in Iowa." Garland found much to praise on the "fortunate coast" of southern California, celebrating it as a sunny refuge from eastern winters, admirably suited to a middle-class life of leisure and the pursuit of comfort.[6]

The discovery of oil at Long Beach in 1919 sparked the great economic boom of the 1920s in California. Speculation in real estate and mineral rights created fortunes overnight, and the prosperity of the region, along with the incessant ballyhoo of the city's boosters, ensured a continued influx of tourists and new residents. Davis describes this process as part of an unprecedented public relations campaign.

> With sunshine and the open shop as their main assets, and allied with the great transcontinental railroads (the region's largest landowners), a syndicate of developers, bankers and transport magnates led by [Harrison Gray] Otis and his son-in-law, Harry Chandler, set out to sell Los Angeles—as no city had ever been sold—to the restless but affluent babbitry of the Middle West.[7]

Such a transformation of the region required, as Davis notes, the continuous interaction of "myth-making" and "crude promotion" (26), and in this capacity it was perhaps the film industry—where the distinctions between myth and reality were already rather loosely drawn—that played the key role in offering an image of Los Angeles to the rest of the country. *Saturday Evening Post* correspondent Garet Garrett remarked that it was "the constant representation of this Southern California environment in moving pictures that must create in people everywhere a desire and longing for it."[8]

Along with the vast numbers of people flocking to southern California to invest in real estate and enjoy its climate were those drawn by the presence of the film industry. The concentration of motion-picture production in southern California that had begun in 1907 was essentially complete by the early 1920s, and by the end of the decade Hollywood had become the "film capital of the world," home to the largest mass-entertainment industry ever created. Los Angeles attracted an ever-growing population of theatrical and vaudeville performers, craftsmen, technicians, artists, and writers, as well as an army of inexperienced film aspirants eager to "crash the movies." To film fans it was Mecca, a pilgrimage spot for the new secular religion of the motion picture, and tourism quickly became a vital subsidiary industry. In a city without the visible traces of history, the most popular tourist attraction became the tour of movie stars' homes, a Hollywood ritual that dates back to as early as 1915.[9]

The rapidity of Los Angeles's growth in the first three decades of the twentieth century was without parallel in national experience. It was, as Garrett observed in his *Saturday Evening Post* article "Los Angeles in Fact and Dream," "a definite social phenomenon of the first magnitude, strictly incomparable."[10] And the strains of this rapid development were increasingly apparent by the 1930s. Garrett noted that the city "perfectly dramatized the common experience of expatriation, or, that is to say, the process of psychic and physical readjustment to a new environment continually taking place in a great majority of the people" (6). As a result of the sudden growth of Los Angeles in the 1920s, there arose in the city a transient, commercial culture often conspicuously lacking a sense of value and purpose derived from a clearly defined sense of historical identity—that is, a sense of connection with the past. According to Garrett, Los Angeles was "a city with no past, ephemeral, each day new again, existing only in the present." "It never grew; it was made all at once. Idea externalized. . . . a Wisconsin or Iowa idea of what a Spanish Village ought to have been in southern California. And since a Wisconsin or Iowa man may never have thought overhead wires unsightly, a beautiful Spanish village, all new, may lie in a forest of poles and cross arms" (134). Drawn by the real-estate promoters' promises of "sunshine and wealth"[11] and by the romance and glamour attached to the motion-picture industry, hundreds of thousands of people poured into southern California over a thirty-year period, and by the 1930s this flood showed no signs of abating.

But the socioeconomic makeup of the immigrants was changing. Whereas the first waves of newcomers to Los Angeles had consisted largely of the prosperous middle and upper middle classes, by the 1930s the Depression had sent many of their less prosperous neighbors in search of the California dream, as well. To those who were out of work, dispossessed by economic circumstance, southern California beckoned as a last hope; it was still relatively inexpensive to live on the West Coast, and the climate was an irresistible attraction to those escaping midwestern dust storms and eastern blizzards. By the thousands such people brought to Los Angeles their unfulfilled dreams of success and the good life.[12] Coming in search of the American dream, they often found it elusive in the open-shop, boom-and-bust economy of southern California, and the resultant loss of hope could lead to bitterness and sullen resignation.

For Garrett, the problem was "the struggle between the idea of soft living" that southern California represented "and the inherited Puritan conscience" characteristic of the midwestern psyche. "In a little while they begin to be troubled. They are uneasy in spirit. A perfect house in a perfect climate, every comfort and pleasure of selfish being realized, and then what? Life recommending itself to all the senses—life, nevertheless, empty."[13] This is a very different regional psychology from that offered by Perley Poore Sheehan only six years earlier, in 1924. It was this sense of Hollywood—and southern California in general—as a place irrevocably cursed by the very aspects of its life that made it so appealing—that informed the fiction of writers such as James Cain, Horace McCoy, and Nathanael West, and led the emigré Bertolt Brecht to describe Los Angeles as an earthly hell.

In Hell too
There are, I've no doubt, these luxuriant gardens

With flowers as big as trees, which of course wither
Unhesitantly if not nourished with very expensive water.
And fruit markets
With great heaps of fruit, albeit having
Neither smell nor taste. And endless processions of cars
Lighter than their own shadows, faster than
Mad thoughts, gleaming vehicles in which
Jolly-looking people come from nowhere and are nowhere bound.
And houses, built for happy people, therefore standing empty
Even when lived in.[14]

Hollywood's cultural metamorphosis from the pastoral "Eden of the movies" into the more sinister suburban nightmare described by Brecht reflected the increasingly dark cultural identity of the entire "southland," for which the commercial sprawl and fantastic clutter of its material landscape became a dominant image. During a 1935 trip to the film capital, the British visitor R. J. Minney recorded very different impressions from the fairy-tale vistas described by Alice Williamson in 1927.

> Hollywood provokes very mixed feelings. Some of it is as repulsive as a sore—the barren wastes by the roadside that serve as parking places for motor cars, the litter of cheap and awful bungalows with walls no stouter than cardboard, the glaring advertisement signs that befoul the mountains, the hideous petrol pumps, even more numerous and awful than the bungalows, the light blue windmills that trademark the Van de Kamp bakeries, the freak architecture of the restaurants, some shaped like bowler hats ("Brown Derbys," they call them), others like oranges and pigs and dogs and monstrous women (you feed under the skirts), massive apartment houses like factories, recurrent open air markets. . . . Hollywood looks raw and unfinished—as though it were hurriedly run up, which of course it was.[15]

Minney, who had come to Hollywood to write a screenplay for Daryl F. Zanuck, published his impressions of the film capital in the trenchant *Hollywood by Starlight*. For him even Hollywood's occasional beauty possessed menace: when he was taken to the top of a Hollywood hill to survey the "glory" of "Hollywood by starlight," his companion pointed out that "from here . . . a girl leapt to her death the other day because she was tired of waiting for a film contract" (35). Such incidents became emblematic of Hollywood in the 1930s. The best-known stormy involved a New York stage actress named Peg Entwistle who committed suicide in 1932 by hurling herself from the "H" of the Hollywood sign, an act whose symbolism was all too apparent. The Hollywood sign was the city's most familiar visual icon. Built in 1923 as part of a realtor's promotional scheme and intended to last only a year or two, the sign had begun to show the ravages of age and vandalism by the late 1930s.[16]

Hollywood's transient character in the 1930s was a result of rapid urban development and of a society made up largely of newcomers, often cut off from their pasts and isolated from one another. The national exodus to southern California that created these conditions forms the social and cultural backdrop of the most compelling Hollywood fiction of the 1930s. These texts, in their attention to the economic hardships faced by extras and by those struggling to get into the film business, as well as in their often bitter attacks upon Hollywood as an industry, reflect the turn toward the social in the literature of the 1930s and can be read as examples of a literary culture of protest and social criticism.[17] During the Depression a new cynicism about Hollywood and the film industry arose, and it was especially evident in Hollywood fiction.

The new dark image of the film capital found expression in a particular narrative formula, which presented an outsider who comes to Hollywood drawn by ambition and unfulfilled personal longings, only to find failure. Variations of this narrative dominated Hollywood fiction in the 1930s, in a series of works exploring the experiences of characters who come to California in pursuit of a better life or who struggle to survive in unimportant jobs on the fringes of the film industry. Arriving in Hollywood in search of a dream, they most often encounter disappointment and a crushing end to their hopes and ideals. The ironic cynicism about Hollywood that characterizes these works usually centers on the realization of a discrepancy between the glamorous Hollywood myth and the often harsh realities of life in the film industry. These stories, artifacts of the Depression era, frequently displayed a bitterness and sense of betrayal aimed toward the fantasy and official optimism that were endemic to Hollywood and were pervasive in the mass culture of the 1930s. Yet these works were also often about *self*-betrayal, about the personal cost of compromise that led with fatalistic inevitability to resignation, despair, and—not infrequently—death. In much of the cultural discourse surrounding Hollywood in the 1930s, the plight of the extra became the emblem of Hollywood's fallen state.

THE PLIGHT OF THE EXTRA

According to one source, in 1923 ten thousand people per month invaded Hollywood to find work in the movie business.[18] Benjamin B. Hampton offered a more conservative figure in *A History of the Movies* (1931). Hampton estimated that from 1919 to 1929 some fifty thousand young women had come to Hollywood seeking a career in motion pictures.[19] As early as the mid-teens, Hollywood had become a magnet for movie hopefuls from all over the country, many of them young women. By the mid-1920s, the image of the movie-struck girl doggedly pursuing a career in Hollywood was familiar enough to become the subject of a popular syndicated comic strip. "Ella Cinders" (an inversion of "Cinderella") began as a daily strip on 1 June 1925 and entered the Sunday comic pages on 1 January 1929. Written by William Conselman, the editor of the *Los Angeles Sunday Times*, and drawn by Charlie Plumb, "Ella Cinders" followed the adventures of a screen-struck young girl seeking a career in movies; it was the first comic strip devoted to life in Hollywood. Hugely popular with readers, within a year it was made into a motion picture starring Colleen Moore in the title role.[20]

Although the exact numbers can only be guessed at, it is evident that the influx of "movie-struck girls" posed a unique social problem. They were often the victims of con men operating phony screen-acting schools, who charged them exorbitant fees for the production of cheaply produced screen tests and the promise to advance their careers.[21] After their eventual failure to make it in the film industry, movie hopefuls often fell into poverty, drawing on the city's economic reserves as charity cases or drifting into petty larceny and prostitution.

In 1916 concerned civic leaders joined with the Young Women's Christian Association to raise funds for the construction of the Hollywood Studio Club, a place where young women could find a temporary home and be properly chaperoned and protected from the more unsavory elements of Hollywood life. The original building, with accommodations for ten, was woefully inadequate from the outset. In 1926 the Studio Club was moved to a more spacious facility, where for the next sixty years it was home to thousands of young women.[22] But the Studio Club was not even an effective stopgap measure, and in 1924 the Hollywood Chamber of Commerce mounted a national publicity campaign to discourage California-bound youngsters by placing ads in newspapers and train stations warning of the poor prospects for success in the film industry.[23]

Still they poured into Los Angeles. "Pretty girls, beautiful girls, encouraged by admiring friends or by the winning of a beauty contest in their home towns, flock to the studios," reported a 1927 article in *Collier's*, entitled "Many Are Called."[24] The article concluded ominously: "Go ahead and chuck your present work for the will-o-the-wisp of movie fame. But give a thought first to the thousands who've done the same thing—and are still only hoping." Writing about the effects of this movie-inspired migration on the moral climate of Hollywood, the Rev. Edwin P. Ryland observed:

> There is enough debauchery here and to spare. There is mammon worship, greed for gain that is coarse and repulsive. There is crime, and impurity cannot conceal its brazen countenance. Our community has attracted far more boys and girls than it can assimilate and the result is moral disease through unemployment and disillusionment that has left depression and abandonment to evil ways.[25]

Such warnings were echoed by the fan magazines, although the message might well be lost amidst all the glamorous evidence to the contrary. As early as 1917 *Photoplay* was asking, "Can the Pretty Girl Without Influence Break into the Movies? Most of the Experts Say 'No!'"[26] In articles such as "What Every Girl Wants to Know" and "What Are the Chances of a Beginner?" *Photoplay* periodically attempted to discourage movie-struck young women from coming west.[27] Those efforts culminated in 1926–27 with a series of articles entitled "The Truth About Breaking into the Movies," written by *Photoplay* correspondent Ruth Waterbury. Waterbury went to Hollywood, ostensibly on a bet with her editor James Quirk, to see if she could get a job as an extra. Predictably, she found it impossible to even get an interview with a casting director until she mentioned her association with *Photoplay*. Waterbury's series offered compelling examples of the hardships faced by newcomers in Hollywood, where extras often starved between jobs and a young woman's willingness to exchange sexual favors for work often made the difference between paying the rent for another month and a humiliating return to her hometown. Altogether it was an extremely bleak view of Hollywood. "No girl knows how desperate a thing ambition is until she gets to Hollywood. No girl knows how dreadful a thing it is to fear everyone until she resides in the film capital. Distrust, suspicion, envy, ruthlessness, despair, they all follow on ambition here."[28] In the last article of the series, entitled "Don't Go to Hollywood!," Waterbury explained that oftentimes a destitute young woman would be helped to return home "by acting as a chaperone to a corpse. The dead are not supposed to travel alone. So when a body must be shipped out from Hollywood, the railroad lets the Chamber of Commerce know, and some girl gets a free ticket for performing this gruesome job. Adventure can not possibly end more abjectly than this. Don't go to Hollywood!"[29]

The plight of the extra in Hollywood could best be explained in the simple economic terms of supply and demand: there were vastly more hopefuls than jobs. Professional extras were lucky if they were employed three days a week at salaries that ranged from $3 per day for crowd work up to $15 a day for "dress extras" who could supply their own wardrobes.[30] By the mid-1920s, when thousands competed for a single job, industry leaders began to seek alternatives to the confusing and often corrupt hiring practices that existed in the studios. A group of film executives commissioned a study by the Russell Sage Foundation, which recommended to the California State Labor Commission the formation of a centralized bureau where extras could register for employment and studios could conveniently hire from a reliable talent pool organized according to physical type.

The Central Casting Corporation was founded by the Association of Motion Picture Producers in 1925, obstensibly both to serve the industry's needs and to protect extras from exploitative hiring practices.[31] For one thing, it eliminated the grueling task of "making the rounds" at the studios by requiring all registered extras to call in once a day. They would then be given a casting assignment or, more likely, simply told, "Nothing." The discouraging finality of that single-word response caused extras to complain until the switchboard operators at Central were persuaded to substitute the somewhat more encouraging phrase "Try later."[32] This system had the unfortunate effect of chaining extras to their telephones. They were afraid to leave home for fear that they would miss a call, which might mean a day's work. According to statistics cited by Ruth Waterbury, in 1927 some fourteen thousand men, women, and children were registered with Central Casting, yet the average daily call from the studios provided work for only 698 of them.[33] And for the beginner Central Casting offered little hope of employment, as it frequently imposed moratoriums on the registering of new names, cutting off movie aspirants from the surest was to get into film work.

Although it had been designed to prevent scandal and eliminate abuses of power in the film industry, there can be little doubt that Central Casting mainly served the interests of the studios as part of a broad policy to regulate and standardize industry practices. As the lowest-paid and therefore most expendable motion-picture workers, extras remained in a condition of economic and personal vulnerability. The dangers of this situation were particularly acute for young women, who undoubtedly were the frequent targets of unwanted sexual advances by those who claimed to be able to help them get ahead in the movie business. While tales of casting-couch seductions and sexual favors exchanged for career advancements have long been central to Hollywood's cultural myth, most of the evidence to support these claims has remained anecdotal and fragmentary. However, one of the most direct attacks on the industry's sexual exploitation of extras came from the novelist Theodore Dreiser in a series of articles entitled "Hollywood: Its Manners and Morals," which appeared in the periodical *Shadowland* in 1921–22.[34] Dreiser offered a stinging exposé of "the extra's fight to exist"—as one of the pieces was subtitled—in a film industry that he depicted as venal and riddled with corruption at every level. "There is no one in the profession today who does not know that sex in one form and another is the principal and hence the determining factor in the rise of most of those of beauty among the women who hope to go far. And that there have been and will yet be many compromises of a decidedly sordid character in order that screen success may be attained. . . ."[35]

Dreiser painted a grim picture of "the moving picture game" entered into by the ambitious beginner, as a life of uncertainty, suspicion, and dependence upon men whose primary interest was to add them to "their already extended harems" (80). With a novelist's interest in the psychology of motivation, Dresser explored the "extra-girl's" willingness to accept deprivation, insult, and physical threat in pursuit of fame and fortune—which, after all, were often the results of luck rather than fitness for the job. But the brunt of his muckraking was directed at the "directors, casting-directors, assistant directors, camera-men, the heavies and even leads of the male persuasion who have anything to do with or can, by any hook or crook, contrive any possible claim upon the time or attention or services of those of the feminine persuasion—the younger and prettier and less experienced, of course—who are seeking to make an ill-paid way of life in this, in the main, gruelling realm" (85–86).

Although he claimed to have as evidence the experiences of no less than "twenty-five aspirants of exceptional beauty and ability," Dreiser's claims remained largely unsupported by corroborating details. In actuality, his efforts to expose the unjust treatment of Hollywood extras reflects a larger concern over the influence of motion pictures and the ethics of the film industry at a time, in the early 1920s, when moral outrage dominated discussions of Hollywood.[36]

By the 1930s the kinds of criticisms that Dreiser had leveled at the film industry were largely taken for granted, having passed into the realm of Hollywood myth. Yet it seems likely that the Depression worsened conditions for those who survived on the fringes of the film industry. Dramatic evidence of this was provided by the publication in 1935 of Max Knepper's strident exposé of life in the film capital, *Sodom and Gomorrah: The Story of Hollywood.* This work was published under the auspices of the Los Angeles branch of the End Poverty in California (EPIC) movement, which had been organized to support Upton Sinclair's bid for the governorship of California in the 1934 election. The election ended in disastrous defeat for Sinclair after the Hollywood film studios, led by Louis B. Mayer of MGM, engineered a massive smear campaign against him, which was financed by contributions extorted from film-industry employees through threats of mass firings if the "socialist" Sinclair was elected. Several studios even threatened to shut down their West Coast production facilities and relocate—in either New York or Florida—if Sinclair won the governorship. MGM went so far as to produce a series of staged "newsreels" designed to discredit Sinclair with the voters, and Mayer blackmailed the theater owners into showing the reels by threatening to withhold MGM films.[37] It was with justifiable bitterness that Sinclair wrote, in his preface to Knepper's tract, that "in the recent election in California the motion picture industry went Fascist".[38] thus, the 1934 California gubernatorial race included one of the first attempts to use the power of the motion-picture medium to directly influence the American electoral process.

Despite the ominous precedent that the studios had set for American politics, Knepper attacked Hollywood as a hotbed not of political reaction but of wanton sexual license, pinning his central arguments on the immorality of the Hollywood film colony and exposing the industry's wholesale sexual exploitation of young women. *Sodom and Gomorrah* begins with a short fictional account of the dangers of movie work, entitled "Adventures of a Beauty Contest Winner in Hollywood." This Hollywood short story concerns a movie-struck young girl from Toledo, Ohio, who is given a ticket to Hollywood after winning a beauty contest sponsored by a cosmetics firm. Once there she encounters rejection and failure. Her desperation to get into the business is compounded by the fact that her father has mortgaged the family home in order to support her while she finds work. Finally she is persuaded to submit to the sexual demands of various film-industry personnel, strung along by promises of a break in pictures if she will "be a good sport."[39] By the end she is disillusioned and defeated, working as a waitress in Hollywood to avoid a humiliating return to her hometown and family.

Knepper offered this story as representing the fates of thousands of young women who had been lured to Hollywood under the false impression that their beauty and charm, or a trophy from some local beauty contest, would land them a job with a studio and an easy path to screen stardom. The message of sexual danger and failure offered by this story represented the essential truth of life in Hollywood for Knepper. In subsequent chapters he mounted a general attack on the sexual content and "bad taste" of Hollywood films. He exposed the immorality of the movie stars and leading executives, claiming (on limited evidence) that the entire industry was "honey-combed by all sorts of depravity and looseness " (82); he wrote of the role of studio publicity departments in covering up Hollywood scandal and foisting on the public untalented performers who had bought their opportunities with sexual favors; he complained about the fan magazine—that "great channel of systematized gossip and false-hood" (146)—and noted the magazines' complicity with the studios in manufacturing a false aura of importance around Hollywood celebrities; he railed against the egotism and megalomania of the Hollywood elite, who in their shortsighted pursuit of pleasure and profit were impeding the artistic development of the motion picture.

It was the plight of the extra-girls—"the starving harem," as the title of one chapter called them—that most clearly embodied the corruption of Hollywood. To his credit, Knepper was more willing than most industry critics to name names and provide documentation for his allegations, but the evidence he provided was still sketchy. Particularly beneficial to his argument was a case in the Los Angeles courts involving an extra-girl who stated that she had submitted to sexual orgies with Dave Allen, the manager of Central Casting, because of his promises to provide her with work (99–100). Knepper reflected on the case:

> The story of the Hollywood extra is essentially a tragic one. . . . It is nothing more than literal starvation, eviction, deferred hope, and frequently the worst kind of moral degradation if the individual persists in sticking. It could hardly be otherwise. The odds against making a living in this field, or of subsequently advancing to stardom, are too great. Consequently there is a huge group of beautiful women, spurred on by ambition and hope, who voluntarily sacrifice them-selves to what at best is a poor livelihood. They form a sort of public harem, their morals being on about the same plane as their economic status. (196–97)

Paradoxically, Knepper observed that the lower costs of living in Los Angeles and the practice of several sharing expenses in "small communistic units" (202) ensured a fairly comfortable standard of living for most Holly-wood extras. "With no more capital or income than the inhabitants of the slum districts, the extras live in a setting of middle-class luxury amid the beautiful Hollywood hills" (199). Still, making ends meet while holding on to the dream of a career in movies could be "nerve-racking in the extreme." Some women supplemented their incomes with outside jobs, while an "amazingly large" group turned to prostitution to help eke out a living

(204). And always they were victims in the climate of rampant sexual appetite that existed in Hollywood. "Almost weekly there is a Hollywood scandal involving members of the picture profession. . . . Of course the vast number of sexual crimes and misdemeanors that go on amongst the film colony are never reported. . . . It is well known that Hollywood is the happy hunting ground of all types of sex perverts" (205–6). While Knepper's stance is that of an outraged social reformer and industry critic his book reveals the same moral self-righteousness that emanated from religious critics of Hollywood, and his judgmental assessments of performers such as Mae West and Jean Harlow reveal a narrow, prudish view of popular culture.

Sodom and Gomorrah is a perfect example of the interweaving of arguments concerning Hollywood's immorality with complaints about the mismanagement of the film business and about the movies as a cultural and artistic form. Looking at Hollywood as an art, as an industry, and as a way of life, Knepper indicted it in the strongest possible terms, characterizing it as "a machine that turns out pseudo-art by formula and on schedule" (82). Such statements aligned Hollywood-as-art with a commercialized mass culture widely thought by intellectuals to be alienating and debased. At the same time, Hollywood-as-place increasingly appeared to be the product of a commercial culture that was prone to quick profit and a flair for the theatrical. Charges of immorality against Hollywood not only buttressed these arguments but served a conservative sexual politics that sought to punish women for career ambitions outside the domestic sphere. In any case, Hollywood was increasingly used to represent the worst features of cultural life under capitalism. Harry Alan Potamkin, a contributing editor to the *New Masses*, wrote in 1931:

> Hollywood is the pimple of the American process, just as America is the pimple of the capitalist process. The process in either case is at the terminal of an impasse. America is vested interest: Hollywood is vested interest. America is ultimate concentration: Hollywood is ultimate concentration. America is frustration: Hollywood is frustration. Hollywood is epitome.[40]

In the Hollywood fiction of the 1930s, complaints about the lives of lowly workers such as screen extras could easily metamorphose into arguments about the mass culture of Hollywood and its colonization of the American psyche. The film capital became the dominant symbol for a condition of cultural crisis and decline, a metaphor for the pathology of mass culture.

THE EXTRA IN HOLLYWOOD FICTION

Literary representations of the Hollywood extra in the 1920s and 1930s served several, often conflicting, cultural purposes. To begin with, they articulated a conservative sexual politics that saw Hollywood as a symbol of the New Woman's emancipation from the domestic sphere and of her desire to pursue career ambitions and compete with men in the workplace. For the extra, as for the star, the drive to work in films and to pursue a career in Hollywood had to be punished. These texts were offered as explicit warnings, fictions charged with the social task of discouraging young women from coming to Hollywood. The Hollywood extra, like the star, became a figure representative of changing social and sexual values and dramatized a rejection of traditional gender roles.

The price of such rebellion was often quite high, as revealed in a series of short stories that dealt with the tragic fates of extra-girls, written by Adela Rogers St. Johns and entitled *The Port of Missing Girls*. The stories appeared monthly in *Photoplay* from March to August of 1927.[41] Each one chronicled the failure of a different Hollywood hopeful—for, as St. Johns wrote, "The story of success is always the same. There is only one story of success. But the story of every failure is different. The one who succeeds wears jewels and rides in a Rolls Royce and her face is a trademark. What becomes of the rest of the ten thousand?"[42]

St. Johns set out to individualize the social phenomenon of "going Hollywood" through a series of fictional cases studies, yet at the same time the central character of each story was held up as a representative figure, a device for the depiction of a social problem larger than the failure of a single individual. St. Johns clearly intended her stories to be taken as "warnings . . . to turn back the hordes of unwelcome, unwanted movie-mad young things" (28) who had been drawn to "Hollywood, Land of Promise, Port of Missing Girls" (30–31). Although the details of background and motivation varied from story to story, the basic narrative pattern was the same. In "Paula," the fourth installment, a beautiful young wife leaves her devoted and simple husband and goes to Hollywood to pursue a career in pictures. Despite her landlady's dismal reaction when she reveals her plans to work at the studios ("God pity you," she remarks), Paula begins her stay in Hollywood with high hopes: "Fame—fortune—romance—adventure—she had come to the land of all these things" (134). Initially Paula believes she has arrived at the Hollywood of cultural myth, yet her inability to find work leads her to doubt. She is courted for a time by a handsome Hollywood leading man, but when she refuses his sexual advances the relationship ends. He tells her, "You've kidded me just about as long as I can be kidded. After all, this is Hollywood—and there are a lot of other beautiful women around" (134). The prostitution motif—which I have argued is a dominant theme in Hollywood fiction—is evident in Paula's reaction, which is to plunge into a series of ill-considered relationships with "a young producer, a very famous Western star, an extremely clever exploitation man, and a scenario writer" (135), all of which, she hopes, will eventually lead to a chance at screen work. (St. Johns's placement of the screenwriter at the end of the list is an undoubtedly ironic comment on the position of the writer in Hollywood.) Finally Paula is forced to confront the reality of her situation when the landlady, herself a former movie star now running a boarding house, advises her that she hasn't a chance in Hollywood. "The market's glutted. I know you're beautiful. What of it? . . . Besides you're too old. . . . Nope, beauty is a drug on the market. So are women—as women. You can't sell yourself in Hollywood. Get that. What the deuce do men want to buy what they can get for nothing every day of the week?" (135–36).

St. Johns's *Port of Missing Girls* stories present Hollywood as operating under a crude system of power relationships based on sexual threat and open contempt for women "as women." And in every case St. Johns offers a domestic solution to the moral and career crises faced by her characters. Paula is rescued by a surprise visit from her husband as she contemplates her failure on a lonely Christmas Eve. With the family reunited and safely under patriarchal protection—and control—once again, St. Johns leaves the reader with the observation that Paula "had never looked so beautiful" (137), her restored physical appearance underscoring the rightness of her renewed domesticity.

A similarly conservative sexual politics is evident in Stella Perry's 1929 Hollywood novel *Extra-Girl*.[43] This grim account of Hollywood disillusionment and failure recounts the experiences of Odile Vaure, a beauty contest winner from Louisiana who develops a romantic obsession with the handsome star Vance Murdock and runs away from family and fiancé to pursue a career in Hollywood. Odile is in some respects a female Merton Gill, inspired more by romantic ideals than by career ambitions, and protected by her strict religious upbringing from the most obvious moral dangers she encounters in the film capital. Still, nothing in her previous experience prepares her for what she encounters in Hollywood, a place where "everyone warned her against something" (53).

For Perry, as for Sherwood and for many who came before and after them, Hollywood represented a paradoxical yoking of opposites, an unstable amalgam of characteristics existing in tension and conflict. For her this was the paradox of Hollywood.

> For there are two, two distinct cities, occupying the same space at the same time, yet never meeting. . . . There is the Hollywood of ideal family life, of protected youth, youth as happy, as safe, as healthy and as fair as anywhere in the world. . . . And there is the Hollywood of youth betrayed, distorted, unnatural, wretchedly brave, gallantly wicked, lonely, hungry, flagrantly daring, or hidden in bluffs and shams, of youth dying on its feet. (39–40)

In this description two mythic versions of Hollywood are set side by side. The first is the healthful "Hollywood" of the studio publicity departments and Chamber of Commerce boosters, who were engaged in a continuous struggle to limit and contain the second, more potent version of the myth— "Hollywood" the devourer of youth and destroyer of dreams. As we have seen, this fundamental dichotomy characterized the cultural arguments that swirled around the film capital in the 1920s and 1930s, and Perry's novel clearly rides these oscillating currents of fascination and fear. "What a strange world!" she wrote, "All this beauty. All the imagination and romance and glory. And all the shame and horror" (91). As it progresses, her novel clearly lends more credence to the latter view, providing literary support for Hollywood's increasingly dark image as "a strange, weird land with indeterminate standards" (282), which the character Odile must attempt to understand and negotiate.

First Odile must accommodate herself to the atmosphere of casual intimacy and cynical resignation that she encounters among the extra-girls with whom she lives. At the parties they take her to, she experiences firsthand Hollywood's climate of sexual expectation and threat, "the pawings and pettings and hectic romances that the unnatural life of the pictures seemed to breed" (68). Odile is able to keep herself out of the sexual carnival that surrounds her, but her friends are not so fortunate: one is raped after a drunken party and then blackmails her attacker, a film executive, into securing a job for her in the scenario department; another, unable to find work and sinking deeper and deeper into poverty, agrees to live with a male extra in order to share expenses, but soon finds herself pregnant and unmarried. Odile's closest friend, Juana Brady, becomes addicted to narcotics under the influence of a sinister assistant producer who uses his supply of drugs to extort sexual favors from her. Unable to free herself from his control, Juana finally kills him and then commits suicide by driving her car over a cliff. For these characters, "going Hollywood" leads only to degradation, exploitation, and death.

Second, Odile is forced to recognize her own inadequacy as an actress and to confront the difficulty of breaking in to the movies as a raw beginner. The novel pays particular attention to the economic insecurities of film work, the boom-and-bust cycles of work and retrenchment at the studios that play havoc with the extras' fragile financial situation (148–50). On more than one occasion, Odile finds herself nearly destitute—a terrifying predicament in that the physical signs of poverty can make it even more difficult for her to find work at the studios. She suffers constant anxiety over her appearance: "Had she begun to look hungry, shabby again?" (154). Her fears are reflected in the desperate efforts of the other extras to keep up appearances. "It was pitiful to walk along the bright Boulevard, seeing them hail one another, so merry and hopeful on the surface, so haunted and frightened back in their eyes" (155). Exploding the Hollywood myth of fame and fortune, the novel presents movie extras as driven, frightened individuals, clinging to their hopes and dreams, which day by day become less tangible as the hard economic realities of life in Hollywood become more apparent. In one scene, Odile observes a young mother dragging her sick child to a studio casting call, and the mingled desperation, fear, and ambition of the people around her become starkly apparent.

> She was seeing with a strange clarity to-day. She could read all these people now, though they all wore the same mask of self-satisfaction. She could place those thanking God for this day's work, these in desperate need hoping to find it, those "well-heeled" taking the game easily, these ambitious dreamers, those in whom dreams and ambitions had died—just let them make a living now!—those who were getting on, those who were letting go. (186)

It is a vision of Hollywood that reveals in cross section the wild hopes of success and the chilling nightmares of failure that jostled one another in the indifferent economic world of American life for which the film capital had become a dominant symbol.

Finally Odile must confront her own romantic illusions, focused upon the handsome leading man Vance Murdock. After the two have a chance encounter at the beach, the thrice-married Murdock pursues Odile. She submits to his attentions only as long as they appear to be motivated by friendship and a shared devotion to the art of motion pictures. This "platonic" affair becomes an extraordinarily complex interplay of desires and misrecognitions: Odile is in love with Murdock's screen persona, a very different sort of person than he actually is but a role he is easily able to play if the situation requires; moreover, Murdock often flatters himself by confusing his screen image with his offscreen life. He grows increasingly infatuated with Odile's innocent "home-girl" qualities and becomes dependent upon her emotionally while at the same time pursuing a destructive sexual relationship with a former child star. Eventually Odile's emotional strength and loyalty cause Murdock to see her as a mother figure, which makes his attempted rape of her appear monstrously incestuous. Gradually Odile comes to recognize Murdock's infantile and depraved character; his crude attempt at seduction, which violates the terms upon which she has allowed their relationship to continue, means "the end of her romantic dream, the dream that had brought her to Hollywood" (257). The shattering of her romantic illusions about Murdock are clearly linked to her growing disillusionment with Hollywood itself, and spring from a painful awareness of the discrepancy between the romantic myth of Hollywood and the actual conditions of life endured by those struggling on the edge of the film industry.

This realization leads Odile to turn her back on Hollywood and embrace the domestic role of wife and mother. She marries a humble publicity agent who has been quietly protecting her from the start, and she abandons her career in order to inhabit "the *other* Hollywood: The one I've always loved. Where the real little homes are. And the real little hopes. And the real little people" (295). Renouncing her excessively romantic desires, which are tied to the romantic myth of Hollywood, Odile embraces the more modest pleasures to be found on "the Street of Babies," the novel's image of domestic fulfillment. The book's culturally conservative admonition was for young women to stay home, get married, and have children rather than pursue an ideal image of themselves as rich, glamorous, and beautiful—an image that was shaped by fan magazines and movies and by powerful but illusory cultural myths about Hollywood.

This ideal image was also about women taking control of their lives by choosing a career independent of marriage. In this respect the narrative of the Hollywood extra could be social criticism that, even as it condemned predatory male sexual behavior in the film industry, attempted to restore and buttress patriarchal control over women. A similar move was repeated in works such as Haynes Lubou's *Reckless Hollywood* (1932) and Donald Henderson Clarke's *Alabam'* (1934), novels that attempted to expose the dangers of "going Hollywood" in the name of a fundamentally conservative sexual politics.

THE COMIC HOLLYWOOD NOVEL

A social and cultural phenomenon on the scale of the national exodus to Hollywood in the 1920s and 1930s was bound to produce a variety of cultural responses, and inevitably the experience of "going Hollywood" was given a comic treatment in a series of popular novels and short stories. As we saw with Wilson's *Merton of the Movies*, the comic Hollywood novel invited readers to laugh at the naive ambitions and romantic fantasies of movie hopefuls even while it appealed to the reader's curiosity about life in Hollywood. In novels such as Homer Croy's *Headed for Hollywood* (1932),

147

Richard Henry Lee's *Nights and Daze in Hollywood* (1934), and Phil Stong's *The Farmer in the Dell* (1935), the film capital's increasingly dark cultural image was partially brightened by the humorous experiences of characters who, unequipped for life in the film capital, made their way through Hollywood's shams and excesses in a series of comic misadventures. The comic Hollywood novel was a satiric attack on the movie industry and the social customs of the film capital, yet its implicitly critical stance was often mitigated by a comedic narrative structure that always ended in marriage for the central character. In this case the domestic sphere was offered not just as an alternative to Hollywood immorality but as an appealing way out for characters who were obviously not talented or attractive enough to make it in the movie business.

An excellent example of the comic Hollywood novel is J. P. McEvoy's *Hollywood Girl* (1929), a brilliant satire of Hollywood during its transition to talking pictures. McEvoy, a syndicated newspaper columnist, utilized an innovative narrative style in which the plot is advanced exclusively through a series of documents, which include telegrams, letters, press releases, newspaper articles, headlines, interoffice memos, diary entries, advertisements, song lyrics, and motion-picture scenarios. The typefaces and page layouts are varied accordingly, and photographs are introduced into the text as well. The complex interweaving of discursive forms and genres make McEvoy's novel a fascinating cultural artifact, highly evocative of the period and the novel's show-business milieu.

Hollywood Girl is a sequel to McEvoy's *Showgirl* (1928), which introduced the central character Dixie Dugan, a wisecracking Broadway chorine with mercenary designs toward men. The lives of chorus girls and the colorful Broadway habitués that populate McEvoy's fiction are subjects that he apparently knew intimately, having worked as a writer for the Ziegfeld Follies in the 1920s. Both novels were made into motion pictures, with *Hollywood Girl* becoming *Showgirl in Hollywood* when Warner Brothers released it in 1930 to capitalize on the already well-known first novel.

Dixie Dugan proved to be an extraordinarily popular character with Depression audiences and was spun off into a popular syndicated comic strip that lasted into the 1960s.[44] In some respects she is a version of the "blonde goddess"—a beautiful and ambitious young woman who uses her sexual charms to control the men around her and to advance her career, a gold digger" and "professional lady" in the same vein as Anita Loos's famous heroine Lorelei Lee in her best-selling novel *Gentlemen Prefer Blondes* (1925).

In *Hollywood Girl*, Dixie leaves Broadway for the West Coast after she is tested by the Colossal Film Corporation at its Astoria studio. The test is the result of an encounter with a Hollywood director, who immediately begins to plot his seduction of her. Yet Dixie is already the object of romantic interest for two other characters: Jimmy Doyle, an unemployed writer, and Jack Milton, a Wall Street banker. Doyle is Dixie's real love, and the novel makes use of his experiences in Hollywood to lampoon the film industry's treatment of writers. But on her way to California Dixie renounces all of her suitors— "To hell with love anyway, I'm going in for a career"[45]—a decision that aligns her with the modern social and sexual freedoms that were becoming available to women in the 1920s, and that displays her frank contempt for men.

Once in Hollywood, Dixie finds that she cannot advance her career unless she submits to the sexual demands of a studio producer. In a compelling stream-of-consciousness diary entry, she describes the fear and despair of young women starving in Hollywood while they await opportunities that are always tied to their willingness to "play ball" sexually.

> my God do I have to be mauled and muzzled over by every man I go out with I'll go for a little of that all in fun but give in baby why should I just to have an option renewed. . . . its a lousy business well life is a lousy business just like the movies it's just a long talking movie that's all with a lot of sound and effects and love is just a big gag. . . . now a girl stays in one of these little furnished apartments with a bed that goes up in the wall and the bear comes along and says hello baby how would you like to go into movies . . . wouldn't you love to be a star . . . wouldn't you love to have a great big house with a big garden and swimming pool. . . . I love the feel of your skin darling. . . . you came out here from New York thinking you were going to knock 'em dead in the movies and where are you. . . . they're not going to call me they're not going to take up my option oh my God. (83–89)

This section of the novel, written in a hallucinatory first person, expresses Dixie's profound bitterness toward both Hollywood and the mass culture of the movies, with their simplistic formula romances and happy endings.

Dixie's experiences in Hollywood lead to a cynical, hard-boiled attitude toward the film industry, which is reinforced through her friendship with a disillusioned former star, Hedda Natchova, one of the book's most memorable creations. Like Norma Desmond in Billy Wilder's film *Sunset Boulevard* (1950), Hedda is planning a comeback picture from the lonely isolation of her "big empty shell of a house on Beverly Hills." Hedda befriends the newcomer Dixie and cautions her about the pervasive atmosphere of illusion and falsehood in Hollywood. "It's all make believe out here and make believe is lying. You get so used to working in lies you never notice when you're living them" (125).

For Hedda, the difference between her former glory days as one of Hollywood's reigning stars and her present fallen state becomes a reminder of failure too painful to live with, and she finally leaps to her death from the window of an apartment building during a Hollywood party. McEvoy uses the event to dramatize a fundamental fact of life in Hollywood: its indifference to the past and to those who have slipped out of the spotlight of publicity and fame. Hedda's literal fall to her death is matched by the falling importance of her death as a news item, as reflected in a series of headlines that begins with a noon edition, where it is the top story ("HEDDA NATCHOVA DIES IN HOLLYWOOD ORGY"), and ends with the five-o'clock edition, where it has become a small item on page 28, under the heading "Ex-Movie Star Dead" (150).

Dixie's fortunes begin to change after Colossal Films undergoes a Wall Street merger that places her longtime admirer Jack Milton in charge of the studio. Dixie gladly accepts his patronage, and he begins to use his considerable influence to win choice parts for her, including Hedda's role in the film that the studio was planning as her comeback vehicle. Anticipating Max Knepper's criticism of film-industry favoritism in *Sodom and Gomorrah*, Dixie's Hollywood career takes off only after she agrees to marry Milton. With devastating irony, McEvoy presents the reader with the official account of Dixie's screen success, as reported in the *Hollywood Daily Screen World:* Dixie's advancement at the studio is offered as evidence that "true ability will always find its just reward out here in Hollywood, the real land of opportunity" (164).

When Dixie completes her first picture, the studio judges it a total flop. The film is finally released after retakes and a high-powered publicity campaign and it surprises everyone by becoming a box-office hit. Launched in a successful film career at last, Dixie has no illusions about herself or about how she managed to succeed in Hollywood. In a letter to her sister she writes candidly about her life there.

> There are at least fifty Hollywoods out here, Nita; the lowest one away down in the sub-basement next to the boilers and then one by one going up to the roof garden where the stars sit in rose lights and munch caviare and flip cigarette butts down on an adoring world. I've been tossing my share over the rail this last few weeks and boy how I love it. This is la vie. . . . How quick you go up in this business. And down too, I guess. (222–23)

From her position as a star, Dixie reflects grimly on the experiences of all those who come to Hollywood and fail to achieve success.

> Hard-faced mothers from all over the country dragging their little girls around to studios ready to sell them out to anyone from an assistant director to a property man just to make a little money off them. Agents with young girls tied up under long term contracts at a hundred a week leasing them to studios for ten times that and pocketing the difference. Hundreds of pretty kids from small towns, nice family girls, church girls, even society pets going broke and desperate, waiting tables, selling notions, peddling box lunches on the street corners—I could tell you stories that would curl your hair. (223–24)

By now it is evident that, despite the novel's hilarious depictions of film-industry waste and ineptitude as the studios struggled to convert to sound, there is an underlying seriousness to *Hollywood Girl*. It is apparent in passages like the preceding one, in which satiric attacks on Hollywood often lead in to expressions of concern about the social and moral implications of an industry that trafficks in youth and beauty.

For Dixie, success becomes a way out of Hollywood and out of the demanding routines of film work. After falling in love with a wealthy aviator, she breaks her contract and leaves Hollywood to become his wife. Far from being a retreat into domesticity, her marriage promises a continuation of the life of luxury and fame that Hollywood has given her, and thus must be read not as a closing off of romantic and pecuniary opportunities but rather of their fuller realization: her marriage provides her with a new and more promising role to play. In McEvoy's novel Hollywood becomes merely a stepping stone in Dixie's career, providing her—as well as the reader—with a glimpse into the dark world of Hollywood failure and success. One of the funniest books about Hollywood, *Hollywood Girl* is also one of the most caustic portraits of the film industry ever penned.

THEY SHOOT HORSES, DON'T THEY?

In the 1930s a series of literary works appeared that offered a vision of Hollywood and southern California colored by an almost metaphysical sense of pessimism and despair. In novels such as James M. Cain's *The Postman Always Rings Twice* (1934), Horace McCoy's *They Shoot Horses, Don't They?* (1934), Richard Hallas's *You Play the Black and the Red Comes Up* (1938), John O'Hara's *Hope of Heaven* (1938), and Nathanael West's *The Day of the Locust* (1939), Los Angeles became a symbolic stage upon which to enact the tragic collision of hope and failure in American life, an event that led, with fatalistic inevitability, to violence and death. Living and writing in Los Angeles, often as employees of film studios, and sharing a stylistic tendency for terse, episodic narratives and an idiomatic, first-person prose, these writers took on the appearance of a regional "school." They were all included in Edmund Wilson's *The Boys in the Back Room*, an important study of contemporary California novelists published in 1941. There can be no doubt that these men were all "serious" writers, and one consequence was that their work never reached the mass audience enjoyed by, say, Harry Leon Wilson or Adela Rogers St. Johns. (Indeed, the two authors I will consider, Horace McCoy and Nathanael West, were initially conspicuous failures in the mass market of American book publishing.)

These novels condensed and refined Hollywood's cultural myths through a highly stylized approach to plot and characterization. With stark economy of narrative, they present individuals who are being swept along by currents of expectation and desire that often originated in the mass culture of fan magazines and movies. Ultimately the characters find themselves trapped in dead-end jobs or destructive relationships, which are indicative of larger social contradictions and moral uncertainties. Reflecting the seedy unrealities of life on the fringes of the film industry, these texts became the definitive literary expressions of the region's dark cultural identity. In Cain's novel, *The Postman Always Rings Twice*, for example, it is Hollywood that first brings Cora to California and establishes the narrative pattern whereby ambition inevitably leads to hopelessness for her. "I won a beauty contest. I won a high school beauty contest, in Des Moines. That's where I lived. The prize was a trip to Hollywood. I got off the Chief with fifteen guys taking my picture, and two weeks later I was in the hash house."[46]

The theme here is a familiar one, as we have seen, yet in the treatment it received from writers such as Cain, McCoy, and West it acquired a depth of significance capable of lifting it to the level of philosophical argument. In their works, Hollywood was not the golden land of opportunity but a place marked by disillusionment and despair. The Hollywood fiction of Horace McCoy, in particular, went far beyond the standard critiques of the film industry to become works of existential protest. In *They Shoot Horses, Don't They?* (1934), the struggle of two Hollywood extras to survive the physical and spiritual degradations of a dance marathon becomes a symbol of existential crisis within a fallen modern world ruled by corrupt commercial forces.[47]

McCoy borrowed heavily from his own Hollywood experiences in writing *They Shoot Horses*. Following stints as a reporter and as an actor in a local theater company in Dallas, Texas, McCoy went to Hollywood in 1931 when an MGM talent scout offered him a screen test.[48] For a year or two he struggled along as an extra, experiencing firsthand the conditions of life in Hollywood during the Depression—a place he referred to in his third novel, *I Should Have Stayed Home* (1938), as "the most terrifying town in the world."[49] At one point he even worked as a bouncer at a marathon dance contest,[50] an experience that became the subject of a short story and then of his first novel, *They Shoot Horses, Don't They?* McCoy finally realized that he could make a better living in Hollywood as a writer. Even before he had left Dallas, he had begun to publish stories in the pulp magazine *Black Mask*, which specialized in the "hard-boiled" detective fiction of Dashiell Hammett and Raymond Chandler.[51] Writing for the pulps, McCoy learned the "cinematic" style of objective realism—with its emphasis on character delineated through violent action and terse dialogue—which became the hallmark of American crime fiction in the 1930s and 1940s. By the end of his life in 1955, McCoy had published only five novels, yet he had received screen credit for nearly fifty films as the result of a long career as a Hollywood screenwriter.[52]

In *They Shoot Horses, Don't They?* two unemployed extras, Robert and Gloria, meet by accident and decide to enter a marathon dance contest, where they are promised "free food and free bed as long as you last and a thousand dollars if you win."[53] Robert, from whose first-person viewpoint the novel unfolds, is a strangely detached and simple person, prone to fantasy and a naive optimism. He has come to Hollywood from Arkansas harboring dreams of becoming a director, and his hopes of breaking out of extra work and finding success contrast sharply with Gloria's cynicism and despair, which are at the center of the novel.

Like McCoy himself, Gloria comes to Hollywood from Dallas, Texas, fleeing a life of sexual abuse that already led her to attempt suicide. In fact, it is while she is recovering in the hospital that she begins to read movie magazines and decides to hitchhike to Los Angeles. In a brief exposition we learn that, after a year in Hollywood, Gloria has managed to find work in only four pictures, in part because Central Casting refuses to register her. Robert immediately sums up her shortcomings: "I could see why Gloria didn't get registered by Central. She was too blonde and too small and looked too old" (20). Yet she clutches at the possibility of success. When Robert asks her, "Why don't you quit the movies?," she replies, "Why should I? I may get to be a star overnight" (23). The marathon becomes her last hope. "A lot of producers and directors go to those marathon dances. There's always the chance they might pick you out and give you a start in a picture . . ." (24). Despite these halfhearted declarations of hope, Gloria's experiences in Hollywood leave her thoroughly embittered, and her anger and cynicism are aimed particularly at the sexual exploitation she has endured. Early in the novel she comments on the sexual favors required of extras in order for them to get ahead in the film industry, and the sexual inversion she describes seems intended to underscore Hollywood's depravity: "I don't know whether the men stars can help me as much as the women stars. From what I've seen lately I've about made up my mind that I've been letting the wrong sex try to make me . . ." (22). Later, she expresses her outrage even more forcefully. "'This motion picture business is a lousy business,' she said. 'You have to meet people you don't want to meet and you have to be nice to people whose guts you hate'" (113). In McCoy's Hollywood, the practice of sexual barter represents an essential fact of life sanctioned by a corrupt film industry. "The hell with pictures," Gloria finally concludes, "I wish I was dead" (103).

The police finally close the marathon following a shooting in which Mrs. Layden, a member of the audience, is killed by a stray bullet fired during a brawl. In Mrs. Layden, McCoy offered a frightening example of Holly-wood's mass audience. She ingratiates herself with Robert and Gloria through small favors and by securing a sponsor for them, but her smother-ing, maternal attitude toward the couple turns sinister when she proposes to Robert that he abandon Gloria and leave the contest in order to live with and be supported by her. The sexual nature of the proposal is implicit yet inescapable. *They Shoot Horses, Don't They?* deploys the sexual subtext of prostitution—almost a generic marker in Hollywood fiction—as a meta-phor for the relationship of the mass audience to popular culture, which is based on a similar exchange of money for pleasure. The monstrous Mrs. Layden becomes a figure of horrifying and unnatural desire, and she embodies the vicarious and highly eroticized relationship of the mass audience to media spectacle. Her death, which is depicted graphically in the novel, is at once an act of senseless, random violence and a ritual sacrifice to the destructive desires of the crowd.

After the contest ends, Gloria and Robert walk out on the pier, from which they can see the glittering lights of the movie stars' homes at Malibu. The contrast of their own lives with those of the stars, so near yet so remote, produces a devastating sense of irony. "Always tomorrow," Gloria muses, "The big break is always coming tomorrow." In a final gesture of defiance she asks Robert to "pinch-hit for God" and kill her by shooting her with a small pistol she produces from her purse, saying, "It's the only way to get me out of my misery" (127). Recalling a childhood memory in which his grandfather was compelled to kill an injured horse, Robert, whose reason-ing is muddled by exhaustion, complies with Gloria's request, and later he explains what has happened to the police officers who arrest him by repeating, "They shoot horses, don't they?"

McCoy utilized an experimental narrative form in the novel by presenting the story in flashbacks interpolated by the words of the judge at the moment of Robert's sentencing for Gloria's death. In progressively larger type we see the legal formula of the death sentence unroll inexorably within the interstices between chapters, in an overall narrative structure that, as one critic observed, "sacrifices suspense for inevitability."[54] The headlinelike graphic quality of these interstitial passages evokes what McCoy's most perceptive critic, Thomas Sturak, has characterized as "the tabloid sordidness of the subject matter." And, as Sturak observes, by beginning and ending with Gloria's death, the novel achieves a pattern of "circular movement permeating the story on all levels,"[55] which formally reproduces the rotations of the dancers around the floor in McCoy's Hollywood dance of death. Before Robert shoots her, Gloria remarks, "I'm going to get off this merry-go-round. . . . I'm through with the whole stinking thing" (125).

In revising an earlier short-story treatment of *They Shoot Horses*, McCoy apparently removed from the text the most topical social references to "breadlines" and the lives of "people who work in factories"[56] in order to pursue a more philosophical and symbolic approach in the work. In this regard, the marathon dance contest becomes the text's organizing trope, a Sisyphean metaphor for meaningless recurrence set against the backdrop of an indifferent social world within which we glimpse the sordid and pathetic lives of the contestants. The marathon is at once a tawdry human spectacle and a stage for ritual sacrifice and mythic drama, in which the brutal dehumanization of the contestants serves the crassly commercial interests of the contest's organizers as well as the voyeuristic "human" interests of the fans.

The marathon is also inescapably, a figure for Hollywood itself, a site of amusement and dissipation for the "Hollywood crowd," which McCoy populated with a number of actual celebrities: Alice Faye, Ruby Keeler, Charlie Chase, William Boyd, Ken Murray. The whirling image of the marathon and, especially, the grueling combats of the "derbies"—in which each night the losing couple is eliminated from the contest—suggest the desperate struggle for fame and fortune in Hollywood, and the vicious and cruel nature of the competition. The marathon also parodies the debased forms of entertainment offered by Hollywood movies, which were built on a similar formula of spectacle and publicity, and thus it implicitly calls into question the values of mass culture. At one point the contest's managers arrange a wedding between two contestants, which McCoy stages as a degraded ritual celebration of consumerism, in that the ceremony becomes a prolonged advertisement for the businesses that have sponsored the event. The huge dance hall, along with the corrupt social world it represents, perches precariously on the shore of the Pacific Ocean, where the incessant motion of the waves comes to signify the presence of an implacable and indifferent Nature.

Admirers of McCoy's novel did not overlook its existential implications, particularly in France, where McCoy was lionized as an American writer of the first rank.[57] Unlike Robert, who seems capable of drifting along quite happily, buoyed only by his improbable fantasies of becoming "the greatest director in the world,"[58] Gloria faces her dilemma with grim resignation and, like a true existentialist hero, refuses to live a life of degradation and diminishing expectations. At times she displays a cosmic sense of her predicament ("I get razzed by an expert. God razzes me . . ." [48]). And in the final moments of her life she seems possessed of a devastating self-awareness, the profundity of which is concealed by McCoy's laconic dialogue. Staring down the shoreline toward Malibu, she remarks, "Oh, what's the use in me kidding myself. . . . I know where I stand" (125); moments later she is dead. In this deeply symbolic novel, McCoy effectively combined a critical portrait of life in Hollywood with a philosophical meditation on human existence, and in so doing he created a work that contributed immensely to Hollywood's increasingly dark literary image.

THE DAY OF THE LOCUST

Nathanael West was one of the many writers who were lured to Hollywood by the promise of steady employment and high salaries in the motion-picture industry after the introduction of sound. Along with F. Scott Fitzgerald, William Faulkner, Dorothy Parker, and Lillian Hellman, West found himself seduced by Hollywood, despite the fact that it seems to have represented for him the epitome of ersatz American culture. In Hollywood, West found a modicum of financial security at a time when his fiction was failing to attract any interest outside of a handful of sympathetic critics and fellow writers. More important, he discovered in Hollywood a key to his ongoing interest in the mass dreams and collective fantasies of the American psyche.

By aesthetic creed a literary modernist, West found himself repeatedly drawn to the materials of popular culture as a way of understanding and representing the predicament of modern life. His modernism—exemplified by his pessimism, his heightened sense of the grotesque, the episodic, fragmentary structure of his narratives, and his carefully crafted, imagistic use of language—is only superficially at odds with his interest in the varieties of cultural expression that proliferated in the burgeoning mass media of the early twentieth century. In a series of brilliant antinovels written throughout the 1930s, West portrayed the tortured inner lives of characters dominated by mass culture, exploring the collective dreams and fantasies of a society on the brink of collapse and exposing the monstrous contradictions and violent impulses at the core of American life.[59] He specialized in an ironic fiction constructed equally upon a cynical, black-comic vision of the world and a profoundly sympathetic understanding of the desperation and pain at the center of modern existence.

For West, Hollywood became the symbol of a mass culture that functioned as both a source of collective fantasy and an instrument of deception and control.[60] All his works explored how human hopes and aspirations, the narrative and aesthetic formulas through which we impose a semblance of meaning on the contingencies of experience, were increasingly derived from a mass culture that offered mere escape and illusion—the false optimism of the *happy ending*. As he wrote in *Miss Lonelyhearts* (1933), "Men have always fought their misery with dreams. Although dreams were once power-full, they have been made puerile by the movies, radio, and newspapers. Among many betrayals, this one is the worst."[61]

The "movies, radio, and newspapers," the dominant mass media of the first half of the century, were the primary instruments of the "business of dreams" against which West railed in all of his fiction. His works persistently expose the tissue of lies and false expectations, fostered by mass culture, that infect his characters' lives. Yet he also recognized the necessity of dreams in the face of a real world filled with human suffering. As he wrote in *The Day of the Locust*, "Any dream was better than no dream and beggars couldn't be choosers."[62] It is the discrepancy between people's lives and their threadbare and fragmentary collective dreams that is the source of the bitterness and violence in all of West's novels.

West first traveled to Hollywood in 1933, after the publication of *Miss Lonelyhearts*, when he accepted an offer from Columbia Pictures to write an original screenplay. He remained less than six months, working on a variety of projects, none of which was ever to see production.[63] In 1935 West again went to Los Angeles, seeking employment as a writer. This time he was to stay until his death in 1940. His first year in Hollywood was marked by unemployment, poverty, and illness, and it was during this time that he first encountered the seedy settings and grotesque, marginal characters that would populate his Hollywood novel—his last published work—*The Day of the Locust*.

Eventually West found steady employment with Republic Studios, famous for its low budgets and quickie production schedules, where he began to learn the techniques of writing for the movies. Many critics have commented on the differences between West's fiction and his screen writing. Jay Martin suggests that West "wrote his novels out of the imagination of personal and collective disaster, but his film scripts out of his imagination of fulfillment."[64] West grasped immediately that the mass dreams and collective fantasies that he had satirized in his novels found perfect expression in the movies, and that if he was to work as a screenwriter he would have to submerge his corrosive vision of America in the saccharine formulas of Hollywood fantasy. Throughout his career in Hollywood, West worked on B pictures, a situation he apparently preferred because such projects made few demands on his creative energies, allowing him to concentrate more fully on his fiction. Yet he approached screen writing with a conscientious, craftsmanlike attitude, and quickly became adept at the techniques of story construction and visualization that made for success in script writing. Eventually he developed a reputation for competence in the film industry, and he graduated to more prestigious studios such as Universal and RKO, where his salary increased, as did the budgets of the films he worked on.

By the time of his premature death in an automobile accident in 1940, West was a recognized Hollywood professional. As a novelist, however, he was a failure. *The Day of the Locust* was a commercial disaster for its publisher, Random House, and a personal defeat for West. It would be twenty years before West's fiction found its audience and the widespread critical acclaim that it so clearly deserved. Today West is widely recognized as one of the most important American writers of the twentieth century, yet his film work is largely forgotten, consigned to the "dream dump" of late-night television.

The Hollywood Metaphor

Los Angeles in the late 1930s provided West with a perfect metaphor for American mass culture. He conceived of the sprawling metropolis as a vast urban extension of the studio back lots, a place where the harsh realities of the Depression could be forgotten in the psychic jungle of cult religions or concealed behind a deceptive facade of architectural fantasy. In fact, the intermingling of illusion and reality in Hollywood is one of the central ideas in *The Day of the Locust.* We see it on the opening page with a description of a Napoleonic army that slowly dissolves into a procession of extras on their way to a sound stage. The movie studios and back lots represent for West a zone of shifting and indeterminate realities, where the presumably stable categories of fact and fantasy soften and melt into each other. And the artifice that the character Tod Hackett observes there finds a parallel in the larger social environment, in the homes and the dress of the people whom he sees on the street, with their "Tyrolean" hats and "miniature Rhine Castle" houses. In Hollywood, the business of illusion-making is not confined by the factory walls of the studios; it spills out into "real" life, where it is taken up as masquerade and facade.

West mounts his subversive vision of American mass culture on a cognitive level. It is a vision that suggests more than just an unsettling of the familiar and the conventional; it implies an erosion, an undermining of the capacity to make any meaningful distinction between the real and the unreal—Hollywood as *simulacrum.* In *The Day of the Locust,* West ushers us into a cultural fun house where what seems real is illusory; yet it is the illusions that are, in some sense, the true reality of Hollywood.

Representing this confusion are the bizarre "Hollywood churches" Tod visits. There the need to believe is deformed through gimmicks and esoteric mysticism into a search for an elusive happiness.

He visited the "Church of Christ, Physical" where holiness was attained through the constant use of chestweights and spring grips;

the "Church Invisible" where fortunes were told and the dead made to find lost objects; the "Tabernacle of the Third Coming" where a woman in male clothing preached the "Crusade Against Salt", and the "Temple Moderne" under whose glass and chromium roof "Brain-Breathing the Secret of the Aztecs" was taught.[65]

In the cult theologies of the Hollywood churches Tod encounters up close the only partially submerged rage of those who followed their dreams to Los Angeles only to find disillusionment. Their messianic fervor represents a final, desperate effort to realize the promises of community, of spiritual and emotional wholeness, that were snatched from them. These were the people who, as West put it, "had come to California to die" (10).

West's focus in *The Day of the Locust*, then, is not on the glamorous aspects of the Hollywood myth—those images of affluence and luxury that made it such an alluring idea in the popular imagination of the 1930s. Rather, he examines the figures on the fringes of the film industry—Faye and Harry Greener, Earl Shoop, Adore Loomis, subalterns in the Hollywood scheme—as well as the looming collective subject of the novel: the mob of movie fans, health faddists, and retired shopkeepers who came to California with their hopes for success and the good life. Through them—especially through their chief representative, Homer Simpson—West explored the fate of those who, throughout the 1930s, were drawn by the golden promises of life on the "fortunate coast" of southern California, and ended up in Hollywood hoping to find some meaning to life in the fleeting glimpse of a film star entering an elegant restaurant or the procession of celebrities at a movie premiere.

The social fact uncovered by West's novel is that, at a time when Hollywood was promoting an ethos of optimism and social fantasy—helping to shape the American dream in its own glamorous image—the conditions of life for most Americans permitted only a vicarious encounter with Hollywood affluence and fame. West went to considerable lengths to explode the idea of Hollywood as a "leisure utopia,"[66] in which the life-styles of the stars served as models of social and economic behavior for society at large. Instead he focused on the experience of those who watched the Hollywood party from outside the gates. Beneath the desire for vicarious experience in the lives of the stars, fueled by fan magazines and a diet of cinematic confections, West sensed the rumblings of envy and bitterness. It was in Hollywood that the whole apparatus of mass fantasy, the strings and wires that animated the dream life of the nation, were most visible and therefore most open to the resentment of those who had been seduced by them. In *The Day of the Locust*, West fashioned Hollywood into a hyperbolic cultural symbol, a metaphoric landscape of American life littered with the unkept promises of mass culture.

The Day of the Locust is a markedly decentered narrative, with Tod Hackett providing only a tenuous connecting presence around which the other characters revolve. In fact, characters in West's fiction rarely appear to be anything more than types. Lacking clearly developed social or psychological identities, they function as representations of collective experience, symbolic everymen, embodying ideas that reveal the tough intellectual core of West's work. His books, as Jay Martin argues, "are truly narratives of ideas,"[67] with characters subordinated to theme and symbol. Yet *The Day of the Locust* presents two possible exceptions to this rule in Tod Hackett and Homer Simpson, perhaps the most developed characters in West's oeuvre. Tod and Homer are linked in significant ways: they are both essentially outsiders and observers, and they bear a notable physical resemblance to each other. More important, the work is structurally divided between them until events draw them together in a dizzying plunge into chaos and violence.

Yet there are significant differences between the two characters, as well. Tod, an artist who has come to Hollywood from the Yale School of Fine Arts to work in the movies, represents a viewpoint much closer to West's own; he is from "back east" and exhibits a critical and aesthetic distance from Hollywood, which suggests that he is closer to the moral center of the book. For Tod, as for West, Hollywood is a rich source of material, and he channels both his fascination and his revulsion for what he finds there into his art. What he finds is a clue ("a painter's clue, that is—a clue in the form of a symbol")[68] to the cultural crisis that Hollywood represents. This symbolic understanding is embodied in his painting "The Burning of Los Angeles."

Homer, on the other hand, represents the limited capacity to understand his own alienation that characterizes "Mass Man." From Wayneville, Iowa, Homer is one of those who, in a desperate search for meaning beyond the empty routine of a dull life, has "come to California to die." His torment is specifically tied his sexual dysfunction. His midwestern moral prudery conceals dangerously repressed sexual urges, symbolized by his hands, monumental and clumsy, which appear to lead a separate life from the rest of his body. He submerges them in a basin of cold water to arouse them from the torpor of sleep, and then they begin to crawl about "like a pair of strange aquatic animals," he hides them in a towel. His disassociation from the gestural ties performed by his hands hints at the force of repression and denial with which he keeps his sexual impulses at bay.

For Homer, the vague romantic and sexual promises of mass culture find an ironic focus in Faye Greener, who takes him to movies and nightclubs. Faye gradually reduces Homer to masochistic submission, wielding a destructive erotic power over him. His sexual and romantic longings, as emasculated and drearily domestic as they are, find inevitable disillusionment with her, and the collapse of his fantasies pushes him finally into complete withdrawal, "uterine flight," a total psychological and physical retreat from the world.

Faye Greener comes to represent the empty promises and hollow fantasies of the mass culture offered by movies, and as such she is a central figure in West's Hollywood metaphor. James Light has observed that, "in her falseness, she suggests the whole Hollywood lie, and her promise, like that of the Hollywood dream-products, leads not to satisfaction, only to increased frustration."[69] An extra and occasional bit player in low-budget comedies, Faye dreams of being a Hollywood star. Her "odd mannerisms" and "elaborate gestures"[70] represent a compendium of celebrity tics culled from movie fan magazines. Like many of the novel's characters, she is a compulsive role player—all surface, studied and mannered, desperately striving to look and act the part she so eagerly wants to play. But in fact she projects only a cheap sexual allure. As Tod observes, "Her invitation wasn't to pleasure, but to struggle, hard and sharp, closer to murder than to love" (19), and on several occasions he fantasizes about raping her. The sexual tension that her presence provokes throughout the novel eventually leads to violence.

Yet, like those fascinated by the incoherent sexual dreams that she arouses, Faye is also in thrall to the mass fantasies of the movies. With Tod she shuffles through the ridiculously improbable stories that make up her "pack of dreams"—concoctions, equally, of her boredom and desire. These narratives, vague wish fulfillments and veiled sexual fantasies, represent debased cinematic versions of her longing for romance, glamour, and success. In Faye Greener the distance between Hollywood dreams and their reality finds its most poignant and most terrifying embodiment. She functions as a symbol both of the essential phoniness of the movies' mass fantasies and of the desperate need for them. For her, "any dream was better than no dream and beggars couldn't be choosers" (61).

Hollywood and Cultural Crisis

As well as embodying a confusion of reality and illusion, West's Hollywood signals a crisis of historical and cultural identity. In West's Hollywood, as David Fine has remarked, "the past is elsewhere; history is in the East."[71] Such critical responses are consistent with Los Angeles's cultural image in the 1930s as "a city with no past . . . like a man without a shadow, unable to demonstrate his own reality."[72] West encountered in Los Angeles a society that made a virtue not of tradition but of newness and novelty. For instance, through its melange of residential architectural styles, which West described, Los Angeles sought to fill the cultural vacuum produced by an absence of history with a sense of romance and fantasy derived from the movies. Architectural historian Charles Lockwood has noted that "architectural purity was not an important consideration in Los Angeles at the time. Nor has it ever been." Instead what mattered was "to achieve a romantic, faraway look, and most architects freely mixed different national, historic, and aesthetic styles on the same house to picturesque, often baffling effect."[73]

The fantastic architecture West shows us becomes a symptom of Hollywood's isolation from history and its distance from established cultural traditions and values. "Only dynamite," Tod muses, "would be of any use against the Mexican ranch houses, Samoan huts, Mediterranean villas, Egyptian and Japanese temples, Swiss chalets, Tudor cottages, and every possible combination of these styles"[74] that he observes in Hollywood. The cottage that Homer Simpson rents is described as "Spanish-Irish," and at one point Tod accompanies Homer and Faye to a nightclub that is built in the shape of a "lady's slipper." The houses described in the novel, like studio sets, are essentially cheap illusions, created from "plaster, lath, and paper." Like Hollywood itself, they represent the desires of people in flight from reality and cut off from the past. This pattern of architectural imagery in the novel suggests not only the need to dream but the spurious forms the dreams are made to assume.

In this respect the studios are only the most acute examples of a more pervasive cultural phenomenon—the impulse to make our dreams our reality by substituting a romanticized and fantastic imitation of the past for the hard realities of the present. It is significant that the films described as being in production on the National (West's fictional studio) lot have titles that suggest big-budget historical epics, such as "Manifest Destiny," "The Great Divide," and "Waterloo," for they point to Hollywood's confusion of history and fantasy.

In one of the most compelling episodes in the book, Tod wanders through the studio back lot, which comes to represent a recapitulation of human history. There, only fragments of the past are preserved in empty facades and half-constructed buildings; like Los Angeles's architectural landscape, the back lot is a hodgepodge of historical periods and styles. He skirts an artificial desert "continually being made larger by a fleet of trucks dumping white sand" (91). He pauses on the porch of the "Last Chance Saloon"; passing through its swinging doors, he enters onto a Parisian boulevard. He walks through a Romanesque courtyard and by a dilapidated Greek temple. As he pushes his way through the jungle of old sets, he sees "a bamboo stockade, an adobe fort, the wooden horse of Troy, a flight of baroque palace stairs that started in a bed of weeds and ended against the branches of an oak, part of the Fourteenth Street elevated station, a Dutch windmill, the bones of a dinosaur, the upper half of the Merimac, a corner of a Mayan temple" (92). It is an ironic vision of history, part museum, part junkyard, and completely in the service of illusion, as the occasional film work that he observes reminds us. And it is also a commentary on the fundamentally fragile nature of historical experience. As one of the central elements in West's Hollywood metaphor, the studio back lot is a symbolic space; it represents a crisis of historical identity and the failure to separate myth from reality within American culture, which is itself a kind of repository of different cultural traditions. The uncertainty and instability at the core of American historical identity reveal a profound anxiety about the

past and our relationship to it—an anxiety that has often led to the conflation of history and myth in the mass dreams of the movies.

More important, the back lot suggests the way in which our relationships
to both the past and present are mediated by mass culture. The objects Tod
stumbles over on the back lot are not authentic historical artifacts—genuine
physical connections to a real, historical past—but mock-ups, cheap props,
flimsy sets, the flotsam and jetsam of the mass fantasies produced by the
film industry. The back lot is the "final dumping ground" of American
culture, the "dream dump" of a culture industry that offers its audiences
an escape from history and from the oppression of the real through fantasies
capable of producing only mediated and inauthentic versions of self and
world. As such, its most salient feature is an artificiality so widespread it
seems to indicate a pervasive crisis of cultural authenticity and value.

The Day of the Locust presents an extremely dark, apocalyptic vision of
American mass culture, a vision that finds it purest expression in Tod's
painting. "The Burning of Los Angeles" is an allegory of cultural crisis, a
portrait of mob violence, which materializes at the end of the book in a riot
at (significantly) a Hollywood premiere. The riot is anticipated earlier in
the novel in another Hollywood setting: the huge set of Mount St. Jean on
which the studio recreates the battle of Waterloo. Here again West points
to the collapse of boundaries between reality and illusion, describing the
scene as if it were a real battle, with only occasional reminders of the
episode's profilmic context—such as an assistant director who repeatedly
rehearses the death of an extra. And when the huge set, which is unfinished,
collapses under the weight of the cast and crew, the scene takes on symbolic
significance. "It was the classic mistake, Tod realized, the same one Napoleon
had made. . . . The result had been disaster for the French; the beginning of
the end" (95).

West parallels the disaster on the Hollywood movie set with the historical
disaster of Waterloo, suggesting a larger historical context for the events of
the novel. Underlying this enlarged frame of reference is a notion of Hollywood as a symbol of American mass culture. In the novel, Hollywood
becomes our Waterloo, "the beginning of the end" for American civilization. The book's conclusion proposes this idea most dramatically.

The eruption of mob violence at a Hollywood premiere at the end of *The
Day of the Locust* is one of the great set pieces of twentieth-century American

literature. The scene ultimately goes beyond the conflicts of individual characters to explore the larger social and cultural contexts for violence with which the novel is concerned. "In America," West wrote, "violence is idiomatic,"[75] and in all of his novels violence is thematized as an essential aspect of American life. The riot in *The Day of the Locust* represents his most sustained treatment of that idea.

Here West confronts us once more with the terrible collective subject of the novel: "the cheated and betrayed" little people who await the arrival of the stars outside Kahn's Persian Palace, the novel's ultimate example of dream architecture. West presents a grim portrait of these "starers" who have come to Hollywood in search of their inflated dreams, only to find, once they arrive, that it cannot possibly support the weight of them. Disillusioned about life, they have become bitter and restless; disillusioned about the dreams that have sustained them, they become savage and brutal; and their disappointment finally finds release in aimless violence. West offers a scathing portrait of these people who followed the map to Hollywood in hopes of arriving at the dream.

> All their lives they had slaved at some kind of dull, heavy labor, behind desks and counters, in the fields and at tedious machines of all sorts, saving their pennies and dreaming of the leisure that would be theirs when they had enough. Finally the day came. They could draw a weekly income of ten or fifteen dollars. Where else should they go but California, the land of sunshine and oranges. Once there, they discover that sunshine isn't enough. They get tired of oranges, even of avocado pears and passion fruit. Nothing happens. They don't know what to do with their time. They haven't the mental equipment for leisure, the money nor the physical equipment for pleasure. Did they slave so long just to go to an occasional Iowa picnic? What else is there? They watch the waves come in at Venice. There wasn't any ocean where most of them came from, but after you've seen one wave, you've seen them all. The same is true of the aeroplanes at Glendale. If only a plane would crash once in a while so that they could watch the passengers being consumed in a "holocaust of flame," as the newspapers put it. But the planes never crashed. Their boredom becomes more and more terrible. They realize that they've been tricked and burn with

resentment. Every day of their lives they read the newspapers and went to the movies. Both fed them on lynchings, murder, sex, crimes, explosions, wrecks, love-nests, fires, miracles, revolutions, war. This daily diet made sophisticates of them. The sun is a joke. Oranges can't titillate their jaded palates. Nothing can ever be violent enough to make taut their slack minds and bodies. They have been cheated and betrayed. They have slaved and saved for nothing.[76]

Despite the crowd's pent-up rage, a grotesque carnival atmosphere spreads through the crush of bodies. Two stout women exchange sexual banter with the men who are pressed tightly against them by the crowd. Trapped within the swells and currents of the mob, Tod overhears one of the women say, "There was a rush and I was in the middle."

"Yeah. Somebody hollered, 'here comes Gary Cooper,' and then wham!"
"That ain't it," said a little man wearing a cloth cap and pullover sweater. "This is a riot you're in." (151)

At this moment the spectacle of mass entertainment is upstaged by the specter of mass violence and social upheaval. West's apocalyptic vision of Hollywood is summed up by this scene of mayhem and terror—a scene that reveals his anxieties about mass culture and its effects upon American life. The "little man wearing a cloth cap and pullover sweater" is a fitting emblem of Hollywood's mass audience, which has been made "savage and bitter" by "boredom and disappointment" (145). In Hollywood—the capital of illusion, the apotheosis of the American dream—West discovered a potent symbol for what he saw as the empty promises of mass culture. Indeed, the scene suggests a culmination of the concerns that pervade all of his novels; it is in the Hollywood riot that "Broad-shoulders," "Sick-of-it-all," and "Desperate," the socially marginalized and powerless in American life, throw down their burdens and seek a violent catharsis. The critique of Hollywood that West presents in this novel suggests a deep insight into the tensions and the contradictions that underlay American life and the mass culture of the 1930s.

In 1939, the year in which West's bitter Hollywood novel was published, the dream factory was at the height of its economic and cultural power. It was a year that film historians often single out as representing the pinnacle of Hollywood's creativity, the apotheosis of the studio system, and the high point of its influence on American society.[77] In the midst of this prosperity and success, West's novel sounded an extraordinarily dark and pessimistic note. Yet in many respects, *The Day of the Locust* was echoing fears about Hollywood and about the cultural influence of the movies that had been widespread since the early 1920s. After novels like *They Shoot Horses, Don't They?* and *The Day of the Locust*, it was difficult to be innocent about Hollywood's glamorous and romantic cultural identity, and the Hollywood fiction that followed reinforced and extended the film capital's negative image.

CHAPTER SIX

ONE THOUSAND DOLLARS A WEEK

Writers in Hollywood Fiction

Unfortunately the Hollywood environment was destructive to novelists. High earnings lulled them into complacence. Some unreality in the atmosphere, a lack of definition of seasons, too much sunshine, too few strong winds to blow alive the sense of frailty of man, the isolation and insulation drugged the senses and numbed the hard edge of purpose. Perhaps the hacks survived best, for Hollywood was their Kingdom of Heaven.

JESSE LASKY, JR.[1]

The figure of the Hollywood writer has long exemplified the fate of the artist in a commercialized mass culture. Working in the film industry, writers found their creative authority circumscribed in a production process that was both hierarchic and bureaucratic, and they seldom received the respect or legal protections that were afforded them as creative artists in the publishing and theatrical worlds. The studios denied them ownership and control over their work, forced collaboration and "writing by committee," and relegated most writers to only a preliminary importance in the creative process. But for all the controls and limitations that writers encountered in Hollywood they were usually very well paid, generally earning more money on a regular basis working for the studios than they ever could as novelists and playwrights, and the economic inducement was difficult to resist. Along with high salaries came the obvious appeals of life in Hollywood and southern California: the pleasant weather, the relatively low cost of living, the satisfaction of owning a comfortable home, and the diversion of working in an industry that was surrounded by an aura of glamour and social importance. "For writers, however, it is Hell, and it is Hell no less if their corner of it, as often happens, is very well run," observed James Cain in 1933.[2] His assessment was echoed by most writers of the period.

Plunged into an environment of swimming pools and starlets, where a life-style based on leisure and consumption was supported by the production of commercially successful films, the Hollywood writer became an emblem of artistic compromise, a well-paid studio "employee" whose artistic talents were expected to serve the company's goal of providing "entertainment" for a mass audience. The figure of the Hollywood writer was an individual divided by irreconcilable conflicts: with his artistic freedom threatened and his sense of cultural importance compromised by the conditions of his employment, he was torn by both a sense of injustice at his treatment by the film industry and guilt at his enjoyment of the good life that resulted from work in the studios—a tense dichotomy of responses indicative of the ambivalence that characterizes so many writers' attitudes toward Hollywood.[3]

Throughout most of the twentieth century Hollywood was an obligatory stopping point for writers, an encounter to be either celebrated or ridiculed by them in articles written for national magazines and in autobiographies, novels, and short stories. Popular conceptions of the Hollywood writer were shaped largely by Hollywood writers themselves, and as a group they were generally critical of the film industry and the movies it produced. But writers were also aware of and often quite excited by the artistic potentials of the medium, and thus for them the fundamental problem of working in Hollywood was often posed as a conflict between commerce and art. The novelist James Farrell observed this tension. "To the writer, the character of the work he does, the way he is employed, the continuous manner in which he is blocked from creating as an artist make it indubitably clear to him that the film is merchandise. But the fact is that the film is both merchandise and art. It is merchandise—a commodity—and it is also an artistic production."[4]

For most writers, the only certainty about working in motion pictures was the understanding that, as Raymond Chandler succinctly put it, "the cards are stacked against the writer." In the struggle between art and commerce that Hollywood came to represent, the inevitable victory of the commercial over the artistic became a leitmotif of writers' complaints. In Chandler's opinion, "the motion picture is a great industry as well as a defeated art."[5] He had little sympathy for the presumed victims of this cultural defeat—Hollywood writers. "They are, to put it bluntly, a pretty dreary lot of hacks, and most of them know it, and they take their kicks and their salaries and try to be reasonably grateful to an industry which permits them to live much more opulently than they could live anywhere else" (51).

The temptation to "sell out" to Hollywood became a crucial test of a writer's talents and personal integrity. Yet what was really under attack in Hollywood, as Richard Fine has shown in his book *West of Eden: Writers in Hollywood 1928–1940*, was not writers' artistic freedoms but rather traditional notions of authorship—which were being redefined within the mass culture of the movies. The significance of the Hollywood writer is that he was among the first cultural workers to experience the consequences of the fact that "the forces of large-scale industrial production at work in the studios were inevitably overwhelming the literary marketplace as well."[6] Hollywood was, in fact, the first clear indication of what mass culture would become; it showed how every aspect of social life could be addressed and influenced through the interlocking media of film, television, radio, and publishing, anticipating the total media "environment" of late-twentieth-century culture.

While the institutions of mass culture certainly recognize the value of the celebrity author from a marketing standpoint, they have shown little interest in preserving the notions of authorship and individual creative genius that long shaped Western ideas about writers and artists. The figure of the Hollywood writer provided one of the first clear indications of how alienating intellectual work could become under the industrial, profit-driven form of cultural production that the Hollywood studio system represented, and thus served to forecast the fate of the artist in the factory of mass culture.

THE HOLLYWOOD WRITER IN FACT AND MYTH

Many early films were produced without any sort of written script, based on a cameraman's or director's rough ideas or on last-minute inspirations during shooting. But by the turn of the century, motion pictures were clearly becoming a narrative art form, and films began to increase in length as their plots became more complex. With the rise of storefront movie theaters around 1905 and the increasing demand for films by audiences, motion-picture firms found it necessary to rationalize and standardize industry practices, and ensuring a steady supply of usable stories became a top priority for production companies. Initially it was the competition within the film industry and the increased need for efficiency and cost cutting in production of filmed narratives that created the need for writers. However, the first studio writing staffs found it difficult to produce a sufficient number of movie plots to meet the voracious needs of the film industry, and by 1908 companies had begun advertising in trade papers for stories and ideas, actively soliciting material from free-lance writers and amateurs. Such practices no doubt contributed to the gold-rush atmosphere of the fledgling movie business and prompted the early skepticism about the film industry among many professional writers.

Such practices could also have unforeseen consequences. As film historian Janet Staiger has noted, "by 1910, free-lancers were flooding the companies with short scripts, resulting in the appearance of manuals and trade advice on how to write the scripts so that they would fit studio requirements."[7] Such manuals and advice columns disseminated the basic pattern of the continuity script and thus served the film industry's need to standardize production of filmed narratives through the use of written scripts. The continuity script, a "blueprint for production," efficiently coor-dinated the activities of all the different workers involved in the making of a film. It thus served the interests of what Staiger has called a "standardized mass-production system" (34) by making all plots conform to a basic structural pattern, the narrative and stylistic features of which have come to be known as the "classical Hollywood cinema."[8] The technical requirements of the continuity script necessitated a knowledge of studio production practices, and both the scenario department and the position of story editor were developed to transform submitted stories into usable screen narratives. By the 1910s, writers were an indispensable component in film production.[9]

While studio scenario departments staggered under an avalanche of unsolicited and mostly unusable manuscripts throughout the teens, some companies approached the problem of supplying story material differently by inviting famous authors to adapt their work for motion pictures and by giving them the "star treatment." Hiring popular novelists and playwrights was one way of attracting the support of middle-class audiences, who were familiar with their works in print or on the stage and who would presumably now be curious to see them translated to the screen. This industry practice of linking motion pictures to the literary and dramatic arts helped to establish their cultural respectability. This was a period of fierce competition in the film business, and promoting movies as adaptations of works by famous authors was an important strategy in product differentiation. Advertising stressed to exhibitors the value of prior literary or dramatic successes; publicity could also be devoted to the author's unique contributions to the filming of his or her work.

The first grand experiment along such lines, and the event that signaled the beginning of the first great migratory wave of writing talent to Hollywood, was the formation of Eminent Authors Pictures by Samuel Goldwyn in 1919. The company's initial talent roster featured an impressive lineup of middle-brow authors, including Gertrude Atherton, Rex Beach, Rupert Hughes, and Mary Roberts Rinehart. Under the terms of the agreement, Goldwyn received a ninety-day option on their forthcoming works, and if a manuscript was selected for production the writer could receive "a $10,000 advance against one third of the film's earnings." As Ian Hamilton has noted in his book *Writers in Hollywood 1915–1951*, "this was real money, betokening a surprising confidence in the usefulness of literary talent."[10]

Yet, after they arrived in Hollywood, many of the "eminent authors" found themselves at odds with the studio over how their manuscripts should be handled, and they usually resented the "studio treatment" their work received. In particular, professional writers objected to the interference of the scenario department, whose task it was to transform every novel or play bought by the studio into a continuity script that would guide the film's production. Such a process never left a manuscript unaltered, and it placed authors in a situation where, as one writer complained, "others change your story, who are not experts at telling stories, and without your permission."[11] In fact, the liberties taken with their work by studio scenario departments were one of the writers' chief grievances. Rex Beach complained, "Until the photoplay producers . . . quit hiring hack scenario writers to plagiarize original writers' stuff, and hash it up as they now do, there will be no improvement in the quality of their material and they will continue to howl about bad business!"[12]

This distinction between "hack" studio writers and "serious" authors, who often worked in the studio for only a short period of time, became a crucial fact of life for writers in Hollywood, where salaries imposed a rigid caste system and the higher-paid visiting authors resented having their work modified, sometimes beyond recognition, by studio script writers who were generally considered little more than technicians. In Hollywood studios, writers of different grades and distinctions rubbed shoulders, sometimes amicably but often with suspicion and mistrust. Moreover, such divisions between writers served the companies' interests. As Staiger points out, "mere technicians need not be paid as much as story originators. Thus only certain writers were worth name-recognition as well as the monetary rewards that went with such billing."[13]

Many authors who worked in Hollywood shared widely held prejudices against motion pictures, which they regarded as a form of entertainment not worthy of serious consideration. Their cultural elitism was evident in their responses to the studio system and to the movies it produced. The novelist Joseph Hergesheimer, who was generally sympathetic toward the film industry, described the attitude of many writers toward the movies as a mingling of condescension and contempt.

> A number of people I knew, men and women who were my inti-
> mates, had no interest at all in either moving pictures or the people
> who made them; they regarded my attraction as either purely
> frivolous or a misguided attempt to make, some day, a great deal of
> money. They denied that the moving picture ever could be an art
> and smiled at the actions of the professions built around it. . . . The
> complacent ignorance of most creative writers about the plainest
> facts of moving pictures was amazing. Their opinion took the form
> of a lofty trinity: any contact with a moving picture was a menace to
> the dignity of their place, they understood moving pictures inti-
> mately, and their supporting them was worth unheard-of amounts
> [of money].[14]

Such attitudes as Hergesheimer describes were aesthetically shortsighted, but they represented a common assessment among writers and intellectuals of the period.

Sometimes, however, writers' complaints against the film industry were entirely justified and not merely the product of their cultural biases. Particularly humiliating for some authors was the fact that they were expected to do a considerable amount of publicity work for the studios, which were eager to cash in on their "prestige value" with the public. Mary Roberts Rinehart complained in her memoirs:

> Whatever its origin, the Eminent Author idea ended as a publicity stunt. . . . According to the press I was making motion pictures; and to support this idea I was being photographed for publicity purposes, on the stage, in the studio garden, on my favorite mount! Nobody believed that compared with me the office boy on the lot was an oriental potentate and the gate-keeper a king. Or that my place on the lot was considerably less definite than that of the waiters in the restaurant.[15]

Some authors found the added attention of publicity humiliating and irrelevant to their jobs as writers, while others rather enjoyed having their photographs taken with pretty actresses at Hollywood premieres. But in either case, most writers who visited Hollywood in the 1920s eventually came to suspect that they were most useful to the studio as figureheads, cultural capital enhancing the studio's reputation with the public. It is uncertain whether the idea to elevate writers to the level of movie-star celebrities was Goldwyn's response to his "chronic inability to develop stars"[16] or instead represented a more high-minded intention "to alter the focus of screen creativity by elevating the importance of the story and dramatic structure in the artistic pattern."[17] What is clear is that the experiment was a commercial failure that was soon abandoned by Goldwyn, and that most of the "eminent authors" returned to the East with considerable contempt for the film industry.[18] However, their negative experiences did little to discourage other authors from making the westward trek when Hollywood called. Indeed, the Eminent Authors experiment served to demonstrate for writers not only how difficult work in Hollywood could be but also how rewarding for those who achieved success.

One example of Hollywood's seductive power over writers in the 1920s can be found in the experiences of the Broadway playwright Cosmo Hamilton. In 1919 Hamilton had gone on record against Hollywood in the pages of *Photoplay,* saying, "I detest the movies!"[19] But by 1921 his views had changed. In a piece for *Photoplay* entitled "The Coast—As Eventually Discovered by Cosmo Hamilton," he laid out the process of his Hollywood conversion. Hamilton's "mission" was "to discover why so many books went in at one end of the studios as originally written and come out at the other end in an absolutely different form,"[20] and he went to Hollywood under contract to produce an original story for the Famous Players Lasky studio. During his stay he was courted by studio executives Jesse Lasky, William DeMille, and DeMille's younger brother Cecil, whom Hamilton described in a moment of impassioned journalism as "masterly and muscular, sitting on a high stool in an agony of thought" while directing a scene with Gloria Swanson (123). This depiction is undercut, however, when Hamilton reveals that the scene DeMille was concentrating on so intently was being shot on a stage between a "prize fight" and a "western shooting match." Such juxtapositions always startled authors because they called into question the seriousness of motion pictures as an art form, and such bizarre contrasts on studio stages served as evidence of Hollywood's "unreality."

Much of Hamilton's article about his trip to Hollywood was devoted to detailed descriptions of the homes and offices of the stars and directors whom he visited, and he was clearly fascinated by the material life of southern California.

> I studied with keen amusement the long line of motor cars which daily ranged themselves up outside the studios with their varied noses pointed to the long low line of buildings bathed in the gorgeous sunlight of California. It was easy to tell which of these cars belonged to Miss Gloria Swanson and which to the Head Carpenter. It need hardly be said that Mr. Cecil deMille's car was a cross between an aeroplane, a Zeppelin and one of those racing implements which tears around tracks leaving a cloud of surprised dust behind it. (124)

Despite such occasional ironic asides, Hamilton found his Hollywood experience to be pleasant and rewarding, and he was entirely pleased with the film of his original story made by the studio. He concluded his article by saying, "I am now to be numbered on that daily growing list of authors who are to be placed among picture fans, and who regard the screen with respect, with the keenest interest and with a considerable amount of awe because of its gigantic public" (124). Hamilton's experiences revealed how seductive "going Hollywood" could be for prominent writers on a short visit to "the Coast": flattered by the attention of studio executives, courted by film stars eager to appear in their films, and receiving weekly salaries in the $1,000 range, many writers found the allures of film work irresistible.

Yet such superficial appeals to the authors' importance disguised the real limitations and controls placed upon them by the studio system. In Hollywood, as a New York literary agent pointed out, "the authors must not forget that their stories are 'goods,' and that they go to the film companies to sell them."[21] Such an arrangement defined authors as employees of the studios, and from this circumstance stemmed all of their basic complaints about working in motion pictures: the forced collaboration and denial of authorship; the loss of ownership and control over their work as artists; the low status of writers in the studio hierarchy.

The second great wave of writing talent to wash over Hollywood began in the late twenties, after the introduction of sound suddenly required the studios to add dialogue to their films. The "talkie revolution" created an overnight demand for writers in Hollywood. In 1929 P. G. Wodehouse noted the disappearance of novelists and playwrights from New York: "They are all in Hollywood, making talking pictures."[22] At the same time, the effects of the Depression on Broadway and on the New York publishing industry led some writers to consider alternative avenues of employment, and many of them went west to seek their economic fortunes in the film industry. This was the period in which Herman Mankiewicz wired his famous telegraph to Ben Hecht announcing the opportunities for writers in Hollywood. "WILL YOU ACCEPT THREE HUNDRED PER WEEK TO WORK FOR PARAMOUNT PICTURES? ALL EXPENSES PAID. THE THREE HUNDRED IS PEANUTS. MILLIONS ARE TO BE GRABBED OUT HERE AND YOUR ONLY COMPETITION IS IDIOTS. DON'T LET THIS GET AROUND."[23]

H. N. Swanson, one of the earliest literary agents to be based in Hollywood, recalled of the early 1930s: "I brought many Eastern writers out to the Coast under writing contracts. Most of them were name writers, who looked upon a trip to California as a vacation; since many of them were short of cash, the experience was a life saver."[24] Often economic considerations dominated the writer's decision to work for the movies, as in the cases of

F. Scott Fitzgerald and Nathanael West, adding elements of desperation and dependence to the author's predicament.

Although the first wave of writers (in the twenties) may have found their creative efforts nullified by studio hacks, their public-relations value ensured that they would at least enjoy the high salaries and social prestige accorded celebrities in Hollywood. In contrast, the second group of writers (in the thirties) was more quickly integrated into the bureaucracy of the studio writing system, and they were welcomed by the studios with considerably less publicity fanfare and monetary reward. It was the experiences of Hollywood writers in the 1930s, during the Depression and including the struggle over the formation of the Screen Writers Guild,[25] that led to the image of the writer as a downtrodden artist exploited by the film industry.

The founding of the Screen Writers Guild in 1933 and its grudging acceptance by the studios in 1941 led to the writers' first effective efforts to challenge their treatment by the studios, but it also enflamed divisions among them. The "Hollywood writers' wars," which accompanied the organization of the Guild, were as much a struggle between writers of different wage scales and political ideologies as it was a conflict between writers and studio bosses. In his 1941 Hollywood novel *What Makes Sammy Run?*, Budd Schulberg created a vivid portrait of the internecine Guild struggles and their effect on writers in Hollywood. He described the conversation at the writers' table in the studio commissary.

> Everybody kidded about the Guild back and forth, but I felt that gagging was really the official court language and that underneath it all you could feel the friction growing.
>
> "Just wait till we join the Author's League, comrades!" Sammy shouted. "Then all us down-trodden writers can become producers and we'll punish the producers by making them get down on their hands and knees—and write!"
>
> Some of the laughter was automatic, some frightened, some reactionary.[26]

For many writers, the Guild struggles created a deep antipathy toward the film industry, and throughout the thirties the conditions of employment in the studios continued to fuel their dissatisfaction and sense of alienation.

A 1929 *Photoplay* article by Leonard Hall, "The Herds of Hollywood," painted a satiric portrait of the fate awaiting writers in Hollywood after the introduction of sound. It presented them as victims of a factory regimen in the studios, subject to an industrial discipline entirely inappropriate for the creative artist. "In the mass production of standardized goods Hollywood has it all over Detroit like a tent," Hall complained. "The whistle blows, and the time clock is punched, and the hands lockstep into the big foundries, just as though they were making gadgets and widgets instead of your entertainment and mine."

> In the New Hollywood, its sunlight filtered through factory smoke and its peace shattered by the clanking of the Talent Mills, the laborers move in herds. . . . When they report for duty at the studios, they are issued a pencil, a dozen sheets of white paper, and a typewriter, and are assigned cells in the writer's corral of the place. . . . Each cubicle bears a name on the door—that of its present inmate. With the trick short-term contracts now in vogue, the names are changed frequently, and washable paints are popular among studios. Often a writer sold down the river meets his successor coming hopefully into the cell he called home for six months.[27]

Such working conditions, Hall suggested, made it impossible for anything but second-rate work to be produced. "With this mass production, Ford-parts method, it is small wonder that Hollywood is getting, these days, just what it seems to want—machine-made stuff" (140). For the serious writer, only one of two possibilities seemed viable.

> He can make up his mind to give in and sink his individuality for the common good—to work as hard as ever he can to give the big bosses in the front offices just exactly what they want in the way of Usable Stuff. . . . Or he can become so disgusted with his herding and goosestepping that he just doesn't give a darn. . . . He goes to an occasional story conference, looks wise, and says little. At the end of his six months he takes his savings, kisses goodbye to nothing, and goes away where he can write as he dad-burned pleases. (140).

Many of the writers' complaints about Hollywood in the 1930s centered on their working conditions: they were often expected to put in regular business hours at the studio in offices that were sometimes cramped and uncomfortable—all of which could seem an affront to their dignity. The novelist Mildred Cram complained that "authors—I am speaking of them as a class—are given dark cubicles in which to work, nasty little offices furnished in mission oak. Sofas are frowned upon as conducive to sleep."[28] P. G. Wodehouse, writing for the *Saturday Evening Post*, commented wryly about writers' working conditions in an article entitled "Slaves of Hollywood."

> In every studio in Hollywood there are rows and rows of hutches, each containing an author on a long contract at a weekly salary. You see their anxious little faces peering out through the bars. You hear them whining piteously to be taken for a walk. And does the heart bleed? You bet it bleeds. A visitor has to be very callous not to be touched by such a spectacle as this.[29]

Wodehouse's facetious sympathy for Hollywood writers in the pages of the *Saturday Evening Post* indicates the ambivalence with which their dilemma was widely received. Added to the affronts to authorial pride and dignity imposed by their working conditions was the generally low status of the writer on the lot. As Cram observed:

> There is no prestige attached to being an author in Hollywood. An author (of standing) in London, in Paris, even in New York, enjoys a certain distinction. He is acceptable. He is even desirable. His opinion is worth something. But when he reaches Hollywood, he finds himself curiously, unexpectedly and completely anonymous. . . . The author is the most unimportant cog in the Hollywood wheel. Executives, big and little, supervisors, directors, dine aloof from the public gaze in a private bungalow. Authors eat at the commissary, in the company of extras, small-part players, camera men, and the boys from the laboratories.[30]

It was not just the writer's sense of social prestige that was bruised by the studio system, but his or her sense of creative freedom as well. As Raymond

Chandler put it, the essence of the studio system was that it sought "to exploit a talent without permitting it the right to be a talent."[31] The writers' loss of control over their work was a continual source of bitterness. In Chandler's assessment, "in Hollywood the screenplay is written by a salaried writer under the supervision of a producer—that is to say, by an employee without power or decision over the uses of his own craft, without ownership of it, and, however extravagantly paid, almost without honor for it" (51). And the playwright Maxwell Anderson wrote:

> If you are a playwright and go to Hollywood, you discover that there are no authors in moving pictures. There are no authors because the picture companies own all the copyrights and are registered in Washington as the writers of the scripts turned out by hired hands on the lot. They can change what you write and they will. After you've written your damnedest, they'll set seven more galley slaves to work on it, singly and in groups, and by the time the product is ready for consumption it will taste like all the rest of the soup in all the other cans labeled with the trade-mark of your studio.[32]

Coupled with writers' loss of control over their work was the difficulty of forced collaboration and "writing by committee." Ben Ames Williams, in a piece for the *Saturday Evening Post* about the writer's role in film production, articulated the complaint of every Hollywood writer: "The author in other mediums has a fierce pride in his work, because it is his own, and his alone; so the circumstance which, above all others, makes the moving-picture market unattractive to him is the necessity for accepting collaboration."[33] Such approaches to screen writing may have served the interests of standardization, but no writer believed that they served the interests of film as art. James Cain wrote in the *American Mercury*, "Imagination is free or it is not free, and here [in Hollywood] it is not free. It serves the medium, instead of the medium serving it, and once that is felt, that is the end of pride, of joy in getting things down on paper, of having them appear in front of your eyes."[34]

For most writers within the Hollywood studio system, the prospects for serious artistic accomplishment seemed hopelessly compromised, and the rewards for the necessary artistic compromises and loss of authority were the dubious benefits of the Hollywood good life. Maxwell Anderson described the trade-off.

> Let us not be too envious of the financial rewards and the tight organization of Hollywood. They are purchased at the price of regimentation—regimentation of the public through block booking and block advertising, regimentation of the artist by divesting him of his copyrights. High salaries in the paradise of the west are the mess of pottage for which the independent artists who work in Hollywood must sell their birthright.[35]

Many writers complained that their sojourns in Hollywood were invariably a type of "exile" within a culturally vapid and soulless factory town, and their complaints were repeated so loudly and so often that they eventually became fixed as popular conceptions of Hollywood. However, they did not go unchallenged. For example, Sam Marx, who was a story editor at MGM in the thirties, wrote (in 1988) of the Hollywood writer, "I believe that, in many ways, the writers who came to Hollywood liked the system of making the movies and were very willing to work under it. It was a very great time of camaraderie; it was a great time of pleasure."[36] On the other hand, anecdotal evidence remained largely negative, as evidenced by Fred Lawrence Guiles's grim account based upon his extensive interviews with Hollywood writers, entitled *Hanging On in Paradise*.[37]

By the 1970s, the image of the beleaguered Hollywood writer came under full-scale attack by several film historians who had begun to question the writers' complaints. Tom Dardis in *Some Time in the Sun* (1975), John Schultheiss in the essay "The 'Eastern' Writer in Hollywood" (1971), and Richard Fine in *Hollywood and the Profession of Authorship, 1928–1940* (1985) all presented revisionist accounts of the writer in Hollywood that challenged the prevailing myth of Hollywood as the destroyer of writing talent.[38]

In *Some Time in the Sun*, Dardis presented five case studies of authors who had worked in the film industry—F. Scott Fitzgerald, William Faulkner, Nathanael West, Aldous Huxley, and James Agee—in order to attack the "commonly held assumption . . . that all the time they spent in Hollywood was lost, wasted time" (8). He argued that employment in the studios provided each of them with a much-needed source of income that supported their literary projects, and that they all managed to do some of their most important writing while living and working in Hollywood. Dardis was centrally concerned with dismantling what he termed "the myth that won't go away," the idea that "selling out in Hollywood" was a process that inevitably led to the corruption and wasting of the writer's talents.[39]

John Schultheiss's essay "The 'Eastern' Writer in Hollywood" similarly examined the myth of the Hollywood writer as "the archetype of the American artist as a success—a betrayer of his talent for the cheap rewards of society"[40]—a conception that Schultheiss attempted to call into question. He surveyed a score of writing careers and concluded that many of the problems writers encountered in the studios were due to their own unwillingness or inability "to understand and utilize the peculiar dramatic mechanism of the cinema" (43). Such arguments had long been made by apologists for the film industry. For instance, Frances Marion, one of the most successful studio writers of the twenties and thirties and the author of a manual on writing for the screen, explained the differences between literary and screen writing in a *Photoplay* article, "Why Do They Change the Stories on the Screen?"

> In the first place, the most delightful narrative cannot be translated to the screen because so often its charm lies in its analyses, its philosophy, its pattern of beautiful word pictures. . . . Because the language of the screen is pantomime, experiences and reactions must be expressed in gestures and physical situations. It is absolutely necessary to have action in our stories.[41]

Both Schultheiss and Dardis cited the cultural elitism of some authors that led them to dismiss the movies as incapable of any serious artistry. They argued that such prejudices often led to a jaundiced, cynical attitude toward motion pictures that could only produce second-rate work. However, after the author's arrival in Hollywood, such an elitist attitude was occasionally reinforced by the business and production practices of the studios. And, despite the assumption of cultural superiority over the movies, the financial incentive to work in Hollywood often made such considerations seem unimportant. For Schultheiss, the dilemma of the

Hollywood writer—"well-fed but creatively impotent"—became a paradigm for the fate of the artist within a commercialized, consumer culture. "The artist, who prior to his Hollywood employment had felt a self-righteous superiority to the materialistic values of society, was now forced to confront the same material temptations he had so easily resisted in theory. Because his material needs were now handily accommodated by his hefty studio paycheck, he found it difficult to pursue his former literary urgings."[42]

The Hollywood writer thus came to embody a kind of cultural surrender—the defeat of the artist by the forces of commercialization and consumption. Dardis and Schultheiss were interested in defining this myth of the Hollywood writer so that they could dismantle it, as part of a revisionist project to show that neither the studio system nor Hollywood social life was inherently antagonistic toward writers or destructive of their talents.

In *Hollywood and the Profession of Authorship* (reprinted as *West of Eden: Writers in Hollywood, 1928–1940*, in 1993), Richard Fine argues that both the popular myth of the Hollywood writer as a downtrodden artist and Dardis's and Schultheiss's attacks on that myth "distort history," in part because they both rely on untenable generalizations about writers' experiences in the studios, which, in fact, were both positive and negative. He concludes, "Not all writers were mangled in Hollywood's machinery. Writers may have been treated cavalierly on occasion, and less frequently with outright hostility, but they were not actively persecuted. Indeed, many did their best writing after reaching Hollywood."[43]

Fine convincingly argues that what was being fought over in Hollywood was not writers or their artistic freedoms but rather the very conception of *authorship* that would define the cinema as a cultural form. As the products of a mass entertainment industry that operated through a careful division of labor within a studio hierarchy, movies were necessarily collaborative and collective in their production, and the notions of artistic vision and control over a work brought to Hollywood by writers made little sense within such a medium. Moreover, writers' attitudes toward Hollywood must be understood within the context of their general loss of cultural authority, as movies increasingly supplanted periodical fiction and "best-selling" novels as the dominant commodity form of narrative fiction. As Fine points out, "the writer's predicament in Hollywood merely fore-shadowed a change in their professional situation generally, as the institutions of the literary marketplace—publishing houses, theatrical production companies, and magazine editorial offices—sought to tap the mass audience in America" (159).

Writers of the twenties and thirties were increasingly aware of and dependent upon the "mass market" that had been created by technology and a triumphant ideology of consumption in American life. Hollywood gave writers the first clear indications of what their work would become within a modern, mass "culture industry." The reccurring themes of Hollywood's writers' complaints—bureaucratization, regimentation, standardization, loss of autonomy—were also the central tropes of a large intellectual debate over the character and effects of mass culture. And this debate was clearly reflected in the image of the Hollywood writer that was constructed in popular fiction, where he was seen as both the victim and the beneficiary of the Hollywood culture industry.

THE HOLLYWOOD WRITER
IN MAGAZINE FICTION

By the early twenties, the difficulties faced by writers in Hollywood were already well known to the readers of fan magazines, which often profiled authors and sometimes provided a forum for their complaints. For example, in 1919 *Photoplay* asked the New York dramatist and theater critic Channing Pollock "to write frankly on the picture business from the author's standpoint."[44] The resulting article, "The Author's Strike," was a diatribe against the film industry and its treatment of writers that set off a controversy in the pages of the magazine.[45] In "The Author's Strike," Pollock canvassed twenty-five prominent authors, all of whom were critical of motion pictures and the film industry. Some of them, including Rex Beach, Gertrude Atherton, and Rupert Hughes, would soon join Sam Goldwyn's Eminent Authors experiment in Hollywood, and a few (most notably Hughes and Cosmo Hamilton) would eventually become enthusiastic supporters of motion pictures. But in 1919 they added their complaints to the chorus of scorn orchestrated by Pollock's article. Pollock concluded by articulating the writer's frustration at the lost opportunities within the cinema "factory."

Here, at the very least, was sweeping criticism from experts; from possessors of the best brains and the best training. Quite plainly, that the 'factory' was turning out third-rate stuff, and, equally plainly, because it was getting no help from producers of first-rate stuff. The cinema, a machine of limitless possibilities promising revolution, promising to popularize good fiction, promising a tremendous and beneficent influence, had developed only as the supplanter of messenger-boy literature and dining-room-girl drama. It might have been—It might be—It was sure to be—Eventually; why not now? (104)

Although it is doubtful that the writers Pollock cited in his article constituted the "best brains" in either the film or the literary world, their complaints certainly echoed a wider debate about the effects of mass culture on society and contributed to the reification of a cultural belief concerning the incompatibility of art and popular entertainment in the movies, at the center of which was the Hollywood writer as he came to be perceived by the public at large. In short stories published in such popular magazines as *Photoplay*, the *Saturday Evening Post,* and *Red Book,* the character of the Hollywood writer became a recognizable type, a cultural figure whose cynicism about the film industry and frequent contempt for the movies were based on a thorough understanding of the system that produced films and of the limitations it placed upon moviemakers. The Hollywood writer as portrayed in popular fiction offered to readers a critical view of Hollywood, which included a skeptical attitude toward the movies and an insider's contempt for the way mass entertainment was ground out in the dream factories.

Unlike most Hollywood fictions, which show little interest in the process of film production, many of the fictional accounts of writers in Hollywood actually focus on working conditions in the studios, generally exploiting them for their comic potential. An early example is the short story "Breaking In," which appeared in *Photoplay* in 1922.[46] Following the rule of early star narratives, "Breaking In" was presented as the "true story of an author's experiences when he went into motion pictures," and was published anonymously in order to protect "a name that would be recognized at once as that of one of the better writers in motion pictures" (49). Such conventions allowed fan magazines to claim that they were providing accurate, firsthand information about motion pictures at the same time as they indulged in explicit myth-making. In magazine fiction the experiences of Hollywood writers were cast in what would soon become a familiar pattern, tracing the arc of their disillusionment with Hollywood.

"Breaking In" chronicles the experiences of an author who agrees to write a scenario after he is taunted with the fact that the head carpenter at the studio earns more in a year than he does writing for the "high-class publications" (50). For this narrator and others like him, the financial advantages of film work over the modest and uncertain living to be made through the literary arts are a constant temptation; the writers in these stories must weigh artistic control and authorial dignity against the monetary rewards to be gained by "going Hollywood." The unlucky author in "Breaking In" soon discovers the psychological cost of such trade-offs, as he endures the various humiliations and frustrations of film work.

He first encounters all of the prejudices against writers held by the film industry. The director with whom he had agreed to work "believes that all writers . . . are just the same as fleas on the dog," and argues during a story conference the "no book is any good"—sentiments presented as typical of directors in Hollywood. After struggling to produce a good script, the writer becomes increasingly frustrated by the director's constant calls for revision. Finally the director instructs him in exactly how to write a motion picture. As the writer tells it, "You simply sat down in a quiet spot and wrote four hundred scenes and about two hundred subtitles. Later on they threw away all the scenes and had a man write new subtitles, and the picture was made" (51). He soon realizes that in Hollywood writing by committee is standard operating procedure, and that the studio's assumption is generally that the more people who work on a script, the better the final film will be.

As the movie nears production, the director asks the writer to collaborate with a "fat little actor," and even the clerk of the hotel where the crew is staying on location contributes fifty scenes to the scenario. Such forced collaborations demoralize the author and make it impossible for him to keep up with the many changes being made in the script. At one point, his loss of control and complete bafflement at the revisions produce in him a state of hallucinatory delirium. When work on the script stops for two days while the writer and director battle over whether the story they are working on is a comedy or a tragedy, the impatient crew begins to blame the writer for deliberately delaying production. Absurd changes are made to the original novel they are adapting; as production gets under way, scene after scene is rewritten, cut, or altered beyond recognition by the director. Finally, the embattled writer reaches the breaking point and quits, on the brink of a nervous breakdown. His adversarial relationship with the director, the continual alteration of his work, and the humiliating collaborations imposed on him are all thoroughly denounced by the anonymous author of "Breaking In."

The artist's confrontation with a production system that often seemed irrational, inefficient, and wasteful was staged again and again in fictions about the Hollywood writer. Frank Condon's short story "New Stuff," which appeared in the *Saturday Evening Post* in 1924, offered one of the most trenchant accounts of a visiting author's experiences working in the strange world of the film studios. Condon began by offering some insight into Hollywood's need for authors in the 1920s.

> The cry was for authors, because at this time, perhaps seven short years ago, the guiding geniuses of the films decided almost overnight to elevate the art, and to stop people, if possible, from sneering at the eager young industry. There was, as the studio managers and production supervisors saw it, entirely too much withering criticism of motion pictures, especially by supercilious book reviewers and dramatic critics who can see no good in anybody but Shakspere [sic] and William James, and not much in them.[47]

The complaints leveled by critics such as Channing Pollock and George Jean Nathan against movies as an art form contributed to the industry's desire to recruit literary talent, as Hollywood strove to achieve cultural respectability in the eyes of an increasingly middle-class audience in the 1920s. In this process, authors often found themselves treated as little more than cultural capital—well-paid figureheads intended to reassure audiences of the movies' cultural value. In Condon's story, this experience is represented in the character of Henry Parkman, the author of a novel about "Chinese politics in the twelfth century" who is brought to Hollywood. Like "Breaking In," "New Stuff" chronicles the studio writer's growing disillusionment. Inexplicably, given Parkman's background, he is assigned to a comedy unit, where he is assured that "from now on the story was the thing. All else was subsidiary to the tale" (10). Initially, all members of the cast lobby him vigorously for important parts in his scenario, which will allow them to showcase their acting abilities. However, after a few days on the set, he realizes that the studio is producing the same movie over and over again, varying details of premise and setting but utilizing the same basic characters and story elements in every two-reel comedy. Parkman notes wryly, "[The studio] generally used the same plot, because there seemed to be nothing wrong with it, and it had proved acceptable and popular in the movie houses" (10). He soon discovers that no matter what he contributes in the way of original ideas, they are reworked and made to serve the formulas of the "Gil and Shorty Comedies" he has been assigned to write.

During his time at the studio, Parkman is assigned two collaborators: a dour scenario writer and a gregarious gag man who never makes a relevant suggestion but maintains a nonstop patter. Again, the process of collaboration imposed by the studio is depicted as an unworkable and inefficient way of producing any writing of worth, let alone of artistic merit. Although Parkman struggles to write an "action-comedy" with an intelligent and well-crafted plot, in production his script is reduced to a series of gags, and when the film is released it displays the same old comedic formulas of every other Gil and Shorty comedy. The obvious irony in "New Stuff" is, in fact, the industry's reliance on old ideas and familiar concepts.

Condon's tale exposed the discrepancy between the film industry's lip service to "screen art" and the conservative commercial forces at work in movie studios that strove to make the "product" familiar and predictable for audiences. As in "Breaking In," the contradictory pressures placed upon writers—to represent art and culture to the public but not to practice them in any meaningful way—leads Parkman to a "nervous breakdown . . . which seizes all authors about their sixth week in Hollywood" (115). A mental collapse before the apparent irrationalities of the studio system is presented as the writer's response to a new medium of popular entertainment that was redefining his role as a creative artist.

Other short stories about writers in Hollywood explored how they were sometimes able to play the studios' game to their own advantage. In "On and Up," which appeared in the *Saturday Evening Post* in 1926, Condon devised a clever tale of one writer's ability to exploit the film industry's practice of hiring celebrity authors to gain cultural respectability.[48] In this tale, Pete Jones, the undistinguished author of an unsuccessful novel called "Robes of the Night"—which he has published under the nom de plum "Fergus Spind"—comes to Hollywood looking for work. Because he is an unknown, Jones can only enter the film industry at the bottom, and he starts out in Poverty Row studios, where he learns the formulas of Hollywood screen writing and slowly advances through the ranks. Jones eventually finds himself working for a major studio, where one day he is given the job of adapting his own novel. The studio has recently purchased it, not knowing that Pete Jones and Fergus Spind are one and the same.

When the movie based on Jones's screenplay is a box-office hit, the director takes all the credit for the film's success, and the humble continuity writer finds himself laid off. Meanwhile, studio executives decide that they must hire the novelist Fergus Spind at any cost. As one of them explains, "The picture is going to be a sensation, and so Fergus Spind will be a sensation. This makes his novel famous, and every motion-picture company will want him to step in and repeat" (201). Jones finally returns to the studio in triumph, after negotiating a $650-per-week contract as the now-famous author Fergus Spind. Condon's comment is clear: in Hollywood, fame is more important than ability.

The temptations of Hollywood life for writers were given a comic turn in Joseph Hergesheimer's 1927 *Saturday Evening Post* story "Forty-Seven Pretty Girls."[49] A year earlier, in 1926, Hergesheimer had visited Hollywood and received the celebrity treatment, an experience that he described for *Saturday Evening Post* readers in a series of articles entitled "Shapes in Light."[50] In Hollywood he had been hosted by dozens of beautiful stars, especially Aileen Pringle, who became his particular favorite. In "Forty-Seven Pretty Girls," Hergesheimer commented upon the "young and seductive feminine loveliness" that had so dazzled him on his visit to Hollywood.[51]

The story concerns an author, Arthur Levis, who, after twenty-five years of writing, unexpectedly produces a best-selling novel and is brought to Hollywood by a film studio to supervise its adaptation. Although he is assured that the film will be faithful to his work, Levis soon discovers that the many "improvements" planned for his story—which include altering the title and changing the age of the central character to a youthful twenty in order to appease the vanity of the star—mean that his book will be completely lost in the adulterated screen version. A studio secretary explains to the somewhat naive author, "Books out here, with us, mean nothing. Probably the man in the Eastern office who got the company to buy it has forgotten its existence. Some girl at a party told him she liked it. . . . Make the girl twenty, call it Black-eyed Susan, and be thankful you're alive" (110).

In the face of such attitudes toward his work, the author suffers "a sense of helplessness, of defeat." However, Levis is soon distracted from the mutilation of his novel by a parade of pretty young women, all of whom scheme to advance their careers by extracting promises of future support from him while managing to evade his tentative romantic moves. Frustrated by the fickle beauties who surround him and horrified by the treatment his novel is receiving, the writer finally quits the studio and flees Hollywood, marrying his studio secretary, "the ugliest girl west of the Sierras" (111), as he leaves town. The writer's escape, however, is undercut by Hergesheimer's portrait of his easy seduction by Hollywood's glamour, affluence, and sexuality.

One of the most acerbic portraits of the Hollywood writer to appear in magazine fiction of the twenties was Milt Gross's satirical day-in-the-life-of "an author in Hollywood today," entitled "Well, Wot Is It?," which appeared in *Red Book Magazine* in 1929.[52] The title refers to the writer's story after it has been changed by the director, a scenario writer, a production supervisor, and assorted gag men, in a process that has taken the writer's original ideas and transformed them alternately into a "dog story," a "mother-and-son story," a "Biblical story," and an "all-negro cast" remake of "Over the Hill." In "Well, Wot is It?," Gross presented a thorough inventory of writers' complaints about working in the film industry, attacking their low status on the lot, their limited creative authority, the cramped offices they were asked to work in, the impossible collaborations the studio demanded, and the endless changes imposed on their work by others.

Despite his frequent threats to leave Hollywood because of his treatment by the studio, the writer in Gross's sketch—who is called simply "the Author"—is actually compliant and eager to please, no matter how absurd the studio's request. This is demonstrated by the increasingly ridiculous publicity stunts he agrees to, which include pictures of him "on top of a camel dressed in a straw vest, polo hat, and overcoat made from beer-bottle tops while Baby Wampas Star throws coconuts" and posing "buried up to his neck in lobster claws while a Hula troop plays native songs on his head with wooden spoons" (71). In "Well, Wot Is It?," Gross showed the writer's complicity, his willingness to pander to the demands of his studio bosses. Rather than presenting the Author as the victim of a production system whose methods often seemed irrational and unfair to writers, Gross depicted him as an individual whose indignant protests against working in movies were nothing more than vain posturing, intended to assuage his offended pride and perhaps to ease his guilty conscience. Like many other representations of Hollywood writers in popular fiction, Gross's depiction of the Author was profoundly ambivalent, in that it exposed the conditions in the studios that gave rise to complaints while at the same time showing the author to be amenable to his own exploitation.

SPIDER BOY

The first Hollywood novel to depict the problems of the writer was Carl Van Vechten's *Spider Boy*, published in 1928 and subtitled *A Scenario for a Moving Picture*. Van Vechten is best known today for the photographic portraiture to which he turned in the 1930s after giving up writing. His multifaceted career as a distinguished music and dance critic for the *New York Times*, as the author of several critically acclaimed novels, and as an outspoken and articulate supporter of the black artists and writers of the Harlem Renaissance made him one of the leading literary figures of the 1920s. Indeed, his prominence ensured that *Spider Boy* was one of the first Hollywood novels to be reviewed by critics, who generally panned it.[53]

Van Vechten had personal experiences with the Hollywood treatment accorded writers upon two occasions. The first was in 1924, when he sold the film rights to his novel *The Tattooed Countess* to Paramount Pictures. Although he knew the studio would make alterations in his story, he was hardly prepared for the changes he encountered.[54] The film was released in 1925 under the title *A Woman of the World* and starred Pola Negri in the title role, in a rare comedic performance that lampooned her then-popular vamp persona. According to his biographer Bruce Kellner, Van Vechten saw the movie only once, "gratefully noting that his name in the credits was in relatively small type."[55]

Van Vechten's second encounter with Hollywood was more positive, although it appears to have reinforced for him many of the stereotypes concerning Hollywood's extravagance and artistic isolation. In January 1927, after returning from a trip to Europe, Van Vechten boarded the Twentieth Century and headed for Hollywood. With no definite business to conduct in the film capital, Van Vechten was, in his own words, "an idler in Hollywood," and this circumstance permitted him the luxury of careful observation as well as full enjoyment of the celebrity treatment given a writer of his reputation. His experiences were recorded in four articles written for *Vanity Fair* from May to August of 1927, in which he related many observations and incidents that would eventually find their way into his novel *Spider Boy*.[56]

Van Vechten was impressed by several features of Hollywood and the film industry, but he always maintained a somewhat mocking tone in his accounts, referring to Hollywood in his first installment as "incredible, fantastic, colossal," a place where there seemed to be "more" of everything: "more money, more sunlight, longer distances, brighter jewels, . . . more oil wells, more fur cloaks (in a climate where they are not required), more work, more poverty and bad luck, more automobiles, more flowers, more police dogs, more heartbreak and courage, more Italian villas and Spanish houses, more beautiful gals . . . and more dissatisfaction than there are anywhere else in the world."[57] Despite the gossipy tone of such pieces, it was the underlying "dissatisfaction" that made Hollywood interesting to him. Like Katharine Fullerton Gerould, everything he wrote on the subject evinced ambivalence: he enjoyed mingling among the glamorous and affluent elite, whom he dubbed "Hollywood Royalty," yet he also recognized that Hollywood's sunny public image was built upon a shallow optimism that concealed an underlying desperation.

> In spite of the dissatisfaction, the discontent, the envy and the inflated values, on top, in the middle, and below, the pretence of perfection must be kept up. All the films are good, all the directors are geniuses,

all the stars are unprecendented—at least till they stop drawing at the box-office. Thus is the Hollywood morale maintained. And every where courtesy and fear. Fear that career is over, fear that it may never begin, for a 'break' in the movies is often a lucky accident. . . . Appearances must be kept in Fabulous Hollywood.[58]

Van Vechten's visit gave him several opportunities to note the position of the celebrity author in Hollywood, a part he relished playing as a guest of Paramount Pictures and of the many motion-picture stars who hosted him during his stay. These included Aileen Pringle, the favored diva of eastern literati Joseph Hergesheimer and H. L. Mencken; Marion Davies, the consort of publishing magnate William R. Hearst; and no lessor Hollywood luminaries than Mary Pickford and Douglas Fairbanks, with whom Van Vechten attended a premiere at Grauman's Chinese Theater, which inspired a scene in *Spider Boy*. In Hollywood Van Vechten observed that, although his reputation as a writer was well known, his works had not been read. At one studio he was introduced to a director as "one of the great authors of the world," whereupon his host immediately made the embarrassed inquiry, "What *have* you written, Mr. Van Vechten?"[59] Such moments, recorded with grace and humor by Van Vechten, accumulated during his visit and indicate the difficult position of the author in Hollywood, where image and reputation often counted for more than talent and ability.

Throughout his stay in Hollywood, Van Vechten continually dodged questions about what he was at work on, noting that "an idle writer" in Hollywood was "so strange a phenomenon . . . as to be almost an object of suspicion." During his stay her contrived several explanations for his presence in the film capital, the most plausible of which was "that I was writing a novel about Hollywood. This statement got into print and *everybody* believed it instantly. It was swallowed so completely, in fact, that I soon began to believe it myself. I think perhaps that there is a very fair chance that I *shall* write a novel the scenes of which will be laid in Hollywood."[60] Whether this is an accurate description of the genesis of Van Vechten's Hollywood novel or is simply his comment upon the self-fulfilling nature of Hollywood publicity, such a backwards arrangement—announcing a book before it is written—exemplified for him the commercial pressures placed on writers in Hollywood. Van Vechten put the befuddled hero of

Spider Boy in a similarly embarrassing predicament in which he finds himself congratulated for a scenario that he has not yet written. Van Vechten filled *Spider Boy* with such autobiographical details and observations, many of which had originally appeared in the *Vanity Fair* series.

Spider Boy chronicles the misadventures of Ambrose Deacon, a shy, mild-mannered author from a midwestern state, working as a newspaperman in New York City, who suddenly finds himself a celebrity after his first play becomes a smash hit on Broadway. Fleeing the glare of publicity and fame, Ambrose boards a train for New Mexico, where an old friend has offered him a haven in which to rest and write. However, heading west on the Twentieth Century, he encounters the supremely glamorous and flamboyantly self-aggrandizing Hollywood star Imperia Starling and her ambitious director Herbert Ringrose. They coerce the weak-willed Ambrose into accompanying them to Hollywood to write a scenario for Imperia's next picture. Upon their arrival, Ambrose becomes a virtual prisoner in Imperia's Beverly Hills villa—a predicament that forces him to escape in a milk wagon on one occasion and to climb through a window and down a tree on another.

As Imperia's "guest," Ambrose witnesses firsthand the hothouse atmosphere of the star's life: the petty intrigues and romantic entanglements, the endless flattery and wheedling of friends and family, the fierce rivalries and violent jealousies that obsess her. Imperia's self-absorption and paranoia make it impossible for her to see beyond the self-invented crisis of the moment. At a party, Ambrose notices that every conversation he overhears is dominated by "the singular personal pronoun. He never heard the word we."[61]

Throughout most of the novel Ambrose has but one goal, and that is to flee Hollywood—"the place where playwrights were seduced to become prostitutes for the motion pictures" (164)—but at every turn he finds his escape blocked. Eventually he accepts the patronage of a rival star, Auborn Six (modeled after Aileen Pringle). After being offered "a sum of money which seemed fantastic" (132), he signs a contract to write an original story for "L.L.B. Studios."

Van Vechten's talents as a writer lay in his cleverly crafted characterizations, embellished by witty dialogue and details of incident and setting that perfectly reveal the absurdities and flaws of his characters. In *Spider Boy* he presents a range of memorable Hollywood figures and locales. Imperia Starling and her director, Herbert Ringrose, are broad, satiric portraits of familiar Hollywood types. Both offer Ambrose their views on the position of the writer in Hollywood in such a way as to maintain their own importance. The director Ringrose proclaims, "Call it an industry, call it an art. . . . Ringrose waved such unimportant distinctions away with his hand. . . . Why quibble? The writer is perhaps the most essential single factor—saving always the director—in Hollywood" (41). Imperia Starling delivers an entire monologue on the need for writers in the film industry.

> Could you but know the difficulties with which I must contend, the louts, the clods of clay with whom I am forced to deal, the stupid scripts which are allotted me by ces sales cochons d'Hollywood!. . . . Next to the artist—she was pensive now—I think it must be the author who is the most important, but what authors they give me! Stories by babes just out of a newspaper kindergarten. Nothing for me to do! (47)

And Imperia taunts him with the power and influence of motion pictures as a mass medium.

> How many people see one of your plays? A few paltry thousands every week, while *millions* look at my pictures, isn't it? And when your play has run its course, it is finished, except for the few, the very few, who can read it in the library. Think what would happen if you wrote for the films . . . wrote a script for *me*. There it would be always gleaming on silver screens all over the globe. (49).

Here Imperia frames her argument in terms of an implicit contest between the visual culture of the motion pictures and a traditional print culture, which is declining in social significance in the face of new technologies that offer writers a larger audience for their work than ever before.

Throughout his stay in Hollywood, Ambrose confesses again and again that he knows nothing about writing motion pictures and has no desire to work in the film industry. During his meeting with Ben Griesheimer, head of L.L.B. Studios, Ambrose declares not less than six times, "I tell you I don't want to write for the films. I don't know anything about pictures" (131), but his candor is interpreted as playing hard to get, and Griesheimer simply offers him more money. Griesheimer is another of Van Vechten's brilliant Hollywood caricatures: a studio executive who plays lip service to film art and delivers stern warnings to writers concerning movie morality, but whose primary interest is the box-office bottom line. Griesheimer's chief concern is that Ambrose write a story suitable for one of his company's stars, and that he stay within rather specific moral boundaries.

> Pretty nearly any story you should write will hit some one. Only remember this: When you write a story for the pictures always keep in mind the great public that sees 'em. Think of the mothers and young girls that's going to sit out front. Purity first, that's the motto of L.L.B. Love, sure—even passion, but keep your story moral. Never forget the wages of sin is death, but if the motives is moral you can get in quite a lot o' necking. (193)

Completely unprepared for Hollywood's assault upon his literary talents and frankly unable to write a story that is suitable for the screen, Ambrose is assigned a studio "bright boy"—a continuity writer—with whom to collaborate. When he still fails to produce a usable story, the bright boy substitutes one of his own, with the unlikely title "Spider Boy." The most trenchant comments about the position of the writer come from this "bright boy" assigned to work with Ambrose, Phil Lawrence. He is a cynical studio hack who is only in the movie business for the money: "I'm out her to clean up . . . and after I get my roll I'll fly back to Broadway et comment!" (196). When Ambrose balks at the idea of claiming credit for a story that he hasn't written, Lawrence gives him a quick lesson in the politics of studio authorship.

> Say, Deacon, get me straight. They wouldn't accept this hokum from me. I'm too unimportant. I'm nobody. But Griesheimer thinks it's sure fire with you name attached to it. . . . If I'm your confidential man and write the continuity I'll swim half way to Honolulu in your reflected glory, but they wouldn't let me enter the race under my own name. . . . All you have to do is to collect the jack. Leave the rest to me. (239–40)

When Ambrose continues to resist Lawrence's arguments, the studio hack fires back.

Can't you see it's your *name* that the firm and Philip Lawrence and everybody else connected with this picture is cashing in on? . . . This is Hollywood, HOLLYWOOD, not the Louvre. Of course I know your name isn't worth a damn in pictures. Griesheimer knows it too. Everybody out here knows it. The point is they want to *think* it is. Why else do you suppose you're hauling in the dough? . . . Did you ever hear of a commodity called class? Well, that's what these cloak and suit clowns are wistful about. They want to pull class into the factory. They buy names to put class into the vivace postcards and then they engage hash-throwers and yeggs like me to take it out. . . . They don't recognize it when they see it—they have to be told about it—but when once they believe in it, they get down on their knees and worship. You represent class to these plumbers and they think your bloody name smeared all over a picture will make it classy. (240–42)

Hollywood's treatment of writers, as Van Vechten shows, emerged from the industry's conflicted desire to produce films that had both cultural prestige and box-office appeal—"class" and "hokum." Such contradictory goals necessitated distinctions between writers, which the studios institutionalized, and ensured that the visiting author was reduced to only a nominal role in the production process.

Ambrose's resistance to Hollywood is undone when he agrees to Lawrence's terms and cashes in on his literary reputation for the rewards of the Hollywood good life. Yet the affronts to his authorial pride have just begun. He is continually embarrassed by different versions of the story he is supposedly collaborating on with Lawrence, which is going through the typical studio rewrites, changing from a "Persian picture" into a "circus story" before finally metamorphosing into a "Russian spy drama." Unable to comprehend the baffling revisions the story undergoes, Ambrose finally comes to understand that it is all simply a "part of the game," an example of the waste and illogic of film making in Hollywood—a realization that is confirmed by his experiences on the set during filming. There Ambrose encounters many examples of Hollywood extravagance, including a director whose reputation at the studio is based on the simple fact that "he has to waste more jack than any other director to maintain his position. In each succeeding picture he has to waste more than he did on the one before" (264).

Despite all of the absurdities and excesses to which Van Vechten exposes his impressionable author, Ambrose finds himself gradually seduced to Hollywood life. After the success of "Spider Boy" (renamed "Love and Danger" by novel's end), Ambrose finds it impossible to resist a career in motion pictures. He marries a young starlet and settles into a comfortable domesticity. Indeed, the most telling aspect of Van Vechten's satiric portrait of Hollywood is the author's gradual capitulation to the gay parties, the pretty women, and the easy money to be found there.

Despite *Spider Boy*'s obvious barbs at Hollywood's treatment of authors, the novel offered only a gently satiric portrait of the film industry, and made the pampered eastern author Ambrose an accomplice in his own seduction and betrayal. Van Vechten concluded his *Vanity Fair* series on a similarly ambivalent note, by sounding the depths of Hollywood's inauthenticity with an architectural metaphor that anticipated Nathanael West's *The Day of the Locust* but stopped far short of West's caustic vision.

> People in Hollywood naturally are much like people anywhere, except that in this instance they are responding to the stimulus of a fantastic environment, for whatever the denizens may tell you—and some there are who boast of the fact—the environment *is* fantastic. The walls of the Hollywood houses are constructed of plaster with wire netting between so that it would be quite possible to kick a hole through the average domicile. A good deal of the Hollywood attitude is equally hollow, but I never found the occasion or discovered the desire to kick a hole through it.[62]

Spider Boy displays Van Vechten's ambivalence toward Hollywood by similarly refusing to "kick a hole" in a film industry that, he clearly recognized, both exploited and was exploited by writers.

QUEER PEOPLE

Presenting a sharp contrast to Van Vechten's mild satire was Carroll and Garrett Graham's raucous Hollywood novel *Queer People*.[63] Published in 1930, this work presented a then-unparalleled portrait of the bawdy dissipations and exuberant excesses of the "queer people" who lived and worked in the "flaming Hollywood" of the 1920s. The Grahams offered frank, often humorous descriptions of the diversions and pleasures that were available in the film capital when three-day parties, all-night speakeasies, high-stakes gambling joints, and exclusive brothels first contributed to Hollywood's reputation for "decadent immoralities and debaucheries" (255). *Queer People* was one of the first books to eschew the usually strident moralism directed at Hollywood's sexual image in favor of a perspective that veered between celebration and cynical acceptance. At heart, however, the book was an attack upon the film industry, and the Grahams repeatedly interrupted their accounts of revelries, in which they took great delight, in order to expose the discontentment, uncertainty, and hazards of life in Hollywood. In fact, *Queer People* attacked so many sacred cows—studio executives, directors and stars, even the Hollywood press corps—that it became something of a local scandal. Budd Schulberg has reported that *Queer People* so deeply offended the sensibilities of some in Hollywood that "it was the sort of thing you would not dare to bring into a motion picture studio unless you hid it in a brown wrapper and locked it in your middle desk drawer."[64] *Queer People* may have offended Hollywood's official view of itself, but it must have delighted readers with its riotous portrait of Hollywood life.

The novel chronicles the exploits of Theodore A. White, or "Whitey" as he is called by friends—an out-of-work newspaperman and occasional author who finds himself stranded in Hollywood, "the oddest city in America."[65] Within his first twenty-four hours Whitey attends a wild Hollywood party, where he becomes so intoxicated that he wakes up the next morning with no memory of the night's events, and only slowly discovers that he has been hired as a scenario writer at a major studio after being mistaken for a prominent Broadway columnist visiting the coast. With the instincts of a con artist, Whitey allows the deception to continue while he collects the impressive salary of $150 per week.

Whitey is a familiar American type: an opportunist and a grifter, constantly figuring the angles to his own advantage but wildly generous with his friends and essentially compassionate to all save those whose selfishness, arrogance, and power threaten others. It is from Whitey's thoroughly amoral but basically humane perspective that the Graham brothers present a grand tour of Hollywood society, from the power politics of the studios to the routines of a Hollywood brothel, from the dissipations of Beverly Hills parties to the desperate lives of struggling extras. One of the principal reasons *Queer People* would become such a seminal text in the canon of Hollywood fictions was its attention to all levels and conditions of life in Hollywood.

Queer People is a picaresque novel that follows its unlikely antihero through a series of episodic adventures, which serve to illustrate the moral turpitude and artistic compromise that the Grahams presented as inescapable features of living and working in Hollywood. The city itself is described in explicitly sexual terms, as an apt environment for "the parade of queer people" who inhabit the film capital.

> The junction of Wilcox and Cahuenga avenues forms the apex of a triangle—unconsciously phallic—of which Hollywood Boulevard is the base. The section contains innumerable apartment houses devoted to the three Hollywood G's—girls, gin, and gynecology. . . . The triangle is Hollywood boiled to its very essence. Homesteads of old residents rub shoulders with the harems of producers' women. Between these streets one can find actors, authors, artists, acrobats, and astrologers, coon-shouters, chorus girls, confidence men, comedians, camera-crankers, Christian Scientists, and call-houses, directors, gagmen, song writers, sadists, psalm singers, soothsayers, and sycophants, press agents, pugilists, policemen, perverts, pickpockets, panhandlers, pimps, playwrights, prostitutes, and parsons and play-girls (both unfrocked), bootleggers, bandits, bookmakers and Babbitts, remittance men, radio announcers and realtors, Jews, Gentiles, Mohammedans and Rosicrucians, all living like Mormons, manicurists, mannikins, misanthropes, misogynists, and masochists, women of all sexes and men of none. (79–80)

Into this sexual carnival, where playwrights stand between pimps and prostitutes, strides Whitey, a satyrlike character, pudgy and moon-faced but irresistible to the procession of extra-girls and actresses he encounters. The "unprincipled, fun-loving, ever-ready" Whitey revels in the sexual atmosphere of Hollywood, an amiable rogue who pursues his pleasures amongst his cronies at the studios and a bizarre assortment of Hollywood characters.

At the same time, however, *Queer People* shows how dangerous such an environment could be for young women, and the novel offers several cautionary examples of their sexual exploitation by directors and studio executives.

Chief among these is the story of Dorothy Irving, "the most beautiful girl in Hollywood" (111). After winning a beauty contest back home in Newton, Iowa, Dorothy accepts a six-month contract to go to Hollywood, where she discovers that success at the studio must be purchased with sexual favors. As beautiful and genuinely talented as she is, Dorothy languishes as a waitress in a Hollywood hash house until Whitey discovers her and comes to her aid. On her behalf, Whitey confronts the powerful studio boss who has been blocking her career for refusing his sexual advances, and blackmails him into giving her a long-term contract. After achieving some success, Dorothy is seduced by a director on the lot, who also introduces her to cocaine. When she discovers the director in the arms of another woman at a Hollywood party, she kills him—a crime for which Whitey, in an act of jazz-age gallantry, shields her from the police. Dorothy Irving's story exemplifies the sexual jeopardy of women in the studio structure and the predatory nature of talent recruitment in the industry during the twenties, as well as the dangers of Hollywood success for those unprepared for its temptations.

For men, the sexual dangers implied by Hollywood were posed as an assault upon a traditional masculine image—a reversal of conventional male and female sexual roles. As the Grahams put it, in Hollywood you could find "women of all sexes and men of none" (80), and *Queer People* provides several instances of Hollywood's threat to traditional masculinity. The most dramatic example concerns Frank Carson, a successful business-man from Duluth who has sold his shoe store and moved to Hollywood to subsidize his wife's screen ambitions. Once she achieves stardom, however, he is reduced to the humiliating role of "a star's husband" (125), emotion-ally and economically dependent upon but ignored by his wife, while she carries on a series of affairs with other men. Carson is a character of growing pathos and complexity, the emblem of an embattled masculinity, as we follow the painful process of his sexual humiliation and emotional collapse. The Grahams' portrayal of Carson's sexual disempowerment reveals a fundamentally conservative sexual ideology, which, by linking women's economic independence to their abandonment of husbands and families, made women's success in Hollywood—and the social, economic, and sexual power that came with it—part of a more widespread social pathology. Ultimately, Carson commits suicide while his wife and her lover attend a glamorous Beverly Hills party, in what is a clear indictment of the "Hollywood system" for its undermining of traditional sexual values.

Queer People displays a marked interest in the ambiguous sexuality of the Hollywood star. Despite the ultramasculine image of male film stars, there was always an implicit threat to traditional constructions of masculinity in the role playing, dissimulation, and attention to personal appearance demanded of Hollywood's leading men. Hollywood actors practiced the "feminine" traits of disguise and masquerade and, like their female costars, focused considerable attention on their "good looks"—the eroticized image of the body as visual spectacle. All of this contradicted traditional notions of masculine behavior in American culture.

The stereotype of the vain, posturing, somewhat effeminate male star is personified in *Queer People* by the character Gilbert Vance, who hosts Whitey's first Hollywood party. Throughout the novel, Vance is a foil to Whitey's aggressive male energy. After the introduction of sound in Hollywood, Vance's tinny voice is deemed unsuitable for the musical numbers he is called upon to perform in his films. In what becomes a revealing sexual irony, the studio hires Whitey to dub Vance's voice. Whitey proceeds to demand a salary equal to the star's, move into his house, and seduce his current mistress. Now the "voice" has replaced the "image" as the source of sexual power on the screen, and Vance's screen posturings contribute even further to the undercutting of his masculine image. All in all, the novel suggests that work in Hollywood is an unavoidably emasculating experience for men. As another actor says, "it's no profession for a grown man. But, what the hell! There's money in it" (146).

The Grahams describe the transition to sound in a montagelike inventory of its effects on Hollywood.

> Voice culture schools sprang up, as thick as bootleggers. Dubious technical "experts" arrived from nowhere, and were engaged by studios at fat salaries. Broken down playwrights and dialogue writers leaped from every westbound passenger and freight train, to the

terror of the literary master minds of the Writer's Club. Famous film stars, without voice or real ability, saw reputations crumble before them. Directors who lacked education, or stage experience, or both, confronted the abyss. Scenario writers whose culture and literary ability had handicapped them for years, came into their own. Actors who had been labeled "All Through" in silent pictures, suddenly found themselves in demand, their salaries sky-rocketing as the microphone revealed their real talents. . . . Hundreds of greater and lesser personages about the studios—executives, directors, writers, cameramen, production managers, supervisors—found themselves swept from jobs in which they had felt secure. A man without a contract was a man doomed.

And all because a New York mammy singer had gambled his time and money on a third-rate picture for a third-rate company, (194–95)

This mocking tone reveals *Queer People*'s attitude toward the possibility of film as art in Hollywood, where artistic compromise often paralleled moral lassitude. The Grahams delighted in exposing the pretentiousness and elitism that surrounded the idea of film as art. In the novel's critical portrait of the studio system, the book delivers its sharpest comments on the role of the writer in Hollywood.

Whitey's experiences provide several glimpses into the life of the Hollywood writer. Early on he is advised that "to hook into the real money" in Hollywood, he should "be a scenario writer." "You don't have to be good. Beat on the table and shout about the premise and the theme and the plot motivation. It doesn't make any difference what you do, the director will hash it up anyway." (149). While in Hollywood, he spends several weeks as a member of a studio scenario department, works on some short stories, writes a few articles about Hollywood for the fan magazines, and even manages to sell an original scenario to a second-rate studio for the princely sum of $5,000, with which he goes on a two-week drinking binge. When the movie based on his script is finally released, Whitey is once again broke and can only study the poster displayed in the theater's lobby, where he discovers his name in "small type" (197).

For a period of time Whitey works as a press agent for an eccentric eastern author—"the craziest author I ever knew" (89)—Madame Rethea Clore. In

Mme. Clore the Grahams created a biting, satiric portrait of the celebrity author in Hollywood; she is a flamboyant character modeled along the lines of Elinor Glyn. Mme. Clore arrives in Hollywood to form a production company that will film her novel, a potboiler she ranks alongside the Bible and Shakespeare. "Although she had never attempted motion pictures before, she was about to demonstrate her all embracing genius by making *The Tigress* the most artistically and commercially successful film production in history" (93–94). Mme. Clore proves to be a vain and arrogant snob, bullying everyone involved in the production with her "impossible demands" and "bizarre ideas" (122). In this character, the Grahams presented a highly unflattering portrait of the celebrity authors that visited Hollywood in the 1920s; Mme. Clore is inflated by a sense of her own importance but limited at every turn by her prejudices against motion pictures and her ignorance about the medium in which she is attempting to work.

The most revealing passages concerning the writer in Hollywood come from Whitey's days as a member of the studio scenario department. There his colleagues range from a relative of the company's president who has obtained his job through studio nepotism to a Columbia graduate who set out to write "the Great American novel" but wound up in Hollywood "rehashing the worst American gags" (46). The centerpiece of this episode is a long description of a typical story conference, one of the book's most hilarious scenes, in which the Grahams gleefully lampooned the studios' collaborative writing process:

> It was all very confusing to Whitey. As far as he could determine, the purpose of a story conference seemed to consist of tearing to pieces any idea forwarded. Occasionally the others paused, momentarily, to ask him for a suggestion. He never got beyond "Well, now I . . .," whereupon one of the other confreres would burst in with a noisy suggestion and bare his throat to the critical fangs of the entire room. . . . At irregular intervals, one of them leaped to his feet, howling like a wounded wolf, and began a series of short, disconnected sentences, sprinkled with oaths and accompanied by wild gestures and grotesque grimaces. It was the accepted method of advancing an idea. . . . Whitey observed that no suggestion was ever completed. Either it was torn to pieces before its creator had told it, or

others interrupting seized upon it, twisted it here and there, mangled it horribly and dressed it up in such fashion that it was entirely strange to its original creator. (50–51)

To Whitey, the irrationality of such a system is obvious, but he slowly comes to realize that such illogical methods of working are the rule within the studio, which at one point he compares to a "lunatic asylum" (41). Gradually he comes to embody the cynical, opportunistic perspective of the "studio hack," the writer whose artistic integrity has been so thoroughly compromised that he no longer holds even a shred of respect for his work or harbors any illusions about its value. It is the studio hack, not the celebrity author, who best knows how to navigate the "bedlam and chaos" (62) of the Hollywood production system; he is the *flaneur* of the studios and boulevards of Hollywood, an individual whose knowledge of the game provides his only security within an industry that relegates him to the lowest levels of significance.

FITZGERALD AND *PAT HOBBY*

Hollywood looms large in the writings of F. Scott Fitzgerald. He authored a score of short stories with Hollywood settings, including the seventeen *Pat Hobby* stories, and a critically heralded Hollywood novel, *The Last Tycoon*, which was left unfinished at the time of his death. Even when Hollywood wasn't an explicit part of one of his stories, its presence could often be felt. There are traces of Hollywood, for example, in Gatsby's elaborate parties at his Long Island estate in *The Great Gatsby*, and Hollywood hovers over the doomed American expatriates on the French Riviera in *Tender Is the Night*.[66] Hollywood was an ideal for Fitzgerald at first, an alluring symbol of youth, beauty, and, most importantly, money. In the twenties he visited Hollywood as a successful author, and received the celebrity treatment from the studio and from the elites of Hollywood society. In the thirties he returned to Hollywood as a writer whose career seemed over, and this time he endured all the frustrations and humiliations to which writers were subjected within the studio system. At the end of his life, Hollywood became a grim reality for Fitzgerald, one that paid his bills but also imposed upon him a "vague sense of competence unused and abilities unwanted."[67]

Underlying both poles of Fitzgerald's response to Hollywood were his mixed feelings toward motion pictures. In 1922 he sold the film rights to his novel *The Beautiful and the Damned* to Warner Brothers for $2,500; a year later he received $10,000 from Famous Players for the rights to *This Side of Paradise* along with his own "treatment" of the novel; in 1927 he came to Hollywood on a $3,500 advance to write an "original" for First National Pictures. Clearly Fitzgerald was interested in the movies, and when Hollywood beckoned he entered into film work eagerly, but the results of his forays were disappointing for him. Critics panned the film version of *The Beautiful and the Damned,* and neither *This Side of Paradise* nor his original scenario ever made it into production.[68] Fitzgerald was disappointed by his lack of success in films, but he was also determined to work in what he saw as an important new medium of artistic expression, despite the limitations it imposed on writers. In his 1936 essay "The Crack Up," he offered an analysis of these limitations in relation to his chosen form, the novel.

> I saw that the novel, which at my maturity was the strongest and supplest medium for conveying thought and emotion from one human being to another, was becoming subordinated to a mechanical and communal art that, whether in the hands of Hollywood merchants or Russian idealists, was capable of reflecting only the tritest thought, the most obvious emotion. It was an art in which words were subordinate to images, where personality was worn down to the inevitable low gear of collaboration. As long past as 1930, I had a hunch that the talkies would make even the best selling novelist as archaic as silent pictures.[69]

Fitzgerald's audacious pronouncement, part aesthetic analysis, part prophetic utterance, was also a clear critique of mass culture ("a mechanical and communal art") by a writer who knew firsthand exactly how far the author's creative powers had diminished within the corporate production hierarchy of the motion-picture studio. For Fitzgerald, as for many writers, the problem with the mass culture of the movies was that within its sphere "words were subordinate to images" and bestselling novelists like himself were becoming "archaic." Fitzgerald recognized that what was occurring in the ascendency of Hollywood was the institutionalization of the culture of the image by an industry geared for mass production and distribution, which meant nothing less than an inevitable decline in the cultural authority of the word and of print culture in general. Such a realization created in Fitzgerald "a rankling indignity, that to me had become almost an obsession, in seeing the power of the written word subordinated to another power, a more glittering, a grosser power."[70] The power of motion pictures, both as an artistic form and as a way of achieving a certain standard of living, was, however, irresistible for Fitzgerald, who throughout his life made repeated attempts to work in Hollywood. His experiences on the West Coast reflected his declining literary fortunes, however; his career seemed to bottom out in Hollywood, where he died in 1940.

Fitzgerald had first arrived, with his wife Zelda, in 1927, at the height of his fame; they had checked into the Ambassador Hotel, staying in the same four-apartment bungalow that Carl Van Vechten and John Barrymore occupied. They kept a heavy social schedule on their first visit; as two of the most celebrated partygoers of the "Roaring Twenties," they outdid even Hollywood residents in their festive excesses on occasion.[71] Although Fitzgerald's work for First National Pictures on his original story "Lipstick" did not lead to the screen success that he had hoped for, the trip to Hollywood did produce a short story called "Magnetism," which appeared in the *Saturday Evening Post* in 1928.[72] In it, a charismatic male star, George Hannaford, finds himself the object of several women's attentions. He is suddenly faced with the possible breakup of his marriage when an ex-lover attempts suicide after a failed attempt to blackmail him, and he begins to question his values and his way of life in Hollywood. Although cast in a familiar romance mold, "Magnetism" was about the dangers of celebrity and was subtly critical of "the almost hysterical egotism and excitability hidden under an extremely thin veil of elaborate good-fellowship" that Fitzgerald had encountered in the film community.

On Fitzgerald's second trip to Hollywood, in 1931, he traveled alone. In fact, he had come because he needed money to pay for Zelda's mounting hospital bills and his daughter's schooling. Fitzgerald's literary reputation was still sufficiently secure in Hollywood to ensure the celebrity treatment. As one commentator noted at the time, "Scott Fitzgerald is almost the only writer who never has cause to complain of his Hollywood welcome. He is famous even in Hollywood, where his meteoric arrivals and departures are discussed in film circles as avidly as they discuss themselves."[73] On this visit he had a five-week contract with MGM at $1,200 per week, but instead of working on an original script he was asked by production chief Irving Thalberg to adapt another writer's novel—Katharine Brush's *Redheaded Woman*. The fact that he was put to work on material derivative of his own best writing only added insult to the injury of forced collaboration with a studio writer. Fitzgerald complained of his work in a letter to his daughter, which reveals the antagonisms that could exist between writers in Hollywood: "I ran afoul of a bastard named de Sano, since a suicide, and let myself be gypped out of command. I wrote the picture and he changed as I wrote. I tried to get at Thalberg but was erroneously warned against it as 'bad taste.' Result—a bad script."[74] Ultimately Fitzgerald was fired, and the script was rewritten by Anita Loos.[75]

On this visit Fitzgerald's social position in Hollywood suffered setbacks, as well. Particularly painful for him was an afternoon tea party at the Thalbergs' home, where an inebriated Fitzgerald embarrassed himself in the impromptu performance of a song. He would later write of the experience in his Hollywood short story "Crazy Sunday," which provides clear glimpses of the doubt and uncertainty that would continue to haunt him while he worked in the film industry. Fitzgerald's central character, Hollywood writer Joel Coles, suffers from a constant insecurity about his job at the studio, at one point observing that "everybody's afraid, aren't they? . . . I just mean generally in Hollywood."[76]

Fitzgerald was fascinated by the personalities and the lives of the people who made films, partly because they moved in a world of affluence and leisure to which he had always aspired, but also because of their flare for the theatrical, their sense of self-as-performance, a quality shared by Fitzgerald characters such as Amory Blaine, Jay Gatsby, and Pat Hobby. At the same time, all of his Hollywood characters were haunted by uncertainty and a tragic air of self-destruction, often suggesting the problems of modern life. In "Magnetism," Kay and George Hannaford are young moderns whose love for each other suffers amid the permissive sexual values of their Hollywood social set. Fitzgerald was interested in the destructive effects of the star's appeal, and he represented the power of this attraction as a force inherently separate from the star's own wishes and desires. Thus, George can only be a passive witness to the emotional devastation that follows him through the story, and for which he feels "partly responsible."[77]

Similarly, in "Crazy Sunday," Fitzgerald makes Jack Coles a witness to the breakup of a marriage between a Hollywood director and his movie-star wife, Miles and Stella Calman (modeled after Irving Thalberg and Norma Shearer). As the writer Coles is drawn deeper into their troubled relationship, the central conflict for him becomes the need to reconcile his growing infatuation with Stella with his respect and loyalty to Calman as a film maker. Fitzgerald's strategy in his fiction for dealing with his ambivalence toward Hollywood was to project all of his admiration for and interest in motion pictures onto a single individual, while maintaining a more critical and reserved view of the industry in general. It was in the nature of Fitzgerald's perception of himself as a writer—and completely in agreement with the psychology of the characters in his novels—to see the solution to the problems of motion pictures as residing in the vision and determination of a single individual, an ironic hero to be sure, flawed as a human being, but nonetheless embodying in his abilities as a film maker the full potential of the cinema. In "Crazy Sunday," we first see Miles Calman as a powerful director and only gradually learn of the infidelities and psychological problems that threaten his marriage to Stella. But his death at the end of the story elevates and ennobles him; he was, for Coles, "the only American-born director with both an interesting temperament and an artistic consciousness,"[78] and the writer becomes a chorus lamenting the passing of the great man. Fitzgerald developed this figure even further in *The Last Tycoon*, where the producer Monroe Stahr represents his most positive assessment of the artistic potential of the Hollywood film industry.

Fitzgerald returned to Hollywood for the last time in 1937, with a six-month contract at MGM that paid him $1,000 a week. The six months extended to a year and a half at the studio, during which time he worked ahead of or behind other writers on a number of films, for only one of which—*Three Comrades*—he would ever receive screen credit. When he was fired for the second time by MGM in 1939, Fitzgerald began to free-lance, picking up two- and three-week rewrite jobs for various studios as he could find them. Meanwhile, his literary fortunes were at an all-time low, with his total book royalties for the year 1939 amounting to only $33.[79]

During the final year of Fitzgerald's life, his most reliable source of income was the series of stories he began to sell to *Esquire* magazine, which presented episodes in the life of a hack writer struggling to maintain a position at a studio where his services were no longer in demand. If characters such as Calman and Stahr represented for Fitzgerald the potentials of film as art, the character of Pat Hobby—the product of his third trip to Hollywood—embodied all of his skepticism and doubts about the movies, and thus suggested a much more critical view of the film industry.

In many ways Pat Hobby was Fitzgerald's alter ego: both had witnessed the decline of their reputations and fortunes and looked back with mingled bitterness and nostalgia to a time in the twenties when they had possessed success. When Fitzgerald wrote of Hobby ("He had once known sumptuous living, but for the past ten years jobs had been hard to hold—harder to hold than glasses"), the words could apply equally to himself. He created Hobby after repeated unsuccessful attempts to establish a career in the film industry, and there can be little doubt that, along with his fictional character, he had come to feel like "a man in the way"—the title of one of the Hobby stories—washed up in and neglected by the industry that he so desperately wanted to be a part of. At one point, Fitzgerald even began to sign telegrams to his editors "Pat Hobby Fitzgerald."[80] Hobby—again, like Fitzgerald—is finally reduced in the stories to only occasional work at the studio, where his salary (that all-important index of a writer's worth) has dropped to a mere $250 a week, exactly the amount Fitzgerald was paid by *Esquire* for each of his Pat Hobby stories.

On the other hand, Pat Hobby, unlike Fitzgerald, is no writer, and he is not above blackmail, bullying, deception, and thievery when it comes to delivering a script. Hobby is a Hollywood type in the same mold as the Grahams' Whitey in *Queer People:* a con man and an opportunist with few scruples to interfere with the pursuit of a job or a drink. But Hobby is a more complex character than Whitey, in part because Fitzgerald is honest about his shortcomings as both a writer and a human being, and this makes him appear more vulnerable. Fitzgerald tells us that Hobby "had been in the business, publicity and script-writing, for twenty years,"[81] and that in "the good old silent days" he had actually headed a scenario department, at a time when writing for the movies meant "you got somebody's plot and a smart secretary and gulped benzedrine 'structure' at her six or eight hours every week. The director took care of the gags" (13). He is a company man, a studio hack trained in the conventions of movie narrative, mistrustful of any innovation on the part of his collaborators, and doggedly loyal to studio hierarchy. "Only a writer—at forty-nine,"[82] Hobby mourns, clearly showing contempt for his lowly position as a studio scribe. But with the introduction of sound in Hollywood and with competition from East Coast novelists and playwrights, Hobby's fortunes at the studio begin to fall, and he ends up representing the Hollywood writer as a comic underdog, defeated as much by his own limitations as by the conditions of studio work. "After talkies came he always teamed up with some man who wrote dialogue. Some young man who liked to work"[83]—like Fitzgerald himself.

Most revealing is Hobby's antagonism toward the authors with whom he is asked to collaborate. He always approaches them with suspicion, and for good reason: their obviously superior talents usually make him look bad. "Perversely," as Fitzgerald noted, "Pat Hobby's sense of justice was with the producer, not the writer" (53), and it is in the relationships between Hobby and the various visiting authors with whom he collides that Fitzgerald presents some of his most telling insights into the position of the writer in Hollywood.

In "Teamed with Genius," Pat is asked to collaborate with an English playwright, Rene Wilcox, recently arrived in Hollywood and unfamiliar with the intricacies of screen writing. Hobby is hired because, in the words of the producer, he "used to be a good man for structure," but he soon begins to panic when the playwright refuses to collaborate and he faces the prospect of writing the script by himself. However, when Wilcox delivers a completed shooting script written without Pat's assistance, the studio hack is stunned by such unorthodox working methods: "Pat sat in a daze. If Wilcox's script was good—but how could a first script be good? Wilcox should have fed it to him as he wrote; then they might have had something."[84] Pat arranges to have a copy of Wilcox's script sent to his office, where he can make the revisions necessary to substantiate a claim of coauthorship, and Fitzgerald gives us a glimpse of the collaborative process at work.

> Working frantically, he made several dozen small changes. He substituted the word "Scram!" for "Get out of my sight!," he put "Behind

the eight ball" instead of "In trouble," and replaced "You'll be sorry" with the apt coinage "Or else!" (36)

Hobby's efforts are to no avail, however. He is outwitted by a clever secretary, secretly in love with the playwright, who switches the scripts, thereby protecting the author's original work from Hobby's hash job. The final, ironic indignity for Hobby is that after his plan is exposed, he manages to retain his studio job only at Wilcox's request, so that he may study Pat as research for a play he plans to write. Such objectifications of Hobby are common in the stories (see "Pat Hobby Does His Bit" and "Fun in an Artist's Studio," for example), and they serve as poignant reminders of the writer's vulnerability and lack of control within the studio system.

In "Mightier Than the Sword," Fitzgerald offered a view of the differences between studio writers and visiting authors that was informed by his own experiences in both roles. When Hobby overhears the complaints of E. Brunswick Hudson, a visiting author who has just been laid off at the studio, he ingratiates himself with the director of the film and begins to collaborate with him on the scenario. But the script is rejected by the front office, and the enraged director lashes out at Hobby. "'Goddam writers!' he said savagely. 'What do we pay you for? Millions—and you write a lot of tripe I can't photograph and get sore if we don't read your lousy stuff! How can a man make pictures when they give me two bastards like you and Hudson?'"[85] After he is fired, Hobby wanders back to his office, only to discover that his name on the door has been replaced by that of E. Brunswick Hudson, now back on the picture. After another blowup with the director leaves Hudson's authorial pride bruised and broken, Hobby offers him ironic consolation.

> "Authors get a tough break out here," Pat said sympathetically. "They never ought to come."
>
> "Who'd make up the stories—these feebs?"
>
> "Well anyhow not authors," said Pat. "They don't want authors. They want writers—like me." (149)

Here Fitzgerald throws the reader's sympathies toward Hobby and other "writers—like me," a category in which, no doubt, he would have placed himself in 1939. But the studio writing system in which Fitzgerald was expected to work meant the end of the great literary solo flights he had performed in his novels of the twenties and the beginning of a constant struggle to preserve any trace of his vision as a writer in a process of forced collaboration that denied him control over his work. For Fitzgerald, finally, it was the cynical has-been Pat Hobby who most clearly saw the reality of writing in Hollywood—that "what people you sat with at lunch was more important in getting along than what you dictated in your office. This was no art, as he often said—this was an industry" (22).

"$1,000 A WEEK"

In his 1941 short story "$1,000 a Week," the novelist James Farrell tells of a writer who has come to Hollywood on a two-week contract because he needs the money. Tom Lambert is a critically successful novelist, but with a family to support and "because my books don't make enough," he comes west to work for "Grandiose Films, Inc," determined "to do the best I can out here."[86] But he quickly becomes demoralized. He is introduced to screen work by another writer, who advises him, "No matter what you do in pictures, it's got to gross at the boxoffice. That's an infallible law of pictures. Many writers don't like it, but it's the fact" (6). He is continually kept waiting for story conferences with his producer, Sidney Klem, and when they finally meet, Klem constantly interrupts their discussions to take phone calls and handle other business. Lambert works hard to incorporate the producer's ideas into his scenario, only to have them tossed out and a new approach asked for in a later conference. The end result of Lambert's work at the studio is disappointing: "The words were his. The ideas belonged to Klem. But he needed money. He needed it badly" (18). At the end of his two weeks Lambert packs up and leaves, feeling "free and liberated for the first time since he had been in Hollywood" (20). Farrell's simple story of one writer's experience in Hollywood presents, in concise narrative form, the frustrations faced by many writers who worked in the Hollywood studio system in the thirties and forties.

Farrell elaborated upon the writer's fate in his 1944 essay "The Language of Hollywood," in which he offered one of the most compelling analyses of the role of the writer within the Hollywood studio system.[87] Arguing from a Marxist perspective, Farrell noted the emergence in America of a powerful "commercial culture" that was increasingly being substituted for a "genuinely popular, genuinely democratic culture," and that constituted a form of "big business." Chief among the "cultural industries"[88] were motion pictures, which, for the novelist, were marked by a "mass production character" and aimed at a "mass audience" (138). It was the desire to ensure the profitability of film making that led to the standardization of production processes in the film industry and the homogenization of film material by the various crafts of the movie studio, including the craft of writing. As Farrell noted, "the bigger our cultural industries become, the greater are the restrictions they must impose on the choice and the handling of subject matter." And the simple fact was that "all must work within this system" (139). The implications for writers were clear.

> Hollywood is not a cause; it is an effect. But the relative purity with which it reveals tendencies now at work in American culture makes it a most illuminating illustration of what I want to convey. The rise of Hollywood to the realm of culture is a phenomenon somewhat analogous to that of the triumph of machine production during the industrial revolution. In the studios many separate crafts and arts are all linked together, mainly under one roof in one serial process. And this requires a large capital investment. This means that we have social methods of artistic creation and of film production carried on for private profits. But those who contribute artistically to this production—with rare exceptions—do not control it. They lose their independence as artists and craftsmen and become employees. Their economic relationship is thereby changed. Most writers, for instance, become wage-working writers. It is true that their wages are generally fantastically higher than those of factory workers, but that is not the decisive factor here. In the economic sense, most writers have a relationship to their employers similar to that of the factory worker to his boss. Just as the worker sells his labour power, so does the writer sell his skill and talent. What he then receives is a wage. All control over the means of his production resides in the employer. Thus, the writer suffers from the same kind of alienation as does the factory

worker. He is alienated from control over his means of production, and over what he produces. (141)

In Farrell's view, the Hollywood "dream factory" was like any other factory, and the creative talents who worked there were subject to the same patterns of industrial exploitation and control as workers in other industries. In the conflict of "commercial versus artistic values" that Hollywood represented to him and to many other writers of the period, it was clearly the forces of commercialism that were defining the movies as a cultural form, reshaping the role of the writer in the process. Hollywood represented for writers the institutionalization of a commercialized mass entertainment industry—what Farrell wryly described as the "grandiose Luna Park of capitalism" (148)—and its ascendancy spelled, more clearly than any subsequent literary theorizing, the "death of the author" within mass culture.

CHAPTER SEVEN

FROM TINSELTOWN TO SUCKERVILLE

Hollywood Crime Novels of the Thirties and Forties

> Hollywood's underworld lives in shiny bungalows amid the
> scent of flowers. Its denizens know no slums. But here is seduc-
> tion, blackmail, dope, theft, suicide, murder. . . . Its apparent
> respectability is the most sinister aspect of this underworld.
>
> RUTH WATERBURY[1]

The association of Hollywood with crime has been a recurrent feature of its
cultural identity from the early 1920s to the present. The belief that the
sunny and glamorous image of the film capital crafted by the studios and
fan magazines concealed a more sinister world of criminality and violence
was, in fact, a central tenet of the Hollywood antimyth. Beginning with the
star scandals of 1921–22, Hollywood's reputation as a place of sexual
danger and immorality gave rise to a perception of the film colony as a
social milieu tainted by an air of general corruption and vice. Such a view
often represented a conservative response to the modern social and sexual
values that were so conspicuously on display in Hollywood. For example,
Photoplay correspondent Ruth Waterbury linked Hollywood's criminal
identity in the late twenties to the "flapper," a symbol of contemporary
women's sexual independence and aggression. "The symbol of Hollywood's underworld is the jazz-baby, gold-crazy, sex-crazy, hard-boiled,
bitter and childishly abandoned to fate."[2] Waterbury's figure of the cynical
sexual opportunist represented an extreme version of modern women's

demands for new personal and economic freedoms in the postwar twenties. Her chief examples of Hollywood crime—the murder of director William Desmond Taylor, the Fatty Arbuckle scandal, and bitplayer Paul Kelly's accidental slaying of his lover's husband in a crime of passion, which briefly enflamed headlines in 1927—were all suggestive of Hollywood's transgressive sexual mores.

Anxieties over the film industry's influence on sexual behavior rested side by side with other concerns. Crime wore a more affluent and respectable face within the film community than elsewhere in the country. In Hollywood, Waterbury continued, criminal activity was planned and carried out "not in a dank cellar as it would have been in any other city, but in a shiny bungalow dressed with new monotonous furniture, in a garden spot where green lawns and the blue sky made a strange frame for muddy imaginings" (29). The notion of the criminal "underworld" that was typical of most urban milieus seemed inappropriate in the bucolic Hollywood of the 1920s. Yet appearances could be deceptive, and the confusion of illusion and reality—the central theme of the cultural discourses surrounding the film capital—could clearly serve the interests of the criminal. For instance, the tendency toward theatricality and performance on the part of those who worked in movies could easily be turned toward deception, disguise, and the concealment of wrongdoing. Because the rewards of success in Hollywood were so great, the temptations to engage in crime were equally compelling, and the wealth of the film industry provided any number of economic motives for criminal activity. Ambition and jealousy, magnified by temperament and ego, could poison personal relationships in a business where success was always uncertain and competition was fierce. And no amount of money could protect the Hollywood star from the withering effects of scandal on a career; hence, ample opportunities for blackmail and extortion existed within the film community. It was the potent appeals of Hollywood's wealth and glamour, combined with the aura of transgressive sexuality that suffused its diversions and dissipations, that made it an apt site for criminal behavior in the popular imagination of the 1920s.

By the 1930s Hollywood had begun to assume a darker, more urban identity as it became a part of sprawling greater Los Angeles, and the entire region of southern California seemed increasingly the product of a secret history of large-scale social crime, which cast a shadow over the city's sunny official image.[3] To begin with, the rapid urban development of the Los Angeles Basin in the twenties and thirties was made possible by a usurpation of the water supply of the Owens Valley, some 250 miles to the north, in one of the most ruthless land grabs in American history. The "rape of Owens Valley," according to Los Angeles historian and newspaperman Morrow Mayo, was "one of the costliest, crookedest, most unscrupulous deals ever perpetrated,"[4] and it made possible the rapid and artificial growth of the "city of angels." Starting in the 1880s, successive waves of immigration into the region led to speculation in real-estate values and produced cycles of boom and bust that often devastated small investors. By the 1930s less prosperous migrants, escaping drought and economic depression in the Middle West, often found themselves facing a hostile social and economic establishment, which had lured many of them to California by promoting the state in national advertising.[5] The discovery of oil at Long Beach in the early twenties created a "get-rich-quick" attitude that fueled the Los Angeles economy throughout the decade. It also led to massive swindles such as the Julian Petroleum scandal, which ruined thousands.[6] Contributing to an image of fraudulence and deception were the religious and health cults that flourished in Los Angeles in the 1920s and 1930s, attracting legions of gullible seekers and health faddists who often became the targets of con artists and charlatans.

The film industry itself was perceived, at least by some, as a disreputable and potentially harmful influence upon city life. Mayo, for instance, in his portrait of the city's growth and development, entitled simply *Los Angeles* (1933), was critical of the ethical and artistic standards of the movie industry, complaining that from the start it had been "almost exclusively in the hands of the lowest type of business man, the lowest type of actors, and the lowest type of writers; to wit, honky-tonk impresarios, hams and hacks."[7] The entwined political economies of real estate, water, oil, and motion pictures drove the rapid development of the city of Los Angeles with a massive campaign of boosterism and promotion, but they also created a vague impression of moral compromise and illegality that seemed to cast a pall over the entire region and was particularly evident in the fiction of the 1930s. For the immigrant writer Louis Adamic, the corruption that he discovered in Los Angeles while working as a laborer in the "Hollywoodland" development was endemic to America as a whole.

Los Angeles is America. A jungle. Los Angeles grew up suddenly, *planlessly*, under the stimuli of the adventurous spirit of millions of people and the profit motive. . . . From Mount Hollywood, Los Angeles looks rather nice, enveloped in a haze of changing colors. Actually, and in spite of all the healthful sunshine and ocean breezes, it is a bad place—full of old dying people, and young people who were born old of tired pioneer parents, victims of America—full of curious wild and poisonous growths, decadent religions and cults and fake science, and wildcat business enterprises, which, with their aim for quick profits, are doomed to collapse and drag down multitudes of people. . . . A jungle.[8]

Into this "jungle" poured an ever-growing population. It spread out across a material landscape increasingly shaped by the automobile into an unplanned urban sprawl, where the various communities that made up greater Los Angeles blurred into a neon labyrinth of apartment houses, bungalow courts, drive-ins, and gas stations. Alongside the presumed misdeeds within the film industry were the opportunities for criminal enterprise to be found among the thousands of new arrivals who poured into Los Angeles during the twenties and thirties. Idealistic and naive newcomers were easy "suckers" for a variety of rackets, ranging from phony acting schools selling "screen tests" and photographic "studios" specializing in pornography to highly organized prostitution and blackmail rings. The irresistible lure of money, fame, and sex served as the magnet for both predator and prey in Hollywood's urban jungle. "Hollywood," Waterbury observed, was "the newest gold coast and the usual scum of camp followers muddy its rising tide."[9] The sociologist Leo Rosten offered a colorful description of this underclass in his landmark study of the film capital, *Hollywood: The Movie Colony, The Movie Makers* (1941).

The hordes which flocked to Los Angeles included a generous assortment of the déclassé: hard men and easy women, adventurers, race-track-touts, quacks and cranks of every delicate shape and hue. Confidence men exploited many who had come to retire; embezzlers fleeced many who had come to invest; "healers" fed on those who had come to recover; evangelists consoled those who had been betrayed. Yogi mystics and swami palm readers, occult fakirs and bold-faced fakers took hasty root in the City of the Angels. Gambling houses and racetracks sprang up to capitalize on the climate and a holiday public eager to reach for the brass ring.[10]

Within such a pervasive atmosphere of fraud and deceit criminals of all classes and categories could take root and flourish. At the same time, their actions were often mirrored by the official corruption found within city government and especially within the Los Angeles Police Department (L.A.P.D.), which was infamous for its abuses of power through "false arrest, brutality with arrest, unlawful detention, incommunicado, and the third degree."[11] Racial and ethnic hatred had long fueled social violence in Los Angeles, and the city's "open-shop" policy toward unions set the stage for some of the most brutal labor struggles in American history.[12] Under the pressures of population growth and rapid urban development, neighborhood and community ties were often tenuous, and Los Angeles led the country in suicides, divorces, and bankruptcies.[13] Discontentment and alienation were endemic to life in Los Angeles, particularly in Hollywood, which was often referred to ironically as "the most unhappy city in the world."[14] Carey McWilliams, in his classic study of the region, *Southern California Country*, depicted Los Angeles as "a vast drama of maladjustment." "Ideas grow rank, coarse, and odorless as geraniums in the freakish environment of Southern California. When so many people have nothing meaningful to do with their time, nothing real with which to occupy their minds, they indulge in fantasy, in silly daydreams, in perversions, and, occasionally, in monstrous crimes."[15]

Hollywood itself was the most monstrous and the most characteristic section of the Los Angeles landscape. The symbolic center of the American film industry and a focal point for representations of sexuality and consumption in American culture, Hollywood was also a social magnet that appeared to systematically lure the young and innocent into an environment dominated by illusion and governed by money, ambition, and power. Indeed, the studios were formidable industrial empires, with their own security forces and legal departments to cover up scandal and safeguard studio interests, and they were run by a handful of extremely powerful men whose decisions could change lives forever. The many crime novels set in

Hollywood that have been published from the 1930s to the present have offered the most extreme version of the Hollywood antimyth, depicting the film industry as simply another Los Angeles "racket." Such wealth and glamour as the film industry displayed inevitably fostered suspicion, greed, and envy in the public imagination, and it was partly as a consequence of this that writers frequently linked Hollywood to an image of criminality and corruption. The writer S. J. Perelman, for example, once described Hollywood as "a dreary industrial town controlled by hoodlums of enormous wealth, the ethical sense of a pack of jackals, and taste so degraded it befouled everything it touched."[16] Newspaperman Harry Carr, in his portrait of the city, *Los Angeles: City of Dreams* (1935), described the mood of Hollywood as like "the struggle between two drowning persons for the last life-belt . . . the cold ruthlessness of a pack of wolves pulling down a wounded buffalo."[17] Hollywood crime novels elaborated upon such views. Within this milieu crime became an organizing metaphor for social and economic relations, and for many writers crime provided a key to understanding the cultural dynamics of Hollywood, condensing all of the vicarious interests and anxieties to which it could give rise into a neat narrative package.

Hollywood's criminal profile within American culture is evident in the fact that crime narratives make up a conspicuously large number of works within the canon of Hollywood fiction. Because of their sheer number, Hollywood crime novels provide an important interpretive context for understanding Hollywood's cultural image, which has long been constructed and understood through a series of scandals and crimes sensationalized in fan magazines and newspaper headlines. It is the Hollywood crime novel that has served as the principal literary form for constructing Hollywood's dystopian image in American culture.

HOLLYWOOD CRIME FICTION:
FROM PUZZLES TO PULPS

The earliest Hollywood crime fictions were works in the tradition of the classic "puzzle" mystery, which focused on the investigation of a crime and its solution by a police detective or special investigator. As a literary form, the mystery is a type of narrative fiction governed by rather specific rules of evidence and scientific logic within which the writer must play fair with the reader. One of the central precepts of the puzzle mystery was that the investigator solved the crime through mental agility and intellectual acumen rather than physical strength or violence. Following in the footsteps of Edgar Allen Poe's Inspector Dupin and Arthur Conan Doyle's Sherlock Holmes came a host of gentleman investigators (and one or two ladies)—often wealthy amateur criminologists—who would methodically lead the reader through their investigations, collecting clues and assessing motives until logical deduction and scientifically gathered evidence pointed to the guilty party. As Julian Symons, a historian of the genre, has noted, the crime in mystery fiction is invariably murder, and the motives are always personal in order that there be a clear and rational basis on which to deduce guilt.[18] Most significant to an understanding of its cultural appeal, as several critics have observed, the classic puzzle mystery is an ideologically conservative literary form that seeks, through the solution of a crime, the restoration of social order and the preservation of the status quo as well as the validation of reason and scientific logic.[19]

As a rule-bound intellectual game, the puzzle mystery all too often seems unable to involve readers emotionally in the characters and their conflicts. Bodies may pile up, but the reader's primary investment in the narrative is with "Whodunnit?" and how the murderer will be revealed by the investigator. Such an appeal suggests a certain moral detachment on the part of the reader, who takes pleasure in both the crime and its punishment, identifying with the perspective of the investigator rather than with the murderer or the victim. Characters are often mere types, frequently defined by crude class, racial, or ethnic stereotypes. Moreover, as Symons notes, the social world of the puzzle mystery is "as fixed and mechanical as that of the Incas,"[20] and society is typically flattened into a generalized backdrop. This was certainly true of Hollywood mysteries, in which it was often considered sufficient to simply mention Grauman's Chinese or the Brown Derby to establish a film-industry setting for the story. Indeed, setting was so completely stylized in the Hollywood murder mysteries that merely the word "Hollywood," resonant with all its multiple and contradictory meanings, could create an evocative frame for crime and its detection.

According to W. H. Auden in his classic essay on mystery fiction, "The Guilty Vicarage," one of the principal requisites for the depiction of milieu in puzzle mysteries was a "closed society so that the possibility of an outside murderer (and hence of the society being totally innocent) is excluded; and a closely related society so that all its members are potentially suspect."[21] Certainly the Hollywood studios provided a densely inter-related society of suspects for the writers of mysteries to work with, but there was never any illusion about Hollywood being a "totally innocent" society; the film capital was presumed guilty from the start, and the Holly-wood crime narrative always recognized the threats to this community from both the unstable mixture of personalities within the studio and the parasites and predators eager to crash into the big money from without.

Despite the second-class literary status that critics have traditionally bestowed upon detective and mystery fiction, it has had a significant cultural impact as a popular literary genre. The figure of the criminal investigator popularized by the puzzle mystery was usually an apostle of scientific rationality and empiricism, and thus an agent of social reform and control. At the same time, the urban detective, as Raymond Williams has argued, emerged in the twentieth century as the cultural figure best able to read behind the deceptive surfaces of modern city life; he is "the man who can find his way through the fog, who can penetrate the intricacies of the streets," and thus the tale of crime and its detection could also reflect the uncertainties and fears attendant upon modernity and urban life. The criminal narrative developed as a genre of urban experience within which "the opaque complexity of modern city life is represented by crime."[22] Moreover, murder, whether factual or fictional, is never without its social and cultural implications, and even the bloodless deaths of the puzzle mystery can point to larger cultural anxieties and social concerns.

The first crime novel to make use of a motion-picture background was Arthur B. Reeve's *The Film Mystery* (1921), which featured the "scientific detective" Professor Craig Kennedy.[23] Set in the East Coast film production centers of New York and New Jersey, *The Film Mystery* evinced an interest in the science and technology of motion pictures similar to that of the pre-Hollywood fictions of Appleton and Hope. The story's premise, though, is one that would be repeated often in subsequent Hollywood mysteries: film star Stella Lamar is murdered on the set while the camera rolls, and the crime is recorded on film. Such an event gave Reeve the opportunity to explore the exotic milieu of the film studio while at the same time demonstrating the scientific uses of motion-picture technology in the detection of crime. Implicit in *The Film Mystery* was a particular ideological agenda: to demonstrate how an analysis of the screen image enables the solution of the crime through a logic of the visible. Like the X ray, the motion-picture image could reveal what was hidden, while the detective laid bare the larger social pathology of the film industry by investigating a series of suspects, all with possible motives for the crime. In *The Film Mystery* these include an unscrupulous movie producer, who has used the star to extort money from wealthy admirers, and the star's ex-husband, an embittered scenario writer who is finally revealed to have masterminded her death. In the novel's denouement, Detective Kennedy pauses before revealing the murderer to make explicit the interconnections of science, motion pictures, and the detection of crimes.

> "I need not tell you, ladies and gentlemen, that this is a highly scientific age in which we live." His tones were leisurely, businesslike, cool. "Your own profession, the moving picture, with all its detail of photography and electricity, its blending of art and drama and mechanics, is indicative of that, but"—a pause for emphasis—"it is of my own profession I wish to talk just now, the detection and prevention of crime." (365–66)

The motif of a murder caught on film was repeated in Edward Stilgebauer's novel *The Star of Hollywood*, a German work published in the United States in 1929.[24] Whether the awkward prose of this work is the fault of the author or of one E. E. Wilson, named as the translator of the English edition, is uncertain. In either case, the book is a clumsily written and highly overblown portrait of the film industry, of which, it seems likely, the author had no firsthand knowledge. Hollywood in *The Star of Hollywood* is more an abstract idea than an actual locale—a sign that Stilgebauer uses to signify corruption and vice in American culture. The novel is mainly interesting for its flamboyant use of the Hollywood setting to articulate a sinister view of the film industry. It begins with a memorable evocation of the Hollywood antimyth.

Hollywood:

On the Pacific, outside the gates of Los Angeles in California, it stands! The City of Illusions! The Cosmos of Cardboard! . . .

The false and compressed passion thinned out by the New World overflows here ceaselessly into a reservoir out of which is fed the hot hunger of millions. . . .

. . . Fever rages through this town. Not the fever born of marshy tracts of the coast, for this kind is unknown in the fortunate climate of California; but the consuming malaria of gold greed and ambition, the rush after fame and vaingloriousness. This malaria slays more quickly and claims its victims more blood-thirstily than does the dreaded epidemic of the tropics.

Here, in the centre of events, stands the possibility of inexhaustible riches and unbreakable power. . . .

In this way Hollywood became what it is to-day. The Mecca of the pilgrims seeking after luck on the stage. The town of cardboard! The nest of desires and vices! To describe it in a single expression, it is: "The Cradle of American Films." (5–6)

Stilgebauer's characterization of Hollywood as the "Cradle of American Films" at the novel's outset is profoundly ironic in light of the tale of drug addiction, insanity, and murder that he then proceeds to unfold. The novel begins with the death of the world-famous "star of Hollywood," Rita Astori, as she performs before the camera at the California Cinema Company. Her death, the result of a morphine overdose, is edited into the release print of the film. All traces of her addiction are discreetly hushed up by a studio physician, who hastily prepares a death certificate in order to save the studio from scandal. Endeavoring to protect the studio's investment in the film, the director selects an unknown extra-girl named Mabel Moon to replace the star because of her physical resemblance to Astori. Yet suspicions are aroused when it is learned that Moon was present on the set the day of Astori's death. Detective Stewart Cheers enters the case after becoming convinced by his careful analysis of the star's death on film that Astori was murdered. He discovers that the fatal overdose was delivered by the extra-girl, who used a prop snake to conceal her actions.

Meanwhile, Moon becomes a screen success overnight, quickly acquiring the wealth and prestige of the Hollywood star whom she has murdered. Moon also becomes addicted to morphine. She develops a morbid obsession with the dead Astori, purchasing and moving into her fabulous villa, which she shares with a mysterious housekeeper and Astori's vicious dog (rendered mute by the severing of his vocal cords). Gothic elements accumulate in the narrative: Stilgebauer depicts the increasingly deranged Moon as drug-addicted, haunted by guilt, and ultimately driven to insanity by her obsession with the dead film star. When detective Cheers finally exposes Moon as the murderer, she follows Astori in death with a fatal dose of morphine.

The Star of Hollywood is a bleak, depressing novel in which the material rewards of screen fame are shown to be powerful inducements to jealousy and violence, with the extra-girl's ambition leading her first to murder and then to suicide. Hollywood wealth and fame are linked metaphorically to the narcotic that addicts and ultimately kills the two women.

One of the most interesting Hollywood puzzle mysteries was Ben Ames Williams's *An End to Mirth*, which was serialized in the *Ladies' Home Journal* in 1930–31.[25] Here again, a murder is committed within the closed world of the film community, but this time it occurs during a party at a Hollywood Hills mansion owned by a successful screen comedian, Ned Brace, who has formed his own production company and enjoys considerable wealth and power in the film industry. Brace, a consummate practical joker, hosts a regular Sunday-evening "bash" at which he stages elaborate hoaxes that are known to shock and outrage even his cynical film-industry friends. For this particular affair Brace has staged his own murder for the diversion of his guests, providing one of them with an opportunity to turn the make-believe into payback. For Williams, the dissipated pastimes of the movie elite presented in *An End to Mirth* exemplified what he called "that quality of exaggeration which the city breeds." However, the high-keyed "mirth" of Brace and his Hollywood guests is brought to an abrupt end when the party's host is found dead of a real gunshot wound.

A central element in *An End to Mirth* is Brace's luxurious hillside mansion, christened "Brace Yourself," which becomes an elaborate metaphor for Hollywood itself. The sprawling home overlooking Los Angeles is a symbol of Brace's wealth and power, with its swimming pool, tennis courts, and extravagantly furnished interior. It is also a kind of fun house, with concealed passages, hidden staircases, secret rooms, and a system of tunnels honeycombing the hillside below it. Brace Yourself provides an architectural metaphor for the deceptiveness of appearances in Hollywood— where, in crime stories, the confusion over what is real and what is illusion always complicates the mystery. Accordingly, Williams presents the murder from the outset as a problem of distinguishing the real from the unreal, and such a view of the crime supports a more general critique of Hollywood's ability to conceal its criminality behind a veil of deception.

Brace has also equipped his mansion with the latest motion-picture equipment, which serves to link technology to the solution of crime. Having recently converted his film studio to sound, Brace has wired his home with recording equipment and loudspeakers, which conveniently capture the sounds of his murder and the responses of the suspects when they discover he is dead. It is indicative of the changes brought about by Hollywood's conversion to sound that in 1930–31 it was a recorded voice, rather than a moving image, that played the crucial role of revealing the murderer in Williams's novel.

An End to Mirth offers a rich gallery of Hollywood types as suspects in the case, revealing the full range of criminal motives within the film industry. As is typical of puzzle mysteries, all of the suspects are shown to have good reasons for wanting Brace dead, and the investigation of the crime leads to the gradual revelation of a "secret history" of sexual relationships among those present. We learn, for instance, that Brace's wife Claire was forced into marriage with him in order to salvage her aging father's career in pictures. Dr. Lesley, the studio physician, has long been in love with Claire, while his wife, Nell Blakeway, openly despises Brace for having ruined her screen career as an ingenue by forcing her to play more mature character roles. Robin Crider is a young, beautiful star whose success is rumored to have been helped along by Brace at the price of certain undisclosed sexual favors. Fanny Aram is a star dubbed "the best-dressed woman in Hollywood" and is married to Gene Aram, a former partner of Brace who has failed to share in the comedian's success and has become cynical and bitter as a result. Because Gene has been taunted by Fanny with a twenty-year-old love affair between her and Brace, the one-time business partner substitutes live ammunition for blanks on the night of the hoax, seeking revenge for his professional failures and sexual betrayal.

Brace's murder raises the specter of scandal for all those gathered in his home. One of the guests, a fan-magazine writer, points out to the assembled Hollywood elite, "Have you read your contracts lately? 'Public scandal or disgrace.' Anyone in the picture game has got to be twice as spotless as Caesar's wife. And there's mud enough in this to splatter us all plenty" (2:17). A studio lawyer is hastily summoned to arrange a cover-up story; however, he fails to convince the district attorney, who sees in a Hollywood murder a chance to grab publicity and advance his own reputation at the film industry's expense. "For here was fame! This would be a case celebrated, a trial reported in every newspaper in the world. His own name would top the headlines day by day. . . . Blackmail. Romance. Wealth. Youth. Beauty. Passion. Jealousy. The glamour of the films—these would all find wide publicity" (4:27).

In *An End to Mirth*, Brace's death and the sexual secrets that are revealed during the investigation of the crime hint at a pervasive corruption within the film community, which comes through despite Williams's attempt to mitigate such a reading by framing the events of the murder with the romance of Brace's daughter Celia and a studio technician, Eddie, who assists the police in solving the crime. At the end of the novel, Celia rejects her father's hillside mansion—a symbol of the wealth and false values that have cost him his life—and embraces a humbler domestic ideal. "'I want,' she said dreamily at last, 'to live in a house just like all the other houses, on a street with all the other people, where folks are always passing by or dropping in. You can be alone on a mountain, Eddie, but you can be lonely, too. I want to be with people. Just like them'" (4:170). This endorsement of a folksy domesticity no doubt appealed to the readers of *Ladies' Home Journal*, but it was also a convenient way for Williams to arrange Hollywood's moral recuperation in the narrative. Still, *An End to Mirth* constructs Hollywood's criminal identity in terms of a secret history of sexually transgressive behavior, which is only partially mitigated by the book's sentimental subplot.

One of the best Hollywood puzzle mysteries, and a work that directly addressed issues of sexuality and gender in the film industry, was Lange Lewis's *The Birthday Murder* (1945). Lewis, who was more adept at characterization than many who worked in the mystery genre, created a complex portrait of a successful woman novelist who becomes a victim of crime in part because of her intelligence and ability. Along with being a renowned author and playwright, Victoria Jason Himes enjoys a seemingly stable and happy marriage with Albert Himes, a Hollywood producer of B movies. Albert, however, is about to make the jump from B pictures to prestige films with his next production, a film version of his wife's latest novel. When Albert is discovered poisoned to death, suspicions are turned toward Victoria, particularly when it is revealed that she and her husband disagreed over the casting of the starlet Moira Hastings in a leading role. When it becomes apparent to investigator Detective Tuck of the L.A.P.D. that Hastings and Albert Himes had been carrying on an affair, it appears likely that Victoria, after learning of her husband's adultery with the beautiful star, poisoned him in a jealous rage.

Throughout the novel Victoria is presented as a serious professional writer and the equal of any man—even of her ultravirile first husband, who arrives mysteriously the night of the murder and becomes a leading suspect in the case. In opposition to his misogynistic views, Victoria's achievements as a woman seem most admirable and positive. Observing her success, her ex-husband reproaches her for becoming "that rather fabulous creature, a self-sufficient woman, functioning like a man in a man's world".[26] Later, another character remarks to her, "You career women interest me; you have a sound practicality, an ability to take care of yourself which I must say I admire. Most women are, to some degree, parasites" (164). Victoria is clearly no "parasite," and her independence and talent have made her a highly respected individual at the studio. There are, however, several examples of women as parasites in the novel, most notably the character Moira Hastings, whom Lewis describes as "a figure standing in for something minted by the hundreds in this strange town, the young actresses, all so much alike in the cool drive of their ambition, differing only in the varying ways which served them to achieve what they wanted" (20). Lacking Hastings's physical charms, Victoria has succeeded in Hollywood on the basis of her intellect and her ability, yet it is precisely because of her "practicality" and cool "male" directness that she becomes a prime suspect in her husband's murder.

The ironic denouement of *The Birthday Murder* reveals once again the difficulty of discerning the real from the unreal in Hollywood: it is finally revealed that Albert killed himself accidentally, and the intended recipient of the poison was Victoria. It was Albert, in fact, who had plotted to murder his wife so that he could star Hastings in the picture based on Victoria's novel. He had used his marriage to Victoria to secure an option on her book as a way out of B-movie work, while pursuing the beautiful and younger Hastings on the side. For the world-weary Detective Tuck, Albert Himes's death exemplifies a familiar Hollywood plot. "The success pattern. The simplehearted dedication of every act to the achievement of a private goal. The simplehearted belief that any means justifies the end" (201). Such ruthless ambition coupled with illicit sexual desires is offered as a defining feature of Hollywood life in *The Birthday Murder*.

While mysteries such as *The Star of Hollywood, An End to Mirth*, and *The Birthday Murder* presented criminality as flourishing within the closed hothouse environment of the film industry, other Hollywood crime novels showed how those working in the industry could be vulnerable to the envy and violence of outsiders. In novels such as Mark Lee Luther and Lillian C. Ford's *Card 13* (1929), Herbert Crooker's *The Hollywood Murder Mystery* (1930), Charles Saxby and Louis Molnar's *Death Over Hollywood* (1937), and Jimmy Starr's *The Corpse Came C.O.D.* (1944), Hollywood characters are victimized by outsiders preying upon the affluence and insecurity to be found in the film community.

In Luther and Ford's *Card 13*, for instance, the outraged moral righteousness of an Iowa tourist leads to the death of a Hollywood screenwriter. When successful studio scribe Tony Gilmore is shot after returning home from a wild Hollywood party, his murder is investigated by his friend, the novelist Arthur Ranleigh, and Inspector Kent of the district attorney's office. Their investigation uncovers a host of possible film-industry suspects and reveals Gilmore's sordid sexual past, which threatens to ruin several prominent screen careers if brought to light. Yet Ranleigh eventually discovers that the murder was committed by Gilmore's matron aunt, Mrs. Barnett—a severe Iowa puritan visiting Los Angeles, who believes that "Hollywood is Sodom and Gomorrah rolled in one" and that "motion pictures are destroying the moral fiber of the nation and the sanctity of the home."[27] The outraged aunt, having witnessed Gilmore's numerous liaisons with starlets and extra-girls, finally snaps when he returns from a party to pick up several bottles of gin (she is an ardent prohibitionist), and kills him in the heat of moral indignation. In a rambling confession, Mrs. Barnett rails against "this ungodly age" (299), exemplified for her by Hollywood's permissive sexual standards; her judgment against the dead screenwriter is simply that "Hollywood ruined him" (301). Thus, in *Card 13* Luther and Ford use Mrs. Barnett's moral outrage against Hollywood as the motive for the murder of her nephew.

In the 1920s, a different kind of crime story began to appear in popular magazines that specialized in the mystery genre—often called "pulps" because they were printed on inexpensive, coarse wood-pulp paper. These new crime narratives reflected a different perspective on criminality from that of the increasingly staid traditional puzzle mystery—which Raymond Chandler, a leading practitioner of the new style, described as an "average, more than middling dull, pooped-out piece of utterly unreal and mechanical fiction."[28] Demonstrating a greater interest in character and setting and marked by violent action and terse colloquial language, the "hard-boiled" school of crime fiction was less interested in solving a mystery than in exploring the dark psychologies of its characters and the even darker social environments in which they moved. As David Madden has noted, the hard-boiled, "tough novels" of writers such as Dashiell Hammett, Horace McCoy, James Cain, and Raymond Chandler reflected the social world of the thirties and forties "in a way that is at once an objective description and an implicit judgement of it."[29] These works were often noted for their greater "realism" in depicting crime and the American criminal social milieu, and they were more frank in their treatment of sexuality and violence. As Chandler noted, the hard-boiled detective story appealed to a different kind of reader, one whose outlook was more pessimistic and more resigned to the casual violence in American life: "people with a sharp aggressive attitude to life. They were not afraid of the seamy side of things; they lived there. Violence did not dismay them; it was right down their street" (234).

Generally written as first-person narratives, hard-boiled novels articulated a cynical view of human relationships and a skepticism about social institutions and moral authorities that had its roots in the changes that took place in American society after World War I. Cynthia Hamilton has described the hard-boiled detective novel as typical of "the big city weariness and wariness of the post-war period; tired of idealism, cynical of reform, it mingles acceptance with outrage as it looks around at a world brutalized and morally bankrupt from a dirty, unheroic war and widespread corruption."[30] In part, the violence and pessimism of hard-boiled fiction was a reflection of social and economic realities in America, which had recently made a catastrophic transition from the boom of the "roaring twenties" to the bust of the Great Depression. Following the frenzy of materialism and consumption of the 1920s, the widespread unemployment and poverty of the 1930s revealed a more brutal and, to some, a more corrupt social order. Prohibition had encouraged the rise of organized crime in America even as it tempted law-abiding citizens into illegality, and by the thirties the gangster had emerged as a powerful yet distinctly ambivalent cultural figure, both despised and admired for his lawlessness.[31] At the same time, the Depression led many to feel that even trusted civic leaders and long-standing social institutions could become elements of a vast criminal conspiracy to victimize and fleece the public. In the 1930 crime became a familiar political metaphor for the prevailing social and economic conditions of American life.

No less an observer of American culture than Katharine Fullerton Gerould analyzed "This Hard-Boiled Era" for *Harper's Magazine* in 1929.[32] She saw the hard-boiled attitude as the product of a hunger for sensation and vicarious experience in a jaded mass audience, and she viewed such trends as a sign of the decadence in American civilization. "We sit at the feet of the hobo, the bruiser, the criminal, and learn, not because of their superior intelligence, but because the nastier detail of their lives is something new to us" (266). Gerould was well aware that violence was an integral part of American social and cultural life.

> Since gangsters have taken to mowing down their enemies in the city streets with machine guns, we can no longer get a "kick" out of the isolated and furtive pistol. . . . We are more prone at the present moment than at any time, these many generations, to assume the casual presence among us of violent and unnatural crimes. . . . We demand knockouts; we get knockouts; and our emotions are roused by nothing less. We deal, easily and habitually, in terms of violence. It is only the super-knockout that makes us really sit up. (267–68)

If one required further evidence of the deleterious effects of the hard-boiled attitude on American culture, according to Gerould, "one need only mention in passing the increasing vogue of fiction dealing plainly with crime" (270). "The immense recent vogue of mystery and detective stories is merely a frank avowal that while we want a 'kick,' we do not want a 'kick' that will start us thinking" (274). Such was often the appraisal of hard-boiled fiction by contemporary literary authorities, yet the themes and style of the pulp writers had parallels in the work of modern authors such as Ernest Hemingway and William Faulkner,[33] and the novels and short stories of the hard-boiled school have proven to be much more durable than the complaints of their critics.

The protagonist of the hard-boiled novel was the private investigator, or P.I. Unlike the investigators of classical mystery fiction, the private detectives of the hard-boiled school solved crimes not through intellect or scientific know-how but through dogged persistence, blind luck, and occasional violence. The P.I. was an individual whose services were for hire to the highest bidder; yet, as a free agent, he could choose to pursue an investigation for his own reasons and was not always guided by the best interests of his clients. One major difference between the puzzle mystery and the hard-boiled crime story was that occasionally the P.I. did not solve the crime, or the solution served to cast guilt upon all who were involved, including the detective. Such narrative resolutions suggested a darker, more pessimistic view of criminality, and the P.I.'s inability to restore justice to a fallen modern world represented the limits of individual agency in a competitive mass society. The P.I. was governed by a code of ethics, a set of loyalties, that often led him to view his clients and criminals with the same jaundiced eye, seeing corruption everywhere. His experiences as a private detective conspired to make of him a loner and a skeptic, yet he was also capable of existential insight and even sentimentality in his compassion for the human suffering that he often witnessed. As David Madden observed in his introduction to a collection of essays on hard-boiled writers, "in a society in which human events daily, on all levels, contradict the preach-ments of institutions," the private investigator was "strategically placed to perceive lies and hypocrisy."[34] He gradually became a figure of intense cultural appeal and importance precisely for his ability to see, behind the glossy, materialistic surface and easy optimism of American life, the under-lying currents of corruption and disintegration.

One feature shared by many hard-boiled crime novels is a California setting. A recent critic of the works of Hammett, Cain, and Chandler has speculated that California became the "favored setting" for their fiction because, as "the first postindustrial economy, it seemed to preview the future."[35] To be sure, Los Angeles has long been viewed as an index of our collective social future, forecasting what is to come in both utopian and dystopian versions. Yet the presence of the Hollywood culture industry also contributed to the place of Los Angeles in the urban symbolism of hard-boiled fiction. This genre often explored the confusion of illusion and reality and the dangers of unrestrained consumption—ideas to which Hollywood and Los Angeles were clearly linked.

One of the first hard-boiled novels to directly explore the Hollywood milieu was Raoul Whitfield's *Death in a Bowl* (1930). Whitfield wrote for the hard-boiled school's leading pulp magazine, *Black Mask*, which was the first publisher of works by Hammett, McCoy, and Chandler.[36] Whitfield brought firsthand experience to his Hollywood crime novel: he had acted in silent pictures before World War I and had lived in Los Angeles on and off for the next twenty years. When *Death in a Bowl* was optioned by Paramount in 1932, Whitfield went to work as a contract writer for the studio, although his efforts produced only one screen credit.[37]

In *Death in a Bowl*, Whitfield created a definitive portrait of the hard-boiled private investigator in Hollywood detective Ben Jardinn, whose laconic observations on life in the film capital constitute a kind of "hard-boiled philosophy" of skepticism and doubt. Jardinn's habit of surveillance makes him aware of a pervasive corruption in the society around him, to which he responds by becoming a loner and a cynic. "'So many humans like to tell lies,' he said almost gently. 'It's hell finding out what really happens.'"[38] Such uncertainties about human actions and their motivations are, of course, magnified in Hollywood, where appearances are always deceptive and artistic temperaments often clash. Yet Jardinn sees behind the facades put in place by wealthy movie stars and powerful directors. "He knew Hollywood. Surface talk meant nothing to him; he got beneath every word" (9). Such an ability serves him well in untangling the complex web of events described in *Death in a Bowl,* in which volatile artistic temperaments and the violent jealousies of a screen star, a writer, and a director create a maze of deceptions for Jardinn to navigate.

The crime, as suggested by the title, is the audacious assassination of a distinguished conductor, Hans Reiner, while he performs in front of a capacity audience at the Hollywood Bowl. Reiner is the brother of a prominent

Hollywood director, Ernst Reiner. Initially his death appears to be at the hands of a disgruntled studio writer, recently fired by the director. But film star Maya Rand becomes a suspect, as well, when it is discovered that she hired a plane to fly over and disrupt the concert, possibly in order to drown out the sound of a rifle shot. The animosities that Jardinn uncovers among his Hollywood suspects create a highly unflattering image of the film community, where temperament and vanity lead to blackmail and murder. And it is a community insulated and protected by its wealth. "Money will buy almost anything—in Hollywood" (12), one character observes. Jardinn acknowledges that the film industry's affluence serves as a shield for its criminality. "'That's what's going to make this hard,' he said. 'There's plenty of money around for the cover-up'" (51).

Despite the novel's indictment of Hollywood corruption, the ironic denouement reveals that Reiner's murderer was Jardinn's own partner, Max Cohn. Having discovered the reason for screen star Maya Rand's hatred of Hans Reiner, Cohn killed Reiner in order to blackmail Rand, whose career is vulnerable to the taint of scandal, with the crime. In *Death in a Bowl*, the diseased social relations in the insulated world of the film community make it vulnerable to the violence and greed of "outsiders"— in this case, from within the private detective's own ranks. It is Jardinn's betrayal by his partner that best exemplifies the novel's hard-boiled ethos, in which all human relationships exist in the shadow of treachery and mistrust. This theme is first announced when Jardinn fires his secretary, "Irish," accusing her of tampering with his watch the night of the murder. But when Irish is found knifed in Jardinn's own apartment, the P.I. faces the inevitable conclusion that he was betrayed by his partner, Cohn. It is this undermining of the integrity of "the agency" that most outrages Jardinn. His professional code of ethics is particularly offended when he learns that Cohn's crimes were motivated by the need to support his mistress, a "Hollywood blonde" who "was always wanting something" (263).

The idea that betrayal would be motivated by the desire for a woman suggests the conservative sexual politics often present in hard-boiled fiction. Jardinn's misogyny is evident on several occasions when he demonstrates brutality toward women. To the lone P.I., emotional entanglements are dangerous, particularly if they lead him to drop his guard or ignore his instincts. A fear of women's sexuality and of their social and economic independence pervades the usually male-dominated social world of the hard-boiled detective. The genre often perpetuated and elaborated upon the dangers of Hollywood's transgressive sexual values through the reccurring figure of the femme fatale.

THE BILL LENNOX STORIES

The September 1933 issue of *Black Mask* featured the first appearance of Bill Lennox, one of the toughest and most cynical hard-boiled detectives to work the Hollywood beat in American pulp fiction. Lennox was the creation of W. T. Ballard, an Ohio newspaperman who had first begun writing short stories for the pulps in the 1920s and had come to Los Angeles in the early thirties to pursue writing jobs at several Hollywood studios. Despite intermittent film work, it was the voracious pulp-magazine market that remained the most stable source of income for Ballard. He began to incorporate his firsthand knowledge of the studios and Hollywood life into his Bill Lennox stories for *Black Mask*.[39]

The first story, "A Little Different," introduced the central characters of the series: Lennox, a former newspaperman, publicity agent, and writer, now a studio "troubleshooter" assigned to deal with the company's more embarrassing problems, such as kidnappings, blackmail, and murder; the beleaguered studio boss Sol Spurck, head of General-Consolidated Films; and Lennox's long-suffering girlfriend, fan-magazine writer Nancy Hobbs, who knows all the Hollywood dirt. She confides to Bill, "I know plenty about this town that I don't print in fan magazines. . . . I get around."[40] Lennox's position as a film-industry insider responsible for doing the studio's "dirty work" produces a jaded attitude toward Hollywood in Ballard's stories. Lennox seems always about to quit his job at the studio in disgust. "I stick around this madhouse and keep things going," he complains to Spurck. "Someday, Sol, I'll quit this louse outfit cold. I'll sit back and watch it go to the devil" (23). Such sentiments seem entirely justified, as Lennox is often fired and rehired by Spurck in the course of protecting the studio's interests.

In "A Little Different," Spurck asks Lennox to locate a prominent male star who has been kidnapped and held for ransom with the result that production on Spurck's latest film has been halted. The search for the missing star takes Lennox on a journey through Hollywood's neon-bathed night life. He explores the seedy clubs and restaurants serving as fronts for the criminal enterprises that cater to the film community's affluence and hunger for excitement. Recurrent settings in the Bill Lennox stories, such as the El Romano Club, the Palace Gambling Ship, and the Three Stars Club, are invariably criminal enclaves run by gangsters who attempt to conceal their illegitimate enterprises behind a facade of Hollywood glamour—emblems, finally, of a corrupt criminal milieu thriving on the film industry's wealth and moral lassitude.

Lennox's work generally involves him in some kind of unlawful activity, usually the concealment of incriminating evidence to protect studio investments or personnel; in other words, he is a master of the cover-up and knows how best to utilize the studio's resources to prevent scandal and expense for the company. His dogged loyalty to the studio frequently blurs easy distinctions between the legal and the illegal, and he often finds himself on the wrong side of the police—who are generally portrayed as bumbling, ineffectual elements in the violent struggle against crime and vice in Los Angeles's urban jungle. Eventually, Lennox exposes a criminal conspiracy operating from within the studio. Spurck's nephew, hired through typical studio nepotism, and a double-dealing Hollywood starlet along with her gangster boyfriend are responsible for the star's kidnapping, which was orchestrated as a means of repaying the nephew's gambling debts. In the Bill Lennox stories, the film industry is in constant need of protection from its own vices and self-destructive elements.

A recurring theme was Lennox's sexual betrayal by a beautiful woman. Here again, the conservative sexual politics of hard-boiled fiction produced an image of women that often said less about them than about male fears and insecurities—for which the narrative frequently compensated by making these women the victims of violent crime. In "A Million-Dollar Tramp," Ballard created an ironic black comedy out of the narrative of sexual betrayal. One of Lennox's unofficial duties at the studio is to keep an eye open for new talent, and when he spots a pretty extra-girl with the ability to achieve success in pictures, he begins to help her career along. However, Lennox soon has to conceal the fact that a man has been murdered in the apartment of the star-to-be, and Lennox's removal of the body from the crime scene endangers him with both the police and the victim's criminal associates, who are looking for a missing $20,000. After saving the star-to-be from both the police and the hoodlums, Lennox receives a brief thank-you note informing him that the pretty extra has decided to return to her hometown sweetheart and live on the $20,000 she has successfully stolen. Played for a sucker by the young woman and deceived by his own illusions about her, Lennox expresses his typical embittered resignation: "You're not the first chiseling tramp that forgot my name after I boosted them into lights, and I don't suppose that you'll be the last."[41]

Bill Lennox appeared in twenty-seven stories in *Black Mask* between 1933 and 1942, and Ballard continued the character in four novels: *Say Yes to Murder* (1942), *Murder Can't Stop* (1946), *Dealing Out Death* (1948), and *Lights, Camera, Murder* (1960). In all of these works Ballard represents Hollywood's excesses and illusions as signs of a larger social disease. As James L. Traylor has observed, Ballard "uses the Hollywood movie colony as a microcosm of the plastic world in which art and artifice keep truth at a distance";[42] Hollywood's illusions conceal its underlying violence and corruption. In the Bill Lennox stories, Hollywood is a town where fantasy disguises criminality, and where a superficial optimism and glamour conceal underlying desperation. "The whole town was flippant and gay," Lennox observes in *Say Yes to Murder,* "a forced gaiety as if people were afraid to be themselves, as if they were all actors on some enormous set";[43] and a little later he remarks to Nancy, "this town can be beautifully dirty, honey—so full of heartbreak and sin" (15–16). The notion of Hollywood as "beautifully dirty" performs an evocative conjoining of cultural responses to the film capital that is typical of Hollywood fiction, where fascination and desire were often mingled with contempt and dread.

LAZARUS #7

The idea of Hollywood as "beautifully dirty"—the symbolic linking of apparent glamour and underlying corruption in the film capital—received its fullest treatment in a work Raymond Chandler described as "a gay and intriguing Hollywoodian gambol"[44]: Richard Sales's bizarre Hollywood crime novel *Lazarus #7* (1942). Sales, like W. T. Ballard, began as a pulp writer before moving to Hollywood to work in motion pictures, and he eventually became the second husband of screenwriter Anita Loos. In *Lazarus #7*, he combined elements of science fiction and mystery to fashion a bitter portrait of Hollywood corruption, embodied in the character of a leprous film star who murders to conceal her disease from the public. The tainted film star—Gloria Gerard—becomes a metaphor for Hollywood's ability to conceal criminality and vice behind a facade of glamour, beauty, and sex appeal. Critic Carolyn See has rightly called *Lazarus #7* "a novel of social criticism" because of its "assumption of a real corruption within the world of the book."[45] "Hollywood is here a sick society," See argues; and the disease that affects it is at once physical, sociological, and moral.

In *Lazarus #7*, as in many Hollywood crime narratives, the solution of the crime depends upon the ability of the investigator to find the truth within a maze of illusions created by the film studio and by an eccentric cast of Hollywood suspects. The investigator of the crime is Dr. Steven Mason, an outsider who recently arrived in Hollywood to visit his old friend Joss Henry, a successful screenwriter. Mason is an M.D. just returned from the Far East, where he has been studying infectious diseases, and his medical and scientific background serves him well in the course of the investigation. At first he is dazzled by the excitement and glamour of Hollywood, as he is pursued by several beautiful women. But after a succession of mysterious deaths, he uncovers mounting evidence of studio corruption and police complicity in the cover-up of a series of cold-blooded murders, possibly involving his old friend Joss and other powerful Hollywood figures.

One index of Mason's growing disenchantment with Hollywood is his reaction to Joss's wild Hollywood life-style and the "deception and depravity and vulgarity" it entails.[46] This first becomes evident to him in the layout of Joss's fabulous "rancho," with its orange groves, tennis courts, and swimming pools but also in the secret doorways and hidden passages (as in Ben Ames Williams's *An End to Mirth*) that lead to Joss's mirrored bedroom, where extra-girls and starlets are led to be seduced. The rancho's elaborate den epitomizes the corrupting influence of Hollywood consumption for Mason.

> Joss' den was—well, I guess you might say, it was what you'd expect. In Hollywood, I mean. It was an astonishing, amazing room. The first thing which impressed you was what it must have cost. This characteristic is definitely Hollywoodian, it is the first consideration. . . .

The walls were of white leather, the desk top was white leather, and the rest of the desk was of zebra wood. The built-in bookcases on one wall were glutted with the finest books in the world . . . ninety per cent of them were still stiff in the bindings and had never been opened. He had to buy them to keep up with the trends in the tinsel town, with what the boys and girls were talking about at the moment, with what was smart to read or own at the time, with what was leading the best-seller lists, with what had been bought by the studios for pictures. (62–63)

Sales, like Edgar Rice Burroughs in *The Girl From Hollywood* and Nathanael West in *The Day of the Locust*, makes the screenwriter's home into an architectural metaphor for the corrupting influence of Hollywood and the superficial values it imposes upon those who work in movies. Mason tells us that in Hollywood Joss's work as a writer "had become very shoddy," and he angrily observes that in the film industry, "mediocrity is a shining star" (64). His aesthetic judgment of Joss's screen writing parallels a more general moral revulsion against the film industry and Hollywood's social life.

This view is shared by the morose police detective Daniel Webster, who protects Mason and helps him to solve the case. Webster is a typical hard-boiled cynic and loner. His name and his nickname, "the Senator"— references to the politician and orator Daniel Webster (1782–1852)—suggest a grounding in traditional American values and institutions. He confesses to Mason, "I don't have many friends. You can't be honest and have friends. I always had a knack of reading people and it made me a lot of enemies and alienated me from everybody and it made me a good detective" (64). It is Webster who best understands the inner dynamics of the Hollywood scene—the interplay of forces in the relations among City Hall, the police, and the film industry. He explains to Mason that "you have to see all the angles or you never find the right one" (65), and his opinion of Hollywood is summed up in a typically laconic judgment: "Everything stinks" (93).

At the center of the novel's indictment of Hollywood is the character Al Roche, a powerful studio functionary who engineers alibis and pays hush money to protect the studio's interests. He is also a procurer, and is not above violence if it helps to further his goals. The aptly named Roche (read "roach") is a feared and despised figure within the film community because of the power and influence he wields—specifically, as Mason observes, because "Al has a lot of things on lots of people" (60). Clearly, Roche is a character who, along with the leprous film star Gerard, comes to symbolize certain aspects of Hollywood itself. Mason describes him to his face.

> "You're deceit and aggression. You're idolatry, egotism, smugness. You're depravity and lust and greed. You're a nonentity where any spiritual or moral value is concerned. As long as there are men like you, there'd be crime and unhappiness and war. You're Adolph Hitler in short pants, my friend, and the mutual lot is your Deutsches Reich and Hollywood is your empire." (102)

Closely associated with Roche is a mysterious studio physician, Dr. Max Lekro. Between his more routine duties, the doctor performs experiments to resurrect the dead, and he has perfected a "cosmetic cure" for leprosy that conceals all signs of the disease. Lekro's chief patient is the beautiful screen star Gloria Gerard, who has used the scientist's quasi-cure to prolong her career after contracting the disease while on location in the South Seas. With her health worsening despite her superficial beauty, the desperate movie star begins murdering all who learn of her malady. First she kills an extra-girl who discovered her secret and has been blackmailing the star in exchange for keeping quiet. Next Gerard murders a studio bodyguard, and then Mason's friend Joss, who was told of the star's condition in a letter mailed by the extra before her death. Gerard's final murder victim is Dr. Lekro himself—whom Mason manages to bring back to life long enough for him to name Gerard as the killer.

Gerard's story in the novel is a parable of Hollywood success and failure. As she remarks to Mason, "It's a hard town and a hard racket, Steve. You don't go up the easy way" (38). Later she admits that fame in Hollywood is won "by being hard sometimes and soft other times, and by not letting anything stand in the way of your success. *Not anything!*" (86). Having come to Hollywood in flight from a life of poverty and abuse at her home in west Texas, Gerard has scratched her way to the top of the studio heap through a strategy of ruthless ambition and moral compromise.

> "You go up every and any way you can, honest or dishonest. You take me. Gloria Gerard, my face gracing every fan magazine on the stands,

243

college boys writing to me in droves, probably dreaming about sleeping with me. I'm not the sweater girl, but I could be. I haven't Dietrich's legs, but mine will do. I have a provocative body and that, with a little real acting, will take an American cinema star as far as she can go. They see me in *Esquire* in an evening gown cut to my navel. They see me at *premieres*, filthy with glamour. I'm the unattainable, so naturally every man—excepting you, Steve—wants to make me and every woman wants to imitate me. That's Hollywood success. . . .

"I made a vow that I'd never be broke and that I'd never be hungry and that nothing would ever knock me off my pedestal but the movie public, and that if anyone tried by hook or crook, it would be too bad." (38–39)

One sign of Gerard's corruption is her aggressive sexuality, and she repeatedly attempts to seduce Steve Mason. In a frank expression of her desire, she says to him, "I told you my life story, and it must have given you an idea of the kind of woman I am. For all the fan-mag buildups, I'm still a woman, and I know reality when I see it. You're real and I like it. . . . You could sleep with me tonight if you wished. Or tomorrow or any time. That's how I feel about you" (68). The problem is that Gloria Gerard isn't "real," although she is superficially beautiful—even in the nude, as Mason observes. Lekro's cosmetic cure conceals the truth about Gerard's disease as the aura of glamour that studio publicity has created around her conceals the depths of her depravity and criminal violence. "A glamorous movie star, her face on every fan magazine in the country, her latest picture playing the Music Hall in New York," Mason observes, "and she turns out to be a leper" (122). Such a revelation serves to call into question the whole edifice of film-industry glamour—the cultural myth of beauty and sexual perfection upon which the star system was based. Gerard becomes a perfect metaphor for the deadly deception of appearances in the Hollywood dream factory.

I WAKE UP SCREAMING

Steve Fisher's classic Hollywood crime novel *I Wake Up Screaming* (1941) combines a meticulous grasp of the details of life in Hollywood with a

grotesque, at times Kafkaesque, view of social relations there.[47] The novel
begins with a brilliant evocation of the Hollywood scene through a series
of images that capture the city's glamour and restless energy, its emptiness
as well as its potential for fulfillment.

> It was a hot Saturday night and I had on a Sy Devore suit and a hand-
> knit tie and sat at the bar in Mike Romanoff's drinking Canadian Club
> old fashioneds. The bar stools were leather and the wall decorations
> had that ultra look and Zsa Zsa Gabor was at a closeby table, her head
> thrown back in laughter, and Gary Cooper and Bing Crosby and Bill
> Holden were at other tables and a couple of blocks away, on the
> corner of Wilshire and Beverly Drive, they were having a premiere
> for the latest Jerry Wald epic: arc lights swinging back and forth,
> limousines arriving, and cops holding back the crowd. I was at long
> last in tinsel town and I was excited. At the same time I felt lonely.
> That sweet, hot loneliness that's like music. I was twenty-seven, had
> a play on Broadway, and now a studio contract at one of the majors
> that was still making big wide screen pictures. Hell, I even had my
> Writer's Guild of America card! I thought about things. Those first
> hard years were over. This was it, I thought. *This is the works!*[48]

For the narrator—a young writer who is never identified by name—this
early euphoria is gradually displaced by a more ambivalent view of
Hollywood. At first he experiences only boredom in the studio's scenario
department, and here the novel offers a telling portrait of the "Hollywood
writer," who, as we have seen, often represented a critical view of the film
industry. In *I Wake Up Screaming* Fisher depicts the studio as rife with fear
and insecurity—a place where "desperate games were being played" (21)
by people with much to lose. Writers, for example, were periodically
tortured by "option jitters" while they awaited the studio's decision on
renewal of their contracts, and stars and directors who slipped at the box
office could find themselves demoted to B-movie work and ultimate
unemployment. Fisher offers many small examples of Hollywood's callous
indifference to, yet desperate fear of, failure—such as this brief observation
made in the studio commissary: "At a small table next to the wall near the
place where waitresses stacked dirty dishes sat a director who had three

weeks to go, but whose option was being dropped. He sat there like a ghost, nibbling at salad. No one wanted any part of him. No one could afford to be seen sitting with failure" (22).

While waiting to be put to work on a script, the young writer meets and falls in love with a beautiful secretary at the studio named Vicky Lynn. Through this romantic liaison he enters into a scheme that leads to Vicky's murder and the devastation of his own emotional and professional life. *I Wake Up Screaming* repeatedly links Hollywood's romantic myth of personal and sexual fulfillment to its ironic antimyth of failure and death. The murder of Vicky Lynn exposes a town in which "up your sleeve or in your shoe you had a dream" (99)—but the dream often turns out to be a nightmare. This is especially so for young women like Vicky who are unwilling to make moral compromises to advance their careers. For "these girls" there is only the hunger "for dreams to come true," while they must "keep eating cheap hamburger and slapping cheap faces and waiting" (59). For the writer the nightmare is "Hollywood's tension, the feverish nights, the rotten little jealousies, the screaming egos, the petty smugness . . . and only a few sweet guys" (134), remembered from his days at the studio. For another character in the novel, an embittered extra, Hollywood is a place where "girls have to sleep with fat slobs to get work . . . and get pregnant and climb the hills and jump off the Hollywoodland sign" (76).

Infatuated with Vicky's beauty and intoxicated by his newfound sense of importance in Hollywood, the young writer decides to make Vicky Lynn into a movie star. He secures the aid of three studio allies, who become his partners in an effort to transform the pretty secretary into a screen goddess: Lanny Craig, an undistinguished writer of B movies with connections to the fan magazines; Hurd Evans, a director of B pictures who arranges for photographs and screen tests of the star-to-be; and Robin Ray, an aging juvenile actor who agrees to have his name romantically linked with the newcomer's, hoping that it will bolster his sagging masculine image with the public. Vicky Lynn is found murdered in her apartment when she is on the brink of Hollywood success, and all four of the would-be star makers become suspects in the ensuing criminal investigation.

When the young writer discovers Vicky Lynn's body, the reader knows that he cannot be the killer. Yet the novel adopts an ambiguous attitude toward the question of his guilt or innocence. It is clear that the writer's plan to transform Vicky into a star led to her death, and Fisher continues to place doubts in the reader's mind through the character of homicide detective Ed Cornell, who becomes convinced early in the investigation that it was indeed the writer who killed Vicky Lynn, out of jealousy over her growing stardom.

In fact, all of the partners in the scheme to make Vicky Lynn a star have compelling motives for committing the crime. Lanny Craig was about to be divorced by his wife and left penniless after she discovered his involvement in the plan to boost Lynn into stardom. Hurd Evans was broke and faced mounting debts, and he had recently taken out a life insurance policy on the young starlet in order to protect his investment in her career. Robin Ray was distraught because Vicky was going to dump him, which would deliver a fatal blow to his image as a screen lover. Despite such clear-cut motives, Detective Cornell persists in accusing the writer, who, he says, was insanely jealous over Vicky's public relationship with Ray. The writer's innocence is further called into question when he begins an affair with Vicky's sister, Jill. Although the writer tries to deny his feelings for Jill throughout most of the novel, after Vicky is murdered the two find their mutual attraction irresistible, and their open expression of love serves to incriminate them further in the mind of Detective Cornell.

In the wake of the investigation, the writer's three partners all find their careers in decline due to their connection with the crime. Yet the young writer finds *his* career suddenly taking off: his option is renewed by the studio, and superficially he seems to enjoy the distractions of life in Holly-wood. (Much of the novel is set during the Christmas season, and an ironic commentary on consumption underlies many of the descriptions of frantic holiday shopping.) Such good fortune as the writer seems to enjoy, however, soon breeds misgivings and doubts in him, and finally the Hollywood life-style is deemed empty.

> For a time I escaped. I remember now that for a long time I wasn't myself. I was a guy caught up in a glorious vortex. I was mad and gay and that isn't me at all. I was in the middle of a silver cyclone and the days and the nights whirled by with a shrill musical screaming. I was a guy in evening dress. Champagne's bright child. I was carried along in a clique of crazy people and I didn't have time to think. I

dined here. I slept there. Table conversation, with a sparkle. Splendid
bedrooms and dialogue in the dark. Breakfasts at noon. It was fun.
But I began thinking of Jill. (73)

As guilt about his complicity in Vicky's death builds, the writer becomes
haunted by a sense of foreboding, especially as regards his growing
romantic attachment to Jill. It is the implacable presence of Detective
Cornell, accusing him of the crime, that ultimately leads to the writer's
breakdown and, for a time, turns him into a hunted fugitive. Cornell is a
symbolic figure in the novel—an emblem of "the Law" and of a puritanical
moral judgment directed against Hollywood's transgressive sexual mores.
Yet he is also sick, literally diseased with consumption, and his pursuit of
the writer is based on an abuse of his authority magnified by a distorted
sense of moral retribution.

The writer first encounters Cornell during the "third degree" he receives
from the police soon after Vicky's death. During the session he is savagely
beaten, and Cornell puts out cigarettes in the palm of his hand in an effort
to extract a confession. When the official investigation subsequently clears
the young writer, an unctuous assistant district attorney makes a smug
official apology; later the writer is outraged when he learns that this
individual earns extra cash by selling crime-scene photos of Vicky's body
to "fact detective" magazines. An opportunistic minor bureaucrat in a
criminal justice system that mingles courtesy with brutality, the assistant
district attorney is another example of the official corruption that is
represented by Ed Cornell and that permeates the social world of the
novel.

Despite the outcome of the official investigation, Cornell takes it upon
himself to pursue the investigation against the writer, following up leads
and working on angles during his off-duty hours. He becomes both a
nemesis and a kind of chorus in the novel, appearing unexpectedly to hurl
accusations of guilt and threats of ultimate punishment at the writer, and
clearly tortured by his own "personal obsession" (47). When Cornell finally
arrives at the studio with an arrest warrant for the writer, the young man
panics and flees, going into hiding with Jill.

Under the pressure of the detective's relentless pursuit, the writer's
perspective becomes increasingly distorted by fear and uncertainty, and the

narrative begins to take on the grotesque features of a nightmare. Hollywood becomes a menacing and "sordid" place: "The glamour . . . and the greed for glamour. The petty hatreds, and the broken hearts, and the bums that hung on" (99). All the desperation and fear that the writer has observed in the film capital now invade his own comfortable existence. Evading the police, he and Jill attempt to change their appearances and assume new identities, living in seedy apartment houses and tourist courts, only to find the police dragnet closing around them.

Yet, even while suffering under the threat of constant pursuit and capture, the two lovers come into a full realization of the depth of their feelings for each other, and Fisher misses no opportunity to develop the irony of their true love. As they attempt to blend in with the crowd on a busy street, Jill pauses to point out a "hunchback midget selling his papers" (92). In a startling juxtaposition of moods, the writer seizes the moment to whisper a proposal of marriage to her. The two fugitives discover emotional fulfillment in the very heart of the desperate circumstances into which they find themselves unjustly thrust. But their happiness is short-lived, as Jill is soon apprehended by the police.

After escaping in a stolen car, the writer begins following up on several aspects of the case, which ultimately lead him to discover Vicky's killer— the sexually repressed and mentally deficient switchboard operator in her apartment house, a young man named Harry Williams, who killed her accidentally when she resisted his clumsy sexual advances. Cornell had learned early on that Williams was the murderer, but had let him escape in order to pursue his own "theory" of the writer's guilt, spun out of his hatred for Hollywood and the sexual desires aroused by the dead girl. When the writer confronts Cornell in his apartment with the facts of the murder and the detective's suppression of the evidence, he discovers just how obsessive Cornell's interest in the case has been: the walls are covered with "cheesecake" publicity photos of the starlet side by side with crime-scene and autopsy shots of her body, while articles of lingerie and half-empty bottles of her perfume, along with other personal items, are heaped in a kind of shrine in the detective's room.

The writer finally proves his innocence to the police, and this turn of events permits a romantic resolution through his marriage to Jill. But the revelation of overwhelming official corruption in the figure of Detective

Cornell and the opportunities for vice and criminality that the writer finds rampant within the studio's star-making machinery still serve to rewrite Hollywood's romantic dream into a nightmare in *I Wake Up Screaming*.

RAYMOND CHANDLER AND HOLLYWOOD: "THE GREAT WRONG PLACE"

Probably the most widely known and most influential representations of Hollywood and Los Angeles are found in the handful of novels written by an ex-oil company executive turned pulp-magazine writer and occasional screenwriter, Raymond Chandler. Born in Chicago in 1888, Chandler was educated in England and served in the First Canadian Expeditionary Corps during World War I before settling in Los Angeles in 1919. There he entered the booming oil business and swiftly became a successful oil-company executive during the lucrative 1920s. This was the decade when the discovery of oil at Long Beach led to a frenzy of drilling, exploration, and speculation in oil stocks, creating a boom-town atmosphere in sleepy rural communities such as Santa Fe Springs, where saloons, brothels, and flop-houses sprang up overnight to serve those who were pouring in to get rich quick in the oil fields. In a social environment dominated by cutthroat competition and a scramble for easy money, crime and corruption flourished, and there can be no doubt that Chandler's pessimistic view of southern California was shaped by these formative experiences in the Los Angeles oil fields.[49]

In 1932, at the age of forty-four, Chandler found himself unemployed and in need of work, so he turned to the uncertain vocation of writing. It was in the burgeoning pulp-fiction market that he first began to sell his stories, publishing regularly in magazines such as *Black Mask* and *Dime Detective* throughout the 1930s. Here he created his own version of the hard-boiled private investigator, Philip Marlowe, who would become the most celebrated example of the cynical urban detective both in mystery fiction and in film.[50] The appeal of Chandler's crime novels lay not in the unraveling of a mystery or in the solution of a crime, but in his acerbic depiction of a particular social milieu—Los Angeles in the thirties and forties—and his exploration of the corruption and criminality there, which, in the world of his novels and short stories, were the city's most characteristic features. Chandler was the novelist of what W. H. Auden called "the Great Wrong Place"; Los Angeles, in his work, represents a fallen modern world filled with routine brutality and anonymous human suffering and dominated by the debased values of a commercialized mass society, where the gangster and the millionaire rule with the complicity of a corrupt and demoralized police force. Chandler's Los Angeles is a place imbued with a sense of moral failure and existential despair, a "cold half-lit world where always the wrong thing happens and never the right."[51] At its symbolic center lay Hollywood, as Chandler makes clear in describing the milieu of his novels.

> The realist in murder writes of a world in which gangsters can rule nations and almost rule cities, in which hotels and apartment houses and celebrated restaurants are owned by men who made their money out of brothels, in which a screen star can be the finger-man for the mob, and the nice man down the hall is a boss of the numbers racket; a world where a judge with a cellar full of bootleg liquor can send a man to jail for having a pint in his pocket, where the mayor of your town may have condoned murder as an instrument of money-making, where no man can walk down a dark street in safety because law and order are things we talk about but refrain from practising.[52]

The language here is general enough to serve as a blanket indictment of American society, while specific references to film stars and famous restaurants owned by gangsters place Hollywood at the center of Chandler's dystopian view of America in the postwar 1940s. The corrupting influence of Hollywood in its relationship to the rest of American society is most fully explored in his novel *The Little Sister* (1949); it and *The Big Sleep* are arguably Chandler's two most important works.[53]

Chandler begins *The Little Sister* by sharply contrasting the natural landscape of the Los Angeles Basin with the man-made corruption endemic to the commercialized culture of the city.

> It was one of those clear bright summer mornings we get in the early spring in California before the high fog sets in. The rains are over. The hills are green and in the valley across the Hollywood Hills you can

see snow on the high mountains. The fur stores are advertising their annual sales. The call houses that specialize in sixteen-year-old virgins are doing a land-office business. And in Beverly Hills the jacaranda trees are beginning to bloom.[54]

This is another example of "beautifully dirty" Hollywood, where the benign climate and fortunate topography of the area, long celebrated by real-estate agents and boosters from the Chamber of Commerce, serves as an ironic frame for the exploitation and despoiling of innocence. A little later Marlowe observes that even "the pale stars" twinkling in the night sky "know enough to keep their distance from Hollywood" (67); here nature stands in opposition to the man-made jungle of Los Angeles and silently passes judgment on the sordid and disordered urban environment. Marlowe understands all too well that the superficial glitter of the city is deceptive, that "the colored lights fooled you" (81) and the real meaning of Hollywood is concealed behind a superficial facade of glamour. "I drove on past the gaudy neons and the false fronts behind them, the sleazy hamburger joints that look like palaces under the colors, the circular drive-ins as gay as circuses with the chipper hard-eyed carhops, the brilliant counters, and the sweaty greasy kitchens that would have poisoned a toad" (79). Marlowe's jaundiced response to Los Angeles culminates in an elegiac meditation on the city's loss of innocence.

> I used to like this town. . . . A long time ago. There were trees along Wilshire Boulevard. Beverly Hills was a country town. Westwood was bare hills and lots offering at eleven hundred dollars and no takers. Hollywood was a bunch of frame houses on the interurban line. Los Angeles was just a big dry sunny place with ugly homes and no style, but goodhearted and peaceful. It had the climate they just yap about now. People used to sleep out on porches. Little groups who thought they were intellectuals used to call it the Athens of America. It wasn't that, but it wasn't a neon-lighted slum either. . . .
>
> Now we get characters like this Steelgrave [a gangster] owning restaurants. . . . We've got the big money, the sharp shooters, the percentage workers, the fast-dollar boys, the hoodlums out of New York and Chicago and Detroit—and Cleveland. We've got the flash

restaurants and night clubs they run, and the hotels and apartment houses they own, and the grifters and con men and female bandits that live in them. The luxury trades, the pansy decorators, the Lesbian dress designers, the riffraff of a big hardboiled city with no more personality than a paper cup. . . .

Real cities have something else, some individual bony structure under the muck. Los Angeles has Hollywood—and hates it. It ought to consider itself damn lucky. Without Hollywood it would be a mail-order city. Everything in the catalogue you could get better somewhere else. (183–84)

Such a view of the city, built upon a stark contrast between an idealized past and a demonized present, works by articulating the competing myths that shaped Hollywood's cultural identity: on the one hand, a bucolic version of an American small town, and on the other, a sinister world of vice and corruption flourishing beneath a facade of glamour, in which Hollywood's image of sexual transgression is depicted in overtly homosexual terms.

In *The Little Sister*, Marlowe becomes involved in a case that ultimately reveals layers of corruption and complicity at every level of society, ranging from the denizens of skid-row flophouses to the elite of Beverly Hills and Hollywood. The "little sister" of the book's title is a prissy, rather straitlaced young woman named Orfamay Quest. She asks Marlowe to locate her brother Orrin Quest, who has apparently disappeared in Los Angeles's urban jungle. Orfamay and Orrin have come to Los Angeles from Manhattan, Kansas. That small midwestern town—named, ironically, after a big city—becomes symbolically linked to Los Angeles in the novel; Hollywood and Manhattan, Kansas, finally, are not that far apart in the levels of criminality and violence revealed by Marlowe's investigation. Marlowe discovers that Orfamay's brother Orrin has been blackmailing another sister, the beautiful screen star Mavis Weld, after discovering that she is romantically linked to a former Cleveland gangster, Steelgrave, now a prominent Hollywood restauranteur. When two small-time crooks learn of Orrin's blackmail scheme and attempt to cut in, he responds by murdering them both with an ice pick at the base of the skull. In Orrin Quest the sheltered small-town life-style of the Middle

West is shown to contain the same potential for corruption and violence as Los Angeles's seedy, urban milieu.

Orfamay, it turns out, has come to Hollywood not out of concern for her brother but because she expects her cut of the blackmail money that he plans to collect from Mavis. When it appears that Orrin may be unwilling to divide the money with her, Orfamay sells him out to the gangster Steelgrave, setting up her own brother to be murdered. Marlowe finally exposes her after discovering that it was she who killed Steelgrave—a crime for which Mavis attempts to take the blame in order to protect her murderous "little sister," at the cost of her own career in Hollywood. The irony of *The Little Sister* is that it is Orfamay and Orrin, products of American small-town values and religious piety, who demonstrate the greatest capacity for violence, always masked by a self-serving moral superiority toward Marlowe and the film industry.

Marlowe's search for the missing brother begins at the bottom of the Los Angeles social ladder, in the Idaho street flophouse that was Orrin's last known address and at the seedy Van Nuys Hotel to which he is summoned by an anonymous call. Chandler's depiction of these shabby urban settings—the worn rugs, peeling wallpaper, cigarette-burned furniture, and unmade "Hollywood" beds—are the outward signs of an underlying social pathology, and Chandler always imbues his settings with moral implications. As the critic Fredric Jameson has written, "All these places are characterized by belonging to the mass, collective side of our society: places occupied by faceless people who leave no stamp of their personality behind them, in short, the dimension of the interchangeable, the inauthentic."[55] It is difficult not to read Chandler's descriptions of these sordid urban settings and the lonely, frightened people who inhabit them as elements of a larger critique of mass society. "Room 332 was at the back of the building near the door to the fire escape. The corridor which led to it had a smell of old carpet and furniture oil and the drab anonymity of a thousand shabby lives."[56]

At the other end of the social scale, and central to the novel's critique of Hollywood, is Chandler's representation of the centers of Hollywood power in the office of talent agent Sherry Ballou and the studio itself, which Marlowe visits in order to interview Mavis Weld. Both Ballou's office and the film studio are noted for being inaccessible and difficult to enter: in both, Marlowe must negotiate a series of hostile secretaries and studio functionaries before he can penetrate the inner sanctum, where he encounters the men who run Hollywood. Sherry Ballou is rendered in the likeness of a decadent aristocrat, indulgent of his clients' occasional wrongdoings and all too willing to cover them up when necessary. "But show business has always been like that. . . . If these people didn't live intense and rather disordered lives, if their emotions didn't ride them too hard—well, they wouldn't be able to catch those emotions in flight and imprint them on a few feet of celluloid or project them across the footlights" (118). Ballou is an apologist for Hollywood's excesses, but he is also a businessman and understands the threats of scandal to career; so he hires Marlowe to protect Mavis Weld.

While visiting the studio to interview Weld, Marlowe inadvertently encounters the studio's top executive, Jules Oppenheimer, a character who has no role in the case and is introduced by Chandler solely as a comment upon the film industry. Marlowe observes him as an "elderly and beauti- fully dressed man" who sits by and watches his three dogs tear up the begonias planted in a well-tended studio flower bed. Particularly fascinat- ing to Oppenheimer is the way his three dogs always urinate in a specific order, a "question of seniority it seems." "'First Maisie. She's the mother. Then Mac. Year older than Jock, the baby. Always the same. Even in my office.' 'In your office?' I said, and nobody ever looked stupider saying anything" (123).

This image of Oppenheimer's dogs peeing in an order determined by rank and age is Chandler's ironic metaphor for the hierarchic and often sexually charged relations of power within the film industry. Oppenheimer himself is a tired businessman who complains that there is "too much sex" in movies (124), and believes that the secret of success in the film business is owning "fifteen hundred theaters." "The motion-picture business is the only business in the world in which you can make all the mistakes there are and still make money," he tells Marlowe, and he dismisses the creative contributions of writers, actors, and directors out of hand. "Doesn't matter a damn what they do or how they do it. Just give me fifteen hundred theaters" (125). Oppenheimer's pragmatic, economic vision of motion pictures reveals Chandler's critical view of the film industry, which was most evident in his outspoken complaints about the treatment of writers in the studio system.[57]

The novel's chief representative of Hollywood corruption is the beautiful and libidinous Dolores Gonzales, a Hollywood starlet and supposed friend of Mavis Weld. In fact, she is consumed with jealousy, both by Weld's affair with Steelgrave, who was once Gonzales's lover, and by Weld's rising screen stardom. Ultimately Marlowe discovers that "Dolores Gonzales" is her Hollywood name and that she is originally from Cleveland, where she was married to a member of Steelgrave's gang. Gonzales is responsible for putting Orrin up to the blackmail scheme, and she sets up Orfamay's meeting with Steelgrave, during which the "little sister" kills the gangster. When the blackmail plot begins to unravel after Orrin's ice-pick murders, Gonzales kills him to prevent the secret of her involvement in the crime from being revealed.

Gonzales embodies all of the sham and treachery to be found in Hollywood, and Chandler depicts her as a nymphomaniacal sexual predator. She continually throws herself at Marlowe and provokes erotic tension in the novel through her nonstop sexual banter. "I do not draw a very sharp line between business and sex," she tells Marlowe at one point. "Sex is a net with which I catch fools."[58] In her lust and ambition, Gonzales clearly serves as a symbol of Hollywood's undermining of conventional sexual and cultural identities.

> Wonderful what Hollywood will do to a nobody. It will make a radiant glamour queen out of a drab little wench who ought to be ironing a truck driver's shirts, a he-man hero with shining eyes and brilliant smile reeking of sexual charm out of some overgrown kid who was meant to go to work with a lunchbox. Out of a Texas car hop with the literacy of a character in a comic strip it will make an international courtesan, married six times to six millionaires and so blasé and decadent at the end of it that her idea of a thrill is to seduce a furniture mover in a sweaty undershirt.
>
> And by remote control it might even take a small town prig like Orrin Quest and make an ice-pick murderer out of him in a matter of months, elevating his simple meanness into the classic sadism of the multiple killer. (158)

Here it is clear that Hollywood is the breeding ground of monsters. Yet these monsters come from other places, from Cleveland and from Manhattan,

Kansas; in other words, Hollywood's criminality is of a piece with a more general social pathology, and all these towns and cities are linked by a common social and cultural disorder. Like many of the works that compose the canon of Hollywood fiction, *The Little Sister* is a novel in which Hollywood is used to frame a larger set of concerns about American mass culture and society.

"Hollywood is easy to hate, easy to sneer at, easy to lampoon," Chandler wrote.[59] But not so the motion picture, or at least its artistic potential, for which Chandler always demonstrated enthusiasm and interest: "Not only is the motion picture an art, but it is the one entirely new art that has been evolved on this planet for hundreds of years."[60] Even more, he admitted— in what must have been a galling concession for a novelist—that motion pictures were "the only art at which we of this generation have any possible chance to greatly excel" (58). Nonetheless, he found working in the Hollywood film industry nearly intolerable, precisely because he believed that the creative abilities of the artist were negated within a creative process based on mass production and driven by commercial imperatives. "Personally I think Hollywood is poison to any writer, the graveyard of talent," he once warned a fellow author,[61] and the reason he gave for this was "the Hollywood system"—the studio system—along with the personalities and false values that seemed to reign there. "Hollywood is not really a civilized community," he wrote in an unpublished "farewell" to the film industry. "It is provincial, inbred, narrow, and immersed in a complication of techniques which were once enough to dominate the world but are no longer enough to dominate even the United States."[62] For Chandler, Hollywood's failure to recognize and develop motion pictures as an art form was symptomatic of its moral and social disorder. In all of his novels and essays, Hollywood appears as "a degraded community," for which he proposed as a suitable motto "NIHIL QUOD TETIGIT NON CORRUPIT (It touched nothing which it did not corrupt)."[63]

Yet this corrupted milieu had tremendous appeal to Chandler as a writer precisely because of its larger implications.

> No doubt I have learned a lot from Hollywood. Please do not think I completely despise it, because I don't. . . . But the overall picture, as the boys say, is of a degraded community whose idealism even is

257

largely fake. The pretentiousness, the bogus enthusiasm, the constant drinking and drabbing, the incessant squabbling over money, the all-pervasive agent, the strutting of the big shots (and their usually utter incompetence to achieve anything they start out to do), the constant fear of losing all this fairy gold and being the nothing they have really never ceased to be, the snide tricks, the whole damn mess is out of this world. It is a great subject for a novel—probably the greatest still untouched. But how to do it with a level mind, that's the thing that baffles me. It is like one of those South American palace revolutions conducted by officers in comic opera uniforms—only when the thing is over the ragged dead men lie in rows against the wall, and you suddenly know that this is not funny, this is the Roman circus and damn near the end of a civilization.[64]

Here Chandler articulates the cultural anxieties that Hollywood fictions had long addressed. For him, as for other writers such as Nathanael West and Horace McCoy, it was nothing less than "the end of a civilization" that was at stake in Hollywood, where the values of mass culture were most fully materialized and followed through to their most extravagant, if logical, conclusions.

Even in the works of less insightful popular novelists and short-story writers who took Hollywood as their subject because of its currency or notoriety, there was a marked tendency to become didactic about the film capital, to define a position either for or against (usually against) it, and the Hollywood crime novel represents the furthest limit of this strain of cultural argument.[65] The fact that the demonization of Hollywood was so often staged within a popular literature that made an equally strong appeal to the reader's interests in and identification with the very social milieu that was under attack exemplifies the divided, ambivalent role of Hollywood in American culture.

In the hands of writers such as Chandler, Hollywood fiction often served as a vehicle for social analysis and cultural argument by posing serious questions about the character and meaning of American mass culture. Hollywood fictions often responded to central issues in American culture and society: shifting moral and behavioral codes, changing gender roles and expectations, the effects of an emerging ethos of leisure and consumption on social values, and a concomitant crisis of cultural authority and authenticity. In many respects Hollywood fiction developed as a dissident literary genre, hostile to the climate of commercialism in American life and critical of consumerist versions of the American dream. At the same time, Hollywood fictions often revealed an underlying conservatism in their suspicion of the moral and aesthetic values of motion pictures, and offered a skeptical view of movies as art, which was indicative of the cultural arguments surrounding the emergence and development of the cinema in the first half of the twentieth century. Transforming Hollywood into a hyperbolic symbol of American civilization, Hollywood fictions provided a popular literary forum for the interrogation and critique of fundamental American ideological values and beliefs.

The postwar forties saw the culmination of the cultural myth of Hollywood, as the life-style it represented—based upon leisure, consumption, and the possibility of escape from a drab, unromantic real world—became increasingly untenable in the face of global political tensions. During and after World War II, it was becoming evident that changes in the patterns of consumption and in the uses of leisure time would occur throughout American society, including Hollywood, which lent both its talent and its production facilities to the war effort. By the end of the war, the film industry was entering a period of retrenchment and transformation that would lead to the collapse of the studio system and to a steady dismantling of the Hollywood myth. After 1946 Hollywood's box-office revenues fell into steady decline, and the 1948 Paramount Consent Decree divested the studios of their lucrative theater chains. Certainly movies continued to play an important role in people's lives, but increasingly they competed with other media, especially television, as well as other forms of recreation, which in the long run had drastic and diminishing effects on the film industry.

Chandler wrote about Hollywood near the end of what would later become enshrined as the golden age of the studio era, when both the cultural anxieties and the utopian longings generated by the film capital were being redefined by a new configuration of cultural forces in American society. Because of Chandler's perspective, his work achieved a rare blend of social criticism and elegy, of outrage and sense of loss. It is the thematic signature of Hollywood fictions to orchestrate such complex patterns of ambivalence—of simultaneous desire for and fear of "Hollywood" and all that it had come to signify in the first half of the twentieth century. Chandler's pessimism, however, is equally characteristic of Hollywood fiction, in which writers as diverse as Edgar Rice Burroughs, Stephen Vincent Benét, Horace McCoy, and Nathanael West all discovered in the film capital a symbol for what they perceived—in quite different ways—to be the collapse of traditional moral, social, and aesthetic values. For these writers, Hollywood became a hyperbolic cultural trope for nothing less than the end of American civilization, a figure that came to embody their profound anxieties over the influence of Hollywood and of a commercialized mass culture on American life and values.

NOTES

INTRODUCTION

1. John Dos Passos, "A Note on Fitzgerald," in *The Crack-Up*, by F. Scott Fitzgerrald, edited by Edmund Wilson (New York: New Directions, 1945), 343.

2. The most systematic and thorough study of Hollywood film making is David Bordwell, Janet Staiger, and Kristin Thompson's *The Classical Hollywood Cinema: Film Style and Mode of Production to 1960*. As the title indicates, the word "Hollywood" has become synonymous with the American film industry.

3. See Kristin Thompson, *Exporting Entertainment: America in the World Film Market, 1907–1934*, 170.

4. Anita Loos, "Hollywood Now and Then," in *Fate Keeps on Happening* (New York: Dodd, Mead & Company, 1984), 153.

5. Based on statistics compiled by Joel W. Finler, *The Hollywood Story*, 280.

6. Richard Koszarski, *An Evening's Entertainment: The Age of the Silent Feature Picture, 1915–1928*, vol. 3 of *History of the American Cinema*, edited by Charles Harpole, 9.

7. James R. Quirk, "Are the Stars Doomed?," *Photoplay*, March 1928, 43.

8. Christopher Finch and Linda Rosenkrantz, *Gone Hollywood*, xi.

9. Perley Poore Sheehan, *Hollywood as a World Center* (title).

10. Hortense Powdermaker, *Hollywood: The Dream Factory*, 17.

11. Leo Rosten, *Hollywood: The Movie Colony—The Movie Makers*, 5.

12. Bruce T. Torrence, *Hollywood: The First Hundred Years*, 47, 49.

13. Notable attempts to place Hollywood in a larger social and cultural context are Rosten, *Hollywood: The Movie Colony—The Movie Makers*; Powdermaker, *Hollywood: The Dream Factory*; Robert Sklar, *Movie-Made America: A Cultural History of American Movies* (New York: Vintage Books, 1975); Garth Jowett, *Film, the Democratic Art* (Boston: Little Brown, 1976); Lary May, *Screening Out the Past: The*

Birth of Mass Culture and the Motion Picture Industry; and Neal Gabler, *An Empire of Their Own: How the Jews Invented Hollywood.* Finch and Rosenkrantz's *Gone Hollywood* attempts an encyclopedic look at life in the film capital, while more specialized studies, such as Charles Lockwood's *Dream Palaces: Hollywood at Home* and Jim Heimann's *Out with the Stars: Hollywood Nightlife in the Golden Era,* attempt to fill the gaps left by more general studies. Garth Jowett's essay "From Entertainment to Social Force: The Discovery of the Motion Picture, 1918–1945," in *Current Research in Film: Audiences, Economics, and Law,* vol. 2 (1986), presents an interesting summary of the broader cultural, social, and political influences of Hollywood and its films.

14. Powdermaker, *Hollywood: The Dream Factory,* 16.

15. Katharine Fullerton Gerould, "Hollywood: An American State of Mind," *Harper's Magazine* 146 (May 1923): 689.

16. Victor Appleton, *Tom Swift and His Wizard Camera; or, Thrilling Adventures While Taking Moving Pictures* (New York: Grosset & Dunlap, 1912). See Nancy Brooker-Bowers, *The Hollywood Novel and Other Novels About Film, 1912–1982: An Annotated Bibliography,* for titles and synopses of the other works in the Appleton and Hope series.

17. Brooker-Bowers, *The Hollywood Novel,* 4.

18. Tom Dardis, "The Myth That Won't Go Away: Selling Out in Hollywood," *Journal of Popular Film and Television* 11, no. 4 (1984): 167.

19. The central characters of Sullivan's *The Glory Road* were introduced in an earlier work, *The Star of the North,* a *Photoplay* serial that ran from September 1915 to May 1916. This novel, which concerns a film company on location in Canada, is similar to Bowers's *Phantom Herd* in its emphasis on the adventure and romance of early film making.

20. "Editor's Note," *Photoplay,* July 1916, 25.

21. Francis William Sullivan, *The Glory Road,* 115–16.

22. In his study of the 1920s, Frederick Lewis Allen cites the social changes produced by "the post-war disillusion, the new status of women, the Freudian gospel, the automobile, prohibition, the sex and confession magazines, and the movies" as being the major contributors to the social revolution known as "the new morality." *Only Yesterday: An Informal History of the Nineteen-Twenties* (New York: Harper & Brothers, 1931), 103.

23. Warren I. Susman, "Culture and Civilization: The Nineteen-Twenties," in *Culture as History: The Transformation of American Society in the Twentieth Century* (New York: Pantheon Books, 1984), 107.

24. This formulation of the mass-culture critique is from Leo Lowenthal, "Historical Perspectives on Popular Culture," in *Critical Theory and Society: A Reader* (New York: Routledge, 1989), 195.

25. Raymond Williams, *Culture and Society* (New York: Columbia University Press, 1960), 300.

26. See J. Corner, "'Mass' in Communication Research," *Journal of Communication*, winter 1979.

27. The interaction of literature and film has produced a considerable body of work in adaptation theory. For many years the leading study was George Bluestone's *Novels into Film: The Metamorphosis of Fiction into Cinema* (Baltimore: Johns Hopkins Press, 1957). More recent work includes Keith Cohen's *Film and Fiction: The Dynamics of Exchange* (New Haven, Conn.: Yale University Press, 1979), and a collection of essays by contemporary novelists, which Cohen has edited, entitled *Writing in a Film Age* (Niwot, Colo.: University Press of Colorado, 1991). See also two collections of essays edited by Gerald Peary and Roger Shatzkin, *The Classic American Novel and the Movies* and *The Modern American Novel and the Movies* (New York: Frederick Ungar, 1978). A more recent history of Hollywood's adaptations of American literary works is Jim Hitt's *Words and Shadows: Literature on the Screen* (New York: Citadel Press, 1992).

28. From 1896 to 1906, roughly the first ten years of commercial film making in the United States, literary fictions had relatively little influence on the emerging medium, which comprised an array of genres and subjects drawn from popular forms of entertainment such as lantern shows, panoramas, Wild West shows, vaudeville, dime museums, comic strips, and amusement parks. The proliferation of storefront theaters from around 1905 created a demand for more films and caused producers to begin rationalizing and standardizing industry practices. It soon became apparent that it was easier and more economical to budget and preplan filmed narratives. The rise of narrative film, with its dependence on popular fiction and drama, is linked to the growth of a mass audience during the nickelodeon period and to the increasing imperative to standardize film production. The first screen adaptation of a popular novel was the Edison Company's version of *Uncle Tom's Cabin*, produced in 1903. Adaptations of popular literary and dramatic works were early seen as a way of attracting middle-class audiences and establishing the cultural prestige of the new medium. Promoting films as adaptations of popular novels and plays became a key strategy in product differentiation, while advertising stressed the value of prior literary or dramatic successes at the same time that it underscored the cultural cachet of these forms. An example of this is D. W. Griffith's *The Birth of a Nation* (1915), which was based on Thomas Dixon's *The Clansman*, a best-selling novel of 1905. For a detailed historical and formal analysis of the interaction between popular fiction and film, see Janet Staiger's "The Hollywood Mode of Production to 1930" and Kristin Thompson's "The Formulation of the Classical Style, 1909–28," in Bordwell et al., *The Classical Hollywood Cinema*, 85–153, 157–240.

29. Despite an explosion of scholarly interest since the 1960s, the serious study of popular (mass) culture was slow to organize and assert itself, particularly in academic circles. Early studies, generally favorable toward mass culture, were done by critics such as Vachel Lindsay (*The Art of the Motion Picture* [New York: Liveright,

1922]), Gilbert Seldes (*The Seven Lively Arts* [New York: Harper & Brothers, 1924]),
and James Agee (*Agee on Film: Reviews and Comments* [Beacon Press, 1941]). During
the 1930s and 1940s, members of the Frankfurt Institute for Social Research such as
Theodor Adorno, Leo Lowenthal, and Herbert Marcuse came to America fleeing
fascism in Europe and began to publish their views on mass culture and the social
effects of mass media. For examples of their thinking, see Adorno, *The Culture
Industry: Selected Essays on Mass Culture* (London: Routledge, 1991); Lowenthal,
Literature, Popular Culture, and Society (Englewood Cliffs, N.J.: Prentice-Hall, 1961);
and Marcuse, *One-Dimensional Man* (Boston: Beacon Press, 1964). Their work set
the tone for much of the scholarly debate about mass culture at mid-century, as
exemplified by Dwight MacDonald's famous essay "A Theory of Mass Culture"
(see Rosenberg and White below). By the 1950s and 1960s, academic interest in
mass culture, often centered in communications and journalism departments,
heated up through a series of conferences and influential anthologies. See *Mass
Culture: The Popular Arts in America*, edited by Bernard Rosenberg and David
Manning White (New York: Free Press of Glencoe, 1957); *Culture for the Millions?
Mass Media in Modern Society*, edited by Norman Jacobs (Princeton, N.J.: D. Van
Nostrand Company, 1959); and Stuart Hall and Paddy Whannel, *The Popular Arts*
(Beacon Press, 1964). At the same time, the work of media theorists such as Marshall
McLuhan and Pop artists such as Andy Warhol led to a new interest in and appreci-
ation of mass culture. This trend was reinforced by sociological studies such as
Herbert J. Gans's *Popular Culture and High Culture: An Analysis and Evaluation of
Taste* (Basic Books, 1974). The study of popular literary genres and cultural forms
acquired a new credibility in the wake of the theoretical and critical movements that
began to reshape the academic fields of anthropology, history, sociology, and
literary studies in the 1960s and 1970s—structuralism and poststructuralism, decon-
struction, new historicism, and the cultural studies movement. The work of critics
such as Roland Barthes and Raymond Williams, as well as that of the scholars
associated with the Birmingham Centre for Contemporary Cultural Studies (Stuart
Hall, Tony Bennett, Dick Hebdige, et al.), have given a new impetus and theoretical
rigor to the study of popular culture. A useful critical analysis of British approaches
to the study of popular culture can be found in Jim McGuigan's *Cultural Populism*
(London: Routledge, 1992). See also John Clarke's "Pessimism versus Populism:
The Problematic Politics of Popular Culture" in *For Fun and Profit: The Trans-
formation of Leisure into Consumption*, edited by Richard Butsch (Philadelphia:
Temple University Press, 1990). Recent studies of popular fiction and literary genres
include Janice Radway, *Reading the Romance: Women, Patriarchy, and Popular Literature*
(Chapel Hill: University of North Carolina Press, 1984); Cynthia S. Hamilton,
Western and Hardboiled Detective Fiction in America: From High Noon to Midnight
(Iowa City: University of Iowa Press, 1987); Bob Ashley, *The Study of Popular Fiction:
A Source Book* (London: Pinter Publishers, 1989); John Fiske, *Reading the Popular*
(Boston: Unwin Hyman Press, 1989); Thomas J. Roberts, *An Aesthetics of Junk Fiction*

(Athens: University of Georgia Press, 1990). For historical surveys of the rise of popular culture studies, see Ray B. Browne, *Against Academia: The History of the Popular Culture Association* (Bowling Green, Ohio: Bowling Green State University Popular Press, 1989), and Chandra Mukerji and Michael Schudson, introduction to *Rethinking Popular Culture: Contemporary Perspectives in Cultural Studies* (Berkeley: University of California Press, 1991). See also *American Media and Mass Culture: Left Perspectives,* edited by Donald Lazere (Berkeley: University of California Press, 1987).

30. Lawrence Levine's *Highbrow/Lowbrow: The Emergence of Cultural Hierarchy in America* (Cambridge, Mass.: Harvard University Press, 1988) provides an important historical analysis of the nineteenth- and twentieth-century culture debates, with an emphasis on the socially hierarchical and class-bound terms and conditions under which these debates have occurred.

31. The seminal essay on the influence of mass production on cultural works is Walter Benjamin's "The Work of Art in the Age of Mechanical Reproduction," in *Illuminations* (New York: Schocken Books, 1969), 217–51. For a discussion of the impact of new technologies of communication and visual representation on the culture and social values of late-nineteenth-century America and an analysis of the ideologies that organize mass culture, see Stuart Ewen and Elizabeth Ewen, "The Bribe of Frankenstein," in *Channels of Desire: Mass Images and the Shaping of American Consciousness,* 2d ed. (Minneapolis: University of Minnesota Press, 1992), 1–21. The "dialectic of mass culture," the Ewens argue, is based on the capacity of mass media to operate both as a vehicle of mass fantasy and escape and as an instrument of social domination and control, an idea often explored in Hollywood fictions.

32. In his essay "Culture Between High and Low," Stanley Aronowitz shows how the arguments over mass culture have made "'strange' bedfellows" of cultural critics generally separated by "conventional ideological divisions." He argues that "the mass culture debate reveals the pervasive *fear* among many intellectuals of the consequences of mass democracy, a fear that transcends and realigns traditional ideological divisions" (80). He goes on to explore similarities in the analysis of mass culture among thinkers as ideologically diverse as Ortega y Gasset, Walter Lippmann, John Dewey, Theodor Adorno, and Herbert Marcuse. *Roll Over Beethoven: The Return of Cultural Strife* (Hanover, N.H.: Wesleyan University Press/University Press of New England, 1993), 63–84.

33. For an analysis and a historical survey of the criticisms of mass culture, see Patrick Brantlinger, *Bread and Circuses: Theories of Mass Culture as Social Decay* (Ithaca, N.Y.: Cornell University Press, 1983).

34. In regard to motion pictures as exemplifying the democratizing potentials of mass culture, two early works stand out: Vachel Lindsay's *The Art of the Motion Picture* (1922) and Gilbert Seldes's *The Seven Lively Arts* (1924). Arnold Hauser, in his essay "The Film Age" in *The Social History of Art* (New York: Vintage Books), speaks of motion pictures as an important contribution to the "democratization of art" in the twentieth century. Although it is often criticized by revisionist film

historians, Garth Jowett's *Film, the Democratic Art* remains the most thorough historical study of the movies as a democratic force in American society.

35. Richard Ohmann, "History and Literary History: The Case of Mass Culture," in *Modernity and Mass Culture*, edited by James Naremore and Patrick Brantlinger (Bloomington: Indiana University Press, 1991), 39. John Clarke has argued that "'culture' in capitalism has been commodified: that is, it has been brought into the realm of objects that are produced and exchanged under capitalist social relations of production. . . . People have to buy their way into popular culture, through the direct purchase of clothes, music, and sporting goods, for example, and through such indirect means as buying television sets. Popular culture now demands an entrance price" ("Pessimism Versus Populism," 31). For a discussion of the role of mass culture in the promotion of an ideology of consumption and leisure, see Stuart Ewen and Elizabeth Ewen, "Consumption as a Way of Life" in *Channels of Desire*, 23–51. See also Stuart Ewen, *Captains of Consciousness: Advertising and the Social Roots of Consumer Culture* (New York: McGraw-Hill, 1976), and Richard Wightman Fox and T. J. Jackson Lears, eds., *The Culture of Consumption: Critical Essays in American History, 1880–1980* (New York: Pantheon Books, 1983).

36. See Nancy Brooker-Bowers, "Fiction and the Film Industry: A Brief History of the Hollywood Novel and a Bibliography of Criticism," *Literature/Film Quarterly* 15, no. 4 (1987): 259–67. For bibliographies of Hollywood fiction, see Carolyn See, "The Hollywood Novel: A Partial Bibliography," *Bulletin of Bibliography* 24, no. 9 (January–April 1966): 208–16; Brooker-Bowers, *The Hollywood Novel*; and Anthony Slide, *The Hollywood Novel: A Critical Guide to Over 1200 Works* (Jefferson, N.C.: McFarland, 1995).

CHAPTER 1. SUNSHINE AND SHADOW

1. Katharine Fullerton Gerould, "The Nemesis of the Screen," *Saturday Evening Post*, 8 April 1922, 157.

2. Kevin Starr, "Stories and Dreams: The Movies Come to Southern California," in *Inventing the Dream: California Through the Progressive Era* (New York: Oxford University Press, 1985), 283–84. Edwin O. Palmer, *History of Hollywood*, vol. 1, *Narrative*, 67; vol. 2, *Biographical*, 3.

3. Perley Poore Sheehan, *Hollywood as a World Center*, 13.

4. Population figures are from Bruce T. Torrence, *Hollywood: The First Hundred Years*, 9, 87.

5. "A sink of iniquity, a modern Sodom" is from "Movie Morals Under Fire," *New York Times*, 12 February 1922, sec. 7, p. 1, col. 7; "the dreamer's dream come true" is from Charles Donald Fox, *Mirrors of Hollywood*, 1; "a decent law-abiding community of good, fine home folk" is from "The Morals of Hollywood," *Literary Digest*, 15 October 1927, 34.

6. Gerould, "Hollywood: An American State of Mind," 689.

7. Quoted in Bordwell et al., *The Classical Hollywood Cinema*, xiii.

8. Kevin Brownlow, *The Parade's Gone By . . .* , 30.

9. Palmer, *History of Hollywood*, vol. 2, 7. See also Pat Dowling, "Who Started Hollywood Anyway?" *Photoplay*, July 1919, 92–93, 134; and Paul Mandell, "David Horsley, Pioneer Picturemaker," *American Cinematographer* 70, no. 3 (March 1989): 44–52.

10. For a discussion of the East Coast end of the film business, see Diana Altman, *Hollywood East: Louis B. Mayer and the Origins of the Studio System*.

11. Jesse L. Lasky, "The Camera Capital: In the East or West?" *Photoplay*, February 1916, 98–99.

12. This account of why Hollywood was selected as a production center was first advanced by Terry Ramsaye in "The Discovery of California," chap. 53 in *A Million and One Nights: A History of the Motion Picture Through 1925* (New York: Simon & Schuster, 1926), 533.

13. Sklar, *Movie-Made America*, 67.

14. Ibid., 68.

15. "The Grand March," *Photoplay*, November 1918, 86–87.

16. Starr, "Stories and Dreams" and "Hollywood, Mass Culture, and the Southern California Experience," in *Inventing the Dream*, 283–339.

17. Neal Gabler, in his book *An Empire of Their Own: How the Jews Invented Hollywood*, makes a similar argument on behalf of the Jewish businessmen who were the film industry's leaders. Excluded from the eastern circles of gentility and status, the Jewish moguls created an alternative social world in Hollywood—"an empire of their own"—where they could recreate themselves "in the image of prosperous Americans." In the process they produced in Hollywood a "'shadow' America . . . a powerful cluster of images and ideas—so powerful that, in a sense, they colonized the American imagination" (6–7).

18. "Better Movies," *Time* 2, no. 6 (8 October 1923): 15. For a sampling of answers to this question, see "What's the Matter with the Pictures?" *Photoplay*, August 1922, 38–41, which carries responses to a letter contest in which *Photoplay* readers were invited to express themselves on this subject. Also of interest is Tamar Lane's idiosyncratic monograph *What's Wrong with the Movies* (Los Angeles: Waverly Company, 1923), which has been reprinted in *Moving Pictures: Their Impact on Society* (a facsimile reprint collection) (Jerome S. Ozer Publisher, 1971).

19. "Movies Arraigned by Senator Myers," *New York Times*, 30 June 1922, p. 9, col. 3. See also "Enemies of the Movies Are Numerous," *New York Times*, 6 January 1921, p. 10, col. 5, and William Sheafe Chase, *Catechism on Motion Pictures in Interstate Commerce* (New York: New York Civic League, 1922), 29.

20. Censorship of motion pictures in the United States first began in 1907, when Chicago passed a city ordinance requiring any person who wished to exhibit a motion picture publicly to secure a permit from the superintendent of police (Ira

H. Carmen, *Movies, Censorship, and the Law* [Ann Arbor: University of Michigan Press, 1966], 186). In December of the following year, New York City mayor George McClellan ordered the closing of some 550 movie theaters and nickelodeons that he had found to be in violation of the Sunday closing laws. At the end of the first decade of commercial film production, producers and exhibitors found themselves confronted by a rising tide of public sentiment in favor of increased regulation and control of motion pictures. The film industry responded by supporting the concept of a nationally centralized advisory committee that would review films and assign classifications, and the National Board of Review was formed in 1909 (John Izod, *Hollywood and the Box Office, 1895–1986*, 21–22). Unfortunately this did not appease the critics of movie morality. In 1911 Pennsylvania enacted the first state censorship legislation; it was followed by Kansas and Ohio in 1913, Maryland in 1916, New York in 1921, and Virginia in 1922 (Neville March Hunnings, *Film Censors and the Law* [London: George Allen & Unwin, 1976], 165). The widening movement for state censorship, coupled with widespread shock and outrage at the star scandals of the early twenties, led concerned leaders of the industry to form the Motion Picture Producers and Distributors Association (MPPDA) in 1922 (Izod 69). Eager to assuage the concerns of critics, the MPPDA appointed former Postmaster General and Republican Party officiary Will Hays president of the association, and Hays launched an aggressive public-relations campaign on behalf of the movies. Throughout the twenties, self-regulation served the motion-picture industry by producing a semblance of moral restraint while at the same time allowing a degree of leniency in the representation of sexual themes and images. Despite revisions to the Production Code in 1927 and 1930, producers continued to push the limits of acceptable screen behavior until 1934 when, under pressure from the Catholic Legion of Decency, the MPPDA amended the code to endow it with enforcement powers (Izod 106).

21. Rupert Hughes, *Souls for Sale*, 5.

22. "How the Movies Got That Way," *Collier's*, 23 September 1922, 11.

23. Gerould, "The Nemesis of the Screen," 12. The "nemesis of the screen" to which Gerould refers in her title is precisely its popularity and success as a form of mass culture.

24. "How the Movies Got That Way," 11. The number of pages devoted to the debate over motion pictures in *Collier's* indicates the degree of interest and concern about this issue in the 1920s. This series of articles, written "by a Producer of Moving Pictures" who was afraid to reveal his identity (presumably because it would jeopardize his position in the film industry), appeared in seven installments in *Collier's* and spared no one, including the movie audience, from criticism. The entire series was: "Why I Am Ashamed of the Movies," 16 September 1922; "How the Movies Got That Way," 23 September 1922; "Little Men Behind the Big Screen," 30 September 1922; "Why I Made That Stupid Film," 7 October 1922; "This Little Film Went to Market," 21 October 1922; "You Can't Censor Nonsense," 4 November 1922; and "You'll Get What You Ask For," 18 November 1922. The

series provoked a flood of followup articles and letters. See also William G. Shepherd, "Will Hays—Witness for the Defense" and "What Mr. Hays Didn't Say," *Collier's*, 2 December 1922; W. W. Hodkinson, "Why You Don't Get Better Films," *Collier's*, 16 December 1922; George Humphrey, "Do the Movies Help or Harm Us?" *Collier's*, 24 May 1924; "What's Happening to the Movies" (editorial), *Collier's*, 28 February 1925; William Allen White, "Are the Movies a Mess or a Menace?" *Collier's*, 16 January 1926; "Here's What's Wrong with the Movies" (the winners of a letter contest), *Collier's*, 22 May 1926. Ironically, while *Collier's* was carrying this debate on motion pictures, it was also publishing numerous articles on various aspects of motion-picture production and human-interest stories on screen personalities that were entirely flattering to the film industry and its products.

25. "Cinemaphobia!" *Photoplay*, May 1920, 125.

26. Maurice Maeterlinck, "The Spiritual Future of America and the Movies," *Photoplay*, April 1921, 36.

27. For examples of these lines of argument, see Randolph Bartlett, "Enemies of the Screen," *Photoplay*, March 1920, 42–43, and James R. Quirk, "We Offer No Apology," *Photoplay*, January 1922, 61–62.

28. White, "Are the Movies a Mess or a Menace?," 6.

29. Humphrey, "Do the Movies Help or Harm Us?," 5.

30. "You'll Get What You Ask For," *Collier's*, 18 November 1922, 10. White made similar arguments in "Are the Movies a Mess or a Menace?"

31. Maeterlinck, "The Spiritual Future of America and the Movies," 108.

32. See John F. Kasson, *Amusing the Million: Coney Island at the Turn of the Century* (New York: Hill & Wang, 1978), and Kathy Peiss, *Cheap Amusements: Working Women and Leisure in Turn-of-the-Century New York* (Philadelphia: Temple University Press, 1986).

33. Helen Bullitt Lowry, "Business Chaperons the Movies," *Saturday Evening Post*, 10 June 1922, 48.

34. "Little Men Behind the Big Screen," *Collier's*, 30 September 1922, 29.

35. "Movie Morals Under Fire," *New York Times*, 12 February 1922, sec. 7, p. 1, col. 7. See also Chase, *Catechism on Motion Pictures in Interstate Commerce*, 115–19. This tract is a compendium of anti-motion-picture and anti-film-industry diatribes, the most heinous of which is Chase's attempt to link Jewish control of the film industry to a Zionist conspiracy aimed at "the domination of the civilized world" (118). Chase wrote, "The few producers which control the motion pictures are all Hebrew. . . . This small group of men have secured the control of a most marvelous power for good or for evil in the world. . . . There is a widespread conviction that this power has been and is being used for selfish commercial and unpatriotic purposes, even that it has been prostituted to corrupt government, to demoralize youth, and break down the Christian religion" (115).

36. Homer Croy, "The Gold Cure," *Collier's*, 8 October 1921, 16. For a humorous treatment of the excesses of spending in the film industry, see the short story by

Sinbad, "Cheap at Twice the Price," *Collier's,* 26 May 1928, 26. Croy went on to write a Hollywood novel, *Headed for Hollywood.*

37. Hodkinson, "Why You Don't Get Better Films," 12.

38. George Randolph Chester, "Too Many Cooks Spoil the Pictures," *Saturday Evening Post,* 18 March 1922, 18.

39. The short stories that appeared in the *Saturday Evening Post* were: "Named by Izzy Isokovitch," 21 April 1923; "Bigger and Better," 12 May 1923; "The Boy Wonder," 26 May 1923; "A Tale of Three Fillums," 16 June 1923; "Fried Eggs," 14 July 1923; "All for the Ladies," 11 August 1923; "Isidor Iskovitch Presents," 8 September 1923; "Fish Eat Fish," 13 October 1923; "Angel Child," 11 November 1923; "The Seven Garments," 1 December 1923; "Them Papers," 2 February 1924; "The Slump," 8 March 1924; "The Yes Man Said No," 19 April 1924; "Below Lay Hollywood," 10 May 1924.

40. David Yallop's *The Day the Laughter Stopped* (New York: St. Martin's Press, 1976) thoroughly discredits the accusations that destroyed Arbuckle's career. Two excellent studies of the Taylor case, the most famous of Hollywood's unsolved crimes, have appeared in recent years. Sidney D. Kirkpatrick's *A Cast of Killers* (New York: E. P. Dutton, 1986) is based on information from a recently discovered investigation of the crime by director King Vidor; Robert Giroux's *A Deed of Death: The Story Behind the Unsolved Murder of Hollywood Director William Desmond Taylor* (New York: Alfred A. Knopf, 1990) is a painstaking reconstruction of the crime based on contemporary accounts. For an account of Reid, see Kevin Brownlow, *Hollywood: The Pioneers,* 111–12. The last word on Hollywood scandal is Kenneth Anger's shadow history of the film capital, *Hollywood Babylon.* No book has gone further in its exploration of the dark side of the Hollywood myth.

41. "Movie Morals Under Fire," *New York Times,* 12 February 1922, sec. 7, p. 1, col. 7.

42. Laurance Hill and Silas Snyder, *Can Anything Good Come Out of Hollywood?* (Hollywood: Snyder Publications, 1923), 2.

43. "Movies Arraigned by Senator Myers," *New York Times,* 30 June 1922, p. 9, col. 3.

44. "The Morals of Hollywood," *Literary Digest* 95 (15 October 1927): 34.

45. James R. Quirk, "Moral House-Cleaning in Hollywood," *Photoplay,* April 1922, 52–53.

46. "Brenon Would End Hollywood Colony," *New York Times,* 6 February 1922, p. 4, col. 2. See also the response to Brenon's remarks by Carl Laemmle, "Defends Movie Colony," *New York Times,* 8 February 1922, p. 6, col. 6.

47. Quoted in Brownlow, *Hollywood: The Pioneers,* 112.

48. "Hays to Try Uplift Out at Hollywood," *New York Times,* 9 December 1922, p. 11, col. 3.

49. "Battle of Two Cities," *Photoplay,* February 1922, 42–45.

50. See "Hollywood Defended," *New York Times,* 12 March 1922, sec. 2, p. 6, col. 6; "Elinor Glyn Thinks Hollywood Abused," *New York Times,* 14 April 1922, p. 17,

col. 5; "Hays Says He Finds No 'Horrors of Hollywood,'" *New York Times*, 30 July 1922, sec. 2, p. 1, col. 2; "Hollywood Colony Praised by Lord Mountbatten," *New York Times*, 15 November 1922, p. 40, no. 3; "Com. Haynes Says There Is No Widespread Use of Drugs and Liquor," *New York Times*, 25 January p. 16, col. 4; "Arlen Defends Hollywood," *New York Times*, 6 January 1926, p. 3, col. 7; "Depicts Hollywood as Homelike City," *New York Times*, 10 September 1926, p. 25, col. 2.

51. "Testimonials to Hollywood Morals," *Billboard*, 28 January 1922, 8. See also Hill and Snyder, *Can Anything Good Come Out of Hollywood?* This ardently pro-Hollywood tract, written and published under the sponsorship of the Hollywood branch of the Security Trust and Savings Bank of Los Angeles, cites an abundance of evidence—statistical, photographic, and anecdotal—to answer the rhetorical question of the title with a forceful "Yes!"

52. "Movie Morals Under Fire," *New York Times*, 12 February 1922, sec. 7, p. 1, col. 7.

53. "Talmadge Sisters, Film Stars, Arrive," *New York Times*, 25 February 1922, p. 9, col. 2.

54. Quirk, "Moral House-Cleaning in Hollywood," 52–53.

55. Kenneth L. Roberts, "Flaming Hollywood," *Saturday Evening Post*, 12 July 1924, 3. See also "The Morals of the Movies," *Photoplay*, July 1920, 46; George Ade, "Answering Wide-Eyed Questions About the Movie Stars at Hollywood," *American Magazine* 93 (May 1922): 52–53; "Horrible Hollywood, Home of Hokum," *Literary Digest* 73 (10 June 1922): 40–46; How Horrible Is Hollywood?" *Literary Digest* 74 (22 July 1922): 40–42; "Hollywood as a City of Work," *Literary Digest* 95 (1 October 1927): 54–57; "The Morals of Hollywood," *Literary Digest* 95 (15 October 1927); O. O. McIntyre, "Unseen Dramas of Hollywood," *Cosmopolitan*, July 1927, 92–93; Elsie Janis, "Who Said Hollywood Was Wild?" *Pictorial Review* 29 (May 1928): 4; Hamlin Garland, "The Fortunate Coast," *Saturday Evening Post*, 5 April 1930, 31.

56. H. L. Mencken, "The Low-Down on Hollywood," *Photoplay*, April 1927, 36–37.

57. "Movie Morals Under Fire." *New York Times*, 12 February 1922, sec. 7, p. 1, col. 7.

58. "The Fair Name of Hollywood," *New York Times*, 27 January 1923, p. 12, col. 4.

59. Gerould, "Hollywood: An American State of Mind," 689–96. For more of Gerould's thoughts on motion pictures, see "Movies," *Atlantic Monthly*, July 1921, 22–30, and "What, Then, Is Culture?," *Harper's Magazine*, January 1927, 190–95.

60. Gerould, "Movies," 22–30.

61. Gerould, "What, Then, Is Culture?," 194.

62. Gerould, "The Nemesis of the Screen," 157.

63. Samuel Merwin, "Fancy Turns," *Red Book Magazine*, August 1924, 58–61.

64. Fox, *Mirrors of Hollywood*, 4. See also the comments of William Faversham in the article "Depicts Hollywood as Homelike City," *New York Times*, 10 September 1926, p. 25, col. 2.

65. "Horrible Hollywood, Home of Hokum," *Literary Digest* 73 (10 June 1922): 40.

66. Mary Pickford, "The Greatest Business in the World," *Collier's*, 10 June 1922, 7–8.

67. Torrence, *Hollywood: The First Hundred Years*, 87.

68. "Why I Am Ashamed of the Movies," *Collier's*, 16 September 1922, 4.

69. Lionel Barrymore, "Will the Movies Ever Be Different?" *Ladies' Home Journal*, May 1927, 225.

70. Carey McWilliams, *Southern California Country*, 3.

71. The dichotomies governing popular responses to Hollywood mirror the similarly divided responses to mass culture. James Naremore and Patrick Brantlinger have argued that "extreme euphoria and extreme despair seem as much products of the mass media as movies or commercials. The tension between these extremes is evident in many of the responses to mass culture in literary and artistic modernism and avant garde movements." "Six Artistic Cultures," in *Modernity and Mass Culture*, 7. Hollywood fiction exemplifies such literary reactions to mass culture. Social and cultural historians have long noted the dichotomy in the cultural responses to Hollywood and Los Angeles. In addition to McWilliams's seminal *Southern California Country*, see Louis Adamic, *Laughing in the Jungle*. More recent is Mike Davis's essay "Sunshine or *Noir*?" in *City of Quartz: Excavating the Future in Los Angeles* (New York: Vintage Books, 1992), 17–97.

CHAPTER 2. "THE EDEN OF THE MOVIES"

1. Perley Poore Sheehan, *Hollywood as a World Center*, 8.

2. Marilynn Conners, *What Chance Have I in Hollywood? Intimate Information Concerning the Movie Capital of the World*. This pamphlet was endorsed by the Los Angeles Chamber of Commerce and produced specifically to stem the flood of new arrivals in Hollywood.

3. Alice Williamson, *Alice in Movieland* (London: A. M. Philpot, 1927), 33.

4. Joan Didion, "I Can't Get That Monster Out of My Mind," in *Slouching Towards Bethlehem* (New York: Simon & Schuster, 1964), 150.

5. Burroughs's only other works with a contemporary American setting, outside of occasional visits by Tarzan, are two obscure novelettes: *The Girl from Farris's*, which was serialized in *All-Story Weekly* beginning 23 September 1916, and *The Efficiency Expert*, which was serialized in *Argosy All-Story Weekly* beginning 8 October 1921. See Robert W. Fenton, "*The Girl From Hollywood* and Other Romances," chap. 12 in *The Big Swingers* (Englewood Cliffs, N.J.: Prentice-Hall, 1967), 113.

6. Quoted in Fenton, *The Big Swingers*, 122–23.

7. Ibid., 120.

8. "Movie Morals Under Fire," *New York Times*, 12 February 1922, sec. 7, p. 1, col. 7. See also Chase's *Catechism on Motion Pictures in Interstate Traffic* (New York: New York Civic League, 1922), 30.

9. Karl Kitchen, "The Morals of the Movies," *Photoplay*, July 1920, 46.

10. Quoted in Fenton, *The Big Swingers*, 122.

11. Samuel Merwin, "Theme with Variations," *Red Book Magazine*, February 1923, 37–40.

12. Arthur Somers Roche, "Alms of Love," *Red Book Magazine*, March 1924, 67–71.

13. Fox, *Mirrors of Hollywood*, 1.

14. Conners, *What Chance Have I in Hollywood?*, 19.

15. Laurance L. Hill and Silas E. Snyder, *Can Anything Good Come Out of Hollywood?* (Hollywood: Snyder Publications, 1923), 15.

16. Williamson, *Alice in Movieland*, 20–21.

17. Conners, *What Chance Have I in Hollywood?*, 51.

18. Fox, *Mirrors of Hollywood*, 3.

19. Williamson, *Alice in Movieland*, 18.

20. According to Roland Marchand, the advertisements of the twenties reflected American life in a kind of "distorted mirror," because "people did not usually want ads to reflect themselves, their immediate social relationships, or their broader society exactly. . . . Advertisers recognized that consumers would rather identify with scenes of higher status than ponder reflections of their actual lives." *Advertising the American Dream: Making Way for Modernity, 1920–1940* (Berkeley: University of California Press, 1985), xvii. Marchand's notion of the "distorted mirror" seems particularly germane to an analysis of Hollywood in this period.

21. Frank Condon, "Hollywood," *Photoplay*, January 1923, 39–43. The story was immediately filmed by director James Cruze for Paramount and released later the same year. Unfortunately, it is now a lost film.

22. Biographical information comes from P. Schuyler Miller's introduction to *The Abyss of Wonders* (Reading, Pa.: Polaris Press, 1953), a collection of Sheehan's short stories.

23. Sheehan, *Hollywood as a World Center*, 2.

24. Fox supplies the following demographic information for Hollywood in the mid-twenties: "**Population.** —115,000 (1925). Native white, 90 per cent; negroes, none; foreign born, 10 per cent; industrial workers, 5 per cent; English reading, 99 per cent; families, 20,000" (51). Certainly, in comparison with other American cities at this time, Hollywood constituted a singularly homogeneous social environment.

25. For an example of this idea, see Douglas Fairbanks's "A Huge Responsibility," *Ladies' Home Journal*, May 1924, 36, where he speaks of the worldwide influence of "the universal language of the American films."

26. It appeared in *Red Book Magazine* from September 1921 to June 1922.

27. The source for my biographical data is James A. Rawley, "Hughes, Rupert," in *Dictionary of American Biography* (Supplement 6). For information on Goldwyn's Eminent Authors Pictures, see A. Scott Berg, *Goldwyn: A Biography*, 91–92. For Hughes's own account of his work at the Goldwyn studios, see "My Adventures in Pictureland," *Photoplay*, November 1919, 72–73, 121–22.

28. Anita Loos, *Gentlemen Prefer Blondes* (New York: Boni & Liveright, 1925).

29. See Jonas Spatz's discussion of this figure in *Hollywood in Fiction: Some Versions of the American Dream*, 114–16.

30. The notion of Hollywood as a "leisure utopia" comes from May, *Screening Out the Past*, 167.

CHAPTER 3. ILLUSION AND REALITY

1. Herbert Howe, "Returning to Hollywood," *Photoplay*, May 1925, 30.

2. Fine continues, "For novelists drawn to the film capital, unreality, impermanence, and instability have been the chief characteristics of the place." David Fine, "Nathanael West, Raymond Chandler, and the Los Angeles Novel," *California History* 68, no. 4 (winter 1982): 196.

3. Edmund Wilson, *The Boys in the Back Room: Notes on California Novelists* (San Francisco: Colt Press, 1941), 57.

4. P. G. Wodehouse, "Slaves of Hollywood," *Saturday Evening Post*, 7 December 1929, 5.

5. "Hollywood Analyzed" (letter from Maurice Widdows), *Saturday Review of Literature* (27 August 1927): 78.

6. The notion of Hollywood as an amusement park, while always implicit in its cultural identity, was finally materialized in the 1980s by the Universal Studio tour and the MGM/Disney Studio theme park. In the latter, the film capital was recreated in Orlando, Florida, hermetically preserved in its "golden age" of the twenties and thirties. There the cultural and social contradictions that had attended the real Hollywood in this period could be sanitized and neatly packaged for consumption by tourists.

7. While it is true that Hollywood produced many different kinds of films in the 1920s—some of them, such as Stroheim's *Greed* (1923) and Vidor's *The Crowd* (1928), intensely realistic and uncompromising—the fact remains that the vast majority of Hollywood films offered to their mass audiences optimism, romance, and the reassurance of a happy ending. An article evaluating the elements of motion pictures that most appealed to audiences ranked "love," "faith," "thrills," "comedy," and "pathos" highest. See Joseph Jefferson O'Neil, "Love Gets the Fadeout But Faith Wins the Crowds," *Collier's*, 7 February 1925, 10–11.

8. See "The City of Make-Believe" (photo essay), *Collier's*, 6 April 1929, 12–13, for a contemporary response to Los Angeles's fanciful material environment. A

recent historical study is Sam Hall Kaplan's *L.A. Lost and Found: An Architectural History of Los Angeles,* particularly chapter 5, "Dream Town" (78–97), which explores Hollywood's influence on the city's architectural identity.

9. *Merton of the Movies* appeared in the *Saturday Evening Post* in consecutive issues from 4 February to 8 April 1922.

10. George S. Kaufman and Marc Connelly, *Merton of the Movies* (New York: Samuel French, 1922). The play opened at the Cort Theater, New York City, on 13 November 1922 and was one of the hits of the 1922–23 season.

11. Paramount's 1924 version of *Merton of the Movies* featured Glenn Hunter, the actor who had starred in the Broadway production. In 1932 the studio remade it as *Make Me a Star,* with Stuart Erwin in the title role. Harold Lloyd's 1932 Paramount film *Movie Crazy* was influenced by *Merton of the Movies,* as well. MGM cast Red Skelton in its 1947 remake, for which the original title was restored.

12. Apparently Wilson found working with Hollywood difficult, although several of his novels were successfully adapted to the screen, including *Ruggles of Red Gap* in 1922 and 1935. In 1935 MGM invited Wilson to Hollywood, at a salary of $1,250 a week, to write a scenario of his book *Ma Pettengill.* Although he needed money at the time, Wilson left after only three weeks' work, fed up with the studio's treatment of his novel. The film was never produced. See George Kummer, *Harry Leon Wilson: Some Account of the Triumphs and Tribulations of an American Popular Writer* (Cleveland: Press of Western Reserve University, 1963), 132–33.

13. Kummer, *Harry Leon Wilson,* 116.

14. Harry Leon Wilson, *Merton of the Movies,* 1.

15. Kummer, *Harry Leon Wilson,* 102.

16. Humphrey, "Do The Movies Help or Harm Us?," 5. For a discussion of the dreamlike quality of motion pictures and the psychological responses they produce in the audience, see Hugo Mauerhoffer's "Psychology of the Film Experience" in *Film: A Montage of Theories,* edited by Richard Dyer MacCann (New York: E. P. Dutton, 1966), 229–35. Discussions of mass culture's capacity to interrupt experience and impose a mediated version of reality upon its presumably passive consumers appear in the work of Frankfurt School critics. For example, see Theodor W. Adorno, "The Culture Industry Reconsidered" in *Critical Theory and Society: A Reader,* edited by Stephen Eric Bronner and Douglas MacKay Kellner (New York: Routledge, 1989), 128–35. Similar arguments are given a postmodern inflection in Jean Baudrillard's *Simulations* (New York: Semiotext(e), 1983).

17. Merton mails off ten cents for his "Ten-Hour Talent Prover, or Key to Movie-Acting Aptitude" test (28). In March of 1922, *Photoplay* found it necessary to warn its readers of the fraudulent claims of a Michigan company that offered, for ten cents, a "twelve-hour talent-tester, or Key to Movie-Acting Aptitude." Scams such as these preyed upon the desires of thousands of movie hopefuls who wanted to make it in Hollywood. See "You Cannot Learn Acting by Mail," *Photoplay,* March 1922, 114.

18. "Hollywood Warns Film-Struck Girls," *New York Times,* 4 December 1923, p. 23, col. 7.

19. "The mass media, with their cult of celebrity and their attempt to surround it with glamour and excitement, have made Americans a nation of fans, moviegoers. The media give substance to and thus intensify narcissistic dreams of fame and glory, encourage the common man to identify himself with the stars and to hate the 'herd,' and make it more difficult for him to accept the banality of everyday existence." Christopher Lasch, *The Culture of Narcissism: American Life in an Age of Diminishing Expectations* (New York: W. W. Norton & Company, 1978), 21.

20. This aspect of the book is cogently discussed by Carolyn See in her unpublished Ph.D. dissertation "The Hollywood Novel: An Historical and Critical Study," (University of California, Los Angeles, 1963), 28. I don't believe that such commentary is as rare in Hollywood fiction as See argues. In fact, many subsequent Hollywood novels simply start from the assumption that Hollywood produces "hokum" (Wilson's term), and therefore do not attempt to prove the claim through a cataloguing of movie banalities in the way that Wilson so obviously delights in doing.

21. Ariel Dorfman, "The Infantilizing of Culture," in *American Media and Mass Culture,* edited by Donald Lazere, 145. Dorfman continues, "It has been constantly observed that the culture industry, tailored to answer the simultaneous needs of immense groups of people, levels off its messages at the so-called lowest common denominator, creating only that which everybody can understand effortlessly. This common denominator (as has also been pointed out frequently) is based on a construct of—what else?—the median, quintessential North American common man, who has undergone secular canonization as the universal measure for humanity. What has not been so clearly stated is this: When that man is reduced to his average, shaved of his adult facilities and conflicting experiences, handed solutions that suckle and comfort him, robbed of his future, what is left is a babe, a dwindled, decreased human being"—an individual resembling, in some respects, Merton Gill.

22. Robert Littell, "A Satire on the Movies," *New Republic* 30 (24 May 1922): 382.

23. Letter to Rosemary Benét dated December 1929, *Selected Letters of Stephen Vincent Benét,* edited by Charles A. Fenton (New Haven: Yale University Press, 1960), 194.

24. See Charles A. Fenton's account of Benét's Hollywood experience, "The Wages of Cinema," chapter 11 in his critical biography, *Stephen Vincent Benét: The Life and Times of an American Man of Letters, 1898–1943* (New Haven: Yale University Press, 1958), 231–40.

25. Letter to Carl Benét dated [23] January 1930. *Selected Letters of Stephen Vincent Benét,* 201.

26. Stephen Vincent Benét, *The Beginning of Wisdom* (New York: Henry Holt & Company, 1921).

27. See Yallop, *The Day the Laughter Stopped*. Also see accounts by Sklar in *Movie-Made America*, 78, and by Brownlow in *Hollywood: The Pioneers*, 108–9.

28. Letter to Rosemary Benét dated December 1929, *Selected Letters of Stephen Vincent Benét*, 197.

CHAPTER 4. FALLING STARS

1. Marquis Busby, "The Port of Missing Stars," *Photoplay*, November 1930, 40.

2. According to Jib Fowles, the use of the word "star" to designate an entertainment celebrity dates from around 1830 (10). Fowles traces the evolution of stardom in the nineteenth and twentieth centuries from the stage to screen, sports, radio, and television. *Starstruck: Celebrity Performers and the American Public* (Washington: Smithsonian Institution Press, 1992). See especially chapter 2, "A Role Is Born (and Endures)."

3. Raymond Durgnat, "Pleading an Aesthetic Excuse," *Films and Feelings* (Cambridge, Mass.: M.I.T. Press, 1967), 138.

4. Alexander Walker, *Stardom: The Hollywood Phenomenon* (New York: Stein & Day, 1970), 13.

5. See Richard Dyer, "Stars as Social Phenomenon," in *Stars* (London: BFI, 1979). Dyer's study of stardom places it within three consecutively tighter frames of reference, where it is seen as a social phenomenon, as a series of media images, and as a sign within specific film texts. Summarizing a tremendous amount of research on stars and celebrity, Dyer's study remains the best starting point for any discussion of this subject.

6. Quoted in David Niven, *Bring On the Empty Horses*, 22.

7. Daniel Boorstin, *The Image: A Guide to Pseudo-Events in America* (New York: Atheneum, 1961), 156.

8. For a fascinating compendium of movie-star success stories, see *How I Broke into the Movies*, edited by Hal C. Herman (Hollywood: Hal C. Herman, 1930). A facsimile edition was published by Yesteryear Press in 1984.

9. See Richard Wightman Fox and T. J. Jackson Lears, eds., *The Culture of Consumption: Critical Essays in American History, 1880–1980* (New York: Pantheon Books, 1983).

10. May, *Screening Out the Past*. See especially chapter 7, "The New Frontier: 'Hollywood,' 1914–1920," 167–99.

11. May, *Screening Out the Past*, 190.

12. Thorstein Veblen, *The Theory of the Leisure Class* (New York: Penguin Books, 1979).

13. "What Thorstein Veblen had theorized as the conspicuous consumption habits of the leisure class were not [in the 1920s] propagated as a democratic ideal within mass advertising"—an ideal that most Americans would not fully realize

until the 1950s, according to Stuart Ewen in his seminal study of consumer culture, *Captains of Consciousness*, 79. While new production processes were making inexpensive manufactured goods available to larger and larger groups of people during this period, mass-produced consumer items were typically designed to approximate in appearance the ornamentation and style of higher-priced, handmade goods. This was a function of the "culture of imitation" in American life that Miles Orvell examines in his study *The Real Thing: Imitation and Authenticity in American Culture, 1880–1940* (Chapel Hill: University of North Carolina Press, 1989). As Orvell notes: "At every level of society individuals sought an elevation of status through the purchase and display of goods whose appearance counted for more than their substance" (49). Orvell's study provides many such examples of the symbolic status of popular consumption.

14. Lowenthal, "The Triumph of the Mass Idols," in *Literature, Popular Culture, and Society*, 109–40.

15. Virtually all popular magazines of the twenties, thirties, and forties contained advertisements for products promoted by film stars. The following are merely a sample culled from the pages of *Ladies' Home Journal* (*LHJ*) and the *Saturday Evening Post* (*SEP*): "How Famous Stars Keep Their Hair Beautiful" (advertisement for Watkins Mulsified Cocoanut Oil shampoo), *LHJ*, March 1922, 39; "Is Your Skin Younger or Older Than You Are?" (advertisement for Pond's cold cream, featuring endorsements by film stars Mae Murray, Mildred Harris, Ruth Roland, and Peggy Wood), *LHJ*, December 1923, 37; "96% of the lovely complexions you on the screen are cared for by Lux Toilet Soap" (advertisement for Lux toilet soap claiming that 417 out of 433 of Hollywood's leading actresses use the product and that "all the great film studios have made it the official soap in their dressing rooms"), *LHJ*, September 1928, 129; "Hollywood's Lovely Clothes" (advertisement for Lux soap, featuring an endorsement by Fay Wray), *LHJ*, February 1929, 51; "What Movie Stars Discovered" (advertisement for Allen-A hosiery, featuring an endorsement by Patsy Ruth Miller), *SEP*, 25 February 1928. Some advertisements relied solely on Hollywood's reputation for glamour and romance, such as the advertisement for Romance chocolates in the April 1926 issue of *Photoplay*, which offered a free trip of Hollywood ("the Land of Romance") (87), or the advertisement for Davis tailor-made clothes in the 23 November 1929 *SEP*, 60, which contained the following ad lines: "To register with a critical public Hollywood stars must have 'IT'—art, charm, personality—call it what you will. Without *it*, the extra never emerges from the mob . . . with it he rises to stardom. In his struggle for recognition, clothes play an important part. . . . That is why Davis Clothes . . . *register*, not only with Hollywood men but with men in all walks of life." Other advertising campaigns relied on the consumer's knowledge of film technique, such as the advertisement for Colgate's dental cream in the December 1923 issue of *LHJ* (43), which asked, "Can Your Smile Stand a 'Close-Up'?" and featured an audience staring at a motion-picture screen filled with a close-up shot

of a smiling starlet. The connections between Hollywood, movie stars, and commercial advertising have yet to be fully explored by film and cultural historians, but an excellent starting place is Charles Eckert's study of film-star "tie-ins," "The Carole Lombard in Macy's Window," *Quarterly Review of Film Studies* 3, no. 1 (winter 1978): 1–21.

16. "Thoughts on Hollywood," *New York Times*, 26 February 1922, p. 2, col. 4.

17. Letter from Mrs. Hettie G. Tell in "What's the Matter with the Pictures?" (letter contest), *Photoplay*, August 1922, 41.

18. For an example of fan-magazine writing that emphasized the hard work of stardom, see Faith Service, "So You'd Like to Be a Star?," reprinted in *Hollywood and the Great Fan Magazines*, edited by Martin Levin (New York: Arbor House, 1970), 142–43. For the opposing viewpoint, see "Those Awful Factories," *Photoplay*, November 1937, reprinted in *The Talkies: Articles and Illustrations from a Great Fan Magazine, 1928–1940*, edited by Richard Griffith (New York: Dover, 1971), 154–55. An interesting article that contrasts both views of the stars' work life is Genevieve Tobin's "An Actress' Working Day," *Screen Guild Magazine*, October 1934, 5. It has been reprinted in *Celebrity Articles from the Screen Guild Magazine*, edited by Anna Kate Sterling (Metuchen, N.J.: Scarecrow Press, 1987), 34–37.

19. Camille Paglia, "Valley of the Doll," *New York Times*, 6 June 1993, sec. 7, p. 12.

20. Richard Dyer, *Heavenly Bodies: Film Stars and Society* (New York: St. Martin's Press, 1986), 7.

21. Ibid., 17.

22. Jib Fowles makes a similar argument. He links the rise of stardom in the late nineteenth century to the loosening of traditional values and ways of life and to the rise of an urban population increasingly cut off from the past and uncertain of its identity in the hectic, modern world of the city. Citing the work of Jackson Lears and Warren Susman, Fowles argues that an interest in and identification with entertainment celebrities was a response to the "anomie and psychic discomfort" of American urban life, and that stars provided "needed models of personality . . . [which] could help in defining the individual against the backdrop of urban anonymity. . . . Stars seemed to exude the perfected, confident behavior than unanchored city dwellers coveted. . . . Performers offered various models of the well-integrated self, at a time of excruciating need, and when other well-wrought exemplars were not forthcoming." *Starstruck*, 26, 27.

23. Service, "So You'd Like to Be a Star?," 214.

24. Louise Brooks, *Lulu in Hollywood*, 58.

25. Christine Gledhill, introduction to *Stardom: Industry of Desire* (London: Routledge, 1991), xiii.

26. Richard deCordova, *Picture Personalities: The Emergence of the Star System in America* (Urbana: University of Illinois Press, 1990).

27. "The Biograph girl" was Florence Lawrence (55–64); "Little Mary" was Mary Pickford (70–72).

28. DeCordova cites three reasons for this resistance: (1) the claims of producers that film actors wanted their identities kept secret in order to protect their professional reputations, an argument that his own research refutes; (2) the struggle over which aspect of film production would emerge as the center of textual productivity and interest—the "brand name" of the film company or the identity of the performer; and (3) the idea that if the performers' identities were revealed it would disrupt the illusion of the screen narrative. *Picture Personalities*, 77–81.

29. *My Strange Life: The Intimate Life Story of a Moving Picture Actress* (New York: Grosset & Dunlap, 1915).

30. DeCordova, *Picture Personalities*, 101.

31. Lennard J. Davis, *Factual Fictions: The Origins of the English Novel* (New York: Columbia University Press, 1983).

32. Robert Kerr, "Loree Starr—Photoplay Idol" (serial), *Photoplay*, February–June 1914.

33. Quoted by Doug McClelland in *StarSpeak: Hollywood on Everything* (Boston: Faber & Faber, 1987), 290.

34. This interest led to two of Hollywood's most memorable self-portraits, both of which emphasize the process of studio star-making: George Cukor's 1932 film *What Price Hollywood?* (RKO/Pathe), and William Wellman's 1937 film *A Star Is Born* (Selznick).

35. Niven, *Bring On the Empty Horses*, 10.

36. Katherine Albert, "Don't Envy the Stars," *Photoplay*, March 1929, 133.

37. See Brooks, *Lulu in Hollywood*; Niven, *Bring On the Empty Horses*; and Pola Negri, *Memoirs of a Star*, 212–13, 233. Negri's autobiography is an eloquent account of the vicissitudes of stardom. She observed, with characteristic grace, "In a way, we were captives of the fantasies that touched so much of our lives. Our joys, our sorrows, our raptures were often defined by the imagistic glossary of the cinematic world to which we belonged" (266). See also, on this subject, the reflections on Bernard Drew in "Heartbreak Hollywood," *American Film*, June 1977, 63–67.

38. Negri, *Memoirs of a Star*, 232.

39. For a brief history of *Photoplay* under Quirk and subsequent editors, see Richard Griffith's introduction to *The Talkies*, xvii–xxiii.

40. "1918" (editorial), *Photoplay*, February 1918, 15.

41. Cited by Quirk, *The Talkies*, vii.

42. See Koszarski on fan-magazine popularity polls in *An Evening's Entertainment*, 259–62. Koszarski notes that the stars favored in fan magazine polls were, curiously, sometimes not the top box-office attractions one would expect them to be. Barbara Gelman makes the same point: "The stars the public wanted to see in a movie and the stars they wanted to know more about were not always the same. In the first half of the twenties, for example, Mary Pickford was still top box office. But fans preferred reading about Clara Bow. Chaplin was the undisputed genius who could pull them into the theaters. But Rudolph Valentino and his troubles

made for much more popular reading material—even when he was flopping at the box office or not making films at all—or even after he'd been dead for years." Introduction to *Photoplay Treasury*, edited by Barbara Gelman (New York: Bonanza Books, 1972), ix. The fact that a dead Valentino could attract more fan interest than a living Chaplin says much about the social and cultural symbolism of stardom as a condition fraught with peril and overshadowed by doom.

43. Jan Vantol, "How Stars Spend Their Fortunes," reprinted in *Hollywood and the Great Fan Magazines*, edited by Martin Levin, 12–13, 172; "How Constance Really Spends Her Money," reprinted in *The Best of Modern Screen*, edited by Mark Bego (New York: St. Martin's Press, 1986); Sara Hamilton, "Hollywood at Play," reprinted in *The Talkies*, edited by Richard Griffith, 106–7, 302–4. For a screen star's response to the fan-magazine treatment accorded them in such articles, see Ann Harding, "'Unique and Extraordinary . . . ,'" *Screen Guild Magazine*, September 1934, 3, reprinted in *Celebrity Articles from the Screen Guild Magazine*, 25–29. The homes of Hollywood stars are described and discussed in Lockwood, *Dream Palaces*. See also three special issues of *Architectural Digest*: April 1990 (Academy Awards Collector's Edition), April 1994 ("Hollywood-at-Home"), and April 1996 ("Hollywood at Home"); they contain a wealth of photographs and information about Hollywood stars' homes. Jim Heimann's *Out with the Stars* provides a fascinating glimpse of Hollywood's social life from the teens through the forties.

44. Sonia Lee, "Motherhood . . . What It means to Helen Twelvetrees," 37–38; Adele Whitely Fletcher, "My Husband Is My Best Friend," 146–47, 215–16. Both were reprinted in *Hollywood and the Great Fan Magazines*, edited by Martin Levin.

45. Griffith, introduction to *The Talkies*, xvii.

46. Katherine Albert, "What's Wrong with Hollywood Love?," reprinted in *Hollywood and the Great Fan Magazines*, edited by Martin Levin, 60–62, 183–84; Kirtley Baskette, "Hollywood's Unmarried Husbands and Wives," reprinted along with *Photoplay*'s apology, which followed a month later, in *The Talkies*, edited by Richard Griffith, 130–32, 320–21. For an account of the controversy this article created, see Niven, *Bring On the Empty Horses*, 28.

47. Louis E. Bisch, "Why Hollywood Scandal Fascinates Us," *Photoplay*, January 1930, 73, 100.

48. Orson Meridan, "Confessions of a Star," *Photoplay*, September 1915, 139–43.

49. Myrtle West, "The Price They Paid for Stardom," *Photoplay*, November 1926, 28–29, 134–36.

50. Herbert Howe, "See Hollywood and Die," *Photoplay*, March 1928, 34, 88.

51. Ruth Waterbury, "Going Hollywood," *Photoplay*, February 1929, 30–31, 104–06.

52. Albert, "Don't Envy the Stars," 32. See also Quirk, "Are the Stars Doomed?," 43, 76, 98–99 (considers the star's precarious economic position in the film industry); Roland Francis, "The Stars Pay and Pay," *Photoplay*, October 1930, 69,

138–39 (considers the cost in privacy and friendship that screen success entails); Busby, "The Port of Missing Stars," 40–41, 138–40 (considers the fate of film stars who have fallen from wealth and fame).

53. Adela Rogers St. Johns, "The Last Straw," *Photoplay*, May 1922, 105.

54. For example, Frank Condon, "Behind the Curtain," *Photoplay*, June 1922; Adela Rogers St. Johns, "The Fan-Letter Bride," *Photoplay*, August 1922.

55. Another version of this theme can be found in Adela Rogers St. Johns's "Miss Dumbell," *Photoplay*, April 1922.

56. Faith Service, "False Faces," *Photoplay*, May 1926, 44.

57. Jean Dupont, "Life for a Night," *Photoplay*, March 1927, 64.

58. Samuel Merwin, *Hattie of Hollywood* (serial), *Photoplay*, July–December 1922, sixth installment, 102–3.

59. The image of the movie star as sexual predator is not nearly as common in the Hollywood fiction of this period as the image of the movie star as sexual victim—usually, as in the case of Hattie, in response to the demands of a powerful director or producer. Two notable exceptions, however, are John V. A. Weaver's *Joy-Girl* (New York: Alfred A. Knopf, 1932) and John Dos Passos's *The Big Money* (New York: Houghton Mifflin, 1933). In both of these novels, ambitious film stars (Lulu Schaeffer and Margot Dowling) use sexual favors to advance their careers and ruin the lives of those around them in the process. A comic treatment of this figure can be found in Lawrence Riley's successful Broadway play *Personal Appearance* (New York: Samuel French, 1935).

60. Although they were often presented in short stories or as secondary characters in novels, male stars were rarely the central characters in Hollywood novels of the twenties and thirties. Of course, the first star novel, the *Photoplay* serial "Loree Starr—Photoplay Idol" by Robert Kerr, published in 1914, featured a male star, a fact that underlines its anomalous position within the canon of Hollywood fiction. It was not until Charles Grayson's *Spotlight Madness* that a male star was presented as the central character in a Hollywood novel. From the forties on, however, the practice became more common.

61. See Allen, "The Revolution in Manners and Morals," in *Only Yesterday*, 88–122. One of the best studies of women and work in this period is Alice Kessler-Harris's *Out to Work: A History of Wage Earning Women in the United States* (New York: Oxford University Press, 1982). See especially chapter 8, "Ambition and Its Antidote in a New Generation of Female Workers," 217–49. Kessler-Harris observes that "women [in the twenties] who escaped or transcended the prevailing social constraints drew mixed admiration and doubts" (235), a response indicative of the ambivalence that surrounded women as film stars.

62. Merwin, *Hattie of Hollywood*, third installment, 94.

63. Joseph Hergesheimer's "Shapes in Light" appeared in three installments in the *Saturday Evening Post*, on March 6, March 20, and March 27, 1926. The passage quoted is from the March 27 installment, 153.

64. Adela Rogers St. Johns, *The Honeycomb*, 111. For more of St. Johns's vivid reminiscences of Hollywood, see as well *Love, Laughter, and Tears: My Hollywood Story*.

65. St. Johns, *The Honeycomb*, 25–26.

66. Ibid., 136.

67. The novel is dedicated to St. Johns's editor at *Cosmopolitan*, Ray Long.

68. Adela Rogers St. Johns, *The Skyrocket* (serial), *Cosmopolitan*, January–April 1925, introduction to first installment, 16.

69. St. Johns, *The Skyrocket*, 33.

CHAPTER 5. "THE MOST TERRIFYING TOWN IN THE WORLD"

1. Quoted in "Dangerous Odds in Hollywood," *Literary Digest* 82 (23 August 1924): 30.

2. R. E. Sherwood, "Hollywood: The Blessed and the Cursed," in *America as Americans See It*, edited by Fred J. Ringel (New York: Harcourt Brace & Company, 1932), 65–77.

3. The best history of Hollywood in this period of technological and economic transition is Alexander Walker's *The Shattered Silents: How the Talkies Came to Stay*.

4. Herbert Howe, "The Daring Days of Hollywood," *Photoplay*, August 1929, 104.

5. Davis, *City of Quartz*, 25.

6. Hamlin Garland, "The Fortunate Coast," *Saturday Evening Post*, 5 April 1930, 31. Writing after a six-month visit to Hollywood, Garland celebrated Los Angeles as a consumer's paradise, linking the region to a modern way of life based on technology and leisure: "Every man, woman, and child appears to own an automobile, and the broad avenues glitter with long lines of polished windshields, nickel-plated lamps and shining fenders. . . . Meanwhile their wives are shopping in spacious and beautiful department stores. [An] atmosphere of leisure pervades even the shops, which are also midwestern. . . . You can depend on freedom from frost and snow, as the beautiful drive-in markets amply prove. Their doors are never closed, and as you drive your motor car into them, you can shop from the running board (31). . . . ['Angelinos'] . . . construct the most beautiful houses and install the most modern conveniences. . . . The ice boxes are electrically cooled and the kitchens are spotless laboratories" (189).

7. Davis, *City of Quartz*, 25.

8. Garet Garrett, "Los Angeles in Fact and Dream," *Saturday Evening Post*, 18 October 1930, 141.

9. Charles Lockwood, "A Tour of the Stars' Homes: Origins of a Popular Hollywood Pastime," *Architectural Digest*, April 1994, 30.

10. Garrett, "Los Angeles in Fact and Dream," 138.

11. Bruce Henstell, *Sunshine and Wealth: Los Angeles in the Twenties and Thirties.* Kevin Starr provides the best history of the region's growth and development in this period, in *Inventing the Dream: California Through the Progressive Era,* and *Material Dreams: Southern California Through the 1920s.*

12. See James N. Gregory, *American Exodus: The Dust Bowl Migration and Okie Culture in California* (New York: Oxford University Press, 1989).

13. Garrett, "Los Angeles in Fact and Dream," 144.

14. Bertolt Brecht, "On Thinking About Hell," in *Bertolt Brecht: Poems 1913–1956* (New York: Methuen, 1976), 367.

15. R. J. Minney, *Hollywood by Starlight,* 36.

16. Anthony Slide, "The 'Hollywood' Sign," in *The American Film Industry: A Historical Dictionary* (New York: Limelight Editions, 1990).

17. See Richard H. Pells, "Literary Theory and the Intellectual" and "Documentaries, Fiction, and the Depression," chaps. 4 and 5 in *Radical Visions & American Dreams: Culture and Social Thought in the Depression Years* (Middletown, Conn.: Wesleyan University Press, 1973), for a discussion of these literary trends.

18. "Hollywood Warns Film-Struck Girls," *New York Times,* 4 December 1923, p. 23, col. 7. See also "Extras in Hollywood," *New York Times,* 13 January 1924, sec. 7, p. 16, col. 1.

19. Benjamin B. Hampton, *A History of the Movies* (New York: Arno Press and New York Times, 1970; originally published 1931), 210.

20. Bill Blackbeard, "Ella Cinders," in *The World Encyclopedia of Comics,* edited by Maurice Horn (New York: Avon, 1976), 232. Blackbeard describes "Ella Cinders" as "one of the most popular strips of all time," and recounts the following story as evidence. "In September [1930], a mail plane carrying a week's originals of *Ella* (October 6–11) from Los Angeles to New York crashed in flames at Warren, Ohio, charring the outside edges of the episodes to a depth of an inch and a half or more. Rushed to the syndicate by the post office, proofs made from the burned originals were sent out to the subscribing papers barely in time for publication and they appeared exactly as rescued from the ruins of the plane: flame-eaten dialogue balloons, panel details and all. Luckily, enough remained of the episodes to make continuity sense; the publicity engendered for the strip was incalculable." Blackbeard concludes his discussion of the strip with the following assessment. "For its first half-dozen years, *Ella Cinders* was a glittering, absorbing body of comic strip work, graphically outstanding and both amusing and gripping as a narrative."

21. Elizabeth Peltret, "The Girl Outside," *Photoplay,* July 1917, 21.

22. Torrence, *Hollywood: The First Hundred Years,* 79–80.

23. "Campaign Started by YWCA and Hollywood Chamber of Commerce to Keep Screen-Struck Girls Away," *New York Times,* 29 April 1924, p. 21, no. 4; see also "Warns Movie-Struck Girls," *New York Times,* 6 August 1927, p. 11, no. 5.

24. Hugh Leamy, "Many Are Called," *Collier's,* 9 April 1927, 19, 46–47.

25. Quoted in "Dangerous Odds in Hollywood," *Literary Digest* 82 (23 August 1924): 31.

26. Peltret, "The Girl Outside," 19.

27. Alfred A. Cohn, "What Every Girl Wants to Know," *Photoplay*, June 1919, 28–31; "What Are the Chances of a Beginner?," *Photoplay*, August 1923, 34–37.

28. Ruth Waterbury, "The Truth About Breaking into the Movies," *Photoplay*, January 1927, 38.

29. Ruth Waterbury, "Don't Go to Hollywood," *Photoplay*, March 1927, 50.

30. For information on salaries and working conditions, see Cohn, "What Every Girl Wants to know," and Marian Spitzer, "A Very Extra Girl," *Saturday Evening Post*, 15 May 1926, 48.

31. For contemporary accounts of the formation of the Central Casting Corporation, see Spitzer, "A Very Extra Girl," 52, and Kenneth L. Roberts, "Movie Mad," *Saturday Evening Post,* 25 September 1926, 151. See also Slide, "Central Casting Corporation," in *The American Film Industry;* Finch and Rosenkrantz, "Extras and Stand-ins," in *Gone Hollywood.*

32. Robert Parrish, *Growing Up in Hollywood,* 46.

33. "At the Central Casting Corporation, the only office in Hollywood to which calls for extra workers come and the only office from which the extra can get work, there are more than 4,000 men registered; more than 6,500 women, more than 3,500 children, some 14,000 people in all. From this group there is an average daily call for 483 men, 195 women, and 20 children, 698 jobs a day for 14,000." Waterbury, "The Truth About Breaking into the Movies," 40.

34. Theodore Dreiser, "Hollywood: Its Morals and Manners," *Shadowland,* November 1921–February 1922. These articles have been reprinted in *The Best of Shadowland* edited by Anna Kate Sterling (Metuchen, N.J.: The Scarecrow Press, 1987), 70–96.

35. Dreiser, "Hollywood: Its Morals and Manners," 82.

36. Dreiser's attack on Hollywood seems to have arisen, in part, out of the resentment he felt for the new medium as a writer. He complained, in one installment, about the "high-salaried and comfortable vice-snoopers" who were afraid to attack the "barons of the movie realm" and thus expended their efforts "hauling before the courts of the land respectable publishers, to say nothing of serious authors whose only crime is that they seek via admirable letters to set forth pictures of the social state of the time" (80). The "vice-snoopers" whom Dreiser castigated certainly were involved in attacks on the film industry, and his remarks sound like the complaints of a print-genre worker faced with the growing cultural authority of the new visual medium.

37. Greg Mitchell, "How Hollywood Fixed an Election," *American Film,* November 1988, 26–31. For a more complete account, see Mitchell's book, *The Campaign of the Century: Upton Sinclair's Race for Governor of California and the Birth of Media Politics* (New York: Random House, 1992).

38. Upton Sinclair, preface to Max Knepper, *Sodom and Gomorrah: The Story of Hollywood*, 6.

39. Knepper, *Sodom and Gomorrah*, 28.

40. Harry Alan Potamkin, "Holy Hollywood," in *Behold America!*, edited by Samuel D. Schmalhausen (New York: Farrar & Rinehart, 1931), 537–52.

41. Adela Rogers St. Johns's *The Port of Missing Girls* (*Photoplay*, 1927) included "No. 1, The Story of Greta," March, 28–31; "No. 2, Patty of the Flappers," April, 32–35; "No. 3, Persis," May, 38–41; "No. 4, Paula," June, 48–51; "No. 5, Judy Keene," July, 49–52; and "No. 6, Marilyn, the Lily Maid," August, 46–48.

42. St. Johns, "The Story of Greta," 28.

43. Stella G. S. Perry, *Extra-Girl* (New York: Frederick A. Stokes Company, 1929).

44. Maurice Horn, "Dixie Dugan," in *The World Encyclopedia of Comics*, edited by Maurice Horn, 211.

45. J. P. McEvoy, *Hollywood Girl*, 43.

46. James M. Cain, *The Postman Always Rings Twice* (New York: Alfred A. Knopf, 1934), 14.

47. Horace McCoy, *They Shoot Horses, Don't They?* (New York: Avon Books, 1970). Originally published by Simon & Schuster, 1935.

48. Mark Royden Winchell, *Horace McCoy*, Boise State University Western Writers Series, no. 51 (Boise, Idaho: Boise State University, 1982), 7.

49. Horace McCoy, *I Should Have Stayed Home*, 3.

50. Lee Server, *Danger Is My Business: An Illustrated History of the Fabulous Pulp Magazines, 1896–1953* (San Francisco: Chronicle Books, 1993), 69.

51. See Philip Durham, "The *Black Mask* School," in *Tough Guy Writers of the Thirties*, edited by David Madden (Carbondale: Southern Illinois University Press, 1968), 51–79.

52. See David Wilt's length discussion of McCoy's work as a screenwriter in *Hardboiled in Hollywood: Five Black Mask Writers and the Movies*, 8–47. Includes filmography.

53. McCoy, *They Shoot Horses, Don't They?*, 24.

54. Winchell, *Horace McCoy*, 41.

55. Thomas Sturak, "Horace McCoy's Objective Lyricism," in *Tough Guy Writers of the Thirties*, edited by David Madden, 150.

56. Ibid., 148.

57. After returning from Paris in 1946, *Vogue* editor Allene Talmey noted, "Everyone in the knowledgeable world talks about American writers, about a curious trinity: Hemingway, Faulkner, and McCoy." "Paris Quick Notes/About Sartre, Gide, Cocteau, Politics/the Theater, and Inflation," *Vogue*, 15 January 1947, 92.

58. McCoy, *They Shoot Horses, Don't They?*, 20.

59. West's novels are *The Dream Life of Balso Snell* (1931), *Miss Lonelyhearts* (1933), *A Cool Million* (1934), and *The Day of the Locust* (1939). *The Collected Works of Nathanael West* (Harmondsworth, England: Penguin Books, 1975).

60. For a discussion of West's critique of mass culture that compares it to the Marxist arguments of the Frankfurt School, see Rita Barnard, "'When You Wish Upon a Star': Fantasy, Experience, and Mass Culture in Nathanael West," *American Literature* 66, no. 2 (June 1994): 325–51. Mathew Roberts has argued, on the other hand, that West's critique of mass culture is more closely aligned with the postwar European avant-garde than with the Marxist analyses of the Frankfurt School critics. See his essay "Bonfire of the Avant-Garde: Cultural Rage and Readerly Complicity in *The Day of the Locust*," *Modern Fictions Studies* 42, no. 1 (spring 1996): 61–90.

61. Nathanael West, *Miss Lonelyhearts*, in *Collected Works*, 224.

62. Nathanael West, *The Day of the Locust*, in *Collected Works*, 61.

63. See "Nathanael West's Film Writing," appendix to Jay Martin, *Nathanael West: The Art of His Life* (New York: Carroll & Graff, 1970), for a detailed discussion of West's film work. Martin's biography provides the most thorough account of West's Hollywood experience, and I have relied on it extensively.

64. Martin, *Nathanael West: The Art of His Life*, 206.

65. West, *The Day of the Locust*, 104.

66. This phrase comes from Lary May, "The New Frontier: 'Hollywood,' 1914–1920," chap. 7 in *Screening Out the Past*.

67. Martin, *Nathanael West: The Art of His Life*, 252.

68. West, *The Day of the Locust*, 29.

69. James F. Light, *Nathanael West: An Interpretive Study* (Evanston, Ill.: Northwestern University Press, 1971), 176.

70. West, *The Day of the Locust*, 49.

71. Fine, "Nathanael West, Raymond Chandler, and the Los Angeles Novel," 196.

72. Garrett, "Los Angeles in Fact and Dream," 134.

73. Lockwood, *Dream Palaces*, 152.

74. West, *The Day of the Locust*, 11.

75. Nathanael West, "Some Notes on Violence," in *Nathanael West: A Collection of Critical Essays*, edited by Jay Martin (Englewood Cliffs, N.J.: Prentice-Hall, 1971), 50.

76. West, *The Day of the Locust*, 145–46.

77. For example, see Ted Sennet's *Hollywood's Golden Year: 1939* (New York: St. Martin's Press, 1989).

CHAPTER 6. ONE THOUSAND DOLLARS A WEEK

1. Jesse L. Lasky, Jr., *Whatever Happened to Hollywood?* (New York: Funk & Wagnalls, 1975), 31.

2. James M. Cain, "Camera Obscura," *American Mercury* 30, no. 118 (October 1933): 138.

3. My use of the masculine pronoun in this chapter is meant to reflect popular conceptions of screen writing as a male-dominated profession, not the actual circumstances in the film industry, where women had long held jobs as writers.

4. James Farrell, "The Language of Hollywood," in *The League of Frightened Philistines and Other Papers* (London: Routledge, 1948), 136.

5. Raymond Chandler, "Writers in Hollywood," *Atlantic Monthly*, November 1945, 52.

6. Richard Fine, *West of Eden: Writers in Hollywood 1928–1940*, 158.

7. Janet Staiger, "'Tame' Authors and the Corporate Laboratory: Stories, Writers, and Scenarios in Hollywood," *Quarterly Review of Film Studies*, fall 1983, 35.

8. See ibid., 38–40. Also see David Bordwell, "Classical Hollywood Cinema: Narrational Principles and Procedures," in *Narrative, Apparatus, Ideology: A Film Theory Reader*, edited by Philip Rosen (New York: Columbia University Press, 1986), 17–34.

9. "By the late teens, the dominant model of the Hollywood scenario department was securely in place. The scenario department assured a constant supply of plots and standardized blueprints for production; the continuity script facilitated interchangeability; the scenario staff divided its labor with some writers contributing plot ideas and others producing the complex script; product differentiation through advertising famous writers or stories induced consumption of the films; the firm owned the story for repeated use of ancillary profits." Staiger, "'Tame' Authors and the Corporate Laboratory," 43.

10. Ian Hamilton, *Writers in Hollywood 1915–1951*, 18.

11. Channing Pollock, "The Author's Strike," *Photoplay*, April 1919, 104.

12. Quoted in ibid., 103.

13. Staiger, "'Tame' Authors and the Corporate Laboratory," 41.

14. Hergesheimer, "Shapes in Light," 141–46.

15. Mary Roberts Rinehart, *My Story* (New York: Farrar and Rinehart, 1931), 292.

16. Fine, *West of Eden*, 49.

17. John Schultheiss, "The 'Eastern' Writer in Hollywood," in *Cinema Examined: Selections From Cinema Journal* (New York: E. P. Dutton, 1982), 41.

18. Notable exceptions are Rupert Hughes (see chapter 2) and Rex Beach, both of whom became successful writer-producers. Fine, *West of Eden*, 51.

19. Quoted in Pollock, "The Author's Strike," 103.

20. Cosmo Hamilton, "The Coast—As Eventually Discovered by Cosmo Hamilton," *Photoplay*, March 1921, 68.

21. R. L. Giffen, "The Prussian Authocracy," *Photoplay*, April 1919, 30.

22. Wodehouse, "Slaves of Hollywood," 5.

23. Ben Hecht, *A Child of the Century*, 466.

24. H. N. Swanson, *Sprinkled with Ruby Dust: A Literary and Hollywood Memoir*, 81.

25. See Nancy Lynn Schwartz, *The Hollywood Writers' Wars* (New York: Alfred A. Knopf, 1982).

26. Budd Schulberg, *What Makes Sammy Run?*, 164.

27. Leonard Hall, "The Herds of Hollywood," *Photoplay*, October 1929, 35.

28. Mildred Cram, "Author in Hollywood," in *The American Spectator Year Book*, edited by George Jean Nathan (New York: Stokes, 1934), 176–77.

29. Wodehouse, "Slaves of Hollywood," 5.

30. Cram, "Author in Hollywood," 177.

31. Chandler, "Writers in Hollywood," 51.

32. Maxwell Anderson, "Cut Is the Branch That Might Have Grown Full Straight," in *Off Broadway: Essays About the Theater* (New York: William Sloan Associates, 1947), 71.

33. Ben Ames Williams, "Lets and Hindrances," *Saturday Evening Post*, 14 June 1930, 166.

34. Cain, "Camera Obscura," 144.

35. Anderson, "Cut Is the Branch That Might Have Grown Full Straight," 73.

36. Sam Marx, "A Mythical Kingdom: The Hollywood Film Industry in the 1930s and 1940s," *Film and Literature: A Comparative Approach to Adaptation*, edited by Wendell Aycock and Micael Schoencke (Lubbock: Texas Tech University Press, 1988), 30. See also Sam Marx, *A Gaudy Spree: Literary Hollywood When the West Was Fun*.

37. Fred Lawrence Guiles, *Hanging On in Paradise*. See also Richard Corless, *Talking Pictures: Screenwriters in the American Cinema* (Woodstock, N.Y.: Overlook Press, 1974); Pat Milligan, ed., *Backstory: Interviews with Screenwriters of Hollywood's Golden Age* (Berkeley: University of California Press, 1986); Lee Server, *Screenwriter: Words Become Pictures* (Pittstown, N.J.: Main Street Press, 1987); Tom Stempel, *Framework: A History of Screenwriting in the American Film* (New York: Continuum, 1988).

38. Tom Dardis, *Some Time in the Sun: The Hollywood Years of Fitzgerald, Faulkner, Nathanael West, Aldous Huxley, and James Agee;* Schultheiss, "The 'Eastern' Writer in Hollywood"; Richard Fine, *Hollywood and the Profession of Authorship, 1928–1940* (Ann Arbor, Mich.: UMI Research Press, 1985), reprinted as *West of Eden: Writers in Hollywood 1928–1940*.

39. Dardis, "The Myth That Won't Go Away," 167–71.

40. Schultheiss, "The 'Eastern' Writer in Hollywood," 54–55.

41. Frances Marion, "Why Do They Change the Stories on the Screen?" *Photoplay*, March 1926, 38. See also Marion's *How to Write and Sell Film Stories* (New York: Covici-Friede, 1937).

42. Schultheiss, "The 'Eastern' Writer in Hollywood," 55.

43. Fine, *Hollywood and the Profession of Authorship, 1928–1940*, 10.

44. Pollock, "The Author's Strike," 31.

45. Pollock's article was rebutted by R. L. Giffen in a piece entitled "The Prussian Authocracy," *Photoplay*, April 1919, 30, and Pollock continued his attack in "Do Married Men Make the Best Husbands?" *Photoplay*, May 1919, 78. Pollock's

views were followed up with an editorial by Arthur Stringer entitled "Herods of the Movies," *Photoplay*, June 1919, 78.

46. "Breaking In," *Photoplay*, March 1922, 49–51.

47. Frank Condon, "New Stuff," *Saturday Evening Post*, 8 November 1924, 10.

48. Frank Condon, "On and Up," *Saturday Evening Post*, 5 June 1926, 18–19.

49. Joseph Hergesheimer, "Forty-Seven Pretty Girls," *Saturday Evening Post*, 22 January 1927, 8–9.

50. Hergesheimer, "Shapes in Light," parts 1–3, *Saturday Evening Post*, 6 March 1926, 3–4; 20 March 1926, 26–27; 27 March 1926, 30–31.

51. Hergesheimer, "Forty-Seven Pretty Girls," 111.

52. Milt Gross, "Well, Wot Is It?," *Red Book Magazine*, February 1929, 70–71.

53. See reviews by Clifton Fadiman, "Spider Boy," *Bookman* 68 (October 1928): 223; R. M. Lovett, "Spider Boy," *New Republic* 56 (12 September 1928): 107; Dorothy Parker, *New Yorker*, August 1928.

54. Among the alterations made to Van Vechten's story was a radical change in the age of his countess, from fifty to a youthful twenty. See Joseph Hergesheimer's response to a screening of *A Woman of the World* in "Shapes in Light," *Saturday Evening Post*, 20 March 1926, 26–27.

55. Bruce Kellner, *Carl Van Vechten and the Irreverent Decades* (Norman: University of Oklahoma Press, 1968), 160.

56. Carl Van Vechten, "Fabulous Hollywood," *Vanity Fair*, May 1927, 54; "Hollywood Parties," *Vanity Fair*, June 1927, 47; "Hollywood Royalty," *Vanity Fair*, July 1927, 38; "Understanding Hollywood," *Vanity Fair*, August 1927, 45.

57. Van Vechten, "Fabulous Hollywood," 54.

58. Van Vechten, "Understanding Hollywood," 78.

59. Van Vechten, "Hollywood Parties," 87.

60. Van Vechten, "Fabulous Hollywood," 54.

61. Carl Van Vechten, *Spider Boy: A Scenario for a Moving Picture*, 97.

62. Van Vechten, "Understanding Hollywood," 78.

63. Howard Hughes purchased an option to film *Queer People*, but studio opposition effectively killed the project before it could get off the ground. See Todd McCarthy, *Howard Hawks: The Grey Fox of Hollywood*, 123, 146.

64. Budd Schulberg, afterword to Graham and Graham, *Queer People* (Carbondale: Southern Illinois University Press, 1976), 280.

65. Graham and Graham, *Queer People*, 17.

66. F. Scott Fitzgerald, *The Great Gatsby* (New York: Charles Scribner's Sons, 1925); *Tender Is the Night* (New York: Charles Scribner's Sons, 1933). Early manuscript versions of *Tender Is the Night* had even stronger ties to Hollywood. See Aaron Latham's discussion of the novel in *Crazy Sundays: F. Scott Fitzgerald in Hollywood*, 76–96.

67. Unpublished letter from Fitzgerald to Leland Hayward, quoted in Latham, *Crazy Sundays*, 17.

68. Latham, *Crazy Sundays*, 34–35; 52–55.

69. F. Scott Fitzgerald, "The Crack Up," in *The Crack Up*, edited by Edmund Wilson (New York: New Directions, 1956), 78.

70. Ibid.

71. Latham, *Crazy Sundays*, 47–50.

72. F. Scott Fitzgerald, "Magnetism," *Saturday Evening Post*, 3 March 1928. It is reprinted in *The Stories of F. Scott Fitzgerald*, edited by Malcolm Cowley (New York: Charles Scribner's Sons, 1951).

73. Dorothy Speare, "Hollywood Madness," *Saturday Evening Post*, 7 October 1933, 60.

74. Fitzgerald in a letter to his daughter, Frances Scott Fitzgerald. *The Letters of F. Scott Fitzgerald*, edited by Andrew Turnbull (New York: Dell Publishing Co., 1966), 29–30.

75. Latham, *Crazy Sundays*, 62–72.

76. F. Scott Fitzgerald, "Crazy Sunday," in *The Stories of F. Scott Fitzgerald*, edited by Malcolm Cowley, 404.

77. Fitzgerald, "Magnetism," 238.

78. Fitzgerald, "Crazy Sunday," 416.

79. Hamilton, *Writers in Hollywood*, 156.

80. Arnold Gingrich, introduction to *The Pat Hobby Stories* (New York: Charles Scribner's Sons, 1962), xv.

81. F. Scott Fitzgerald, "A Man in the Way," in *The Pat Hobby Stories* (New York: Collier Books, 1988), 13.

82. F. Scott Fitzgerald, "No Harm Trying," in *The Pat Hobby Stories*, 103.

83. Fitzgerald, "A Man in the Way," 14.

84. F. Scott Fitzgerald, "Teamed with Genius," in *The Pat Hobby Stories*, 34.

85. F. Scott Fitzgerald, "Mightier Than the Sword," in *The Pat Hobby Stories*, 147.

86. James T. Farrell, "$1,000 a Week," in *$1,000 a Week and Other Stories* (New York: Vanguard Press, 1942), 5.

87. Farrell, "The Language of Hollywood" and "More on Hollywood," in *The League of Frightened Philistines and Other Papers*, 133–71.

88. Farrell, "The Language of Hollywood," 133. It should be noted that Farrell's phrase "cultural industries" in this essay precedes by three years the publication of Theodor Adorno's *The Dialectic of Enlightenment*, with its famous essay on the "culture industry."

CHAPTER 7. FROM TINSELTOWN TO SUCKERVILLE

1. Ruth Waterbury, "The Underworld of Hollywood," *Photoplay*, September 1927, 29.

2. Ibid., 28.

3. For a portrait of Los Angeles in the late twenties as it was assuming a more urban identity, see Bruce Bliven, "Los Angeles," *New Republic*, 13 July 1927, 197–200. A more recent history is Bruce Henstell's *Sunshine and Wealth*.

4. Morrow Mayo, *Los Angeles*, 245.

5. Ibid., 74–106, 128–36. Gregory, *American Exodus*, 19–26.

6. The definitive account of the corrupting influence of oil speculation in southern California is Jules Tygiel's *The Great Los Angeles Swindle*.

7. Morrow Mayo, *Los Angeles*, 251.

8. Adamic, *Laughing in the Jungle*, 220.

9. Waterbury, "The Underworld of Hollywood," 114.

10. Rosten, *Hollywood: The Movie Colony—The Movie Makers*, 19.

11. Ernest Jerome Hopkins, quoted in Mayo, *Los Angeles*, 195.

12. See Richard Perry and Louis Perry, *A History of the Los Angeles Labor Movement* (Berkeley: University of California Press, 1963). For information on labor struggles within the film industry, see Mike Nielsen and Gene Mailes, *Hollywood's Other Blacklist: Union Struggles in the Studio System*.

13. McWilliams, *Southern California Country*, 239.

14. Harry Carr, *Los Angeles: City of Dreams*, 265.

15. McWilliams, *Southern California Country*, 239.

16. Cited by Gil Reavill, *Hollywood and the Best of Los Angeles* (Oakland, Calif.: Compass American Guides, 1994), 18.

17. Carr, *Los Angeles*, 264.

18. Julian Symons, *Bloody Murder: From the Detective Story to the Crime Novel: A History* (New York: Viking, 1985), 94–95.

19. See ibid., 115; William O. Aydelotte, "The Detective Story as a Historical Source," *Yale Review*, 1949–50, 76–95.

20. Symons, *Bloody Murder*, 96.

21. W. H. Auden, "The Guilty Vicarage," in *The Dyer's Hand and Other Essays* (New York: Random House, 1962), 149.

22. Raymond Williams, *The Country and the City* (New York: Oxford University Press, 1973), 227.

23. Arthur B. Reeve, *The Film Mystery* (New York: Harper & Brothers, 1921).

24. Edward Stilgebauer, *The Star of Hollywood* (Cleveland: World Syndicate Publishing Company, 1929).

25. Ben Ames Williams, *An End to Mirth*, parts 1–4, *Ladies' Home Journal*, December 1930, 3–5; January 1931, 16–17; February 1931, 21; March 1931, 27.

26. Lange Lewis, *The Birthday Murder*, 151.

27. Mark Lee Luther and Lillian C. Ford, *Card 13*, 22.

28. Raymond Chandler, "The Simple Art of Murder," in *The Art of the Mystery Story*, edited by Howard Haycroft (New York: Biblo & Tannen, 1976), 225.

29. David Madden, introduction to *Tough Guy Writers of the Thirties*, xvii.

30. Hamilton, *Western and Hardboiled Detective Fiction in America*, 25.

31. See David E. Ruth, *Inventing the Public Enemy: The Gangster in American Culture, 1918–1934* (Chicago: University of Chicago Press, 1996).

32. Katharine Fullerton Gerould, "This Hard-Boiled Era," *Harper's Magazine* 158 (February 1929): 265–74.

33. See Madden, introduction to *Tough Guy Writers of the Thirties*, xxii–xxiii.

34. Madden, introduction to *Tough Guy Writers of the Thirties*, xviii.

35. William Marling, *The American Roman Noir: Hammett, Cain, and Chandler* (Athens: University of Georgia Press, 1995), xiv.

36. See Durham, "The *Black Mask* School," 51–79.

37. William F. Nolan, *The Black Mask Boys: Masters in the Hard-Boiled School of Detective Fiction* (New York: William Morrow & Company, 1985), 129–33.

38. Raoul Whitfield, *Death in a Bowl*, 137.

39. James L. Traylor, "Tod Ballard: An Appreciation," in *Hollywood Troubleshooter: W. T. Ballard's Bill Lennox Stories*, edited by James L. Traylor (Bowling Green, Ohio: Bowling Green University Popular Press, 1985). All references to the Bill Lennox stories are from the collection.

40. W. T. Ballard, "A Little Different," in *Hollywood Troubleshooter*, edited by James L. Traylor, 29.

41. W. T. Ballard, "A Million-Dollar Tramp," in *Hollywood Troubleshooter*, 24.

42. Traylor, "Tod Ballard: An Appreciation," 3.

43. W. T. Ballard, *Say Yes to Murder*, 12.

44. Chandler, "The Simple Art of Murder," 235.

45. Carolyn See, "The Hollywood Novel: The American Dream Cheat," in *Tough Guy Writers of the Thirties*, edited by David Madden, 207–8.

46. Richard Sales, *Lazarus #7*, 79.

47. In 1960 Fisher published a revised paperback edition of the novel that modernized certain Hollywood settings. All references are to the 1960 version of the novel, reprinted in 1991 by Vintage Crime/Black Lizard.

48. Steve Fisher, *I Wake Up Screaming*, 3.

49. The details of Chandler's life can be found in Frank MacShane's *The Life of Raymond Chandler* (Boston: G. K. Hall & Company, 1976). For an examination of his work in the context of his oil-field experiences, see William Marling, "Raymond Chandler, Oil Executive," in *The American Roman Noir*, 188–201.

50. See William Luhr, *Raymond Chandler and Film*, 2d ed. (Tallahassee: Florida State University Press, 1991).

51. Raymond Chandler, *The Little Sister* (New York: Vintage Books, 1988). The book was filmed by MGM in 1969 under the title *Marlowe*.

52. Chandler, "The Simple Art of Murder," 236.

53. Critic Herbert Ruhm has argued that *The Little Sister* is "Chandler's best novel" and "by far the most accurate of Hollywood novels" in his essay "Raymond Chandler: From Bloomsbury to the Jungle—and Beyond," in *Tough Guy Writers of the Thirties*, edited by David Madden, 182–83.

54. Chandler, *The Little Sister*, 3.

55. Fredric Jameson, "On Raymond Chandler," *Southern Review* 6 (summer 1970): 630.

56. Chandler, *The Little Sister*, 48.

57. See Chandler, "Writers in Hollywood," 50–54.

58. Chandler, *The Little Sister*, 159.

59. Chandler, "Writers in Hollywood," 50.

60. Raymond Chandler, "Oscar Night in Hollywood," *Atlantic Monthly*, March 1948. Citation is from reprint in *Sight and Sound: A Fiftieth Anniversary Selection*, edited by David Wilson (London: Faber & Faber, 1982), 58.

61. Letter from Raymond Chandler to George Harmon Coxe, in *Selected Letters of Raymond Chandler*, edited by Frank MacShane (New York: Dell, 1981), 6.

62. Raymond Chandler, "A Qualified Farewell," in *The Notebooks of Raymond Chandler*, edited by Frank MacShane (New York: Ecco, 1976), 66.

63. Letter from Raymond Chandler to Carl Brandt, in *Selected Letters*, 146.

64. Letter from Raymond Chandler to Alfred Knopf, in *Selected Letters*, 64.

65. The work of contemporary writers such as John Gregory Dunne (*True Confessions*, 1977; *Playland*, 1994), Thomas Sanchez (*The Zoot-Suit Murders*, 1978), James Ellroy (*The Black Dahlia*, 1987; *The Big Nowhere*, 1988; *L.A. Confidential*, 1990), and Michael Tolkin (*The Player*, 1988) have continued this tradition of the Hollywood crime novel as a work of social criticism.

BIBLIOGRAPHY

BOOKS

Adamic, Louis. *Laughing in the Jungle.* New York: Harper & Brothers, 1932.

Albert, Katherine. *Remembering Valerie March.* New York: Simon & Schuster, 1939.

Altman, Diana. *Hollywood East: Louis B. Mayer and the Origins of the Studio System.* New York: Carol Publishing Group, 1992.

Anger, Kenneth. *Hollywood Babylon.* San Francisco: Straight Arrow Books, 1975.

Anonymous. *My Strange Life: The Intimate Story of a Moving Picture Actress.* New York: Grosset & Dunlap, 1915.

Balazs, Andre. *Hollywood Handbook.* New York: Rizzoli, 1995.

Balio, Tino. *The American Film Industry.* Rev. ed. Madison: University of Wisconsin Press, 1985.

———. *Grand Design: Hollywood as a Modern Business Enterprise, 1930–1939.* Vol. 5 of *History of the American Cinema.* New York: Charles Scribner's Sons, 1993.

Ballard, W. T. *Dealing Out Death.* Philadelphia: David McKay Co., 1948.

———. *Say Yes to Murder.* New York: G. P. Putnam's Sons, 1942.

Baum, Vicki. *Falling Star,* New York: Doubleday, 1934.

Baxter, John. *The Hollywood Exiles.* New York: Taplinger, 1976.

———. *Hollywood in the Thirties.* London: Tantivy Press, 1968.

Beardsley, Charles. *Hollywood's Master Showman: The Legendary Sid Grauman.* New York: Cornwall Books, 1983.

Beauchamp, Cari. *Without Lying Down: Frances Marion and the Powerful Women of Early Hollywood.* New York: Scribner, 1997.

Belfrage, Cedric. *Promised Land: Notes for a History.* London: Gollancz, 1938.

Bemelmans, Ludwig. *Dirty Eddie.* New York: Viking Press, 1947.

Benét, Stephen Vincent. *The Beginning of Wisdom.* New York: Henry Holt & Co., 1921.

Berg, A. Scott. *Goldwyn: A Biography.* New York: Alfred A. Knopf, 1989.

Bordwell, David, Janet Staiger, and Kristin Thompson. *The Classical Hollywood Cinema: Film Style and Mode of Production to 1960.* New York: Columbia University Press, 1985.

Bower, B. M. *The Phantom Herd.* New York: Grosset & Dunlap, 1916.

Brooker-Bowers, Nancy. "The Hollywood Novel: An American Literary Genre." Ph.D. diss., Drake University, 1983.

———. *The Hollywood Novel and Other Novels About Film, 1912–1982: An Annotated Bibliography.* New York: Garland, 1985.

Brooks, Louise. *Lulu in Hollywood.* New York: Alfred A. Knopf, 1983.

Brownlow, Kevin. *Hollywood: The Pioneers.* New York: Alfred A. Knopf, 1979.

———. *The Parade's Gone By. . . .* New York: Alfred A. Knopf, 1968.

Burroughs, Edgar Rice. *The Girl from Hollywood.* New York: Macaulay, 1923.

Carr, Harry. *Los Angeles: City of Dreams.* New York: D. Appelton-Century Company, 1935.

Cendrars, Blaise. *Hollywood: Mecca of the Movies.* Translated by Garrett White. Berkeley: University of California Press, 1995.

Chandler, Raymond. *The Little Sister.* Boston: Houghton Mifflin Co., 1949.

Chester, George Randolph, and Lillian Chester. *On the Lot and Off.* New York: Harper & Brothers, 1924.

Cini, Zelda, and Bob Crane. *Hollywood: Land and Legend.* Westport, Conn.: Arlington House, 1980.

Clarke, Donald Henderson. *Alabam'.* New York: Vanguard, 1934.

Conners, Marilynn. *What Chance Have I in Hollywood? Intimate Information Concerning the Movie Capital of the World.* Hollywood: Famous Authors Imprint, 1924.

Crooker, Herbert. *The Hollywood Murder Mystery.* New York: Macaulay Co., 1930.

Crowther, Bosley. *Hollywood Rajah: The Life and Times of Louis B. Mayer.* New York: Holt, Rinehart and Winston, 1960.

Croy, Homer. *Headed for Hollywood.* New York: Harper & Brothers, 1932.

Crump, Irving. *Our Movies' Makers.* New York: Dodd, Mead & Company. 1940.

Dardis, Tom. *Some Time in the Sun: The Hollywood Years of Fitzgerald, Faulkner, Nathanael West, Aldous Huxley, and James Agee.* New York: Charles Scribner's Sons, 1976.

Davis, Mike. *City of Quartz: Excavating the Future in Los Angeles.* New York: Vintage Books, 1992.

Davis, Ronald L. *The Glamour Factory: Inside Hollywood's Big Studio System.* Dallas: Southern Methodist University Press, 1993.

Day, Beth. *This Was Hollywood: An Affectionate History of Filmland's Golden Years.* Garden City, N.Y.: Doubleday & Company, 1960.

Dos Passos, John. *The Big Money.* New York: Harcourt Brace, 1936.

Easton, Carol. *The Search for Sam Goldwyn.* New York: William Morrow, 1975.

Eyman, Scott. *The Speed of Sound: Hollywood and the Talkies Revolution*. New York: Simon & Schuster, 1997.

Fernett, Gene. *American Film Studios: An Historical Encyclopedia*. Jefferson, N.C.: McFarland, 1988.

Field, Rachel, and Arthur Pederson. *To See Ourselves*. New York: Macmillan, 1937.

Finch, Christopher, and Linda Rosenkrantz. *Gone Hollywood*. Garden City: Doubleday & Company, 1979.

Fine, David, ed. *Los Angeles in Fiction: A Collection of Original Essays*. Albuquerque: University of New Mexico Press, 1984.

Fine, Richard. *West of Eden: Writers in Hollywood 1928–1940*. Washington, D.C.: Smithsonian Institution Press, 1993.

Finler, Joel W. *The Hollywood Story*. New York: Crown, 1988.

Fisher, Steve. *I Wake Up Screaming*. New York: Dodd, Mead & Company, 1941.

Fitzgerald, F. Scott. *The Last Tycoon*, edited by Edmund Wilson. New York: Charles Scribner's Sons, 1941.

Florey, Robert. *Filmland: Los Angeles et Hollywood les Capitales du Cinema*. Paris: Editions de Cinemagazine, 1923.

Fox, Charles Donald. *Mirrors of Hollywood*. New York: Charles Renard Corp., 1925.

Friedrich, Otto. *City of Nets: A Portrait of Hollywood in the 1940's*. New York: Harper & Row, 1986.

Gabler, Neal. *An Empire of Their Own: How the Jews Invented Hollywood*. New York: Crown, 1988.

Gardner, Ann. *Reputation*. New York: Burt, 1929.

Garnett, Tay. *Light Your Torches and Pull Up Your Tights*. New Rochelle, N.Y.: Arlington House, 1973.

Gibbons, Cromwell. *Murder in Hollywood*. New York: David Kemp & Company, 1936.

Gomery, Douglas. *The Hollywood Studio System*. New York: St. Martin's Press, 1986.

Goodman, Ezra. *The Fifty-Year Decline and Fall of Hollywood*. New York: Simon & Schuster, 1961.

Gorman, John. *Hollywood's Bad Boy*. Hollywood: Brewster, 1932.

Graham, Carroll, and Garrett Graham. *Queer People*. New York: Vanguard, 1930.

Graham, Sheilah. *Hollywood Revisited*. New York: St. Martin's Press, 1984.

Grayson, Charles. *The Show Case*. New York: Green Circle Books, 1936.

———. *Spotlight Madness*. New York: Horace Liveright, 1931.

Greig, Maysie. *Romance for Sale*. New York: Doubleday, 1934.

Guiles, Fred Lawrence. *Hanging On in Paradise*. New York: McGraw-Hill Book Company, 1975.

Hallas, Richard. *You Play the Black and the Red Comes Up*. London: Cassell & Company, 1938.

Hamilton, Ian. *Writers in Hollywood 1915–1951*. New York: Harper & Row, 1990.

Haver, Ronald. *David O. Selznick's Hollywood*. New York: Bonanza Books, 1980.

Hecht, Ben. *A Child of the Century*. New York: Simon & Schuster, 1954.

Heimann, Jim. *Hooray for Hollywood: A Postcard Tour of Hollywood's Golden Era*. San Francisco: Chronicle Books, 1983.

———. *Out with the Stars: Hollywood Nightlife in the Golden Era*. New York: Abbeville Press, 1985.

Henstell, Bruce. *Sunshine and Wealth: Los Angeles in the Twenties and Thirties*. San Francisco: Chronicle Books, 1984.

Higham, Charles. *Hollywood at Sunset*. New York: Saturday Review Press, 1972.

———. *Merchant of Dreams: Louis B. Mayer, M.G.M. and the Secret Hollywood*. New York: Donald I. Fine, 1993.

Hughes, Rupert. *Souls for Sale*. New York: Harper & Row, 1922.

Izod, John. *Hollywood and the Box Office: 1895–1986*. New York: Columbia University Press, 1988.

Kaplan, Sam Hall. *L.A. Lost and Found: An Architectural History of Los Angeles*. New York: Crown, 1987.

Knepper, Max. *Sodom and Gomorrah: The Story of Hollywood*. Los Angeles: Max Knepper, 1935.

Kobal, John. *Hollywood: The Years of Innocence*. New York: Abbeville Press, 1985.

———. *People Will Talk*. New York: Alfred A. Knopf, 1985.

Koszarski, Richard. *An Evening's Entertainment: The Age of the Silent Feature Picture, 1915–1928*. Vol. 3 of *The History of the American Cinema*. New York: Charles Scribner's Sons, 1990.

Landery, Charles. *Hollywood Is the Place!* London: J. M. Dent & Sons, 1940.

Lane, Tamar. *Hey Diddle Diddle*. New York: Adelphi Press, 1932.

Lasky, Jesse, and Don Weldon. *I Blow My Own Horn*. Garden City, N.Y.: Doubleday, 1957.

Latham, Aaron. *Crazy Sundays: F. Scott Fitzgerald in Hollywood*. New York: Viking Press, 1971.

Lee, James. *Hollywood Agent*. New York: Macaulay, 1937.

Lee, Richard Henry. *Nights and Daze in Hollywood*. New York: Macaulay, 1934.

Lewis, Lange. *The Birthday Murder*. Indianapolis: Bobbs-Merrill Company, 1945.

———. *Meat for Murder*. Indianapolis: Bobbs-Merrill Company, 1943.

Lockwood, Charles. *Dream Palaces: Hollywood at Home*. New York: Viking Press, 1981.

Lokke, Virgil L. "The Literary Image of Hollywood." Ph.D. diss., University of Iowa, 1955.

Loos, Anita. *Cast of Thousands*. New York: Grosset & Dunlap, 1977.

———. *Kiss Hollywood Good-by*. New York: Viking Press, 1974.

Lubou, Haynes. *Reckless Hollywood*. New York: Armour, 1932.

Luther, Mark Lee, and Lillian C. Ford. *Card 13*. Indianapolis: Bobbs-Merrill Company, 1929.

———. *The Saranoff Murder*. Indianapolis: Bobbs-Merrill Company, 1930.

Mabie, Mary Louise. *The Root of the Lotus.* New York: Scribner, 1938.

Marion, Frances. *Minnie Flynn.* New York: Boni & Liveright, 1925.

Marx, Samuel. *A Gaudy Spree: Literary Hollywood When the West Was Fun.* New York: Franklin Watts, 1987.

———. *Mayer and Thalberg: The Make-Believe Saints.* New York: Random House, 1975.

May, Lary. *Screening Out the Past: The Birth of Mass Culture and the Motion Picture Industry.* Chicago: University of Chicago Press, 1980.

Mayo, Morrow. *Los Angeles.* New York: Alfred A. Knopf, 1933.

McBride, Joseph. *Frank Capra: The Catastrophe of Success.* New York: Simon & Schuster, 1992.

McCarthy, Todd. *Howard Hawks: The Grey Fox of Hollywood.* New York: Grove Press, 1997.

McCoy, Horace. *I Should Have Stayed Home.* New York: Alfred A. Knopf, 1938.

———. *They Shoot Horses, Don't They?* New York: Simon & Schuster, 1935.

McEvoy, J. P. *Hollywood Girl.* New York: Simon & Schuster, 1929.

McGrath, Keane. *Hollywood Siren.* New York: W. Godwin, 1932.

McWilliams, Carey. *Southern California Country: An Island on the Land.* New York: Duell, Sloan & Pearce, 1946.

Minney, R. J. *Hollywood by Starlight.* London: Chapman & Hall, 1935.

Moore, Colleen. *Silent Star.* Garden City, N.Y.: Doubleday & Company, 1968.

Morden, Ethan. *The Hollywood Studios: House Style in the Golden Age of the Movies.* New York: Alfred A. Knopf, 1988.

Negri, Pola. *Memoirs of a Star.* Garden City: Doubleday & Co., 1970.

Nielsen, Mike, and Gene Mailes. *Hollywood's Other Blacklist: Union Struggles in the Studio System.* London: British Film Institute, 1995.

Niven, David. *Bring On the Empty Horses.* New York: G. P. Putnam's Sons, 1975.

———. *Hollywood Doesn't Live Here Anymore.* Boston: Little, Brown & Company, 1988.

O'Flaherty, Liam. *Hollywood Cemetery.* London: Gollancz, 1935.

O'Hara, John. *Hope of Heaven.* New York: Harcourt, Brace, 1938.

Palmer, Edwin O. *History of Hollywood.* 2 vols. Hollywood: Arthur H. Cawston, 1937.

Parrish, Robert. *Growing Up in Hollywood.* Boston: Little, Brown & Company, 1976.

Perry, Stella. *Extra-Girl.* New York: Stokes, 1929.

Pickford, Mary. *Sunshine and Shadow.* Garden City, N.Y.: Doubleday & Company, 1955.

Pollack, James S. *The Golden Egg.* New York: Henry Holt & Company, 1946.

Powdermaker, Hortense. *Hollywood: The Dream Factory.* New York: Little, Brown & Company, 1950.

Preston, Jack. *Screen Star.* Garden City, N.Y.: Doubleday, Doran & Company., 1932.

Priestly, J. B. *Albert Goes Through.* New York: Harper & Brothers, 1933.

Rivkin, Allen, and Laura Kerr. *Hello Hollywood*. Garden City, N.Y.: Doubleday & Company, 1962.

Robbins, Harold. *The Dream Merchants*. New York: Alfred A. Knopf, 1949.

Robinson, David. *Hollywood in the Twenties*. London: A. Zwemmer, 1968.

Rolfe, Lionel. *Literary L.A.* San Francisco: Chronicle Books, 1981.

Rosenberg, Bernard, and Harry Silverstein. *The Real Tinsel*. London: Macmillan Company, 1970.

Rosenstein, Jake. *Hollywood Leg Man*. Los Angeles: Madison Press, 1950.

Rosten, Leo. *Hollywood: The Movie Colony—The Moviemakers*. New York: Harcourt, Brace & Company, 1941.

St. Johns, Adela Rogers. *The Honeycomb*. Garden City, N.Y.: Doubleday & Company, 1969.

———. *Love, Laughter, and Tears: My Hollywood Story*. Garden City, N.Y.: Doubleday & Company, 1978.

———. *The Skyrocket*. New York: Cosmopolitan, 1925.

Sale, Richard. *Benefit Performance*. New York: Simon & Schuster, 1946.

———. *Lazarus #7*. New York: Simon A& Schuster, 1942.

Saxby, Charles, and Louis Molnar. *Death Over Hollywood*. New York: E. P. Dutton & Company, 1937.

Schatz, Thomas. *The Genius of the System: Hollywood Filmmaking in the Studio Era*. New York: Pantheon Books, 1988.

———. *Old Hollywood/New Hollywood: Ritual, Art, and Industry*. Ann Arbor, Mich.: UMI Research Press, 1983.

Schickel, Richard. *The Stars*. New York: Bonanza Books, 1962.

Schulberg, Budd. *Moving Pictures: Memories of a Hollywood Prince*. New York: Stein & Day, 1981.

———. *What Makes Sammy Run?* New York: Random House, 1941.

Scott, Evelyn F. *Hollywood: When Silents Were Golden*. New York: McGraw-Hill Book Company, 1972.

See, Carolyn. "The Hollywood Novel: An Historical and Critical Study." Ph.D. diss., University of California, Los Angeles, 1963.

Seldes, Gilbert. *The Movies Come from America*. New York: Charles Scribner's Sons, 1937.

Sheehan, Perley Poore. *Hollywood as a World Center*. Hollywood: Hollywood Citizen Press, 1924.

Shippey, Lee. *If We Only Had Money*. Boston: Houghton, Mifflin, 1939.

Shorris, Sylvia, and Marion Abbott Bundy. *Talking Pictures*. New York: New Press, 1994.

Spatz, Jonas. *Hollywood in Fiction: Some Versions of the American Myth*. The Hague: Mouton, 1969.

Spear, Dorothy. *The Road to Needles*. Boston: Houghton Mifflin, 1937.

Sperling, Cass Warner, and Cork Millner. *Hollywood Be Thy Name*. Rocklin, Calif.: Prima, 1994.

Staiger, Janet, ed. *The Studio System*. New Brunswick, N.J.: Rutgers University Press, 1995.

Starr, Jimmy. *The Corpse Came C.O.D.* Hollywood: Murray & Gee, 1944.

Starr, Kevin. *Endangered Dreams: The Great Depression in California*. New York: Oxford University Press, 1996.

———. *Inventing the Dream: California Through the Progressive Era*. New York: Oxford University Press, 1985.

———. *Material Dreams: Southern California Through the 1920s*. New York: Oxford University Press, 1990.

Steen, Mike. *Hollywood Speaks! An Oral History*. New York: G. P. Putnam's Sons, 1974.

Stong, Phillip. *The Farmer in the Dell*. New York: Harcourt, Brace, 1935.

Swanson, H. N. *Sprinkled with Ruby Dust: A Literary and Hollywood Memoir*. New York: Warner Books, 1989.

Taylor, John Russell. *Strangers in Paradise: The Hollywood Émigrés, 1933–1950*. New York: Holt, Rinehard and Winston, 1983.

Thompson, David. *Beneath Mullholland Falls: Thoughts on Hollywood and Its Ghosts*. New York: Alfred A. Knopf, 1997.

———. *Showman: The Life of David O. Selznick*. New York: Alfred A. Knopf, 1992.

Thompson, Kristin. *Exporting Entertainment: America in the World Film Market 1907–1934*. London: BFI, 1985.

Torrence, Bruce T. *Hollywood: The First Hundred Years*. New York: Zeotrope, 1982.

Tully, Jim. *Jarnegan*. New York: Albert & Charles Boni, 1926.

Turnbull, Margaret. *The Close-Up*. New York: Harper, 1918.

Tygiel, Jules. *The Great Los Angeles Swindle: Oil, Stocks, and Scandal During the Roaring Twenties*. New York: Oxford University Press, 1994.

Van Loan, Charles. *Buck Parvin and the Movies*. New York: George H. Doran, 1917.

Van Vechten, Carl. *Spider Boy: A Scenario for a Moving Picture*. New York: Alfred A. Knopf, 1928.

Vasey, Ruth. *The World According to Hollywood, 1918–1939*. Madison: University of Wisconsin Press, 1997.

Vidor, King. *A Treee Is a Tree*. Hollywood: Samuel French, 1981.

Wade, Horace. *To Hell with Hollywood*. New York: Dial, 1931.

Walker, Alexander. *The Shattered Silents: How the Talkies Came to Stay*. New York: William Morrow & Company, 1979.

Wanger, Walter. *You Must Remember This: Oral Reminiscences of the Real Hollywood*. New York: G. P. Putnam's Sons, 1975.

Webb, Michael, ed. *Hollywood: Legend and Reality*. Boston: Little Brown & Company, 1986.

Webster, Henry Kitchell. *Real Life.* Indianapolis: Bobbs-Merrill Co., 1921.

Wells, Walter. *Tycoons and Locusts: A Regional Look at Hollywood Fiction of the 1930s.* Carbondale: Southern Illinois University Press, 1973.

West, Nathanael. *The Day of the Locust.* New York: Random House, 1939.

Whitfield, Raoul. *Death in a Bowl.* New York: Knopf, 1931.

Wilkerson, Tichi, and Marcia Borie. *The Hollywood Reporter: The Golden Years.* New York: Coward-McCann, 1984.

Williamson, Alice M. (Mrs. C. N. Williamson). *Alice in Movieland.* London: A. M. Philpot, 1927.

Wilson, Harry Leon. *Merton of the Movies.* Garden City, N.Y.: Doubleday, Page & Company, 1922.

———. *Two Black Sheep.* New York: Cosmopolitan, 1931.

Wilt, David. *Hardboiled in Hollywood: Five Black Mask Writers and the Movies.* Bowling Green, Ohio: Bowling Green State University Popular Press, 1991.

Winchester, Clarence. *An Innocent in Hollywood.* London: Cassell & Company, 1934.

Zierold, Norman. *The Moguls: Hollywood's Merchants of Myth.* Los Angeles: Silman-James Press, 1969.

SHORT STORIES, SERIALS, AND ARTICLES

Adams, Frank R. "—And a Woman." *Photplay,* June 1925.

———. "Celluloid Boulevard." *Photoplay,* August 1923.

———. "The Chinese Jane." *Photoplay,* July 1925.

———. "The Comedian." *Cosmopolitan,* November 1921.

———. "The Double Quits." *Good Housekeeping,* June 1923.

———. "The Good Little Bathing Girl." *Cosmopolitan,* August 1921.

———. "Le Jongleur of Hollywood." *Cosmopolitan,* September 1922.

———. "Liar's Lane." *Photoplay,* January 1924.

———. "Scandal Street." *Cosmopolitan,* June 1923.

———. "The Stuffed Shirt." *Photoplay,* 23 October, 1923.

Albert, Katherine. "Eggs and Onions." *Photoplay,* 1 September, 1928.

———.. "The Whip." *Photoplay,* June 1929.

Andrews, Charlton. "A Hollywood Cinderella." *Photoplay,* November 1925.

Anonymous. "Breaking In." *Photoplay,* March 1922.

Bakerston, Stewart. "Higher Hire." *Photoplay,* September 1927.

Barrington, Vivian. *Laura Leonard—Heart Specialist* (serial). *Photoplay,* July–December 1914.

Beatty, Jerome. "All Was Ambrosial." *Collier's,* 8 June 1929.

———. "One-Eyed Jacks Are Wild." *Cosmopolitan,* December 1929.

———. "The One Man Pigeon." *Collier's,* 3 May 1930.

———. "Pickles and Pictures." *Photoplay,* December 1929.

———. "Sound Business." *Collier's*, 27 July 1929.

———. "Stout Heart." *Collier's*, 12 October 1929.

———. "Take Your Time." *Collier's*, 3 August 1929.

———. "Texas Good Girl." *Collier's*, 29 March 1930.

———. "The Yodeling Lady." *Collier's*, 2 November 1929.

Biggers, Earl Derr. *Love in Hollywood* (serial). *Ladies' Home Journal*, April–June 1921.

Birchard, Robert S. "Hollywood at 100." *American Cinematographer* 68, no. 7 (July 1987): 28–32.

Boylan, Malcolm Stuart. "Funny Old Fool." *Photoplay*, May 1928.

Brackett, Charles. "The Lioness and the Mouse." *Saturday Evening Post*, 10 August 1929.

Bretherton, Vivien R. "It Happened in Hollywood." *Photoplay*, September 1929.

Brooker-Bowers, Nancy. "Fiction and the Film Industry: A Brief History of the Hollywood Novel and a Bibliography of Criticism." *Literature/Film Quarterly* 15, no. 4 (1987): 259–67.

Chester, George Randolph. "All for the Ladies." *Saturday Evening Post*, 11 August 1923.

———. "Angel Child." *Saturday Evening Post*, 3 November 1923.

———. "Below Lay Hollywood." *Saturday Evening Post*, 10 May 1924.

———. "Bigger and Better." *Saturday Evening Post*, 12 May 1923.

———. "The Boy Wonder." *Saturday Evening Post*, 26 May 1923.

———. "Fish Eat Fish." *Saturday Evening Post*, 13 October 1923.

———. "Fried Eggs." *Saturday Evening Post*, 14 July 1923.

———. "Isidor Iskovitch Presents." *Saturday Evening Post*, 8 September 1923.

———. "Named by Izzy Iskovitch." *Saturday Evening Post*, 4 April 1923.

———. "The Seven Garments." *Saturday Evening Post*, 1 December 1923.

———. "The Slump." *Saturday Evening Post*, 8 March 1924.

———. "A Tale of Three Fillums." *Saturday Evening Post*, 16 June 1923.

———. "Them Papers." *Saturday Evening Post*, 2 February 1924.

———. "The Yes Man Said No." *Saturday Evening Post*, 19 April 1924.

Cohen, Octavus Roy. "Arabian Nights." *Photoplay*, December 1926.

———. "Ball and Jane." *Saturday Evening Post*, 6 September 1930

———. "The Bathing Booty." *Saturday Evening Post*, 4 October 1924.

———. "Battle Scared." *Saturday Evening Post*, 12 June 1926.

———. "Ben Hurry." *Photoplay*, August 1926.

———. "Between Halves." *Saturday Evening Post*, 5 March 1927.

———. "Black Beauty." *Saturday Evening Post*, 28 April 1928.

———. "The Bright Shadow." *Collier's*, 22 March 1930.

———. "The Call of the Riled." *Saturday Evening Post*, 6 March 1926.

———. "The Claws in the Contract." *Saturday Evening Post*, 6 February 1926.

———. "Comin' Through the Sky." *Saturday Evening Post*, 8 March 1930.

———. "The Cookie Pushers." *Photoplay*, August 1924.

——. "Crude Interest." *Saturday Evening Post*, 26 March 1927.

——. "Custard's Last Stand." *Saturday Evening Post*, 18 October 1930.

——. "Cut and Dried." *Saturday Evening Post*, 12 October 1929.

——. "Damaged Good." *Saturday Evening Post*, 18 July 1925.

——. "Double Double." *Saturday Evening Post*, 27 September 1924.

——. "Double Double." *Collier's*, 3 March 1928.

——. "Double or Nothing." *Saturday Evening Post*, 19 November 1927.

——. "Endurance Vile." *Saturday Evening Post*, 5 December 1925.

——. "Every Little Movie." *Saturday Evening Post*, 30 August 1924.

——. "5000 Feet Make One Smile." *Saturday Evening Post*, 4 January 1930.

——. "French Leave." *Photoplay*, June 1927.

——. "Ham and Exit." *Saturday Evening Post*, 18 December 1926.

——. "Hams Aplenty." *Saturday Evening Post*, 4 September 1926.

——. "Happy Daze." *Photoplay*, January 1926.

——. "Honeymoon." *Ladies' Home Journal*, October 1930.

——. "Inside Inflammation." *Saturday Evening Post*, 1 November 1924.

——. "The Lion and the Uniform." *Saturday Evening Post*, 31 January 1925.

——. "A Little Child." *Saturday Evening Post*, 18 October 1924.

——. "Loon Wolf." *Saturday Evening Post*, 1 March 1930.

——. "Love and Defection." *Photoplay*, October 1926.

——. "Love and Let Love." *Photoplay*, September 1923.

——. "Low But Sure." *Saturday Evening Post*, 6 November 1926.

——. "Mate in America." *Saturday Evening Post*, 8 January 1927.

——. "Mercy, Monsieur." *Saturday Evening Post*, 8 May 1926.

——. "Miss Directed." *Saturday Evening Post*, 11 April 1925.

——. "Neapolitan Scream." *Saturday Evening Post*, 14 August 1926.

——. "On Account of Monte Cristo." *Photoplay*, November 1926.

——. "The Party of the Worst Part." *Saturday Evening Post*, 15 February 1930.

——. "The Pay of Naples." *Saturday Evening Post*, 17 July 1926.

——. "The Pull by the Horns." *Saturday Evening Post*, 7 May 1927.

——. "The Roman Nose." *Photoplay*, April 1927.

——. "Safe and Seine." *Photoplay*, May 1927.

——. "Skin and Groans." *Saturday Evening Post*, 9 January 1926.

——. "The Slappeyan Way." *Saturday Evening Post*, 7 September 1929.

——. "Star or Wife?" *Photoplay*, September 1924.

——. "Stews Company." *Saturday Evening Post*, 5 February 1927.

——. "10,000 Pictures Can't Be Wrong." *Saturday Evening Post*, 9 November 1929.

——. "Tres Sheik." *Saturday Evening Post*, 16 October 1926.

——. "Troupers." *Collier's*, 25 January 1930.

——. "Write and Wrong." *Saturday Evening Post*, 7 March 1925.

Condon, Frank,. "Adam's Other Apple." *Photoplay*, February 1927.

——. "Beefsteak and Onions." *Photoplay*, December 1923.

———. "Behind the Curtain." *Photoplay*, June 1922.

———. "Behold the Sheik." *Saturday Evening Post*, 12 February 1927.

———. "The Best Minds." *Saturday Evening Post*, 2 May 1925.

———. "Big Names." *Saturday Evening Post*, 4 April 1925.

———. "Brownie." *Saturday Evening Post*, 29 November 1924.

———. "The Camera Never Lies." *Photoplay*, April 1924.

———. "Directed by Andy." *Saturday Evening Post*, 20 December 1924.

———. "A Far Cry." *Collier's*, 1 June 1929.

———. "The Fighting Rabbit." *Saturday Evening Post*, 21 November 1925.

———. "Finders Keepers." *Saturday Evening Post*, 27 December 1924.

———. "Flashback." *Collier's*, 8 September 1928.

———. "Gentlemen of the Box Office." *Saturday Evening Post*, 9 April 1927.

———. "Hear and See." *Saturday Evening Post*, 1 June 1929.

———. "Hollywood." *Photoplay*, January 1923.

———. "The Legend of Hollywood." *Photoplay*, March 1924.

———. "Little Drops of Water." *Saturday Evening Post*, 25 April 1925.

———. "Love Letters." *Collier's*, 26 October 1929.

———. "Man at Work." *Collier's*, 12 January 1929.

———. "Minor Changes." *Saturday Evening Post*, 6 June 1925.

———. "Mud." *Saturday Evening Post*, 12 September 1925.

———. "New Stuff." *Saturday Evening Post*, 8 November 1924.

———. "On and Up." *Saturday Evening Post*, 5 June 1926.

———. "Picture Feet." *Collier's*, 16 July 1927.

———. "Rain or Shine." *Photoplay*, January 1925.

———. "The Repeater." *Saturday Evening Post*, 20 October 1928.

———. "The Retake Man." *Saturday Evening Post*, 19 June 1926.

———. "Story by —." *Saturday Evening Post*, 10 December 1927.

———. "They Also Eat Fish." *Saturday Evening Post*, 17 March 1926.

———. "Trouble with Women." *Photoplay*, December 1924.

———. "Words and Pictures." *Collier's*, 15 March 1930.

Corbaley, Kate. "A Pair of Blue Rompers." *Ladies' Home Journal*, January 1920.

Courtney, Basil. "Retake." *Collier's*, 21 May 1927.

Craig, Johnstone. "The Picture Gang." *Photoplay*, August 1915.

Dale, Virginia. "Came the Dawn." *Red Book Magazine*, January 1927.

———. "Dear Diary." *Red Book Magazine*, November 1926.

———. "Dear Diary." *Red Book Magazine*, December 1926.

———. "The Girl Who Was Too Beautiful." *Red Book Magazine*, December 1928.

———. "I Think I'll Get Married." *Red Book Magazine*, February 1927.

———. "I Was So Insulted." *Red Book Magazine*, April 1927.

———. "Not That Kind of Girl." *Red Book Magazine*, August 1926.

———. "The Woman Pays." *Red Book Magazine*, June 1927.

De Mille, Anna George. "Stars." *Photoplay*, October 1927.

Didion, Joan. "I Can't Get That Monster Out of My Mind." In *Slouching Towards Bethlehem*. New York: Simon & Schuster, 1968.

——. "In Hollywood." In *The White Album*. New York: Simon & Schuster, 1979.

Dreiser, Theodore. "Hollywood: Its Morals and Manners." In *The Best of Shadowland*, edited by Anna Kate Sterling. Metuchen, N.J.: Scarecrow Press, 1987.

Dupont, Jean. "Life for a Night." *Photoplay*, March 1927.

Early, Dudley. "The Movies Are Like That." *Photoplay*, November 1928.

Edington, Arlo, and Carmen Edington. "Father Knows Best." *Photoplay*, September 1929.

——. *The Studio Murder Mystery* (serial). *Photoplay*, October 1928–May 1929.

Evans, Ida M. "Mr. Bray Casts." *Red Book Magazine*, July 1927.

——. "A Yacht Darling." *Red Book Magazine*, December 1925.

Farrell, James T. "The Language of Hollywood" and "More on Hollywood." In *The League of Frightened Philistines*. London: Routledge, 1948.

Fitzgerald, F. Scott. "Magnetism." *Saturday Evening Post*, 3 March 1928.

——. "A Millionaire's Girl." *Saturday Eveing Post*, 17 May 1930.

Fletcher, Adele Whitely. "The Old Shoe." *Photoplay*, April 1929.

Franklin, Edgar. "Oh, Jr Jones!" *Photoplay*, October 1930.

Gatlin, Dana. "It's Different in Life." *Photoplay*, December 1928.

Gebhart, Myrtle. "The Gimme Girl." *Photoplay*, January 1930.

Gelzer, Jay "Apron Strings." *Collier's*, 17 November 1928.

Gerould, Katharine Fullerton. "Hollywood: An American State of Mind." *Harper's Magazine* 146 (May 1923).

Glass, Montague. "A Good Job for Julius." *Cosmopolitan*, January 1928.

——. "He Always Wrote Her Everything." *Cosmopolitan*, February 1930.

——. "Yes, Mr. Rosenthal." *Cosmopolitan*, June 1926.

Goldman, Raymond Leslie. "Twinkle Twinkle." *Photoplay*, March 1923.

Goldwater, France. "Everything But." *Photoplay*, May 1929.

Green, Karl. "Wedding Knells." *Photoplay*, March 1926.

Griffin, Eleanore. "The Big Break." *Photoplay*, June 1930.

——. "Just a Cute Trick." *Photoplay*, August 1930.

Gros, Milt. "Well, Wot Is It?" *Red Book Magazine*, February 1929.

Hancock, Vesta Wills. "Ambitious Baby." *Photoplay*, May 1930.

Hellman, Sam. "Borgia, Behave." *Red Book Magazine*, September 1927.

——. "Dumb as She Is." *Red Book Magazine*, November 1927.

——. "Glam." *Red Book Magazine*, October 1927.

——. "Movies Make the Man." *Red Book Magazine*, August 1927.

——. "Once You Click." *Red Book Magazine*, December 1927.

Hergesheimer, Joseph. "And Now the Story." *Saturday Evening Post*, 16 April 1927.

——. "The Extra Consideration." *Saturday Evening Post*, 19 March 1927.

——. "Forty-seven Pretty Girls." *Saturday Evening Post*, 22 January 1927.

——. "Parent to a Star." *Saturday Evening Post*, 26 February 1927.

———. "A School for Acting." *Saturday Evening Post*, 19 February 1927.

———. "The Supercherub." *Saturday Evening Post*, 2 April 1927.

Hughes, Rupert. "Shop!" *Cosmopolitan*, July 1928.

———. *Souls for Sale* (serial). *Red Book Magazine*, September 1921–June 1922.

Ilif, Roy Milton. "Be Yourself." *Photoplay*, November 1923.

———. "Star Stuff." *Photoplay*, July 1923.

Johnson, Nunnally. "Away from It All." *Saturday Evening Post*, 15 February 1930.

———. "The Hero." *Saturday Evening Post*, 14 March 1925.

———. "The World's Shortest Love Affair." *Saturday Evening Post*, 27 October 1928.

Johnston, Agnes Christine. "Community Clothes." *Photoplay*, July 1926.

———. "The Failure's Wife." *Photoplay*, December 1925.

———. "A Hollywood Promise." *Photoplay*, October 1929.

———. "The Movie Hound." *Photoplay*, April 1928.

———. "The Politest Man in Hollywood." *Photoplay*, February 1929.

Kerr, Robert. *Loree Starr—Photoplay Idol* (serial). *Photoplay*, February–June 1914.

Kirk, R. G. *Stars of Steel* (serial). *Collier's*, 16, 23 April 1927.

Kummer, Frederic Arnold. "Beating Them to It." *Photoplay*, February 1918.

———. "The Big Scene." *Photoplay*, November 1917.

———. *It Can't Be Done* (serial). *Photoplay*, February 1918.

———. "The Devil's Camera." *Photoplay*, May 1918.

———. "Jimmy Stars at Last." *Photoplay*, June 1918.

———. "The Rejected One." *Photoplay*, March 1918.

———. "Signing Up Cynthia." *Photoplay*, January 1918.

———. *The Studio Secret* (serial). *Photoplay*, April–September 1923.

———. "The Test." *Photoplay*, December 1918.

———. *That Terrible Thorne Girl* (serial). *Photoplay*, May–October 1925.

Lardner, Ring W. "The Jade Necklace." *Cosmopolitan*, November 1926.

Lea, Fanny Heaslip. *Happy Landings* (serial). *Saturday Evening Post*, March 29–May 3, 1930.

Lessing, Bruno. "Five Men with Whiskers." *Cosmopolitan*, September 1924.

Loos, Anita. *The Better Things of Life* (serial). *Cosmopolitan*, June 1930–March 1931.

———. "Hollywood Now and Then." In *Fate Keeps On Happening*. New York: Dodd, Mead & Company, 1984.

Lowe, Corinne. "The Hope That Springs." *Photoplay*, August 1920.

Mack, Grace. "Better Than Pickford." *Photoplay*, February 1928.

———. "Brains and Sex Appeal." *Photoplay*, March 1929.

———. "Girl Fodder." *Photoplay*, March 1930.

———. "The Girl from Woolworth's." *Photoplay*, May 1929.

———. "The Golden Fleecer." *Photoplay*, July 1929.

———. "An Old Fashioned Girl Steps Out." *Photoplay*, August 1929.

———. "Stepping Stones." *Photoplay*, June 1928.

———. "Why Sheiks Go Wrong." *Photoplay*, November 1929.

Mack, Grace, and Will Chappel. "Lucky Girl." *Photoplay*, June 1930.

Malloch, G. R. "The Desert Island." *Collier's*, 4 September 1926.

Markey, Gene. "A Promising Young Actress." *Photoplay*, February 1926.

McGaffey, Kenneth. *Mollie of the Movies* (serial). *Photoplay*, June 1915–January 1916.

McMurdy, Charles. "Co-Stars." *Photoplay*, February 1918.

McMurtry, Larry. "The Hollywood Novel, the Hollywood Film." *American Film* 2, no. 5 (March 1977): 67.

McNutt, William Slavens. "The Love Hunch." *Photoplay*, July 1927.

———. "The Wild Way." *Photoplay*, October 1926.

Merwin, Samuel. "Fancy Turns." *Red Book Magazine*, August 1924.

———. *Hattie of Hollywood* (serial). *Photoplay*, July–December 1922.

———. "More Stately Mansions." *Red Book Magazine*, October 1924.

———. "Theme with Variations." *Red Book Magazine*, February 1923.

Miller, Henry. "Soiree in Hollywood." In *The Air-Conditoned Nightmare*. New York: New Direction, 1945.

Mitchell, Ruth Comfort. "Blood and Tears." *Red Book Magazine*, February 1925.

Morris, Gouverneur. "The Bird in the Bush." *Cosmopolitan*, April 1927.

Nathan, George Jean. "After-Thoughts on Hollywood." In *The Morning After the First Night*. Rutherford, N.J.: Fairleigh Dickinson University Press, 1971.

Orcutt, George. *Beauty to Burn* (serial). *Photoplay*, January–June 1915.

O'Reilly, Edward S. "Branded by Cupid." *Photoplay*, February 1918.

———. "Hydrant-Headed Reform." *Photoplay*, January 1918.

———. "Revenge Is Sweet." *Photoplay*, April 1918.

———. "Temperamental Tim." *Photoplay*, October 1917.

———. "A Whack at the Muse." *Photoplay*, November 1917.

Pascal, Ernest. "Discipline." *Photoplay*, December 1930.

Pelley, William Dudley. "Poise Will Be Poise." *Photoplay*, August 1928.

Pelswick, Rose. "Does It Pay Girls?" *Photoplay*, August 1927.

Perelman, S. J. "Back Home in Tinseltown." In *Eastward Ha!* New York: Simon & Schuster, 1977.

Peterson, Herman. "More Than Hunger." *Photoplay*, December 1927.

Pinkerton, Katherine, and Robert Pinkerton. *Not in the Scenario* (serial). *Photoplay*, November 1923–February 1924.

Poole, Ernest. "This Girl Wished for a Palace." *Cosmopolitan*, February 1926.

Potamkin, Harry Alan. "Holy Hollywood." In *Behold America!*, edited by Samuel D. Schmalhausen. New York: Farrar & Rinehart, 1931.

Priestly, J. B. Chap. 10 in *Midnight on the Desert*. New York: Harper & Brothers, 1937.

Putnam, Nina Wilcox. "Ankle Along!" *Saturday Evening Post*, 8 January 1927.

———. "Applesauce." *Cosmopolitan*, March 1925.

———. "Doubling Cupid." *Saturday Evening Post*, 13 December 1924.

———. "Good Scout." *Collier's*, 19 April 1930.

———. "I Knew Him When." *Saturday Evening Post*, 9 November 1929.

———. *Laughter, Ltd.* (serial). *Saturday Evening Post,* 12 August–23 September 1922.

———. "Making the World Safe for Junior." *Saturday Evening Post,* 14 October 1922.

———. "Some Boloney." *Cosmopolitan,* May 1925.

———. "Speak for Yourself." *Cosmopolitan,* January 1930.

———. "Theme Song." *Saturday Evening Post,* 25 January 1930.

———. "Travel at Your Own Risk." *Saturday Evening Post,* 25 October 1924.

———. "Vox Potpourri." *Saturday Evening Post,* 27 March 1920.

———. *West Broadway* (serial). *Saturday Evening Post,* 7 May–25 June 1921.

———. "Where the Road to Mandy Lay." *Saturday Evening Post,* 6 December 1924.

Quigley, Martin J. "Just an Old One-Reeler." *Photoplay,* January 1924.

Ramsey, Walter. "Five-Fifty-and Fate." *Photoplay,* December 1930.

———. "The Ten-Dollar Bill." *Photoplay,* July 1930.

———. "A True Short Story." *Photoplay,* May 1930.

Reichenbach, Harry L. "The Big Fade-Out." *Photoplay,* March 1917.

———. "The Flash Back." *Photoplay,* April 1917.

———. "Sexes and Sevens." *Photoplay,* June 1928.

Robertson, Stewart. "The Broad A Baby." *Photoplay,* March 1929.

———. "Hollywood Hight Hat." *Photoplay,* November 1929.

———. "Hot Tamale." *Photoplay,* February 1930.

———. "It Gets a Guy Sore." *Photoplay,* February 1929.

———. "A Little Deal for Dora." *Photoplay,* June 1929.

———. "Make Way for a Genius." *Photoplay,* April 1930.

———. "Mr. Hoople Stays in Character." *Photoplay,* October 1928.

———. "Monahan the Menace." *Photoplay,* August 1929.

———. "Rosie Rolls Her Eyes." *Photoplay,* July 1929.

———. "Sheila in Person." *Photoplay,* March 1930.

———. "Sing a Soothin' Song." *Photoplay,* October 1929.

———. "Weight and Hope." *Photoplay,* July 1930.

Roche, Arthur Somers. "Alms of Love." *Red Book Magazine,* March 1924.

———. "Sacrifice." *Collier's,* 10 May 1930.

———. "Where You Find It." *Red Book Magazine,* May 1924.

St. Johns, Adela Rogers. "The Amazing Choice." *Good Housekeeping,* March 1927.

———. "Beautiful But Dumb." *Cosmopolitan,* May 1924.

———. "Borrowed Plumes." *Cosmopolitan,* November 1923.

———. "The Burden of Beauty." *Cosmopolitan,* September 1924.

———. "Dog in the Manger." *Photoplay,* September 1921.

———. "Dolls." *Cosmopolitan,* July 1923.

———. "Eyes of the Blind." *Good Housekeeping,* August 1923.

———. "The Fan-Letter Bride." *Photoplay,* August 1922.

———. "The Great God Four-Flush." *Cosmopolitan,* May 1923.

———. "A Hollywood Love Story." *Good Housekeeping,* September 1923.

———. "Jailbait." *Cosmopolitan,* November 1925.

———. "Kitty Shinn's Husband." *Cosmopolitan*, March 1924.

———. "The Last Affair of Lalun Chang." *Cosmopolitan*, July 1925.

———. "The Last Straw." *Photoplay*, May 1922.

———. *The Love Dodger* (serial). *Photoplay*, March–July 1924.

———. "Maggie Qunanne." *Cosmopolitan*, February 1923.

———. "Miss Dumbbell." *Photoplay*, April 1922.

———. "The One Motto for a Married Woman." *Cosmopolitan*, December 1922.

———. "The Port of Missing Girls: Judy Keene." *Photoplay*, July 1927.

———. "The Port of Missing Girls: Marilyn, the Lily Maid." *Photoplay*, August 1927.

———. "The Port of Missing Girls: Patty of the Flappers." *Photoplay*, April 1927.

———. "The Port of Missing Girls: Paula." *Photoplay*, June 1927.

———. "The Port of Missing Girls: Persis." *Photoplay*, May 1927.

———. "The Port of Missing Girls: The Story of Greta." *Photoplay*, March 1927.

———. "The Romance of a Great Man." *Collier's*, 1 February 1930.

———. "Sense of Humor." *Cosmopolitan*, October 1930.

———. *The Skyrocket* (serial). *Cosmopolitan*, January–April 1925.

———. "Starring Mrs. Tim Hale." *Cosmopolitan*, October 1922.

———. "Talkie." *Cosmopolitan*, September 1929.

———. "They Always Do." *Good Housekeeping*, August 1924.

———. "Thumbs Down." *Cosmopolitan*, September 1923.

———. "The Tramp." *Cosmopolitan*, August 1922.

———. "The Worst Woman in Hollywood," *Cosmopolitan*, February 1924.

Sanborn, Ruth Barr. "The Wagon and the Star." *Collier's*, 20 September 1930.

Sangster, Margaret E. "The Extra Boy and the Star." *Good Housekeeping*, June 1928.

———. "In a Gold Frame." *Photoplay*, September 1925.

———. "The Stars That Never Made It: Chinese New Year." *Photoplay*, January 1929.

———. "The Stars That Never Made It: The Madonna." *Photoplay*, August 1928.

———. "The Stars That Never Made It: Nice Baby." *Photoplay*, October 1928.

———. "The Stars That Never Made It: The Portrait." *Photoplay*, September 1928.

———. "The Stars That Never Made It: Tinsel." *Photoplay*, December 1928.

———. "The Stars That Never Made It: To the Manner Born." *Photoplay*, November 1928.

———. "Wicked?" *Photoplay*, June 1926.

Saxby, Charles. "In Person." *Red Book Magazine*, December 1923.

Schulberg, Budd. "The Hollywood Novel." *American Film* 1, no. 7 (May 1976): 28–32.

See, Carolyn. "The Hollywood Novel: The American Dream Cheat." In *Tough Guy Writers of the Thirties*, edited by David Madden. Carbondale: Southern Illinois University Press, 1968.

———. "The Hollywood Novel: A Partial Bibliography." *Bulletin of Bibliography* 24, no. 9 (January–April 1966): 208–16.

Service, Faith. "False Faces." *Photoplay*, May 1926.

———. "The Synthetic Star." *Photoplay*, December 1926.

Sherwood, Robert E. "Hollywood: The Blessed and the Cursed." In *America as Americans See It*, edited by Fred J. Ringel. New York: Harcourt Brace & Company, 1932.

Shumat, Harold. "Portraits of Three Women." *Saturday Evening Post*, 8 March 1930.

Sinbad. "Cheap at Twice the Price." *Collier's*, 26 May 1928.

Speare, Dorothy. "His Royal Sigh." *Ladies' Home Journal*, July 1930.

Sullivan, Francis William. "The Gas Girl." *Photoplay*, August 1917.

———. *The Glory Road* (serial). *Photoplay*, July 1916–February 1917.

Synon, Mary. "Good Trouper." *Ladies' Home Journal*, September 1928.

Tate, Lucile N. "Just an Old Fashioned Girl." *Photoplay*, August 1925.

Tildesley, Alice L. "Good Girl." *Photoplay*, January 1929.

Turnbull, Hector. "Picture Stuff." *Collier's*, 30 April 1921.

Tuttle, Margaretta. "Before I Wake." *Saturday Evening Post*, 9 February 1929.

———. *Little Girl* (serial). *Saturday Evening Post*, June 2–16, 1928.

Vale, Rena. "Play Houses." *Photoplay*, May 1928.

Wagner, Rob. *A Girl of the Films* (serial). *Red Book Magazine*, July–December 1922.

———. "The Quickie." *Saturday Evening Post*, 20 November 1926.

———. "A Tame Story." *Saturday Evening Post*, 2 July 1928.

Warren, William. "Alice in Movieland." *Photoplay*, January 1922.

Widmer, Kingsley. "The Hollywood Image." *Coastlines* 17, no. 5, pt. 1 (1961): 17–27.

Wilcox, Roy. "Doubling for Death." *Photoplay*, January 1930.

Wiley, High. "Bonanza." *Red Book Magazine*, March 1927.

———. "Once a Bridge Man." *Collier's*, 17 May 1930.

Williams, Ben Ames. *An End to Mirth* (serial). *Ladies' Home Journal*, December 1930–March 1931.

Williams, Frank (Francis William Sullivan). *The Star of the North* (serial). *Photoplay*, September 1915–May 1916.

Williams, Margaret K. "Sheik-bite." *Collier's*, 24 July 1926.

Willson, Dixie. "Baby Blue Eyes." *Photoplay*, October 1930.

———. "Miss Master Mind." *Photoplay*, November 1930.

———. "A Queen Goes Fishing." *Photoplay*, September 1930.

Wilson, Harry Leon. *Merton of the Movies* (serial). *Saturday Evening Post*, 4 February–8 April 1922.

Winslow, Thyra Samter. "Just a Sweet Girl." *Cosmopolitan*, September 1927.

Witwer, H. C. "Bee's Knees." *Cosmopolitan*, May 1924.

———. "That Big Punch Climax." *Collier's*, 23 January 1926.

———. *Bigger and Better* (serial). *Collier's*, 22 October 1927–23 February 1929.

———. "Came the Dawn." *Cosmopolitan*, January 1926.

———. "A Comedy of Terrors." *Collier's*, 29 August 1925.

———. *The Shooting Stars* (serial). *Collier's*, 11 June 1921–29 April 1922.

———. "The Square Sex." *Cosmopolitan*, April 1924.

———. "The Wages of Cinema." *Cosmopolitan*, October 1922.

———. "When Kane Met Abel" (from *The Leather Pushers* serial). *Collier's*, 19 February 1921.

———. "Yes Man's Land." *Cosmopolitan*, January 1927.

Worts, George F. "The Breaks in the Game." *Saturday Evening Post*, 4 October 1930.

———. "The Heart of a Cameraman." *Saturday Evening Post*, 6 September 1930.

INDEX